# DIGITAL TECHNOLOGY
## Principles and Practices

**GERALD E. WILLIAMS, P.E.**

**Riverside City College**

 SCIENCE RESEARCH ASSOCIATES, INC.
Chicago, Palo Alto, Toronto, Henley-on-Thames, Sydney, Paris, Stuttgart

A Subsidiary of IBM

**Library of Congress Cataloging in Publication Data**

Williams, Gerald Earl, 1931–
    Digital technology.

    Includes index.
    1.   Electronic digital computers.
2.   Logic circuits.      3.   Digital electronics.
I.   Title.
TK7888.W49          621.3819′58′2          76-47660
ISBN  0-574-21500-X

## DEDICATION

With the pride that only a satisfied parent can know, I dedicate this book to two of the finest young men I know—my sons Geoffrey and Kelly, who have filled my life with the magic and beauty of love.

# PREFACE

This text is designed for a one-semester beginning course in digital technology for students enrolled in electronics technology programs in technical institutes and in two- and four-year colleges. Important prerequisites are an understanding of electronics fundamentals and a knowledge of semiconductor fundamentals. In each chapter learning objectives are stated and student problems are provided. Troubleshooting hints are distributed throughout the text, and a laboratory manual is available. The coverage of programmable logic and bus-system organizing concepts contributes to the primary goal of the text, which is to give the student both a solid grounding in modern digital integrated circuits and a foundation for future study of microprocessors. The concluding chapter, which gives a general orientation to the microprocessor scene, forms a bridge between hard-wired logic systems and software microprocessor systems.

Chapter 1 introduces logic fundamentals, including gates, truth tables, logic diagrams, timing diagrams, and simple Boolean equations. Basic Boolean laws, including the laws of De Morgan, are also covered.

Chapter 2 examines the internal circuitry and characteristics of modern integrated circuit logic gates (TTL, MOS, C-MOS, ECL, and I²L). Discussion includes the illustration and explanation of schematics of gate circuits, important electrical parameters, and a comparative analysis of the characteristics of the different standard logic families. Some troubleshooting hints are included.

Chapter 3 introduces truth tables and Boolean algebra demonstrating how they are used to analyze and design logic circuits. Practical methods for minimizing the amount of hardware required to perform a given logic task are covered.

Chapter 4 introduces flip-flops, examining the principal integrated-circuit types and presenting the theory of operation of each basic flip-flop with emphasis on type $D$ and $J-K$ flip-flops. A guide to the selection and comparison of commercial flip-flop packages is provided.

Chapter 5 discusses the generation, shaping, and delaying of logic pulses, including astable and monostable multivibrators, as well as other kinds of pulse-generating oscillators. The newer types of integrated circuit oscillator packages and modern logic gate oscillators are emphasized. Simple methods of interconnecting gates of different logic families are also discussed.

Chapter 6 introduces the binary and other computer-oriented number systems and number codes and presents both human and computer methods for translating from one number system into another.

Chapter 7 is a comprehensive study of binary counter circuits, with emphasis on integrated-circuit techniques and commercial integrated-circuit counter packages. A counter comparison and selection guide is included that compares characteristics of the most common commercial units.

Chapter 8 examines the theory and practice of using flip-flops connected as shift registers. Areas discussed include bidirectional circuits and counter circuits formed from shift registers. A shift register comparison and selection guide is also included.

Chapter 9 examines number representation schemes, computer arithmetic, and the circuitry used in the computer to perform arithmetic operations. Addition, subtraction, multiplication, and division are discussed both in terms of arithmetic methods and logic circuitry.

Chapter 10 investigates the various kinds of computer memories, including read/write (RAM), read-only (ROM), and large-scale shift register memories. Discussion includes the theory of operation of each type of memory cell, as well as the details of cell organization in complete memory systems. Core and other forms of memory are briefly discussed, but the emphasis is on integrated-circuit memories.

Chapter 11 (interfacing) concerns methods, circuits, and special integrated circuits for connecting standard integrated logic circuits to outside-world devices. Special data communications codes (ASCII and EBCDIC) are discussed, and a CRT television-type alphanumeric visual display system is described in some detail. Several sections in the chapter are concerned with connecting integrated circuit chips to data bus lines and transmission lines. Special integrated circuits for driving visual readout devices are also discussed.

As mentioned above, Chapter 12 is designed to bridge the gap between hardware-oriented logic systems and the software/firmware orientation of the microprocessor.

# ACKNOWLEDGMENTS

I would like to thank the following people for their invaluable help: My wife Patty, whose industry and talent kept wolves and creditors from the door, and gave me a heady taste of creative freedom; Judy Otten, who performed the impossible task of maintaining order in the midst of my literary anarchy and did a fine job of manuscript typing; Mat and Phyllis Fletcher for their help with drawings and manuscript.

Because an author's greatest asset is a team of knowledgeable and thorough reviewers, I wish to thank the following scholars for their critical and constructive evaluations of the manuscript:

Vincent Cavanaugh of St. Louis Community College, Floressant Valley

John Keown of Southern Technical Institute

Sol Libes of Union County Technical Institute

Neal D. Voke of Triton College

My thanks to Glen Grahm for his help in the microprocessor chapter and the sections on digital voltmeters.

To William H. Hudelson Jr., my appreciation for his photographic help, and for permission to use the photograph in Figure 2-5.

My appreciation also goes to R. L. Randall and Bud Nicol for their fine technical work on the laboratory manual.

Last, because his is a hard act to follow, my thanks to Alan W. Lowe of Science Research Associates—every inch the competent professional editor, with a patience that fans of Job could not help but admire.

Gerald E. Williams

# CONTENTS

# INTRODUCTION

This text about digital logic begins with the most elementary logic gates and concepts and culminates with an introduction to the ultimate logic system, the microprocessor. The study properly begins with the simplest logic gates and progresses through a series of increasingly complex and powerful logic forms. At each level of complexity different logic forms are required to meet the needs of that level.

The first level involves circuits that can be conveniently constructed using integrated circuit packages with less than a dozen gates per package. Included at this level is the simplest memory element, the flip-flop.

The next level of complexity requires IC packages containing between 12 and 100 gates. At this medium-scale integration level we find medium-scale logic circuits, counters, and shift register memories on a single chip, as well as the same circuits composed of a number of small-scale chips.

At the upper end of the medium-scale range we find complexities in data selectors, multiplexers, and arithmetic units that are too great for small-scale IC chips to be practical. It is also at this second level that we begin to take an interest in programmable logic. Here we have a kind of universal logic package that contains a certain number of gates. The package has several programming inputs that are connected (or switched) to +5 volts or ground, and the circuit in the chip can be programmed to be any standard logic circuit that can possibly be made from the number of gates in the package. We also find counters that can be programmed to count in any desired fashion, replacing (in some applications) a number of specialized counters.

Because of the extra logic circuitry required for programmed devices, they are at the upper end of the medium complexity level and are seldom fabricated from smaller gate packages.

The third level (large-scale integration) is largely the domain of MOS field effect (and injection logic) devices. Packages contain hundreds to thousands of logic gates. At this level conventional bipolar logic gives way to MOS (and $I^2L$) devices. Bipolar logic is much faster and has a number of other advantages over MOS. However at this level conventional bipolar logic is too power hungry, takes up too much chip space per gate, and exceeds practical chip heat-dissipation capabilities. There are a few bipolar devices on the lower end of this scale of complexity.

Most of the devices at this level are programmable. They are primarily memory systems, arithmetic units, and a few special purpose devices. The memory devices are of three kinds: read/write, read-only, and shift register memories. Memories, by definition, are programmable devices. Arithmetic units are programmable in the sense that they must be told to add, subtract, or perform some other operation.

The fourth complexity level is still classified as large-scale integration from the standpoint of the number of gates on a chip. It is reasonable, however, to call this the fourth level of logic. This is the microprocessor level where programmable logic circuits, counters, registers, some memory, and arithmetic systems are all represented. The microprocessor is a fully programmable computer central processor. With the addition of some external memory and input/output devices, it becomes a full-fledged, programmable, general-purpose digital computer. This so-called microcomputer is micro only in size. Its computing capability is every bit as great as many earlier room-sized machines. The important thing about microprocessors is their small size and low cost.

The microcomputer is a digital computer in a shoebox size that is available for $100 or less. By simply programming the device it becomes any desired form of logic system—the universal logic system.

Of equal importance to the microprocessor are the simpler circuits. Not only are they the basis of large-scale circuitry, but they also take care of a great many peripheral chores essential to microprocessor operation. In addition, there are many relatively simple logic systems that don't demand microprocessor sophistication.

CHAPTER **1**

# THE LANGUAGE OF LOGIC

*Learning Objectives. Upon completion of this chapter you should understand the following:*
1. *What a logic diagram is and why it is used.*
2. *What a truth table is, how it is constructed, and how it is used.*
3. *What a timing diagram is and its use.*
4. *What a Boolean equation is and how it is used.*
5. *What an AND gate is, its characteristics, and its truth table.*
6. *What an OR gate is, its characteristics, and its truth table.*
7. *What NAND and NOR gates are, their characteristics, and truth tables.*
8. *The properties of an inverter.*
9. *The basic Boolean laws.*
10. *DeMorgan's laws and the system of logic duals.*
11. *How bubble notation works.*

## INTRODUCTION

Digital circuits, no matter how complex, are composed of a small group of identical building blocks. These blocks are either basic gates or special circuits such as Schmitt triggers, special memory cells, and other structures for which gates are less suitable. The vast majority of the functional building blocks are gates or combinations of gates. A flip-flop, for example, can be considered as a functional block, but it too is composed of standard gates interconnected within the package.

A counter is a more complex functional unit than a flip-flop and is composed of flip-flops and control gates connected inside the package to perform a particular counting function. The flip-flops are made up of combinations of basic gates.

At a much higher level of organization, the microprocessor is the central processing unit of a computer in a package using thousands of gates, flip-flops, and memory cells. Even the memory cells are modified versions of basic gates.

In this chapter we will examine the functional (logical) properties of basic gates. In the next chapter we will examine the electronic properties of the most important gate circuits. In subsequent chapters we will see how these basic gates can be integrated into larger systems to

1

perform all of the computing, counting, and control functions required by computers, as well as smaller scale digital systems.

In most electronics systems the schematic diagram is our most valuable symbolic tool. We also use *block* diagrams to explain systems behavior. In logic systems the schematic diagram is often an unsatisfactory form of communication because of the large number of individual circuits involved and because modern integrated circuits are fairly complex. Schematic diagrams of digital systems would be difficult to follow and to draw simply because of the vast number of components involved. There are only a half dozen or so basic circuits for which we normally draw schematics. In this chapter we will be concerned with logical gates, but later we will encounter some building blocks that are not made up of basic gates alone.

## THE LOGIC DIAGRAM

Gates are the basic universal *logic* building blocks. Each gate has a special symbol that represents the circuitry in the gate. These logic symbols will be combined to form block diagrams called *logic diagrams*.

Although the logic diagram will be our primary method of symbolizing logic systems, there are also some supplementary forms of notation that serve to interpret the operation of logic circuits and systems.

While the logic diagram indicates how the various gates are interconnected, the supplementary forms tell us exactly what the particular logic circuit is intended to do and when.

## THE TRUTH TABLE

One of the best statements of exactly what a particular circuit does (and does not do) is called a *truth table*. The truth table is a formal specifications sheet that describes the exact circuit behavior for every possible set of conditions. Logic circuits normally have a number of inputs and one or more outputs.

Each input signal can be only one of two possible values designated as 1 or 0 in a logic discussion and as *high* or *low* when electronic conditions are being emphasized. All input signals are usually independent of each other so that $2^n$ possible combinations of input 0's and 1's exist. The base (2) is used because there are two possible input conditions, 0 or 1. The exponent ($n$) is the number of independent inputs to a given circuit. Each output can produce one of two values (0 or 1) and is a function of the various combinations of input signals. The truth table, then, shows all possible combinations ($2^n$) of input conditions and the resultant condition of each output for all the input conditions.

The truth table is a *complete* statement of logic circuit functions because no condition can exist that is not included in the truth table.

### THE BOOLEAN EQUATION

*Boolean algebra* is a special logical algebra which provides the same information as the truth table in the form of equations. It has specific rules for manipulating equations to discover several alternate logic structures that will perform the desired function. In addition, Boolean notation, in conjunction with a special kind of truth table, provides a tool to insure that any given logical requirements are met with an absolute minimum number of gates.

### THE TIMING DIAGRAM

The logic diagram shows how the logic gates are interconnected to form the specific logic system, truth tables, and Boolean equations to describe what the gates and the system accomplish. The timing diagram tells us *when* each gate or each part of the system responds with respect to a standard timing signal called the *clock* signal.

These four systems—the logic diagram, the truth table, the Boolean equation, and the timing diagram—provide the methods of describing and explaining logic systems on paper and make up the symbolic *language of logic*.

## 1-1 Logic Functions and Conventions

Logic circuits are composed of combinations of high speed electronic switches called *gates*. These gates are the electronic equivalent of simple conventional switches connected in series or parallel. Various systems combine groups of these series and parallel switches. We will use simple switches only for the purpose of explaining the basic logic functions and combinations.

In most digital circuits we cannot use mechanical switches (or relays) because they are much too slow. Electronic switches have been designed that can switch in much less than a microsecond ($10^{-6}$ sec) and, in most cases, in a few nanoseconds ($10^{-9}$ sec). To give you some idea of how fast this is, light travels at a speed of 186,000 miles per second or 982,080,000 feet per second. In 1 microsecond light will cover a distance of 982 feet, and in 1 nanosecond it will cover a little under 1 foot (0.982 ft). Many modern electronic switches are capable of switching in the time it takes light to travel the length of a man's stride.

Input voltages used to represent logic 0's and 1's in electronic gates can be any pair of distinctly different voltage levels. However, in practice they have been well standardized, eliminating much of the confusion that existed at one time. There are two logic conventions in use: *positive logic* and *negative logic*. In positive logic a logic 1 is represented by the most positive of the two levels, and a logic zero is represented by the less positive level. In current transistor-transistor-logic (TTL) technology positive logic universally uses +5 volts for a logic 1 and zero volts for logic 0. The less common emitter-coupled logic family uses positive logic but a −0.8 volt = logic 1 and −1.9 volts = logic 0. The level −0.8 volt is more positive than −1.9 volts.

In the *P*-channel field-effect family of logic circuits the output voltages are negative for both levels, as they are in emitter-coupled logic. The absolute voltage levels are somewhat more variable and will be examined later. The logic is positive.

In the *N*-channel field-effect family the levels are +5 volts = logic 1 and 0 volts = logic 0. These are the same levels used in the TTL family.

Since nearly all modern logic circuits use positive logic, negative logic devices are becoming increasingly rare. In negative logic, the most negative of the two voltage levels represents a logic 1 and the less negative voltage represents a logic 0. These two definitions are fairly recent and other definitions may sometimes be found in older texts.

## SWITCHING CIRCUIT CONVENTIONS

    a. An open switch is designated 0. If some switch *A* is open, *A* = 0.
    b. A closed switch is designated 1. If some switch *A* is closed, *A* = 1.
    c. If lamp *f* is lit, we designate that lit condition as a 1.
    d. If lamp *f* is dark, we designate it by: *f* = 0.

(See Figure 1-1a.)

## GATE-CIRCUIT CONVENTIONS

    a. A 1 on the input of an electronic gate can also be designated *High, Hi,* or *H*.
    b. A 0 on the input of an electronic gate can also be designated *Low, Lo,* or *L*.
    c. A 1 on the output of an electronic gate can also be designated by *High, Hi, or H,* and a 0 can be represented by *Low, Lo,* or *L*.
    d. Inputs will be labeled *A, B, C,* and so forth, and the output of a gate will be called *f* (for *function*).

## BOOLEAN ALGEBRA CONVENTIONS

There are only three basic logical functions in digital circuits and Boolean algebra: AND, OR, and NOT. Variables in Boolean algebra

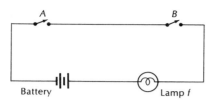

a. The two-variable AND switching circuit

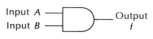

b. The AND gate symbol

c. Equation: $f = (A \cdot B)$

| m | Switch A | Switch B | f (lamp) |
|---|----------|----------|----------|
| 0 | open | open | not lit |
| 1 | open | closed | not lit |
| 2 | closed | open | not lit |
| 3 | closed | closed | lit |

d. The two-variable switching-circuit truth table

| m | A | B | f |
|---|---|---|---|
| 0 | 0 | 0 | 0 |
| 1 | 0 | 1 | 0 |
| 2 | 1 | 0 | 0 |
| 3 | 1 | 1 | 1 |

$f = (A \cdot B)$

e. The standard truth table

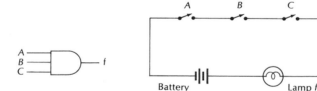

f. The three-input AND gate

g. A three-switch AND circuit

| m | A | B | C | f |
|---|---|---|---|---|
| 0 | 0 | 0 | 0 | 0 |
| 1 | 0 | 0 | 1 | 0 |
| 2 | 0 | 1 | 0 | 0 |
| 3 | 0 | 1 | 1 | 0 |
| 4 | 1 | 0 | 0 | 0 |
| 5 | 1 | 0 | 1 | 0 |
| 6 | 1 | 1 | 0 | 0 |
| 7 | 1 | 1 | 1 | 1 |

Equation:
$f = A \cdot B \cdot C$

h. The three-input AND gate truth table

| m | A | B | C | f |
|---|---|---|---|---|
| 0 | L | L | L | L |
| 1 | L | L | H | L |
| 2 | L | H | L | L |
| 3 | L | H | H | L |
| 4 | H | L | L | L |
| 5 | H | L | H | L |
| 6 | H | H | L | L |
| 7 | H | H | H | H |

i. The three-input AND gate truth table in terms of High and Low input levels

**Figure 1-1** AND Circuit, Gate, and Truth Tables

correspond to the input conditions on a gate (or gates). They are designated $A$, $B$, $C$, and so on and can have only a value of either 0 (low) or 1 (high). Boolean expressions are normally written as equations with an $f$ used (generally by itself) on the left side of the equal sign. The $f$ corresponds to the output function of a gate (or system of gates) and can have either one of two values, 0 or 1. (See Figure 1-1b and c.)

Equations consist of variables joined by operators: ( $\cdot$ ) the Boolean *product* symbol and (+) the Boolean *sum* symbol, along with an equal sign and the $f$ (function). For example, $f = (A \cdot B) + (A \cdot C)$ is read as $f$ equals ($A$ *and* $B$) *or* ($A$ *and* $C$).

It is important to understand that the ( $\cdot$ ) and (+) symbols do not describe the same operation as ordinary arithmetic multiplication and addition.

The ( $\cdot$ ) symbol is called AND. The equation $f = A \cdot B$ is read as $f$ equals $A$ AND $B$. The (+) symbol is called the OR symbol. The equation $f = A + B$ is read as $f$ equals $A$ OR $B$.

### THE COMPLEMENT

The complement or NOT function is the third Boolean operator. A bar over a variable, constant, or operator ($\cdot$ or +) indicates a NOT or complemented variable, constant, or operator.

$$\text{If } A = 1, \bar{A} \text{ (not } A) = 0.$$
$$\text{If } B = 0, \bar{B} \text{ (not } B) = 1.$$

### SUMMARY

1. The AND function (symbolizing the AND gate):

$$f = A \cdot B$$
$$\text{Read as: } f = A \text{ AND } B$$
$$f = AB$$

2. The OR function (symbolizing the OR gate):

$$f = A + B$$
$$\text{Read as: } f = A \text{ OR } B$$

3. The *complement* or NOT function (symbolizing the *inverter*):
   Indicated by a bar over a variable (or larger segments of an equation). For example, $\bar{A}$ would be read as NOT $A$.

There are no squares, square roots (or any other roots or powers) in Boolean algebra nor are there any fractions or division operations. There are only two possible values for constants and two possible values for variables, 0 or 1.

## TRUTH TABLE CONVENTIONS

(See Figure 1-1e.)

### Columns

The truth table will have the following columns: one for each variable ($A$, $B$, $C$, $D$, and so on), one or more $f$ columns, and one $m$ column. The $m$ column simply numbers the rows, always beginning with 0.

### Rows

The rows contain every possible combination of 0's and 1's, with each row containing one combination. The number of rows on a given truth table depends on the number of variables involved in the corresponding Boolean equation. The number of rows $= 2^n$, where $n$ is the number of variables.

**Example** In the equation $f = (A \cdot B) + (A \cdot C)$ there are three variables: $A$, $B$, and $C$. The number of rows is as follows: $n = 2^n$ where $n = 3$, and $n = 2^3 = 8$ rows. These would be numbered 0 through 7.
We will use these conventions throughout the text.

## 1-2  The AND Gate

### FUNCTIONAL DEFINITION

The AND gate will produce a 1 (high) output *if and only if* there is a logical 1 (high) on *all* inputs at the same time.
The Boolean representation of the AND gate is $f = A \cdot B$ and is read $f = A$ AND $B$.
The AND gate is the electronic equivalent of series-connected switches. Figure 1-1 shows the AND switching circuit, the AND gate symbol, two forms of truth table, and the equation for a two-input and a three-input AND function. The AND gate can have any number of inputs.

**Example** To start a car with an automatic transmission, you must put the shift lever out of gear (*neutral* or *park*) AND turn the key to start the car. The conditions are: key turned to "start" AND "shift lever out of gear" equals start. Both conditions must exist at the same time if the car is to start. The equation for this example is as follows: start = neutral · key on.

### TIMING DIAGRAMS

Digital circuits are normally driven by pulses derived from a master oscillator called a *clock*. Diagrams of these pulses in different parts of the system are called *timing diagrams*. Timing diagrams are often a convenient way to illustrate graphically the behavior of a digital circuit. The timing diagram for a two-input AND gate is illustrated in Figure 1-2.

The input and output conditions are shown on the timing diagram in the same order as they are listed on the truth table.

## 1-3 The OR Gate

The OR gate is the electronic equivalent of switches connected in parallel. Figure 1-3 shows the OR switching circuit, the OR gate sym-

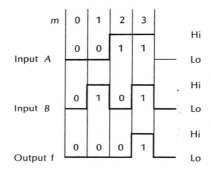

**Figure 1-2** Two-Input AND Gate Timing Diagram

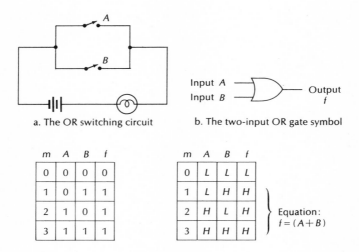

a. The OR switching circuit

b. The two-input OR gate symbol

| m | A | B | f |
|---|---|---|---|
| 0 | 0 | 0 | 0 |
| 1 | 0 | 1 | 1 |
| 2 | 1 | 0 | 1 |
| 3 | 1 | 1 | 1 |

| m | A | B | f |
|---|---|---|---|
| 0 | L | L | L |
| 1 | L | H | H |
| 2 | H | L | H |
| 3 | H | H | H |

Equation:
$f = (A + B)$

c. Truth tables

**Figure 1-3** The OR Function

bols, the truth tables, and the equations. The truth table indicates that a logic 1 (high) on one or more inputs at the same time will produce a 1 (high) output. The OR gate will output a 0 *only* when *all* inputs are 0 (low) at the same time. The OR gate can have any number of inputs.

Figure 1-4 shows a four-input OR switching circuit, gate symbol, truth table, and equation. Figure 1-5 is the timing diagram for a two-input OR gate. The extension *wings* in Figure 1-4b are sometimes used to prevent the input lines from appearing too crowded on the drawing.

The AND gate symbol may also be extended in a similar fashion as shown in Figure 1-6. These extension lines can also have a special

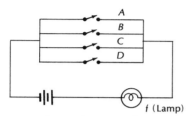

a. The switching equivalent

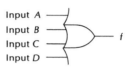

b. The four-input OR gate symbol

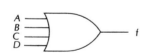

c. Four-input OR gate; alternate symbol

Equation: $f = A + B + C + D$

| | A | B | C | D | f |
|---|---|---|---|---|---|
| $m_0$ | 0 | 0 | 0 | 0 | 0 |
| $m_1$ | 0 | 0 | 0 | 1 | 1 |
| $m_2$ | 0 | 0 | 1 | 0 | 1 |
| $m_3$ | 0 | 0 | 1 | 1 | 1 |
| $m_4$ | 0 | 1 | 0 | 0 | 1 |
| $m_5$ | 0 | 1 | 0 | 1 | 1 |
| $m_6$ | 0 | 1 | 1 | 0 | 1 |
| $m_7$ | 0 | 1 | 1 | 1 | 1 |
| $m_8$ | 1 | 0 | 0 | 0 | 1 |
| $m_9$ | 1 | 0 | 0 | 1 | 1 |
| $m_{10}$ | 1 | 0 | 1 | 0 | 1 |
| $m_{11}$ | 1 | 0 | 1 | 1 | 1 |
| $m_{12}$ | 1 | 1 | 0 | 0 | 1 |
| $m_{13}$ | 1 | 1 | 0 | 1 | 1 |
| $m_{14}$ | 1 | 1 | 1 | 0 | 1 |
| $m_{15}$ | 1 | 1 | 1 | 1 | 1 |

d. Truth table

**Figure 1-4**  The Four-Input OR Gate

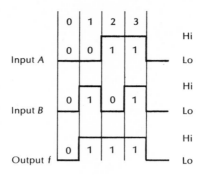

**Figure 1-5** Two-Input OR Gate Timing Diagram

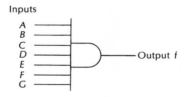

**Figure 1-6** AND Gate Symbol with Extensions to Accommodate Several Inputs without Crowding the Drawing

symbolic meaning as an indication that the gate shown is actually constructed of more than one gate. When more inputs are required than are available in a readily obtainable gate package, several gates may be connected to function as a single basic gate. Only experience can tell you whether this meaning is intended in a given situation.

## 1-4 The Inverter

The inverter, the simplest of the three gates, has one input and one output. The output is always the complement of the input. The complement of a 1 is 0; the complement of 0 is 1. A 1 (high) at the input of an inverter produces a 0 (low) at the inverter output. A 0 (low) input produces a 1 (high) output.

Notice that Figure 1-7 shows two different symbols, one with a circle on the input and the other with the circle on the output. The circle,

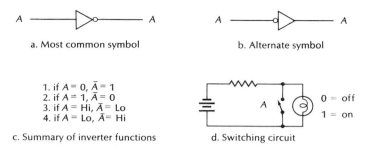

a. Most common symbol                    b. Alternate symbol

1. if $A = 0$, $\bar{A} = 1$
2. if $A = 1$, $\bar{A} = 0$
3. if $A = $ Hi, $\bar{A} = $ Lo
4. if $A = $ Lo, $\bar{A} = $ Hi

c. Summary of inverter functions         d. Switching circuit

$0 = $ off
$1 = $ on

**Figure 1-7**   The Inverter

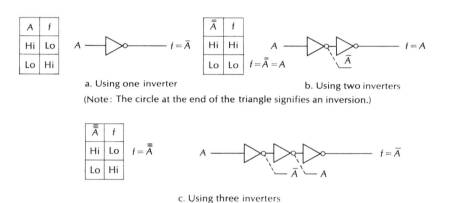

a. Using one inverter                       b. Using two inverters

(Note: The circle at the end of the triangle signifies an inversion.)

c. Using three inverters

**Figure 1-8**   Inverter Truth Tables and Diagrams

often called a *bubble,* is always a part of the inverter symbol, and identifies the symbol as an inverting amplifier.

In the case of multiple inverters in series: (1) An *even* number of inverters yields the same results as no inverters at all, and (2) an *odd* number of inverters is equivalent to a single inverter. (See Fig. 1-8.) Figure 1-9 shows the inverter timing diagram.

## BASIC PROPERTIES OF BOOLEAN ALGEBRA

Because Boolean equations are such a common and useful form for describing digital circuits, it is important to be familiar with the basic laws of Boolean algebra and how they are applied to digital circuits. Some of these properties have already been briefly examined but now we will formalize the already familiar ones and examine some that we have not yet encountered in this text.

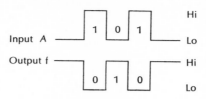

**Figure 1-9** Inverter Timing Diagram

### BINARY NUMBER SYSTEM

In any digital system where computing is involved we find ourselves dealing with two distinctly different binary systems. One is the *binary number system* and the other is a *binary logical algebra* called Boolean algebra.

Ordinary algebra is a symbolic extension of our familiar decimal number system and its manipulations obey the same rules that apply in the number system. This is not true with respect to binary arithmetic and Boolean algebra.

It may seem confusing at first to use the same symbols in both systems when they have a different meaning in each, but you will soon find that in practice it proves to be no problem. In this chapter we will be dealing only with Boolean algebra. As long as we keep in mind that the laws and theorems we are examining are necessarily different from those of ordinary algebra and number systems, there should be no confusion.

## 1-5 Basic Boolean Operations

1. The AND Operation Equation:

$$f = A \cdot B$$

This operation is often called the Boolean Product. The AND function is unique to Boolean algebra and should not be confused with binary arithmetic multiplication. Table 1-1 shows the truth tables for Boolean product combinations.

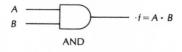

**Figure 1-10** Electronic Implementation of *A* AND *B*

**Table 1-1**   Tables of Boolean Product Combinations

| | A | B | f |
|---|---|---|---|
| 0 | 0 | 0 | 0 |
| 1 | 0 | 1 | 0 |
| 2 | 1 | 0 | 0 |
| 3 | 1 | 1 | 1 |

a. Operations A AND B

| | AND | | f |
|---|---|---|---|
| 0 | A | A | A |
| 1 | 1 | A | A |
| 2 | A | 1 | A |
| 3 | 0 | A | 0 |
| 4 | A | 0 | 0 |

b. Mixed variables and constants

**Table 1-2**   Tables of Boolean Sum Combinations

| | A | B | f |
|---|---|---|---|
| 0 | 0 | 0 | 0 |
| 1 | 0 | 1 | 1 |
| 2 | 1 | 0 | 1 |
| 3 | 1 | 1 | 1 |

a. Operations A OR B

| | OR | | f |
|---|---|---|---|
| 0 | A | A | A |
| 1 | A | 1 | 1 |
| 2 | A | 0 | A |

b. Mixed variables and constants

2. The OR Operation Equation:

$$f = A + B$$

The OR operation is referred to as a Boolean sum. Again, this is a unique Boolean function not to be confused with arithmetic addition. Figure 1-11 shows the electronic implementation of the OR functions and Table 1-2 provides truth tables of Boolean sum combinations.

3. The NOT Operation and the Laws of Complementation:
First law of complementation:

$$\text{If } A = 0, \overline{A} = 1$$
$$\text{If } A = 1, \overline{A} = 0$$

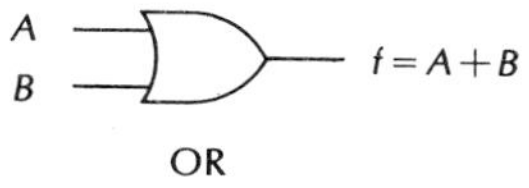

$$f = A + B$$

OR

**Figure 1-11**   Electronic Implementation of the OR Function

Second law of complementation:
$$A \cdot \bar{A} = 0$$
Third law of complementation:
$$A + \bar{A} = 1$$
Law of double complementation:
$$\bar{\bar{A}} = A$$

Figure 1-12 illustrates the electronic interpretation of the laws of complementation.

## 1-6   The Commutative Laws

There are two commutative laws in Boolean algebra, one for the logical AND function and one for the logical OR function. Both commutative laws state that order is not important, that $A$ may be OR'ed or AND'ed to $B$, or $B$ OR'ed or AND'ed to $A$ with the same result.
Commutative law for the OR function:
$$A + B = B + A$$
Commutative law for the AND function:
$$A \cdot B = B \cdot A$$

## 1-7   The Associative Laws

The associative laws apply when three or more variables (or constants) are to be combined by the AND or OR function. The associative laws state that the variables may be combined in any order without changing the outcome.
Associative law for the OR function:
$$A + (B + C) = C + (A + B)$$

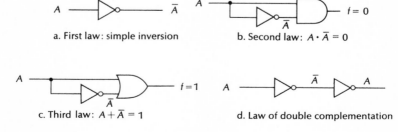

a. First law: simple inversion

b. Second law: $A \cdot \bar{A} = 0$

c. Third law: $A + \bar{A} = 1$

d. Law of double complementation

**Figure 1-12**   Electronic Interpretation of the Laws of Complementation

Associative law for the AND function:

$$A \cdot (B \cdot C) = C \cdot (A \cdot B)$$

## 1-8   The Distributive Laws

In addition to specifying rules for grouping and ''multiplying out,'' the distributive laws also lead to a kind of ''factoring'' that will prove to be of value later on in this course.
First distributive law:

$$A \cdot (B + C) = (A \cdot B) + (A \cdot C)$$

Second distributive law:

$$A + (B \cdot C) = (A + B) \cdot (A + C)$$

## 1-9   The Laws of Tautology

First law of tautology:

$$A \cdot A = A$$

$$\text{because: If } A = 1, 1 \text{ AND } 1 = 1, \text{ and}$$
$$\text{If } A = 0, 0 \text{ AND } 0 = 0$$

Second law of tautology:

$$A + A = A$$

$$\text{because: If } A = 1, 1 \text{ OR } 1 = 1, \text{ and}$$
$$\text{If } A = 0, 0 \text{ OR } 0 = 0$$

When constants are involved:

$$A \cdot 1 = A$$
$$A \cdot 0 = 0$$
$$A + 1 = 1$$
$$A + 0 = A$$

## 1-10   The Laws of Absorption

First law of absorption:

$$A \cdot (A + B) = A$$

Second law of absorption:

$$A + (A \cdot B) = A$$

In both cases in Figure 1-13, a 1 on $A$ will produce a 1 at $f$. $B$ can be either 1 or 0 without affecting the output at $f$. If there is a 0 on $A$, the output will be 0 for either $B = 0$ or $B = 1$. The $B$ has no influence over the output result and can be dropped from the system.

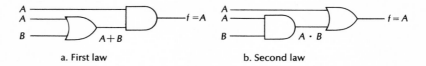

a. First law              b. Second law

**Figure 1-13**   Electronic Interpretation of the Laws of Absorption

## 1-11   DeMorgan's Laws

DeMorgan's laws describe the dual nature of Boolean algebra. When DeMorgan's laws are applied to the implementation of Boolean functions using electronic gates, they can be interpreted to mean: *Any Boolean function can be accomplished using either AND gates and inverters or OR gates and inverters.*

Boolean expressions are often written initially in a form that implies the use of all three gate forms (AND, OR, Invert) to implement the function. DeMorgan's laws provide the basis for the use of most modern electronic gate families. These commercial gate families are based on, for example, an AND gate and a built-in inverter. In this example the OR gate would exist in the family but would probably be more expensive and not as frequently used.

DeMorgan's laws imply that the OR gate would not actually be necessary and that any circuit requirements could be met using only the AND-inverter gate package.

### DEMORGAN'S LAW: CASE 1

$$\overline{A \cdot B} = \overline{A} + \overline{B}$$

Figure 1-14 shows the gate circuits corresponding to the expression on each side of equation 1. The truth tables shown are identical. Because every possible condition is included on the truth table, identical truth tables provide *proof* that the two circuits are functionally identical.

The truth table entries in Figure 1-14a show all of the possible conditions of 0's and 1's for inputs $A$ and $B$. Under the heading "$A \cdot B$, output," the entries define the functional operation of any AND gate.

The bar over $A \cdot B$ ($\overline{A \cdot B}$) means that the entire expression is complemented by "passing" it through an inverter. The complete logic function $\overline{A \cdot B}$ requires the use of an AND gate and an inverter as shown in Figure 1-14a.

The rightmost column in the truth table, the result of the complete function, is the defined function. The column adjacent (to the left) of the $\overline{A \cdot B}$ column is shown here for the purpose of explanation only. It

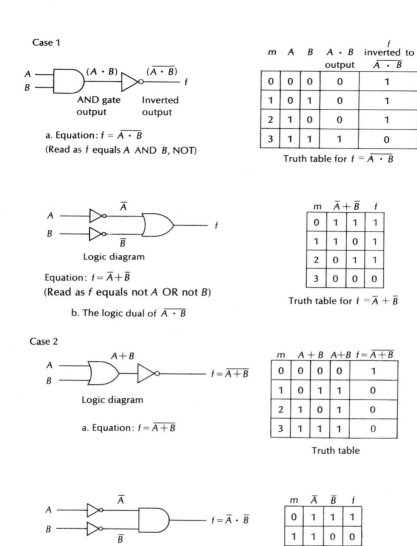

Case 1

| m | A | B | A · B output | f inverted to $\overline{A \cdot B}$ |
|---|---|---|---|---|
| 0 | 0 | 0 | 0 | 1 |
| 1 | 0 | 1 | 0 | 1 |
| 2 | 1 | 0 | 0 | 1 |
| 3 | 1 | 1 | 1 | 0 |

Truth table for $f = \overline{A \cdot B}$

AND gate output    Inverted output

a. Equation: $f = \overline{A \cdot B}$
(Read as f equals A AND B, NOT)

Logic diagram

Equation: $f = \overline{A} + \overline{B}$
(Read as f equals not A OR not B)

b. The logic dual of $\overline{A \cdot B}$

| m | $\overline{A} + \overline{B}$ | f |
|---|---|---|
| 0 | 1 | 1 |
| 1 | 1 | 0 | 1 |
| 2 | 0 | 1 | 1 |
| 3 | 0 | 0 | 0 |

Truth table for $f = \overline{A} + \overline{B}$

Case 2

Logic diagram

a. Equation: $f = \overline{A + B}$

| m | A + B | A+B | $f = \overline{A + B}$ |
|---|---|---|---|
| 0 | 0 | 0 | 0 | 1 |
| 1 | 0 | 1 | 1 | 0 |
| 2 | 1 | 0 | 1 | 0 |
| 3 | 1 | 1 | 1 | 0 |

Truth table

Logic diagram

b. Equation: $f = \overline{A} \cdot \overline{B}$

| m | $\overline{A}$ | $\overline{B}$ | f |
|---|---|---|---|
| 0 | 1 | 1 | 1 |
| 1 | 1 | 0 | 0 |
| 2 | 0 | 1 | 0 |
| 3 | 0 | 0 | 0 |

Truth table (inverted)

**Figure 1-14**  De Morgan's Laws: Case 1 and Case 2

would not normally be included because it merely represents one of the steps in obtaining the desired function $f = \overline{A \cdot B}$.

Figure 1-14b shows the logic diagram for $f = \overline{A} + \overline{B}$. The truth table shows the headings of the two leftmost columns as $\overline{A}$ and $\overline{B}$. Each 1 appearing in the truth table in part a of this figure, columns $A$ and $B$, shows up as a zero in the table in part b. Each 0 in the truth table in part a (columns $A$ and $B$) shows up in part b as a 1. The $f$ column defines the functional behavior of any OR gate for all possible combinations of 0's and 1's for variables $A$ and $B$.

These two configurations are called logic duals because, although they are structurally different, they perform identical functions.

### DEMORGAN'S LAW: CASE 2

$$f = \overline{A + B} = \overline{A} \cdot \overline{B}$$

Figure 1-14, Case 2a shows the truth table and logic diagram for this pair of duals. In both cases of DeMorgan's laws the following applies:

| Inverted Output Positive Logic | Inverted Input Logic Dual |
|---|---|
| $f = \overline{A \cdot B}$ | $f = \overline{A} + \overline{B}$ |
| $f = \overline{A + B}$ | $f = \overline{A} \cdot \overline{B}$ |

### SUMMARY OF FUNDAMENTAL LAWS

1. Laws of tautology
   (1) $A \cdot A = A$
   (2) $A + A = A$
   *Constants*
   (1) $A \cdot 1 = A$
   (2) $A \cdot 0 = 0$
   (3) $A + 1 = 1$
   (4) $A + 0 = A$

2. Laws of complementation
   (1) $A \cdot \overline{A} = 0$
   (2) $A + \overline{A} = 1$
   (3) $\overline{\overline{A}} = A$ (double complement)

3. DeMorgan's laws
   (1) $\overline{A \cdot B} = \overline{A} + \overline{B}$
   (2) $\overline{A + B} = \overline{A} \cdot \overline{B}$

4. Commutative laws
   (1) $A \cdot B = B \cdot A$
   (2) $A + B = B + A$

5. Distributive laws
   (1) $A \cdot (B + C) = (A \cdot B) + (A \cdot C)$
   (2) $A + (B \cdot C) = (A + B) \cdot (A + C)$

6. Associative laws
   (1) $A \cdot (B \cdot C) = C \cdot (A \cdot B)$
   (2) $A + (B + C) = C + (A + B)$

7. Laws of absorption
   (1) $A \cdot (A + B) = A$
   (2) $A + (A \cdot B) = A$

## 1-12   The NAND Gate

Two of the most popular modern gate structures are the NAND (not AND) and the NOR (not OR) gates. Any digital circuit can be constructed using only NAND gates and inverters or only NOR gates and inverters.

The NAND gate is an AND gate with a built-in inverter in the output line. Figure 1-15 shows the NAND gate symbol, its AND-inverter equivalent circuit, and how the law of the double complement can be used to convert a NAND gate into an AND gate. The bubble on the output represents the built-in inverter and is part of the NAND symbol. The AND function is not directly accessible in the NAND gate package.

In Figure 1-15b, notice that the equivalent circuit (and equation) is identical to Figure 1-14, Case 1a.

## 1-13   The NOR Gate

The NOR gate is an OR gate with a built-in inverter in the output line. The NOR gate is a NOT-OR gate. The OR function is not available from a NOR gate. Figure 1-16 shows the NOR gate symbol, its OR-inverter equivalent circuit, and how the law of the double complement can be used to obtain the OR function from a NOR gate. The bubble on the output is an integral part of the NOR gate symbol.

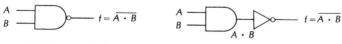

a. NAND gate symbol               b. AND inverter equivalent of the NAND

c. Taking advantage of the double complement
to convert a NAND gate into an AND

**Figure 1-15**   The NAND Gate

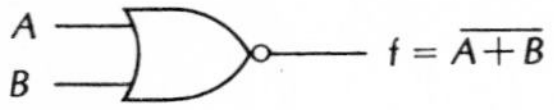

a. NOR gate symbol

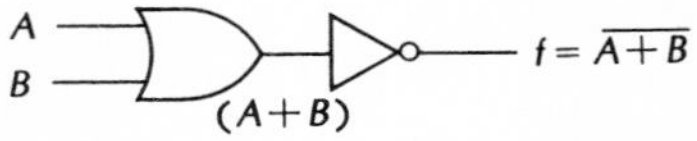

b. The OR — inverter equivalent of the NOR

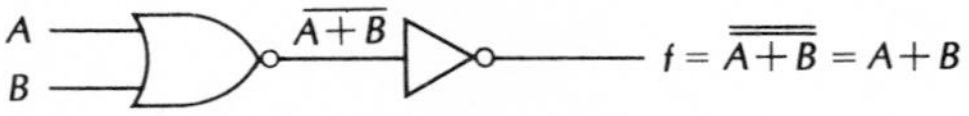

c. Taking advantage of the double complement
law to convert a NOR gate into an OR

**Figure 1-16**    The NOR Gate

Notice that the NOR equivalent circuit (Fig. 1-16b) is identical to the Case 2 a logic diagram and equation in Figure 1-14. (Note: Properly connected either the NAND gate or the NOR gate can serve as an inverter. Most logic families that feature NAND or NOR gates as the primary gate form also provide inverters for use when it is more convenient to use them.)

## 1-14    Using NAND and NOR Gates as Inverters

The following drawings indicate methods for using NAND and NOR gates as inverters. It is important that unused inputs on any gate be tied to some low-impedance source—generally to the positive side of the power supply or ground. An open input circuit *sees* a nearly infinite driving impedance and is an invitation for noise or unwanted pulses to sneak in. A circuit may function in a lab with an open OR gate input, for example, but may become erratic in the field where electrical noise levels are higher (see Figure 1-17).

## 1-15    Bubble Notation

The use of bubble notation makes logic diagrams less cluttered, easier to read, and easier to draw.

### SOME RULES FOR BUBBLE NOTATION

1. The bubble on the output of a gate is a part of that particular symbol and the indicated inverter is built into the gate.

2. The input bubbles do *not* indicate whether the inverters are internal to the gate or connected externally. In general, for basic gates the inverters are connected externally and are *not* a part of the gate circuit. The best interpretation of an input bubble is to con-

Preferred method

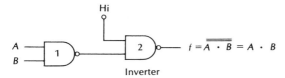

Note: The High (Hi) on the upper leg of gate 2 is normally
a fixed voltage power supply line, in most cases the
same line that supplies power to the gates.

Alternate method

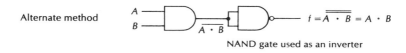

NAND gate used as an inverter

a. $(A \cdot B)$ synthesized with NAND gates

Preferred method

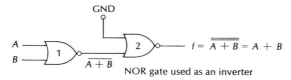

Note: The GND (Lo) on the upper leg of gate 2 is normally
a fixed voltage power supply line, in most cases the
same line that supplies power to the gates.

Alternate method

$$f = \overline{\overline{A + B}} = A + B$$

NOR gate used as an inverter

b. $(A+B)$ synthesized with NOR gates

**Figure 1-17**  Synthesized Gates

sider that input as a *low* active input. It takes a zero (low) instead
of a one (high) on a bubbled input leg to activate that input. Some
logic circuits, particularly flip-flops, do have built-in low active
inputs.

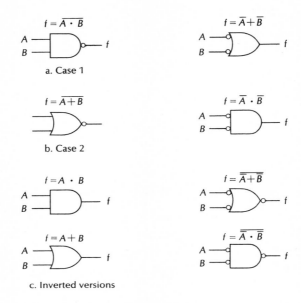

a. Case 1

b. Case 2

c. Inverted versions

**Figure 1-18**  De Morgan's Theorem Gate Equivalents

## 1-16  DeMorgan's Theorem and Logic Gate Equivalents

The equivalent circuits in Figure 1-18 are based on the two cases of DeMorgan's theorem:

$$\text{Case 1:}\quad \overline{A \cdot B} = \overline{A} + \overline{B}$$
$$\text{Case 2:}\quad \overline{A + B} = \overline{A} \cdot \overline{B}$$

Figure 1-18 shows the equivalent logic gates (logic duals) based on the two cases of DeMorgan's theorem. The symbols differ from Figure 1-13 in that inverters are symbolized by circles on the inputs and outputs of the gates. This method of presentation is called bubble notation, derived from MIL-STD 806B and The American National Standards Institute (ANSI) y32.14.

## SUMMARY

Figure 1-19 summarizes NAND and NOR gates and their various equivalent forms.

### Problems

1. Why are schematics used infrequently in describing logic systems?

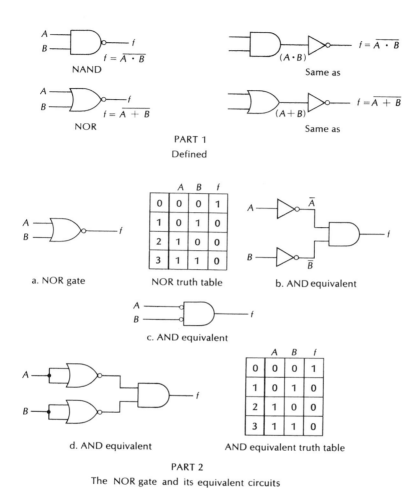

PART 1
Defined

a. NOR gate    NOR truth table    b. AND equivalent

c. AND equivalent

d. AND equivalent    AND equivalent truth table

PART 2
The NOR gate and its equivalent circuits

**Figure 1-19**   NOR and NAND Gate Circuits and Equivalents

2. Match the following to items (1) through (4) below:
    a. Boolean equations        d. Timing diagrams
    b. Schematic diagrams    e. Truth table
    c. Logic diagrams
   (1) Tells *how* logic elements are interconnected
   (2) Tells *when* a gate is expected to operate
   (3) Provides a tool for describing logic circuit organization and discovering other equivalent organizations
   (4) Specifies all possible operating conditions for a given logic circuit
3. Describe the AND function in words.

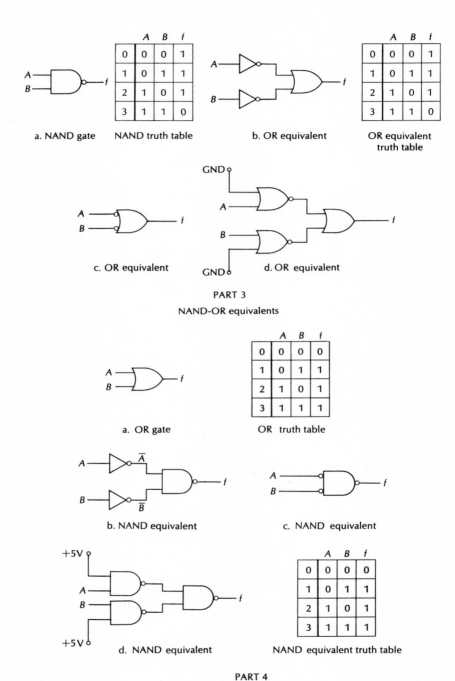

| | A | B | f |
|---|---|---|---|
| 0 | 0 | 0 | 1 |
| 1 | 0 | 1 | 1 |
| 2 | 1 | 0 | 1 |
| 3 | 1 | 1 | 0 |

a. NAND gate  NAND truth table

b. OR equivalent

| | A | B | f |
|---|---|---|---|
| 0 | 0 | 0 | 1 |
| 1 | 0 | 1 | 1 |
| 2 | 1 | 0 | 1 |
| 3 | 1 | 1 | 0 |

OR equivalent truth table

c. OR equivalent

d. OR equivalent

PART 3

NAND-OR equivalents

a. OR gate   OR truth table

| | A | B | f |
|---|---|---|---|
| 0 | 0 | 0 | 0 |
| 1 | 0 | 1 | 1 |
| 2 | 1 | 0 | 1 |
| 3 | 1 | 1 | 1 |

b. NAND equivalent

c. NAND equivalent

d. NAND equivalent   NAND equivalent truth table

| | A | B | f |
|---|---|---|---|
| 0 | 0 | 0 | 0 |
| 1 | 0 | 1 | 1 |
| 2 | 1 | 0 | 1 |
| 3 | 1 | 1 | 1 |

PART 4

The OR-NAND equivalents

Figure 1-19 continued

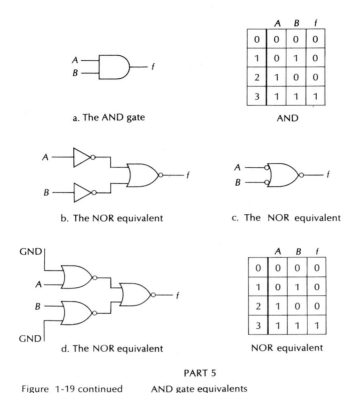

a. The AND gate

| | A | B | f |
|---|---|---|---|
| 0 | 0 | 0 | 0 |
| 1 | 0 | 1 | 0 |
| 2 | 1 | 0 | 0 |
| 3 | 1 | 1 | 1 |

AND

b. The NOR equivalent

c. The NOR equivalent

d. The NOR equivalent

| | A | B | f |
|---|---|---|---|
| 0 | 0 | 0 | 0 |
| 1 | 0 | 1 | 0 |
| 2 | 1 | 0 | 0 |
| 3 | 1 | 1 | 1 |

NOR equivalent

PART 5

Figure 1-19 continued    AND gate equivalents

4. Write the Boolean equation for the AND function, draw the AND gate symbol, and write the truth table for the AND function.
5. Write the Boolean equation, the truth table, and draw the logic symbol for the OR function.
6. Describe the OR gate function in words.
7. Explain the NOT operation. What is the logic gate called that performs the NOT function?
8. Draw the logic symbol for a NAND gate, and draw a logic diagram of its equivalent using:
   a. AND's inverters     c. OR's inverters with bubble notation
   b. OR's inverters       d. OR's, NOR's
9. Draw the logic symbol for a NOR gate, and draw a logic diagram of its equivalent using:
   a. OR's inverters      c. AND's inverters with bubble notation
   b. AND's inverters    d. AND's, NAND's
10. Write the two cases of DeMorgan's theorem.
11. Write the truth table for a NAND gate.

# CHAPTER 2

# INTEGRATED LOGIC CIRCUITS

*Learning Objectives.    Upon completing this chapter you should:*
1. *Be able to compare speed and power consumption among the various logic circuits.*
2. *Know the logic levels and power supply requirements of each logic circuit.*
3. *Know which class of applications involve which logic circuit forms.*
4. *Know the meaning of the terms; fan-out, fan-in, compatibility, dynamic and static logic, LSI, MSI, SSI, speed, Schottky, noise immunity, and interfacing.*
5. *Be able to identify each of the logic circuits presented in the chapter.*
6. *Be familiar with data manual symbols.*
7. *Know the basic rules for power supply decoupling.*
8. *Know what dynamic and static testing are.*
9. *Be able to define storage time.*
10. *Know what factors limit logic circuit speed.*
11. *Know what a totem-pole circuit is and why it is used.*
12. *Be familiar with the most important operating parameters of TTL, MOS, C-MOS, and MTL.*
13. *Understand the theory of operation for each of the major logic circuits.*

In most applied digital logic we are not too concerned about the internal circuitry of a gate package. We are far more involved with input and output characteristics, operating levels, gate propagation times, loading rules, and so on. Still, there is some justification for spending time in examining the internal schematics of typical gate structures, because many of the input-output and transfer characteristics are dictated by internal circuitry.

This chapter is concerned with the practical considerations necessary to make real circuits work. It also briefly covers the theory of operation of basic integrated circuit gates.

## 2-1   Integrated Circuits

Nearly all modern logic circuits and subsystems are monolithic* integrated circuits. Transistors, diodes, resistors, and small capacitors are formed on small chips of silicon—from about 0.1 inch to 0.5 inch on a side (dimensions approximate). Individual components are interconnected by aluminum or gold wiring patterns that resemble ordinary printed circuit wiring.

Here we will examine briefly how integrated circuits are fabricated and assembled. This is not intended to be a comprehensive coverage and will necessarily be simplified.

The procedure begins with the development of the artwork for fabricating glass photographic masks. Each mask controls the areas on the silicon wafer (substrate) where various levels of *doping* (defined in next paragraph) are required for transistor bases, collectors, field effect channels, resistors, and so on.

Each mask pattern is developed photographically on a silicon wafer. The wafer is then heated to the point where it almost melts but where surface tension still holds it in a solid form. Impurity elements are diffused into the silicon like butter diffusing into hot toast. The process of adding controlled amounts of certain impurity elements to the silicon crystal is called *doping*. Several masks are used to control the areas of diffusion, one mask for each doping level. One set of masks is designed for a circuit consisting of anywhere from a few to thousands of gates connected in an array ranging from a few individual gates to a complete microcomputer. (The term microcomputer refers to the machine's physical size not its computing capabilities.) Figure 2-1 shows IC transistor cross-sections.

A silicon ingot some two inches (more or less) in diameter is sliced into wafers a few mils thick. Each wafer will eventually have as many as several hundred complete *independent* circuits on it. At the end of the diffusing and interconnecting wiring operations, the wafer is diced by laser cutting, scribing and breaking, or by a diamond saw. This yields up to several hundred chips, each a complete integrated circuit. Each die or chip is then mounted on a header similar to that shown in Figure 2-2. Tiny hairlike gold wires that connect input, output, and power pads on the chip are welded (under a microscope) to pins on the header. Each chip and its gold leads are molded in a plastic block (or housed in some other case). The header strip is then cut apart, the leads formed and the type number stamped on the case. Figure 2-3 shows some typical case styles. There are, of course, a number of quality control

---

* Circuits are fabricated on a slab of semiconductor material by selectively altering the conductivity (at the molecular level) of the semiconductor material. Various conductivity levels correspond to the transistor elements, base collector, etc.

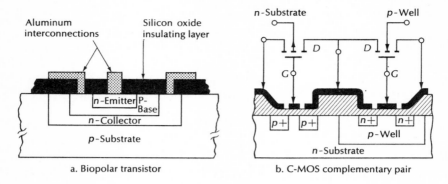

**Figure 2-1**  Cross-Sections of Bipolar and C-MOS Integrated Circuit Transistors

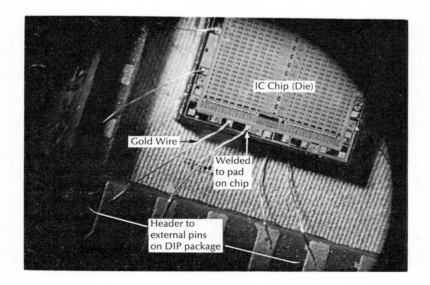

**Figure 2-2**  IC Chip (Die) Connected to Header

and testing steps involved in producing the highly reliable integrated circuits currently available.

Individual integrated circuits are then mounted on etched circuit boards. Figure 2-4 shows an unassembled circuit board, and Figure 2-5 shows one with the components in place. Figure 2-6 shows a complete microcomputer on a single circuit board.

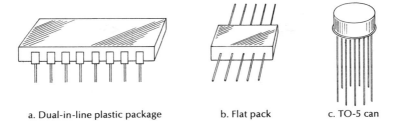

a. Dual-in-line plastic package    b. Flat pack    c. TO-5 can

**Figure 2-3**  Typical Case Styles

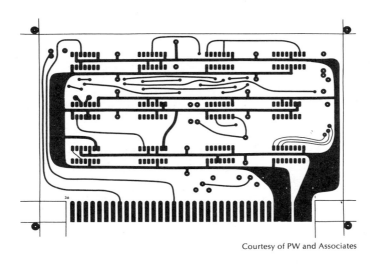

Courtesy of PW and Associates

**Figure 2-4**  Circuit Board for Interconnecting IC's

## 2-2  Bipolar and MOS Integrated Circuits

There are two basic types of integrated circuits; one is based on bipolar transistors and the other is built around *metal-oxide-semiconductor* (MOS) field effect transistors. In both technologies transistors or parts of transistors are used as diodes, resistors, and capacitors. The amount of functional capability on a given chip is generally defined by the number of operational gates on the chip even though the number of *components* may differ from one kind of gate to another.

**Figure 2-5**   Assembled Board with IC's and Other Components Mounted

### SSI

The acronym SSI stands for *small-scale integration* and identifies integrated circuit packages that contain less than twelve logic gates.

### MSI

The acronym MSI, *medium-scale integration,* identifies logic packages containing more than 12 but less than 100 logic gates.

Courtesy of Motorola Semiconductor Products, Inc. © 1975

**Figure 2-6** Complete Circuit on a Circuit Board

## LSI

*Large-scale integration* is defined as any integrated circuit with more than 100 gates in a single package. In many cases an LSI chip may contain several thousand gates.

An important consideration about any logic family is that all logic circuits—gates, flip-flops, counters, and so on—are compatible. This means that the output(s) of any gate in the family can be connected to the input(s) of any other gate (or more complex structures) without elaborate buffering circuits, voltage level changers, or other interface circuitry.

Each of the popular families provides a remarkably complete set of logic building blocks, and because of the concept of compatibility, members of each family can be assembled in almost any combination required, as long as a few simple rules are followed. Whenever circuits using one family are connected to circuits based on a different family, some problems often arise requiring that extra circuitry be added to bridge the gap. This extra hardware is called *interface* circuitry.

Digital integrated circuits (except for some special LSI circuits) are divided into logic families, each of which is based on one particular type of transistor circuit. The same basic circuit is used for all gates, inverters, and flip-flops. MSI and LSI circuits of considerable complexity are composed of interconnected arrays of standard gates.

All devices in a given logic family use the same logic levels, operate from the same power supply voltage, and the output of one device can supply the proper amount of voltage and current to drive the input of another. Because each logic family uses a different circuit, any two given logic families are generally not totally compatible with each other. In addition to the basic logic elements and MSI or LSI circuits, each logic family contains special circuits, such as level translators (for interfacing to the circuits of another logic family), signal conditioning circuits (Schmitt triggers and multivibrators), display driver circuits (for interfacing a logic circuit to visual display), and other circuits for special applications.

The compatible logic families based on bipolar technology cover most SSI and MSI logic needs. MOS technology is more often the basis of LSI systems, such as memories, microprocessors, calculators, digital clocks (the time-of-day kind), and other specialized products. These circuits are not defined as families. Complementary MOS is used for a fairly complete family in direct competition with bipolar logic circuits. C-MOS is relatively slow compared with bipolar circuits, but it is fairly compatible with both large-scale MOS circuits and bipolar logic.

## 2-3   Comparison of Logic Families

Each logic family has its particular strengths and weaknesses. The most common comparison characteristics are as follows:

### Speed-Propagation Delay

Propagation delay is the time required for a change in level at the input to a logic circuit to result in a stable change at the output. The delay is generally measured in nanoseconds. Two figures may be given, one for the time needed for the gate to switch from *high* to *low,* and one for a *low* to *high* transition.

Speed, measured in megahertz, is a measure of how fast a flip-flop can be driven into changing states without error. A given family usually contains more than one kind of flip-flop and each may have its own speed limitation.

### Fan-Out and Fan-In

Each family has a basic gate circuit (NAND, NOR, and so on) that is considered the standard gate for that family. The input current (at the appropriate input voltage) for an input on the standard gate is considered to be a unit load for that family. The fan-out number for a gate defines the number of standard gate inputs it can drive. A gate with a fan-out of 10 can drive 10 standard inputs.

A single unit load is typical of a simple gate input, but reset operations for an MSI counter or other circuit may require that several gate inputs (internally connected) be driven at the same time, counting as more than one unit load. If such an input requires three unit loads, it is said to have a fan-in of 3 and will require three fan-out units to drive it.

### Power Dissipation

Power dissipation is a measure of circuit power dissipated in heat, plus the working power required by a gate or system of gates. It is often rated in milliwatts per gate.

### Noise Immunity

Noise immunity defines the amount of noise that can be superimposed on a gate input signal (high or low) without causing the gate to produce an incorrect output (measured in mV or volts). Table 2-1 compares the following modern logic families with respect to these parameters:

> TTL: transistor-transistor logic
> ECL: emitter-coupled logic (also called *current-mode logic*)
> C-MOS: complementary metal-oxide-semiconductor logic
> DTL: diode-transistor logic
> RTL: resistor-transistor logic (obsolete)
> HTL: high-threshold logic (specialized)

## 2-4 Transistor-Transistor Logic (TTL)

### THE EVOLUTION OF TTL LOGIC

The TTL circuit is the culmination of several years of development and improvement in the electrical characteristics of logic gates.

Diode logic (a pre-integrated circuit form) has excellent switching characteristics, good isolation among inputs, a small input capacitance,

**Table 2-1**  Comparison of Logic Families

| Circuit Form | Standard TTL | High-Speed TTL | Low-Power TTL | Schottky TTL | Low-Power Schottky TTL |
|---|---|---|---|---|---|
| Positive logic function of basic circuit | NAND | NAND | NAND | NAND | NAND |
| Typical fan-out (number of inputs of the same family that can be driven) | 10 | 10 | 10 | 10 | 10 |
| Supply voltage | 5.0V ± 10% | 5.0V ± 10% | 5.0V ± 10% | 5.0V ± 10% | 5.0V ± 10% |
| Typical power dissipation per gate | 12mW | 22mW | 1mW | 19mW | 2mW |
| Immunity to external noise | Very good | Very good | Very good | Good | Good |
| Propagation delay per gate | 10ns | 6ns | 33ns | 3ns | 9.5ns |
| Typical clock rate for flip-flops | 35MHz | 50MHz | 3MHz | 125MHz | 45MHz |

and some inherent noise immunity. The fact that no amplification takes place makes each driven gate a heavy load on the driving gate.

Adding an amplifier stage to the diode logic circuit yielded the basic DTL diode-transistor-logic circuit in Figure 2-7. DTL gates are still found in digital systems, but they are being replaced by TTL in most new equipment.

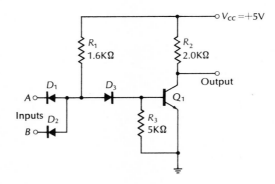

**Figure 2-7**  DTL NAND Gate Schematic Diagram

**Table 2-1** continued

| HTL | Complementary MOS | 4-ns ECL | 2-ns ECL | 1-ns ECL | DTL |
|---|---|---|---|---|---|
| NAND | NOR or NAND | OR/NOR | OR/NOR | OR/NOR | NAND |
| 10 | 50 or higher | 25 | 25 inputs or 50 ohms | 10 low-Z inputs or 50 ohms | 8 |
| 14 to 16V | 3 to 18V | $-5.2V \pm 10\%$ | $-5.2V \pm 10\%$ | $-5.2V \pm 10\%$ | $-5.2V \pm 10\%$ |
| 55mW | 0.01mW static $\approx$ 1mW at 1MHz | 22mW | 25mW + load | 60mW + load | 8mW or 12mW |
| Excellent | Very good | Fair | Fair | Fair | Good |
| 150ns | 70ns | 4ns | 2ns | 1ns | 30ns |
| 4MHz | 5MHz | 70MHz | 125MHz | 400MHz | 12 to 30MHz |

The basic TTL circuit is shown in Figure 2-8. The introduction of the multi-emitter transistor considerably reduced the cost and chip space required for an integrated circuit logic gate as well as providing performance superior to that of DTL.

The TTL circuit still retains the excellent diode switching properties, because each emitter forms a junction diode with the single collector of

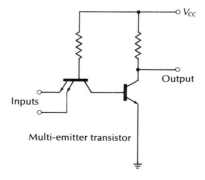

**Figure 2-8**   (Simplified) Basic TTL Circuit

the multi-emitter transistor. The collector-base junction voltage drop provides additional noise immunity by increasing the input switching threshold voltage.

One other refinement has been added to TTL circuits in the form of a push-pull (generally called a *totem-pole* configuration) output stage. (See Figure 2-9.) This output stage provides a low impedance drive to other gate inputs allowing one gate to drive ten or more gate inputs. In addition, switching time is significantly reduced and made more predictable. There are two principal factors that tend to limit switching speed in a transistor—input capacitance and carrier storage within the depletion zone at the transistor collector-base junction.

### CAPACITANCE

There is always some input capacitance that has to be charged before the transistor can switch. Part of the capacitance is simply stray-wiring capacitance, but generally more important is the collector-base junction capacitance when the transistor is turned off. The capacitance is the result of a reverse-biased junction that consists of two areas that contain an abundance of free carriers separated by a layer (the depletion layer) that has been swept clear of carriers and behaves as a dielectric. The base-collector junction, in the reverse-biased condition, behaves as a capacitor between collector and base. Proper design of the transistor can minimize this capacitance, but there is another factor involved. The

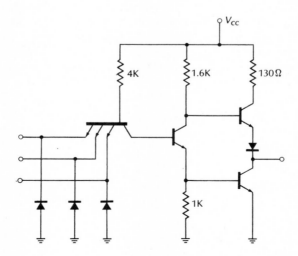

**Figure 2-9** TTL NAND Gate Circuit with Totem-Pole Output Stage Note: Input diodes protect against negative input voltages.

transistor does have voltage gain during the switching transition; and, because of the *Miller effect*, this small interelectrode capacitance appears to the driving gate as the voltage gain—interelectrode capacitance *product*. It might appear that voltage gain is a negligible factor because the steady-state input and output voltages are so nearly equal, a fact that would seem to imply near unity voltage gain. However, when we talk about propagation delays, we are actually referring to the time the transistor takes to *slew* from the *off* state to the *on* state and from the *on* state to the *off* state. The total gate delay is the sum of the two transition times. During these changes in conduction states there is voltage gain involved, and the interelectrode capacitance is effectively amplified.

## STORAGE TIME

Once the transistor is driven into a full *on* condition, called *saturation*, the collector-base junction is forward biased and the depletion zone is saturated with carriers. When the time comes to switch the transistor from full conduction (saturation) into the *off* (no conduction) state, a finite time is required to sweep these carriers out of the depletion zone. The time required to clear these carriers out of the depletion zone is called *storage time*, which contributes to the overall gate propagation delay time.

## THE IMPORTANCE OF THE TOTEM-POLE OUTPUT STAGE

On the rising part of the drive pulse one of the two totem-pole transistors provides a large charging current to charge input capacitances rapidly. On the falling part of the drive pulse the other transistor provides a low-impedance capacitor discharge path that also helps clear stored charges more rapidly. This action is known as *active pull-up* and *pull-down*. Pull-up involves a resistor or transistor that pulls the output *up* towards $V_{cc}$. Pull-down involves a device that provides a low-impedance path, pulling the output down towards ground.

### Problems

1. Define LSI.
2. Define SSI.
3. Define MSI.
4. Define *compatibility*.
5. Define *interface*.
6. Are most logic families completely *compatible* with most other logic families? Why?
7. What is propagation delay and what is the unit of measurement?
8. Define *noise immunity*.

9. What is meant by *speed* when applied to a given logic family?
10. Define *fan-out*.
11. Define *fan-in*.
12. List the 6 most popular logic families.
13. What two factors are most important in limiting the operating speed of a transistor switching circuit?
14. What is the purpose of adding a totem-pole output stage to the basic TTL gate?
15. What is the standard Vcc for the TTL family?

# Characteristics and Parameters of TTL

### THE 54/74 TTL FAMILY

There are two basic series of TTL logic—the 5400 series, which was originally designed to meet military requirements, and the 7400 series commercial variety. The 5400 series has an operating temperature range of from −55°C to +125°C and conforms to military documentation, testing, and reliability requirements. The 7400 series commercial grade TTL has a temperature range of from 0°C to 70°C. A military grade package can always be used as a direct replacement for its commercial equivalent although such a substitution is generally prohibitively expensive. A typical catalog number might read as 54/7404, indicating that the 5404 military grade and the 7404 commercial grade are both available. All manufacturers use the same numbers for equivalent devices, although a particular manufacturer may use a one- or two-letter prefix company symbol or an *in-house* number in addition to usual 7400 or 5400 series numbers. For example, the SN 7475 and 9375/7475 are both quad latches and are direct substitutes for one another.

TTL logic is the most widely used SSI and MSI logic family. Nearly every major manufacturer has a TTL product line, and most common TTL integrated circuits are produced by a number of companies. The TTL product line consists of the following subfamilies:

Standard TTL
Low-Power TTL
High-Speed TTL
Schottky-Clamped TTL
Low-Power Schottky TTL

### VARIATIONS ON THE BASIC TTL CIRCUIT

The basic TTL circuit is the most common and popular of bipolar logic forms, but there are several variations of the basic circuit to satisfy special logic needs. All of the variations, however, have the following properties in common:

1. Supply voltage: $V_{cc} = 5.0$ volts
2. Noise immunity: 1.0 volts
3. Fan-in per gate input: 1 unit
4. Fan-out: 10

### STANDARD TTL

Figure 2-10 shows a standard logic circuit, a three-input NAND gate. The circuit operates from a single +5 volt power supply and is compatible with circuits of *all* other TTL subfamilies (as well as that of DTL logic). It has a typical gate delay of 10 ns, a power dissipation of 10 mW per gate, and a maximum operating frequency (for flip-flops) of 35 MHz.

## 2-5 Operating Theory and Characteristics of the 7400 NAND Gate

We will examine the 7400 two-input NAND gate because it is the basis for the entire TTL family and the most often used member of the family. The NAND gate has a positive (high) output when either input is grounded (low). The output is low (ground) only when both inputs are high (positive).

The following are the NAND rules:

| *Output* | *Input Conditions* |
|---|---|
| Positive (high) | Either or both inputs grounded (low) |
| Grounded (low) | Both inputs positive (high) |

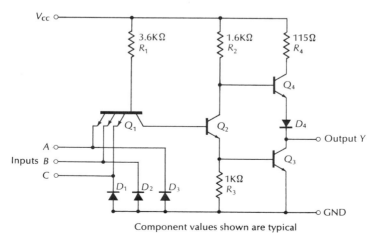

Component values shown are typical

**Figure 2-10**   Standard Logic Circuit Three-Input TTL NAND Gate

## INPUT AND OUTPUT LEVELS

*Input levels* typically range from an absolute minimum of 2.4 volts to a typical maximum 3.5 volts. The inputs can tolerate voltages of up to +5 volts but negative voltages can damage the gate and must be avoided. An input left unconnected behaves as though there were +2.4 to +5 volts being applied. However, inputs should not be left open in practice because it allows noise injection and erratic operation.

When an input is grounded, approximately 1.6 milliamperes (mA) of current flows along the input to ground path. If there is an appreciable resistance in the input to ground path, a voltage drop will be developed that can prevent the input from pulling near enough to ground for reliable operation. The resistance from input to ground should not exceed 500 ohms. The maximum voltage for the input to be effectively grounded is 0.8 volt and is normally closer to 0.6 volt.

*Output levels* range typically from 0.6 volt for a low (ground) to 3.5 volts for a high. These output levels satisfy the input requirements of less than 0.8 volt for a low and greater than 2.4 volts for a high. The output of a TTL gate can be (and almost always is) directly connected to the inputs of other TTL gates.

When the output is driving the input of another TTL gate at the low (0.6 volt) level, it must be capable of sinking 1.6 mA. Standard TTL can sink 16 mA and can drive 10 standard TTL inputs.

When the output is driving the input of another TTL gate at the high (positive) level, input diodes in the driven TTL gate are reverse-biased. The driving gate need supply only a small leakage current while holding the voltage level at 2.4 volts or greater (typically closer to 3.3 volts). Table 2-2 summarizes input-output conditions.

## THEORY OF OPERATION

Figure 2-11 shows the schematic diagram for the 7400 standard TLL two-input NAND gate.

### Both Inputs Unconnected

Assume that both inputs are open (not connected to anything). There is no current flowing out of either of the emitters in the dual emitter transistor, $Q_1$. There is no transistor action and the collector-base junction is forward-biased. Current flows from the +5 volt $V_{cc}$ source, through the forward-biased junction, and into the base of $Q_2$. This turns $Q_2$ and $Q_3$ *on*. Heavy conduction through $Q_2$ shunts nearly all available current away from the base of $Q_4$. $Q_4$ turns *off*. The *output* drops to about 0.6 volt, a logic low level. In this condition the output can sink up to 16 mA. For this reason TTL is often called *current-sinking* logic.

**Table 2-2** Summary of TTL Input-Output Conditions

| | Input Logic 0 (Low) | Input Logic 1 (High) | Output Logic 0 (Low) | Output Logic 1 (High) |
|---|---|---|---|---|
| Minimum | 0V | 2.4V | 0.4V | 2.4V |
| Typical | 0.6V | 3.3V | 0.6V | 3.3V |
| Maximum | 0.8V | 5.0V | 0.8V | 3.6V |

a. Voltages

| | | | | |
|---|---|---|---|---|
| Typical | 1.6mA | | Sinks | |
| | | | 16mA | |

b. Currents

**Both Inputs Connected to Positive**

Now assume that *both* inputs are connected to a voltage between 2.4 and 5.0 volts. This condition simply drives the base-emitter junction deeper into reverse bias. The results are the same as when both inputs are left unconnected. Remember that even though the same results can

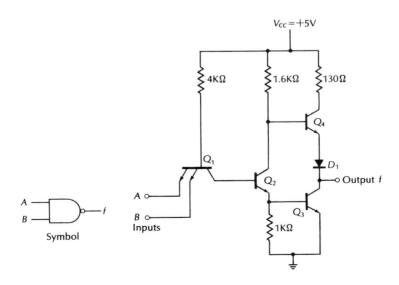

**Figure 2-11** Standard 7400 TTL NAND Gate Circuit

be had by either unconnected inputs or inputs connected to positive, leaving inputs unconnected is poor practice because of the possibility of noise pickup.

### One Input Grounded and One Positive

In this case the grounded emitter biases the emitter junction forward. $Q_1$ now behaves like a transistor and a large collector current flows through the 4K base resistor, out of the emitter to ground. This pulls $Q_1$'s collector to near ground potential, turning $Q_2$ *off*. The collector voltage of $Q_2$ rises to approximately $V_{cc}$ turning $Q_4$ *on*. The output goes *high*. The voltage output is about 3.3 volts because of the drop across the 130 ohm resistor, the collector-emitter drop of $Q_4$, and the diode ($D_1$) junction potential.

### Both Inputs at Ground

When both inputs are connected to ground, both emitter-base junctions of $Q_1$ are potentially forward-biased. But because the two junctions are never absolutely identical, one will conduct more heavily than the other and *hog* the available current, holding the other junction in a reverse-bias condition. Only one of the input junctions is forward-biased at any given time, and one is all that is required.

So far we have paid very little attention to $Q_1$ as a transistor. For the most part it functions as a diode array, and calling it a transistor is more a matter of structural fabrication than function. When all emitters are *high,* the hFE is less than unity.

If you carefully inspect the *low* to *high* (input) voltages, you will see that total current drain from the power supply varies during each phase of operation. This fact is important because these current variations can be reflected down both the $V_{cc}$ and *ground* lines. The particular phase in which $Q_2$, $Q_3$, and $Q_4$ are all *on,* followed within fractions of a nanosecond by $Q_3$'s turning off, generates a current spike of about ten times the normal current.

Table 2-3a summarizes the 7400 operation and part b shows common symbols as they are generally found in the manufacturer's data manual. Typical values for TTL are also indicated on the table.

## 2-6    Decoupling

The current spike generated by the on-to-off or off-to-on switching transition of a TTL gate is necessary for fast operation, but if these spikes are allowed to propagate down the $V_{cc}$ line, they can cause the system to malfunction.

To prevent current spikes from being reflected down the $V_{cc}$ line, decoupling capacitors are used to store energy to supply the brief (spike) current demand. These capacitors are essential in all but the simplest TTL systems.

Actual values are less critical than the way in which they are distributed on the circuit board. For example, a single $0.2\,\mu$F capacitor would be less effective than four $0.05\,\mu$F capacitors properly distributed. Further, since electrolytic capacitors and wound mylar capacitors tend to be highly inductive, wound mylar capacitors should be avoided in favor of disc capacitors. Electrolytic capacitors should be of the tantalum type and bypassed by a $0.05$ to $0.1\,\mu$F disc.

The following represent typical decoupling capacitor usage:

1. One $0.01$ to $0.1\,\mu$F disc from $V_{cc}$ to ground for every four small-scale IC's
2. One $0.01$ to $0.1\,\mu$F disc for each pair of MSI IC's
3. One tantalum $10\,\mu$F 10 volt capacitor where the $V_{cc}$ line enters the circuit board
4. A $0.01$ to $0.1\,\mu$F capacitor near any IC package that is more than 7.5 centimeters (about 3 inches) from the nearest decoupling capacitor

All leads should be kept as short as possible and capacitors should be placed close to the IC packages.

## 2-7  Troubleshooting Procedures and Equipment

Logic systems can be tested in two modes, static and dynamic. Static testing is the simpler of the two methods and should be tried first.

Static tests are performed by sequencing the system through the conditions on its truth table and comparing actual results with those indicated in the truth table output ($f$) column. A bounceless pushbutton is a simple but essential piece of equipment for delivering manual pulses to the inputs. (See Chapter 4.) Output levels can be indicated by an electronic voltmeter, DC oscilloscope, or one of a variety of commercially available logic probes. The simplest logic probe consists of a light-emitting diode and a current-limiting resistor. This kind of logic probe is not always satisfactory because it demands (typically) 5–15 mA current.

A TTL gate can sink 16 mA so the simple probe can represent as much as 10 TTL loads by itself, leaving very little current available to drive other gates. The use of this kind of probe on an already loaded gate can cause the gate to appear faulty when it is actually working properly. More sophisticated probes are available that do not load the circuit significantly. Some probes have built-in short-term memory or holding circuits that permit the detection of pulses that occur faster than the eye can respond to. Probes that can detect ground faults are

**Table 2-3**    Table of TTL Gate Operating Characteristics

| Input A | Input B | Output |
|---|---|---|
| Unconnected | Unconnected | Logic 0<br>Low (ground) |
| + | + | Logic 0<br>Low (ground) |
| + | 0<br>Gnd | Logic 1<br>High (+) |
| 0<br>Gnd | + | Logic 1<br>High (+) |
| 0<br>Gnd | 0<br>Gnd | Logic 1<br>High (+) |

a. Summary of 7400 NAND Gate Operation

Definition of Terms:

$V_{cc}$    Power supply voltage: 5.0V $\pm$10% ($\pm$5% for 5400 series)

$V_{IH}$    High-level input voltage: voltage required for logic 1 at an input. It is a guaranteed minimum of 2.0V.

$V_{IL}$    Low-level input voltage: voltage required for a logic 0 at an input. It is a guaranteed maximum of 0.8V.

$V_{OH}$    High-level output voltage: voltage level output from an output in the logic 1 state. It is a guaranteed minimum of 2.4V.

$V_{OL}$    Low-level output voltage: voltage level output from an output in the logical 0 state. It is a guaranteed maximum of 0.4V.

$I_{IH}$    High level input current: the current flowing into an input when a logic 1 voltage is applied to that input

$I_{IL}$    Low-level input current: the current flowing from an input when a logic 0 voltage is applied to that input

$I_{OH}$    High level output current: the current flowing from the output while the output voltage is at logic 1

$I_{OL}$    Low-level output current: the current flowing into an output, while the output voltage is at logic 0

Logic High State

$V_{IH}$    must be 2.0V or greater
$I_{IH}$    will not exceed 40 $\mu$A
$V_{OH}$    will be 2.4 V or greater
$I_{OH}$    will source at least 400 $\mu$A

Logic Low State

$V_{IL}$    must not exceed 0.8V
$I_{IL}$    will source at least 1.6mA
$V_{OL}$    will not exceed 0.4V
$I_{OL}$    will sink at least 16mA

b. TTL Characteristics

**Table 2-3** continued

| Circuit Form | $V_{cc}$ | Typical Power Dissipation per Gate | Fan-out | Propagation Delay per Gate | Immunity to External Noise | Clock Rate |
|---|---|---|---|---|---|---|
| Standard TTL (NAND) | 5V | 12mW | 10 | 10nS | 1V Guaranteed 0.4V | 35MHz |
| High-speed TTL (NAND) | 5V | 22mW | 10 | 6nS | Guaranteed 0.4V | 50MHz |
| Low-power TTL (NAND) | 5V | 1mW | 10 | 33nS | Guaranteed 0.4V | 3MHz |
| Schottky TTL (NAND) | 5V | 20mW | 10 | 3nS | 0.4V | 125MHz |
| Low-power Schottky TTL (NAND) | 5V | 2mW | 10 | 10nS | 0.4V | 45MHz |

c. Table of TTL Gate Operating Characteristics

particularly useful since ground faults are fairly common and can produce symptoms that are difficult to diagnose.

An extremely useful device is a special IC clip that clamps onto all pins of an IC and brings them out to convenient test pins. Some of these clamps feature a separate built-in logic probe for each of the 16 pins on a dual-inline (DIP) package.

Static techniques generally provide no clue to timing faults, noise problems, or poor circuit design problems.

Dynamic testing is accomplished with the circuit in normal operation by observing the pulse voltages with an oscilloscope. The scope *must* have a triggered sweep and a frequency response of at least 5 MHz. A frequency response as high as 125 MHz may be required for the faster Schottky versions of the TTL circuit. Dual trace inputs are also quite useful. Some dynamic testing can be done with a logic probe by observing the relative brightness. Experience is required to use the probe effectively for even *rough* dynamic indications.

**2-8 D**

TTL gates, a simple resistor
it would not
nces of

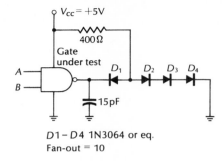

$D1 - D4$ 1N3064 or eq.
Fan-out = 10

**Figure 2-12**   Dummy Load for TTL Logic Gates

## 2-9   Noise Immunity

TTL circuits generally are considered to be immune to noise of 1 volt in amplitude, although as much as 1.5 volts of noise is seldom a problem. The guaranteed DC noise margin is 0.4 volt at all temperatures within the operating range. Because of the high switching speed of TTL circuits, most noise pulses are so slow by comparison that considering them to be DC is generally a realistic approach. Figure 2-13 illustrates TTL switching and noise immunity levels.

# TTL SUBFAMILIES

In addition to the standard TTL family, there are four (common) distinct subfamilies: high-speed TTL, low-power TTL, Schottky-clamped TTL, and special TTL gates.

## 2-10   High-Speed TTL (High Power)

The high-speed TTL circuit uses a Darlington driver which improves the current drive to the totem-pole output to increase switching speed. The resistor values are lower than in the standard TTL and, consequently, the high speed TTL has a hi̶g̶h̶ ̶̶ ̶ ̶ ̶ ̶ ̶22 mW, as compared to the standard TTL's 1̶3̶ ̶ ̶ ̶ ̶ ̶ ̶ ̶ ̶̶ ̶ ̶ ̶ has a 6 ns delay time and a flip-fl̶o̶ ̶ ̶ ̶ ̶ ̶ ̶ ̶ ̶ ̶ ̶ ̶ ̶n̶- dard TTL has a propag̶ ̶ ̶ ̶ ̶ of 35 MHz.

The hi̶ ̶ ̶ ̶ ̶

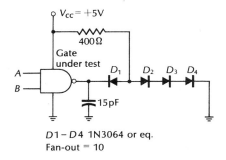

**Figure 2-12**   Dummy Load for TTL Logic Gates

## 2-9   Noise Immunity

TTL circuits generally are considered to be immune to noise of 1 volt in amplitude, although as much as 1.5 volts of noise is seldom a problem. The guaranteed DC noise margin is 0.4 volt at all temperatures within the operating range. Because of the high switching speed of TTL circuits, most noise pulses are so slow by comparison that considering them to be DC is generally a realistic approach. Figure 2-13 illustrates TTL switching and noise immunity levels.

## TTL  SUBFAMILIES

In addition to the standard TTL family, there are four (common) distinct subfamilies: high-speed TTL, low-power TTL, Schottky-clamped TTL, and special TTL gates.

## 2-10   High-Speed TTL (High Power)

The high-speed TTL circuit uses a Darlington driver which improves the current drive to the totem-pole output to increase switching speed. The resistor values are lower than in the standard TTL and, consequently, the high speed TTL has a high power consumption, 22 mW, as compared to the standard TTL's 12 mW. The high-speed TTL has a 6 ns delay time and a flip-flop operating speed of 50 MHz. The standard TTL has a propagation delay time of 10 ns and a flip-flop speed of 35 MHz.

The high-speed unit provides roughly twice the speed of standard TTL at the expense of approximately twice the power consumption. The fan-out of the high-speed TTL is 10, but its fan-in is about 1.3. A standard TTL gate can drive no more than 7 high-speed TTL gate

**Table 2-3** continued

| Circuit Form | $V_{cc}$ | Typical Power Dissipation per Gate | Fan-out | Propagation Delay per Gate | Immunity to External Noise | Clock Rate |
|---|---|---|---|---|---|---|
| Standard TTL (NAND) | 5V | 12mW | 10 | 10nS | 1V Guaranteed 0.4V | 35MHz |
| High-speed TTL (NAND) | 5V | 22mW | 10 | 6nS | Guaranteed 0.4V | 50MHz |
| Low-power TTL (NAND) | 5V | 1mW | 10 | 33nS | Guaranteed 0.4V | 3MHz |
| Schottky TTL (NAND) | 5V | 20mW | 10 | 3nS | 0.4V | 125MHz |
| Low-power Schottky TTL (NAND) | 5V | 2mW | 10 | 10nS | 0.4V | 45MHz |

c. Table of TTL Gate Operating Characteristics

particularly useful since ground faults are fairly common and can produce symptoms that are difficult to diagnose.

An extremely useful device is a special IC clip that clamps onto all pins of an IC and brings them out to convenient test pins. Some of these clamps feature a separate built-in logic probe for each of the 16 pins on a dual-inline (DIP) package.

Static techniques generally provide no clue to timing faults, noise problems, or poor circuit design problems.

Dynamic testing is accomplished with the circuit in normal operation by observing the pulse voltages with an oscilloscope. The scope *must* have a triggered sweep and a frequency response of at least 5 MHz. A frequency response as high as 125 MHz may be required for the faster Schottky versions of the TTL circuit. Dual trace inputs are also quite useful. Some dynamic testing can be done with a logic probe by observing the relative brightness. Experience is required to use the probe effectively for even *rough* dynamic indications.

## 2-8 Dummy Loads

Because of the totem-pole output in most TTL gates, a simple resistor cannot be used as a dummy load. Even if it worked, it would not simulate the nonlinear input characteristics or input capacitances of TTL inputs. Figure 2-12 shows a satisfactory dummy load that simulates ten *unit-load* gate inputs—a fan-in of 10.

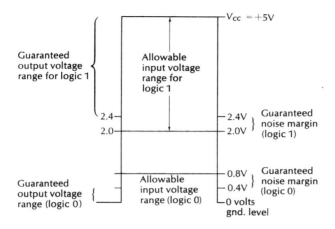

**Figure 2-13** TTL Switching Levels and Noise Immunity

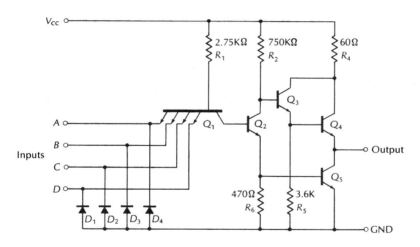

**Figure 2-14** High-Speed TTL NAND Gate

inputs. High-speed TTL is gradually being replaced by the more recent Schottky TTL gates. Figure 2-14 shows the high-speed TTL circuit. A 74H04 is the number designation for the high-speed version of the standard 7404.

## 2-11 The Low-Power TTL

The circuit for the low-power TTL is essentially the same as for the standard TTL except that resistor values have been increased, reducing the power consumption from 12 mW to 1 mW, with a decrease in speed from 10 ns for the standard TTL to 33 ns for the low-power version. Number designations containing an *L* indicate low power; for example, 74L04 is the low-power version of the standard 7404.

The low-power TTL gate has a fan-out of 10. It will drive ten low-power TTL inputs but only one standard TTL input. The low-power TTL gate is meeting considerable competition from complementary MOS (C-MOS) devices, such as the RCA 4000 series (COSMOS) and the Motorola MC 1400 and 74C00 series.

## 2-12   The Schottky-Clamped TTL

The Schottky-clamped TTL is the fastest member of the TTL family. With a 3 ns propagation time and a 125 MHz clocking rate, it is a serious rival to the fastest available logic (ECL) family with its 1 to 4 ns propagation times.

The Schottky TTL also compares favorably with ECL (emitter-coupled logic) in power consumption and cost, as well as being com-

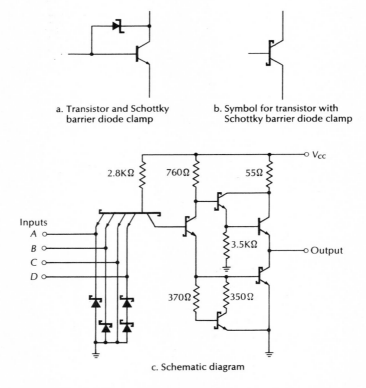

a. Transistor and Schottky
   barrier diode clamp

b. Symbol for transistor with
   Schottky barrier diode clamp

c. Schematic diagram

**Figure 2-15**   The Schottky Diode Clamped TTL NAND Gate

patible with the other members of the TTL family. The secret of this circuit's high speed is the elimination of storage-time delay by clamping the collector of each transistor to its base with a Schottky barrier diode. This prevents the collector-base junction from going into saturation in which the junction becomes heavily forward biased, drawing carriers into the depletion zone that must be cleared before the transistor can be turned off. The use of a clamping diode between collector and base to prevent saturation is not a new idea, but ordinary junction diodes also have some storage problem. The Schottky diode has no storage problems and virtually eliminates transistor carrier storage when used as a collector-base clamp. Figure 2-15 shows a Schottky-clamped transistor, the special symbol for a Schottky transistor, and the schematic diagram of the Schottky TTL *NAND* gate. There is also a low-power Schottky circuit with the same speed as the standard TTL, but with a power requirement of only 2 mW per gate as opposed to the 12 mW for a standard TTL gate. Table 2-4 compares the several TTL subfamilies with respect to speed and power consumption.

## 2-13   Special TTL Gates

### THE 4000 AND 8200 SERIES

In general the Motorola 4000 series TTL devices and the Signetics 8200 series devices are interchangeable with 7400 devices. There may be slight electrical differences and the pinout of equivalent devices in the two series may be different. When in doubt, consult the data manual.

### OPEN COLLECTOR GATES

Most TTL gates use a totem-pole output stage. The outputs can be tied together only via the inputs of another gate. They cannot be tied di-

**Table 2-4**   Comparison of TTL Subfamilies

| TTL Subfamily | Gate Power (milliwatts) | Propagation Time (nanoseconds) | Upper Counting Frequency Limit (Megahertz) |
|---|---|---|---|
| Standard | 10 | 10 | 35 |
| High-speed | 22 | 6 | 50 |
| Low-power | 1 | 33 | 3 |
| Schottky | 19 | 3 | 125 |
| Low-power Schottky | 2 | 10 | 45 |

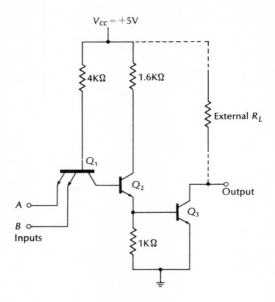

**Figure 2-16**    Open Collector TTL NAND Gate

rectly together because if one output goes high while another goes low, the direct connection will yield an indeterminate output level. In addition, gate damage is a very likely result.

Some TTL gates are available using a single output transistor with an uncommitted collector. Figure 2-16 is a typical example of an *open collector* gate.

Outputs of open collector devices can be connected together to a common external load resistor. For example, all of the outputs of a 7405 Hex inverter (six inverters in a package) can be connected in this way to get a six-input NOR gate.

If two 7401 open collector and two input NAND gates are connected as shown in Figure 2-17c, the result is not a four-input NAND gate but rather the following logic function:

$$f = \overline{(A \cdot B) + (C \cdot D)}$$

The wired output configuration is not very popular with designers for several reasons: open collector circuits are much slower than totem-pole output devices; the noise problem in open collector circuits is greater than in totem-pole devices; and troubleshooting hard wired groups of open collector gates is next to impossible without serious damage to the circuit board.

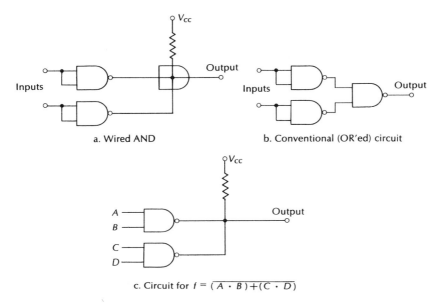

a. Wired AND

b. Conventional (OR'ed) circuit

c. Circuit for $f = \overline{(A \cdot B) + (C \cdot D)}$

**Figure 2-17** Hard-Wired Open Collector Gates

## AND GATES

An AND gate can easily be obtained by inverting the output of a NAND gate. Combining two gates adds additional propagation delay, power consumption, and stray wiring capacitance. By building the inverter into the IC, we can form an AND gate that adds only about 4 ns delay and 5 mW of power consumption and eliminates external wiring problems. Input-output characteristics are the same as for the NAND gate.

## NOR GATES

A similar approach could be taken to fabricate OR or NOR by combining NAND's on a chip but the total propagation delay would be greater than would be acceptable if such a gate were to be used with other gates having much shorter propagation times. Instead, the NOR gate uses a slightly different circuit but does have the same basic input and output circuits to insure compatibility with the rest of the TTL family.

## AND-OR-INVERT AND EXPANDER GATES

There is another group of gates that provide moderately complex logic functions in a single package. These expander gates (AND-OR-Invert) are infrequently used.

## SCHMITT-TRIGGER NAND GATES

Because many data sources are comparatively slow and (or) produce waveforms that are not acceptable to high-speed logic circuits, a NAND gate with a Schmitt trigger is available. The 5413/7413 Schmitt NAND accepts almost any input waveform and produces an output waveform fully compatible with the requirements of TTL circuits.

## GATES WITH TRI-STATE OUTPUTS

The tri-state output gate was designed for systems where a large number of gates must tie to a common bus. The open collector devices have proved unsatisfactory for this application. Minicomputers, for example, are organized with a data-bus system in which many gate outputs are tied to a common line. Tri-state logic uses the two standard logic levels and has an added third state that is not a logic level but an open-circuit condition that effectively disconnects the output of the gate from the bus. The gate does not interract with the bus in any way unless it is *enabled* by a signal on a special *enable* input. In the two normal logic states a totem-pole circuit provides active pull-up and pull-down with the speed of standard TTL gates. When tri-state gates are used, two of them on the same bus must not be enabled and allowed to go to opposite logic levels at the same time. Since totem-pole output circuits cannot operate in this mode, this problem of "fighting for the bus" is one that must be carefully avoided. Figure 2-18b shows four tri-state devices on a common bus.

Tri-state devices are not used indiscriminately; but where they are necessary, there is no good substitute. Because of the extra *enable* inputs, a given package contains fewer tri-state gates than would be usual for ordinary TTL.

### Problems

16. What is the maximum input voltage in TTL for a logic 0 output?
17. What is the minimum input voltage for a logic 1 in TTL?
18. What is maximum output voltage for a logic 0 in TTL?
19. What is the minimum output voltage for a logic 1 in TTL?
20. What is the guaranteed noise margin for a logic 0 in TTL? For a logic 1?
21. What are the differences between the 5400 and 7400 series TTL?
22. To which subfamily does each of the following belong?
    a. 7400    b. 74H00    c. 74S00    d. 74L00
23. When high speed is required, what must be traded for it? (See Table 2-4.)

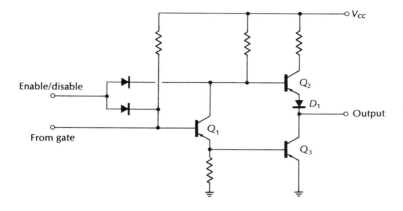

a. One version of the TTL tristate output circuit

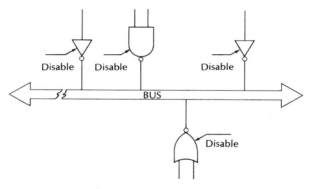

b. Tristate devices on a bus

**Figure 2-18**   Four Tri-State Devices on a Common Bus

24. Define the following:
    a. $V_{cc}$      d. $V_{OH}$      g. $I_{IL}$
    b. $V_{IH}$      e. $V_{OL}$      h. $I_{OH}$
    c. $V_{IL}$      f. $I_{IH}$      i. $I_{OL}$
    Find the value of each in the data manual for the 7400.
25. Why must unused gate inputs be returned to ground or $V_{cc}$?
26. Why is power supply line decoupling so important in TTL systems?
27. Wound mylar capacitors are not satisfactory for decoupling purposes. Why?

28. On a TTL power supply bus there is a 10 $\mu$F and a 0.1 $\mu$F disc capacitor. They are in different places along the line but effectively in parallel. Why can't the 0.1 $\mu$F be removed?
29. What is the difference between static and dynamic testing in troubleshooting digital systems?
30. What are the three levels in a TTL tri-state output device?
31. Draw the schematic diagram of a two-input open collector TTL NAND gate.
32. Draw a logic diagram showing six open collector TTL gates in a wired AND configuration, with the node driving a single NAND gate.
33. What makes the Schottky-clamped gate faster than the standard TTL gate?

## 2-14   Emitter-Coupled Logic (ECL)

The 2 ns ECL, which has become widely accepted, optimizes speed and power consumption to make ECL easier to use. Figure 2-19 illustrates the 2 ns ECL logic element circuit, a gate that performs both an OR as well as a NOR function. The basis of the circuit is a differential amplifier $Q_3/Q_4$ and $Q_5$ that conducts current through one or the other of its sides ($Q_3/Q_4$ or $Q_5$), depending on the level on the input lines $A$ and $B$. The circuit requires a nominal $-5.2$ volt power supply, connected to $V_{EE}$. A constant bias voltage $V_{BB}$ at the base of $Q_5$ sets the switching point between logic 1 and 0. With a $-5.2$ volt power supply the logic 1 and 0 levels are approximately $-0.9$ volt and $-1.7$ volts.

ECL does not operate in a saturated mode and produces no switching transients. Because of its higher cost and high speed, ECL is most often found in large, expensive computers.

## 2-15   MOS and C-MOS

A variety of metal-oxide-semiconductor field effect (MOS) devices are available. MOS devices are available in $P$-channel, the newer $N$-channel devices, and complementary MOS devices. Complementary MOS uses an $N$-channel/$P$-channel pair of MOS devices in a kind of class $B$ operating mode. The gate draws appreciable current only during the switching operation. The C-MOS family contains gates, counters, and the like in an almost one-to-one correspondence with available packages in the TTL family.

C-MOS is compatible with TTL in that it can be operated at 0 volt + 5 volt levels. A C-MOS gate can drive any (single) low-power TTL gate or a single standard TTL if two of the C-MOS gate inputs are tied together. A CD 4049 C-MOS buffer can be used to interface C-MOS

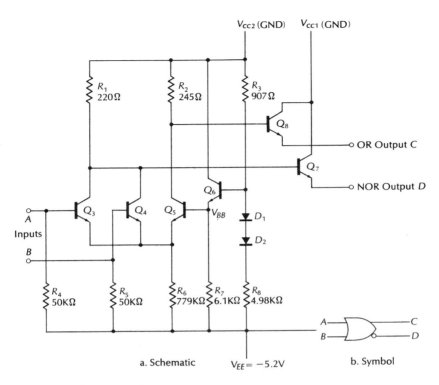

**Figure 2-19**  The 2-ns ECL Circuit

to standard TTL without tied inputs. We will go into the problems of interfacing among families in a later chapter.

C-MOS is providing stiff competition for low-power TTL and even for standard TTL in systems where its relatively slow speed is tolerable and where very low power operation is required.

Because of greater gate complexity and the corresponding greater chip space per gate, the C-MOS family consists almost entirely of SSI and MSI packages.

Single-ended P-MOS and N-MOS are devoted almost entirely to MSI and LSI, memories, registers, arithmetic elements, and complete microprocessor units. Table 2-5 compares important characteristics of the various popular logic types.

## P-MOS

The older metal gate P-MOS requires a +12 volt and −12 volt power supply, has a high threshold voltage, and is comparatively difficult to

**Table 2-5** Comparison of MOS and Bipolar Logic Types

| Gate Process | | Relative Chip Complexity | Power Dissipation per Gate | Threshold Voltage | Supply Voltage ($V_{GG}$) ($V_{CC}$) ($V_{DD}$) | Propagation Delay (ns/gate) | Freq. (MHz) (Max.) | Noise Margin "1" | "0" |
|---|---|---|---|---|---|---|---|---|---|
| P-channel | | | | | | | | | |
| High threshold | Med. power | 1 | 1.7mW | $-3.5$ to $-5$ | $+12V, -12V$ | 75nS | 2 | 3 | 1.5 |
| | Low power | 1.2 | 0.45mW | $-3.5$ to $-5$ | $+12V, -12V$ | 300nS | 500 KHz | 3 | 1.5 |
| Silicon gate | | 1.3 | 1.0mW | $-1.5$ to $-2.5$ | $+5V, -12V$ | 60nS | 5 | 2 | 0.7 |
| Ion implant, depletion loads | | 1.3 | 1.5mW | $-1.5$ to $-5$ | $+5V, -12V$ | 35nS | 5 | 1.5 | 1 |
| N-channel MOS | | | | | | | | | |
| Metal gate | | 1.3 | 1.0mW | 1 to 2 | $+5V$ | | 10 | 1 | 1 |
| Silicon gate | | 1.6 | 1.0mW | 1 to 2 | $+5V$ | | 10 | 1 | 1 |
| Complementary (C-MOS) | | | | | | | | | |
| Metal gate | | 0.3 | 50nW | $(\pm)1.5$ to $(\pm)2.5$ | $+5V$ | 40nS | 20 | $V_{DD}/2.2$ | |
| Silicon gate | | 0.4 | 50nW | $\pm0.5$ to $\pm2.5$ | $+5V$ | 25nS | 25 | $V_{DD}/2.2$ | |
| Bipolar lines | | | | | | | | | |
| TTL (standard) | | 40 | 15mW | | 5.0V $+20\%$ $-10\%$ | 10nS | 60 | 1.2 | 1.2 |
| ECL | | 20 | 25-35mW | | 5.2V $+20\%$ $-10\%$ | 1nS | 400 | 0.4 | 0.4 |
| DTL | | 20 | | | 5.0V $\pm10\%$ | 30nS | | | |
| Low-power TTL | | 40 | 1.0mW | | 5.0V $+20\%$ $-10\%$ | 33nS | 3 | 1.2 | 1.2 |

interface to TTL. It is also the slowest of the MOS devices, from 75 to 300 ns.

### SILICON-GATE P-MOS

Most of the newer P-MOS devices use a silicon gate in place of the earlier metal gate. The silicon gate reduces the threshold voltage and allows the use of a +5 volt power supply providing output levels that are more easily interfaced to TTL. Flip-flop frequency is increased from about 2 MHz to 5 MHz over the metal gate P-MOS.

### N-MOS

N-MOS devices are more recent than P-MOS devices but are finding increasing applications and designer acceptance. N-MOS devices are from five to ten times faster than P-MOS devices, use a single 5 volt power supply, and can drive a single standard TTL load without any additional interfacing components. Of all the MOS devices, the N-MOS devices are the most compatible with TTL.

### C-MOS

C-MOS has an advantage over single MOS devices because it consumes power only during logic transitions. C-MOS generates almost no switching noise and is the quietest of the most common gates. (ECL is also a quiet logic form.)

## 2-16   MOS Gate Theory of Operation

Figure 2-20 shows the basic MOS static inverter. The NAND and NOR gates are basically inverters with added MOS FET transistors. We will examine the theory of operation for the inverter, since it is the basic gate in the MOS family. (Refer to Figure 2-20 as you read the following discussion.)

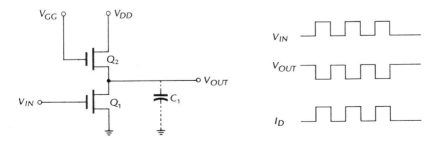

**Figure 2-20**   MOS Static Inverter

In the single-channel MOS transistor, $Q_1$ is the switching transistor. $Q_2$ serves as a fixed load resistor and does not take an active part in the switching operation. When the signal $V_{IN}$ turns $Q_1$ *on*, current begins to flow from the power supply ($V_{DD}$). The output voltage is a function of the ratio of the *on* resistance value of $Q_1$ and the fixed resistance of $Q_2$. The output voltage can never go all the way to zero. The operation is essentially the same as any common source MOS FET amplifier. $Q_2$ is used as a load resistor instead of a fixed value resistance because a larger effective resistance value can be obtained in less chip space, and because it eliminates the need for a separate resistor processing step in manufacture.

## 2-17   C-MOS Theory of Operation

Figure 2-21 shows the basic C-MOS inverter circuit. Assume that the input signal is low (ground); the $N$-channel transistor $Q_1$ is *off*, and the $P$-channel device is *on*. The output is approximately $+V_{DD}$ (frequently $+5$ volts).

If the load being driven by the output of the gate is the input to another MOS gate, almost no current is drawn from the power supply. The input resistance of an MOS gate is very nearly infinite. When the input goes high, $Q_1$ is turned *on* and $Q_2$ is turned *off*. No DC current flows from the power supply and the output is pulled to ground by the low *on* resistance of $Q_1$. The output levels are very close to 0 volts and $+V_{DD}$ volts.

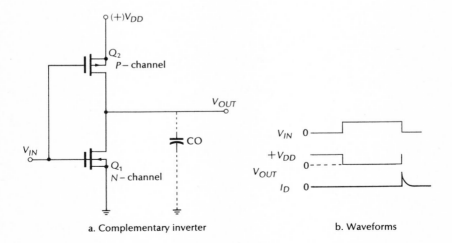

a. Complementary inverter     b. Waveforms

**Figure 2-21**   C-MOS Inverter

In C-MOS gates the turn-on threshold is a function of the power supply voltage, $V_{DD}$. The turn-on threshold is given by:

$$\frac{V_{DD}}{2.2} \approx 45\% \; V_{DD}$$

For a $V_{DD}$ of 5 volts, an input high would have to be at least 2.25 volts to switch the gate.

There are two sets of C-MOS devices, the 4000 series and the 54C/74C series. The 4000 series, the earlier version, is gradually being replaced by the 54C/74C series in most applications. The 54C/74C series is typically 50 percent faster and sinks 50 percent more current than the 4000 series devices. The 54C/74C devices are *pin-for-pin* and *number-for-number* functional equivalents of 7400 series TTL devices and feature approximately the same switching speed as low-power TTL. Table 2-6 compares 54C/74C and TTL 7400 series devices.

The 54C/74C temperature ranges are

$$54C: -55°C \text{ to } +125°C$$
$$74C: -40°C \text{ to } +85°C$$

The 54C/74C series devices can be operated with $V_{cc}$ values up to 15 volts with increased speed and power dissipation.

## NOISE IMMUNITY

C-MOS has excellent noise immunity. A spurious signal of up to 0.45 $V_{cc}$ will not cause a logical output signal (2.25 volts of noise immunity at $V_{cc} = 5$ volts).

**Table 2-6**  Comparison of TTL and CMOS (54C/74C)

| Family | $V_{cc}$ volts | $V_{in}$ (0) Max | $V_{in}$ (1) Min | $V_{out}$ (0) Max | $V_{out}$ (1) Min | Propagation Delay (nS) | $I_{out}$ (0) | $I_{out}$ (1) | Power Dissipation per Gate |
|---|---|---|---|---|---|---|---|---|---|
| 54/74 | +5 | 0.8V | 2.0V | 0.4V | 2.4V | 15 | 16mA | 40$\mu$A | 10mW |
| 54L/74L | +5 | 0.7V | 2.0V | 0.3V | 2.4V | 35 | 2mA | 100$\mu$A | 2.25mW |
| 54C/74C | +5 | 0.8V | 3.5V | 0.4V | 2.4V | 50 | 360A | 100$\mu$ A | 1.25mW |
| 54C/74C | +10* | 2.0V | `8.0V | 1.0V | 9V | 30 | — | — | 5mW |

*$V_{cc}$ up to 15 volts can be used with C-MOS when TTL devices are not a part of the system.

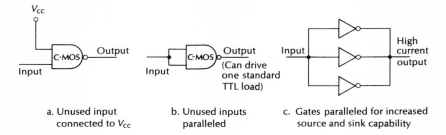

a. Unused input
connected to $V_{cc}$

b. Unused inputs
paralleled

c. Gates paralleled for increased
source and sink capability

**Figure 2-22** Paralleling C-MOS

### UNUSED INPUTS

Unused inputs on a NAND gate may be tied to $V_{cc}$ or they may be paralleled with active inputs as shown in Figure 2-22, parts a and b. If they are paralleled, the source current is increased to nearly 1.6 mA, enough to drive one standard TTL input. The parallel connection increases the input capacitance, which may pose some high frequency problems. Although the current that the output of the 54C/74C devices can sink is not increased by paralleling the inputs, this is not necessary for driving TTL. When increased drive current in both directions (source and sink) is required for driving LED indicators or similar devices, C-MOS can be connected as shown in Figure 2-22c.

### POWER SUPPLY CONSIDERATIONS

Because C-MOS is such a low-power device, it is ideal for battery-operated devices. Because of its controlled (gradual) rise time, power supply filtering, decoupling, and regulating are less critical in C-MOS than in TTL. Figure 2-23 shows the schematic diagram of C-MOS (54C/74C) NAND and NOR gates.

## 2-18 Dynamic MOS Logic

A form of logic circuit is possible in MOS circuits that has no counterpart in bipolar circuits. Dynamic logic is a sampling type of logic that works only because the input to an MOS transistor is almost completely capacitive. A logic circuit driving the input of an MOS transistor needs only to provide a current path for the short time required to charge the input capacitance. Once charged, the capacitor can hold the transistor in an *on* state until the charge leaks off. This dynamic form of operation demands power only during switching and only enough to charge the very small capacitors involved.

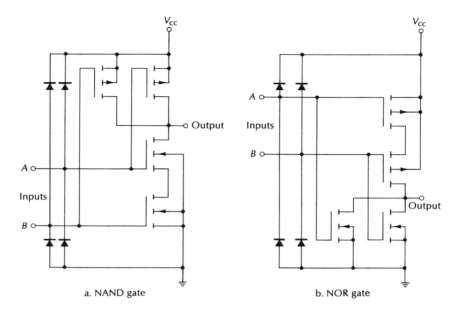

a. NAND gate          b. NOR gate

**Figure 2-23**   C-MOS Gates

The transistors provide the necessary rapid charge and discharge paths. Figure 2-24 shows a basic MOS dynamic inverter. Notice that two clock pulses are required to control the operation of the gate. The phase 1 and phase 2 clock pulses are 180° out of phase and not only serve to control the transfer of data but also control the energy so that they periodically refresh the capacitor charge that leaks off. The clocks must run continuously and the capacitors must be *refreshed* every few milliseconds. When the circuit is first started up (initialized), the first pair of clock pulses, Ø 1 and Ø 2, gate in *precharge* current for $C_1$ and $C_2$. In an IC with a large number of gates, the precharge operation demands the largest current of any phase of the operation.

The following is a step-by-step description of the dynamic MOS inverter in Figure 2-24.

1. At $t_1$ the pulse from the phase 2 (Ø 2) clock turns on $Q_3$, causing the charge on $C_1$ to be transferred to $C_2$. $C_1$ is much larger than $C_2$ so the transfer can be made with no significant drop in the $C_1$ voltage.

2. At $t_2$ $V_{IN}$ turns $Q_1$ *on*, and the Ø 1 clock pulse turns $Q_2$ *on*. This causes a partial discharge of $C_1$. The discharge condition is not transmitted to $C_2$ because $Q_3$ is *off*.

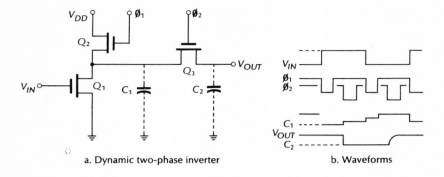

a. Dynamic two-phase inverter     b. Waveforms

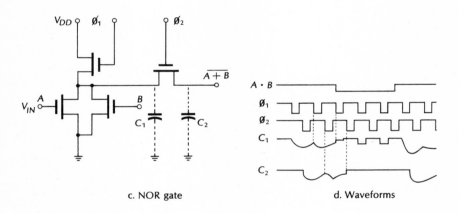

c. NOR gate     d. Waveforms

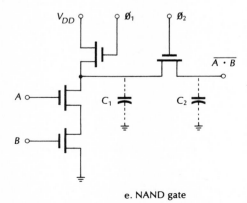

e. NAND gate

**Figure 2-24**   Dynamic MOS Logic

3. At $t_3$ the $\emptyset$ 1 clock turns $Q_2$ *off*. A partial charge remains on $C_1$ and is subsequently discharged through $Q_1$, which remains turned *on* by $V_{IN}$.

4. At $t_4$ the $\emptyset$ 2 clock turns $Q_3$ *on*, and $C_2$ is also allowed to discharge through $Q_1$ to ground.

5. Drain current flows at $t_1$ (to charge up $C_1$) and during the short period that $Q_1$ and $Q_2$ are *on* simultaneously (from $t_2$ to $t_3$).

**Problems**

34. What do the Schottky gates have in common with ECL gates that improves their speed?
35. Which member of the ECL family is most popular?
36. Compare C-MOS and TTL with respect to the following parameters:
    a. speed
    b. propagation delay time
    c. $V_{cc}$
    d. noise immunity
    e. cost per gate
    f. fan-out
    g. chip space required per gate
    h. power consumption per gate
37. Match the following to items (1) through (4) below (more than one may be correct):
    a. N-MOS        b. P-MOS        c. C-MOS
    (1) Uses both *N*- and *P*-channel devices on the same chip
    (2) The earliest and slowest member of the MOS group
    (3) Used primarily at MSI and SSI levels
    (4) Uses a single power supply and is used primarily for LSI structures
38. What is the chief advantage of silicon-gate over metal-gate devices?
39. Is N-MOS compatible with TTL? Explain.
40. Is P-MOS compatible with TTL? Explain.
41. Is C-MOS compatible with TTL? Explain.
42. What is the basic gate structure in MOS?
    a. AND        c. NOR        e. Inverter
    b. OR        d. NAND        f. None of these
43. What kind of drain load resistor is used in MOS gates?
44. Which of the MOS devices consumes the least power?
45. In C-MOS the smallest noise voltage that will falsely turn on a gate is how many volts?
46. Explain the difference between static and dynamic MOS logic.

47. What is the purpose of the two-phase (2 $\emptyset$) clock pulses as used with dynamic MOS logic?
48. What is *precharge* in dynamic MOS logic? Why is it necessary?

## 2-19 Integrated Injection Logic ($I^2L$)

Integrated injection logic is a recent form of bipolar logic that is as simple to fabricate and as inexpensive to produce as MOS. It is particularly well suited to LSI processes, requires less chip space than MOS, and rivals the speed of TTL.

Bipolar logic faced some formidable problems in LSI packages. Circuits were too complex, occupied far too much chip space per gate, and required power dissipations that all too easily exceeded the modest practical limit of one-half watt per chip. The complexity of gate structures also made interconnection of individual gates difficult. Attempts to find ways to alter the geometry of existing bipolar logic circuits were doomed to failure from the beginning. The chief culprit was the passive load resistor required by each gate. The load resistors occupied the lion's share of the chip space and pushed the heat dissipation to the point of requiring exotic cooling methods for any significant number of gates.

Once the load resistor was replaced by a constant current source in the form of an active transistor, the injection logic gate became a reality. The injector transistor is a *PNP* transistor in the common base configuration—the same basic circuit frequently found as the active emitter resistor in differential amplifiers and other linear circuits.

Figure 2-25 illustrates the relative chip space occupied by a bipolar transistor and a passive load resistor. The illustration provides some insight into the magnitude of the space problem created by passive load resistors.

Next, the collector and emitter were exchanged on the chip resulting in a multicollector transistor operating in an inverse mode. With the upside-down transistor configuration, common emitter circuits can operate in a common *N* type silicon bed. This eliminates the need for isolation space between transistors and allows one injector transistor to service several gate transistors.

The chip space required for isolation in right-side-up bipolar IC's is frequently twice as great as that required for a transistor. The inverted configuration allows the substrate to become a part of the interconnecting wiring rather than simply presenting an isolation problem. Those interconnections handled within the substrate minimize the complexity of the upper surface wiring pattern, reducing the cost still further. Figure 2-26b shows the basic inverter structure along with the *PNP* injector transistor. Figure 2-26a illustrates the simplicity of fabrication.

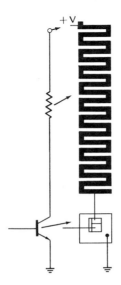

**Figure 2-25** Relative Chip Space Occupied by Transistor and Passive Load Resistor

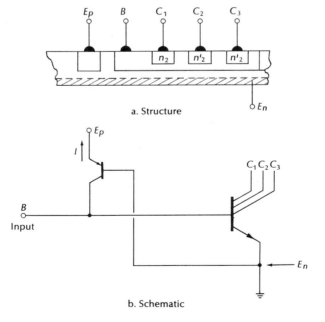

a. Structure

b. Schematic

**Figure 2-26** Merged Complementary Bipolar Logic

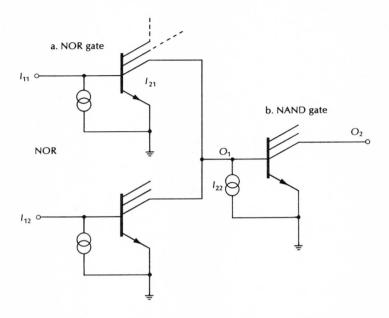

**Figure 2-27** Inverters Combined to Form NOR and NAND Gates

Because of the way in which the transistors are "merged" within the substrate, the structure is often called *merged complementary bipolar logic*. The abbreviation MTL for merged transistor logic is used synonomously with $I^2L$.

By hard-wiring the collectors, more complex structures can be formed. Figure 2-27a shows how two inverters can be connected to form a NOR gate. Figure 2-27b is a NAND gate structure. The load is actually the driven gate, and the collector current for the driving gate is supplied by the injector transistor connected to the base of the driven transistor.

### MTL IS TTL COMPATIBLE

Table 2-7 compares the speed of MOS, TTL ($T^2L$), and MTL gates.

### Problems

49. $I^2L$ (MTL) is a form of which kind of logic?
    a. Bipolar    b. MOS    c. Hybrid
50. Why is the gate transistor in $I^2L$ formed upside-down on the chip?
51. What circuit component was the major factor in holding back the development of bipolar LSI?

**Table 2-7**  Gate Propagation Time for the Major
Gate Forms

| Technology | Gate Propagation Time |
|---|---|
| P-MOS | 1 MS |
| N-MOS | 100-25 ns |
| C-MOS | 100 ns |
| C-MOS On Sapphire | 100-25 ns |
| I²L (MTL) | 25-10 ns |
| Standard T²L (TTL) | 10 ns |
| Schottky T²L (TTL) | 10-1 ns |
| I²L Schottky | 10-1 ns |

52. In I²L logic what has been used to replace the component mentioned in problem 51?
53. Compare the speeds of P-MOS, N-MOS, C-MOS, TTL, and MTL.

## SUMMARY

Bipolar TTL and C-MOS dominate the small-scale and medium-scale integration (SSI and MSI) digital scene. Both families provide circuit packages ranging from a few simple independent gates to fairly complex counters, adders, and many gate, general, and special purpose logic structures. They have invaded the field of large-scale integration only to a relatively small extent. Neither form lends itself well to large-scale integration because of gate complexity and, in the case of TTL, excessive power dissipation.

TTL is considerably faster than C-MOS but consumes far more power. Where speed is the primary consideration, TTL has been the most popular choice. Both TTL and C-MOS can be operated from a single supply (+5 volts for TTL and typically 5 to 18 volts for C-MOS).

P-MOS and N-MOS are dedicated primarily to large-scale integration. The newer N-MOS is faster than P-MOS, uses a single +5 volt power supply, and is generally more compatible with both I²L and C-MOS. P-MOS is an older process and requires a +5 volt and −12 volt power supply, making it more difficult to interface to TTL. P-MOS is also slower than N-MOS or C-MOS.

Both P- and N-MOS are far more conservative in their power demands than TTL. C-MOS requires the least power of any presently available forms. Arithmetic systems, memories, and microprocessor units (the heart of a computer) are the special province of P-MOS and N-MOS. Individual gate packages, counters, and the like are not generally available in P-MOS and N-MOS.

Dynamic logic is a veritable miser when it comes to power consumption. It is more complex to operate because of the requirement of two or more clock signals. The timing required is fairly critical and speed is limited. This form of logic has been largely restricted to two kinds of large memory circuits and is not common in other applications.

Merged transistor logic (MTL or $I^2L$) is a recent bipolar logic that promises MOS simplicity and low cost with TTL speed.

In any logic circuit there is always a tradeoff between speed and power consumption. Each family has its own speed-power product, and process modifications can improve this product to some extent. However, for a given process an increase in speed is always obtained at the cost of increased power consumption.

# CHAPTER 3

# ASYNCHRONOUS LOGIC

*Learning Objectives. Upon completion of this chapter you should:*
1. *Be familiar with basic gates and their duals.*
2. *Be able to write equations from a truth table.*
3. *Be able to plot an equation on a truth table.*
4. *Be able to draw logic diagrams from equations or write a truth table from a logic diagram.*
5. *Be familiar with the terms minterm and maxterm.*
6. *Be able to simplify equations with up to four variables using a Karnaugh map.*
7. *Be able to plot a simplified equation on a truth table.*
8. *Be able to design and analyze data selector logic circuits.*
9. *Be able to design and analyze folded data selector logic circuits.*
10. *Know what ROM logic is and when it is used.*

A logic circuit is composed of one or more logic gates. The inputs to the gates consist of a *high* or *low* voltage, representing logic 1's and logic 0's. Circuit outputs are also either *high* or *low,* logic 1 or logic 0. There are two kinds of logic: combinatorial (also called asynchronous or direct logic) and sequential or synchronous logic. Synchronous logic (discussed in Chapter 4) responds to the input conditions only at specific times controlled by a master pulse generator called a *clock.* Circuit operation is synchronized to the clock. Asynchronous logic (the topic of this chapter) responds as the input conditions change. No clock input is provided and the circuit is not synchronized with the system clock.

We will examine logic operations starting with very basic ones and working up to fairly complex systems. At each level of complexity we will study the most appropriate methods of representing and manipulating equations and logic diagrams. At the lowest level of complexity we will examine the relationship among truth tables, equations, and logic diagrams. We will also investigate the dual nature of logic at this level.

At the next level of complexity we will work with Karnaugh mapping and simplification methods. Because simplification methods using Karnaugh maps become cumbersome as systems become more complex, we will examine a tool called *data selector* (or *multiplex*) logic that is appropriate to this higher level of complexity. Finally, we will study the highest level method, called *ROM* (read-only memory) logic.

The various levels of complexity are dictated by the commercial availability of logic circuits, rather than purely by logic considerations. Certainly logic considerations have influenced manufacturing decisions, but their influence was tempered by practical considerations. Each method is best suited to a fairly specific complexity level and is either very difficult or completely impossible to use for greatly different levels.

## 3-1 Single-Input Logic

There is only one valid logic function for a single input gate—inversion. Because there are two possible input values, 0 and 1, and two output values (also 0 and 1), we can make truth tables representing four different single-input gate functions as shown in Table 3-1. Truth tables 1 and 2 are useless because the output condition is not influenced by input conditions and thus performs no logic function. Table 3 is a logic "do-nothing" circuit because the output condition simply follows the input condition. Although the circuit represented by truth table 3 is a useful circuit element in the form of a non-inverting buffer amplifier, it cannot be considered as a logic element. The number 4 truth table is the table that describes the inverter function. Table number 4 is the only table which represents a valid logic function.

## 3-2 Two-Input Logic

For two-input devices it is possible to write sixteen different truth tables. Six of them are useless, six are common and most often used, and the remaining four are used only in very unusual situations.

The following are the useless truth table forms:

1. Where all outputs are always 0.
2. Where all outputs are always 1.
3. Where the outputs are identical to input $A$.
   Here input $B$ does not affect the output under any condition. The circuit is, in effect, a single-input circuit with input $A$.
4. Where the outputs are identical to the inputs on $B$.
   In this case, we have a single-input circuit with input $B$.

**Table 3-1**  All Possible Single-Input Logic Functions

| 1 | | | 2 | | | 3 | | | 4 | |
|---|---|---|---|---|---|---|---|---|---|---|
| $A$ | $f$ | | $A$ | $f$ | | $A$ | $f$ | | $A$ | $f$ |
| 0 | 0 | | 0 | 1 | | 0 | 0 | | 0 | 1 |
| 1 | 0 | | 1 | 1 | | 1 | 1 | | 1 | 0 |

5. Where the outputs are all inversions of input $A$.

The circuit has degenerated into a single-input inverter for input $A$.

6. Where the outputs are the inversion of input $B$.

Here we have a single-input inverter with input $B$.

These cases—in which the two-input circuit degenerates into a single-input non-inverting amplifier or an inverter—are useful in practice even though their logical significance is trivial.

Because actual IC gate packages come with several gates to a package, it is often practical, for example, to use an extra NAND gate in an existing package rather than adding an additional inverter package.

## 3-3 Logic State Definitions

There are two kinds of logic: positive and negative.

Positive Logic Definition

$$+ = \text{Logic } 1$$
$$\text{Ground} = \text{Logic } 0$$

Negative Logic Definition

$$\text{Ground} = \text{Logic } 1$$
$$+ = \text{Logic } 0$$

We stated earlier that TTL and most other modern logic circuits are positive-logic devices. This is true in the sense that manufacturers define their products' functions in terms of the positive-logic definition. If a manufacturer had been making 7400 NAND gates and arbitrarily decided to change the logic definition from positive to negative, the 7400 would have to be listed in the new data manual as a NOR gate. The same electronic circuit with a different logic definition performs a different logic function. Fortunately, manufacturers do not take such arbitrary liberties with the logic definition; however, it is often desirable for us to alter the logic definition for our own convenience.

## 3-4 Gates and Logic Duals

The concept of logic duals allows the selection of whichever logic definition best fits the problem at hand. The justification for logic duality is contained in the two laws of DeMorgan.

### LOGIC DUAL DEFINED

From here on we will adopt the following definition for logic duals: *Two logic circuits are defined as logic duals when both have identical logic truth tables, but opposite logic definitions*. One is defined as positive logic, the other is defined as negative logic.

With the preceding definition in mind, let us examine each of the most useful and common two-input logic circuits and their duals.

In Figure 3-1a is the truth table for an AND gate. It is independent of any logic level definition. The logic diagrams in parts b, e, f, and g are also independent of the logic definition, as is the equation in part c. The truth tables in parts d, h, and j are, however, oriented to the logic definition. The negative-OR truth table indicates that a positive-AND gate is equivalent to a negative-OR gate if we are content with having all output voltages inverted. In practice, the basic gates in nearly all families have inverting amplifiers (inverters) as an internal part of the gate. Notice that the NOR outputs (with negative logic inputs) as shown in the truth table (Figure 3-1j) are identical to the outputs for the positive AND gate. Compare the f column in tables h and j. The input levels are inverted and meet the negative logic requirements. A careful examination of Figure 3-2 will show that the same kind of duality applies for the positive AND circuit. The importance of the information contained in Figures 3-1 and 3-2 will become apparent in the next section.

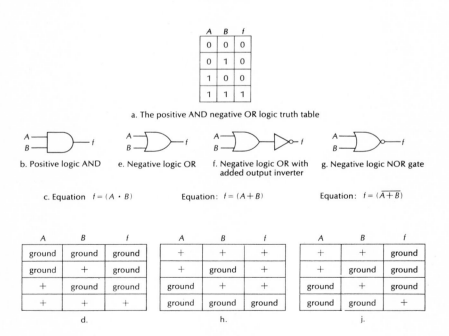

| A | B | f |
|---|---|---|
| 0 | 0 | 0 |
| 0 | 1 | 0 |
| 1 | 0 | 0 |
| 1 | 1 | 1 |

a. The positive AND negative OR logic truth table

b. Positive logic AND  e. Negative logic OR  f. Negative logic OR with added output inverter  g. Negative logic NOR gate

c. Equation  $f = (A \cdot B)$    Equation: $f = (A + B)$    Equation: $f = (\overline{A + B})$

| A | B | f |
|---|---|---|
| ground | ground | ground |
| ground | + | ground |
| + | ground | ground |
| + | + | + |

d.

| A | B | f |
|---|---|---|
| + | + | + |
| + | ground | + |
| ground | + | + |
| ground | ground | ground |

h.

| A | B | f |
|---|---|---|
| + | + | ground |
| + | ground | ground |
| ground | + | ground |
| ground | ground | + |

j.

DeMorgan's Law:  $\overline{A \cdot B} = \overline{A} + \overline{B}$

**Figure 3-1**  Logic Duals

## 3-5 Minterm and Maxterm Forms

Minterm and maxterm are two common forms for logic equations and the associated arrangement of logic gates, one or both of which is the basis for every asynchronous logic circuit. The names refer to an obsolete form of truth table and are abbreviations of the full names which are no longer used—minimum-area-term and maximum-area-term. Figure 3-3 shows the equation and logic diagram for the minterm and maxterm forms. In practical circuits, inverters (when called for) are generally found in series with selected input lines. Figure 3-4 shows the same circuits as Figure 3-3 but with inverters used to obtain the desired inverted input signals. In Figure 3-4a inputs are shown connected together—A on gate 1 to A on gate 2 and B on gate 1 to B on gate 2. In Figure 3-4b the connections are implied by the letter designations. Both are common methods of drawing the logic diagram. The minterm circuit in Figure 3-3a and the maxterm circuit shown in part b both perform the same logic function.

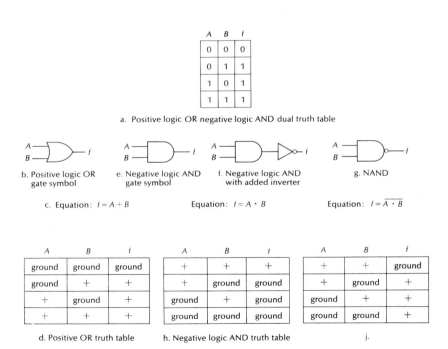

a. Positive logic OR negative logic AND dual truth table

| A | B | f |
|---|---|---|
| 0 | 0 | 0 |
| 0 | 1 | 1 |
| 1 | 0 | 1 |
| 1 | 1 | 1 |

b. Positive logic OR gate symbol

e. Negative logic AND gate symbol

f. Negative logic AND with added inverter

g. NAND

c. Equation: $f = A + B$

Equation: $f = A \cdot B$

Equation: $f = \overline{A \cdot B}$

| A | B | f |
|---|---|---|
| ground | ground | ground |
| ground | + | + |
| + | ground | + |
| + | + | + |

d. Positive OR truth table

| A | B | f |
|---|---|---|
| + | + | + |
| + | ground | ground |
| ground | + | ground |
| ground | ground | ground |

h. Negative logic AND truth table

| A | B | f |
|---|---|---|
| + | + | ground |
| + | ground | + |
| ground | + | + |
| ground | ground | + |

j.

DeMorgan's Law:  $\overline{A + B} = \overline{A} \cdot \overline{B}$

**Figure 3-2**  Logic Duals

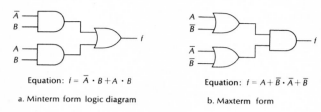

Equation: $f = \overline{A} \cdot B + A \cdot B$

a. Minterm form logic diagram

Equation: $f = A + \overline{B} \cdot \overline{A} + \overline{B}$

b. Maxterm form

**Figure 3-3**   Minterm and Maxterm Forms

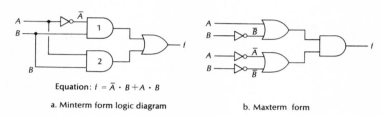

Equation: $f = \overline{A} \cdot B + A \cdot B$

a. Minterm form logic diagram

b. Maxterm form

**Figure 3-4**   Minterm and Maxterm Circuits with Inverters

## EXAMPLES OF MINTERM AND MAXTERM EQUATIONS

The minterm form may be identified as a sum-of-products form.

**Examples**

1. $f = (\overline{A} \cdot \overline{B} \cdot C) + (A \cdot \overline{B} \cdot C) + (A \cdot B \cdot C)$
2. $f = (A \cdot \overline{C}) + (B \cdot D) + (\overline{A} \cdot \overline{C} \cdot D) + (A \cdot B \cdot \overline{C} \cdot D)$
3. $f = (AB\overline{C}) + (B\overline{C}D) + (ABCD) + (A\overline{D})$
4. $f = (A \cdot \overline{B} \cdot \overline{C}) + (\overline{A} \cdot \overline{B} \cdot C) + (B \cdot C) + (A \cdot \overline{B})$

The maxterm form may be identified as a product-of-sums form.

**Examples**

1. $f = (A + B + \overline{C}) \cdot (\overline{A} + B + C) \cdot (\overline{A} + \overline{B} + C)$
2. $f = (\overline{A} + C) \cdot (\overline{B} + \overline{D}) \cdot (A + B + D) \cdot (\overline{A} + \overline{B} + C + \overline{D})$
3. $f = (\overline{A} + \overline{B} + C) \cdot (\overline{B} + C + \overline{D}) \cdot (\overline{A} + \overline{B} + \overline{C} + \overline{D}) \cdot (\overline{A} + D)$
4. $f = (\overline{A} + B + C) \cdot (A + B + \overline{C}) \cdot (\overline{B} + \overline{C}) \cdot (\overline{A} + B)$

As a direct result of DeMorgan's law:

1. *Any logic operation can be implemented in either a minterm or a maxterm form.*
2. *Any minterm form logic circuit can be converted into a maxterm circuit.*
3. *Any maxterm form logic circuit can be converted into a minterm circuit.*

**Table 3-2** Minterm Truth Tables, Equations, and Logic Diagrams

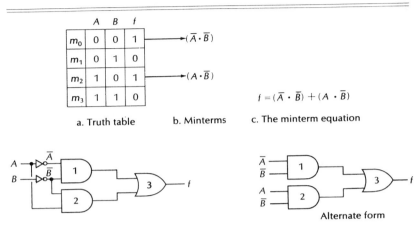

| | A | B | f |
|---|---|---|---|
| $m_0$ | 0 | 0 | 1 | → $(\overline{A} \cdot \overline{B})$ |
| $m_1$ | 0 | 1 | 0 |
| $m_2$ | 1 | 0 | 1 | → $(A \cdot \overline{B})$ |
| $m_3$ | 1 | 1 | 0 |

a. Truth table　　b. Minterms　　c. The minterm equation

$$f = (\overline{A} \cdot \overline{B}) + (A \cdot \overline{B})$$

d. The logic diagrams

**Table 3-3** Truth Table

| m | A | B | C | f | Minterms |
|---|---|---|---|---|---|
| 0 | 0 | 0 | 0 | 0 | |
| 1 | 0 | 0 | 1 | 1 | $(\overline{A} \cdot \overline{B} \cdot C)$ |
| 2 | 0 | 1 | 0 | 0 | |
| 3 | 0 | 1 | 1 | 0 | |
| 4 | 1 | 0 | 0 | 0 | |
| 5 | 1 | 0 | 1 | 1 | $(A \cdot \overline{B} \cdot C)$ |
| 6 | 1 | 1 | 0 | 1 | $(A \cdot B \cdot \overline{C})$ |
| 7 | 1 | 1 | 1 | 0 | |

The two forms are *complementary*. In order to understand what is meant by *complementary*, let us examine Tables 3-2 and 3-3.

In Table 3-2 we have made a truth table for some arbitrary function. Later we will deal with more realistic situations.

## THE MINTERM FORM

The minterm type equation, often called the sum-of-products form, can be written directly from the truth table by interpreting a 0 under the A heading as $\overline{A}$ and a 1 in the A column as A. Entries under the B heading

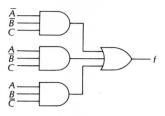

**Figure 3-5**   Logic Diagram for
Truth Table 3-3

are treated in the same way. The conditions in the $A$, $B$, and other
columns are interpreted and written only for rows in which there is a 1
in the $f$ column. In Table 3-2a the $m_0$ row has a 1 in the $f$ column. The 0,
0 under $A$, $B$ is written as $(\overline{A} \cdot \overline{B})$. This is the first minterm. The next 1
entry in the $f$ column is row $m_2$ and is written as $(A \cdot \overline{B})$, as shown under
the heading *minterms*. The final equation is formed by joining the minterms (AND-terms) with OR (+) symbols as shown in part c of this
table. This is the minterm, or sum-of-products form, equation.

The logic diagram for the equation in $c$ is shown in two equally
acceptable arrangements. The two input gates (1 and 2) are AND gates
with the necessary inverters (shown or implied) to form the hardware
equivalent of the two minterms. The OR gate joins the two products in
the way indicated by the equation.

**Example**   Write the equation and draw the logic diagram as described
by the truth table 3-3. If we combine the terms to form an equation we
get:

$$f = (\overline{A} \cdot \overline{B} \cdot C) + (A \cdot \overline{B} \cdot C) + (A \cdot B \cdot \overline{C})$$

Figure 3-5 shows the logic diagram.

**Problems**

Given the following equations, construct a truth table like the one in
example 3-1 for each problem (with a blank $f$ column). Complete the
$f$ column to correspond to each equation.
1. $f = (\overline{A} \cdot \overline{B} \cdot \overline{C}) + (A \cdot \overline{B} \cdot C) + (\overline{A} \cdot B \cdot C)$
2. $f = (\overline{A} \cdot B \cdot C) + (A \cdot \overline{B} \cdot \overline{C})$

Given the following logic diagrams (Figure 3-6), write the equation
for each.

**THE MAXTERM FORM**

Although the minterm form is the most common, the maxterm form is
often used, so it is necessary to be able to translate from one form into
the other. Truth tables can be assumed to be minterm truth tables

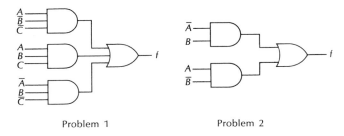

Problem 1                    Problem 2

**Figure 3-6**   Logic Diagrams for Problems 1 and 2

unless otherwise specified. The maxterm truth table is primarily used only as an aid in translating from one form to another or for other special purposes.

In Table 3-4a we have repeated the minterm truth table from 3-2. Table 3-4b is the complementary (maxterm) truth table. Truth table b is formed by inverting all entries. All 0's are changed into 1's and all 1's become 0's. The maxterms in c are written from the maxterm truth table. The completed maxterm, or product-of-sums equation, is formed by joining the *sum* terms (maxterms) by an AND symbol as shown in Table 3-4d. The maxterm logic diagram is constructed as shown in Figure 3-7.

It is important to understand that the two logic circuits, the minterm and the maxterm forms, perform identical logic functions. From a functional logic standpoint, they are identical and completely interchangeable.

**Example** Given the following maxterm equation, convert it into its minterm equivalent:

**Table 3-4**   Maxterm Truth Tables, Equations, and Logic Diagrams

| | A | B | f | | | | | | | |
|---|---|---|---|---|---|---|---|---|---|---|
| $m_0$ | 0 | 0 | 1 | | $M_0$ | 1 | 1 | 0 | | |
| $m_1$ | 0 | 1 | 0 | | $M_1$ | 1 | 0 | 1 | $(A+\bar{B})$ | |
| $m_2$ | 1 | 0 | 1 | | $M_2$ | 0 | 1 | 0 | | |
| $m_3$ | 1 | 1 | 0 | | $M_3$ | 0 | 0 | 1 | $(\bar{A}+\bar{B})$ | $f = (A+\bar{B})\cdot(\bar{A}+\bar{B})$ |

| a. Minterm truth table (repeated from Table 3-2) | b. Maxterm (complemented) truth table | c. Maxterms | d. Maxterm equation |

Note: Lower-case *m* indicates minterm and
upper-case *M* indicates Maxterm

Equation : $f = (A + \overline{B}) \cdot (\overline{A} + \overline{B})$

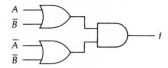

**Figure 3-7** Maxterm Logic Diagram

a. The equation:

$$f = (\overline{A} + B + \overline{C}) \cdot (A + \overline{B} + \overline{C})$$

b. The maxterm truth table is shown in Table 3-5a.

c. Inverting all entries in the maxterm table a yields table b, the minterm table. The minterms corresponding to the 1 entries in the minterm table $f$ column are indicated in part c. Connecting the minterms by + (OR) symbols yields the equation:

$$f = (\overline{A} \cdot \overline{B} \cdot \overline{C}) + (\overline{A} \cdot \overline{B} \cdot C) + (\overline{A} \cdot B \cdot \overline{C}) +$$
$$(A \cdot \overline{B} \cdot \overline{C}) + (A \cdot B \cdot \overline{C}) + (A \cdot B \cdot C)$$

On the surface it would appear that the minterm equation is far more complex than the maxterm version. What has actually happened is that a number of redundant terms are included that can be easily eliminated.

When a term accomplishes nothing that is not already accomplished by other terms, it is said to be *redundant* and can be dropped from the equation. We will find little or no difference between the complexity of

**Table 3-5** Maxterm and Minterm Truth Tables

| | A | B | C | f | | | A | B | C | f | |
|---|---|---|---|---|---|---|---|---|---|---|---|
| $M_0$ | 1 | 1 | 1 | 0 | | $m_0$ | 0 | 0 | 0 | 1 | $(\overline{A} \cdot \overline{B} \cdot \overline{C})$ |
| $M_1$ | 1 | 1 | 0 | 0 | | $m_1$ | 0 | 0 | 1 | 1 | $(\overline{A} \cdot \overline{B} \cdot C)$ |
| $M_2$ | 1 | 0 | 1 | 0 | | $m_2$ | 0 | 1 | 0 | 1 | $(\overline{A} \cdot B \cdot \overline{C})$ |
| $M_3$ | 1 | 0 | 0 | 1 | $(A + \overline{B} + \overline{C})$ | $m_3$ | 0 | 1 | 1 | 0 | |
| $M_4$ | 0 | 1 | 1 | 0 | | $m_4$ | 1 | 0 | 0 | 1 | $(A \cdot \overline{B} \cdot \overline{C})$ |
| $M_5$ | 0 | 1 | 0 | 1 | $(\overline{A} + B + \overline{C})$ | $m_5$ | 1 | 0 | 1 | 0 | |
| $M_6$ | 0 | 0 | 1 | 0 | | $m_6$ | 1 | 1 | 0 | 1 | $(A \cdot B \cdot \overline{C})$ |
| $M_7$ | 0 | 0 | 0 | 0 | | $m_7$ | 1 | 1 | 1 | 1 | $(A \cdot B \cdot C)$ |

a. Maxterm truth table for $f = (\overline{A} + B + \overline{C}) \cdot (A + \overline{B} + \overline{C})$ 
b. Inverting to a minterm table 
c. Minterms

the minterm and maxterm equation once redundant terms are eliminated. In the next section we will examine formal simplification (minimization) techniques that are used to eliminate the redundant terms. Redundancies can crop up in either or both forms of the equation.

**Problems**

Given the following maxterm equations, use an inverted truth table to convert them into minterm form. Draw the logic diagram for the given maxterm and the derived minterm equation.

3. $f = (\overline{A} + B + C) \cdot (\overline{A} + \overline{B} + C) \cdot (A + B + \overline{C}) \cdot (A + \overline{B} + \overline{C}) \cdot$
$(\overline{A} + \overline{B} + \overline{C})$

4. $f = (\overline{A} + B + C) \cdot (\overline{A} + \overline{B} + C) \cdot (A + B + \overline{C}) \cdot (\overline{A} + \overline{B} + \overline{C})$

5. $f = (A + \overline{B} + C) \cdot (A + B + \overline{C})$

6. $f = (A + \overline{B} + \overline{C}) \cdot (\overline{A} + \overline{B} + C) \cdot (A + B + C)$

7. Design logic circuits to perform the above functions:
   a. Write a minterm truth table
   b. Write the minterm equation
   c. Draw the minterm logic diagram
   d. Write the maxterm truth table
   e. Write the maxterm equation
   f. Draw the maxterm logic diagram

8. There are 3 starting lanes $(A, B, C)$ at a racecourse. A logic circuit is required that sounds an alarm whenever there happens to be an odd number of cars at the starting gates or if there are no cars at all at the gate. Let a 0 stand for no car at a gate and a 1 represent a car waiting in its lane at the gate.

9. In a particular building there are 3 doors. Fire regulations are such that there must never be one and only one door open at any given time. Design a logic circuit that produces a 1 output whenever the forbidden condition occurs.

## 3-6 Simplification

The process that we have been using to derive equations and logic diagrams from truth tables always yields valid results. But more often than not circuits derived from the truth table contain more hardware than is really necessary to get the job done. The problem is simply one of overlapping functions where part of a term will do the work of two or more complete terms. Suppose we have the equation: $f = (A \cdot B \cdot C) + (A \cdot B \cdot \overline{C})$. The equation says that we get the desired function when we have $(A \cdot B)$ combined with either $C$ or $\overline{C}$. If either $C$ or $\overline{C}$ will do, and every possibility includes one or the other, the term $C$ is useless (complemented or uncomplemented). It can therefore be dropped from the equation. This leaves: $f = (A \cdot B) + (A \cdot B)$. Because the two terms are identical, one of them is a duplicate, or redundant, term. Therefore, we keep only one of them. The function can be performed by simply $f = (A \cdot B)$ just as well as by the more complex $f = (A \cdot B \cdot C) + (A \cdot B \cdot \overline{C})$.

## AN ANALOGY

$f =$ the requirements for driving a nail:

$f =$ (a nail AND a hammer AND an apron) OR (a nail AND a hammer AND NO apron). The apron is obviously unimportant. Forgetting about the apron, we have:

$f =$ (a nail AND a hammer) OR (a nail AND a hammer). Obviously what we need is simply a nail and a hammer.

$f =$ (a nail AND a hammer)

The analogy is fine as far as it goes, but we need to build on a more rigorous premise. We find the foundation for simplification methods in the basic Boolean laws we examined in Chapter 1. The third law of complementation, $A + \overline{A} = 1$, forms the foundation for the discussion that follows.

## THE RULES FOR COMBINING TERMS

Two terms may be combined whenever:
   a. each term contains exactly the same variables
   b. the terms to be combined are identical with the exception that one—and only one—variable appears in the complemented (barred) form in one term and in the uncomplemented form in the other.

### Examples

   1. $f = (A \cdot B \cdot C) + (\overline{A} \cdot B \cdot C)$

Because A appears in both complemented and uncomplemented forms and because $A + A = 1$, the $A$ drops out, leaving $f = (B \cdot C) + (B \cdot C)$. Because the two new terms are identical, one of them is said to be redundant and is dropped. The final simplification of the equation is $f = (B \cdot C)$.

   2. $f = (\overline{A} \cdot B \cdot \overline{C} \cdot D) + (\overline{A} \cdot B \cdot C \cdot D)$

The $C$ appears in the complemented form in the first term and in the uncomplemented form in the second term. The $C$ drops out, leaving $f = (\overline{A} \cdot B \cdot D) + (\overline{A} \cdot B \cdot D)$. Because the two terms are identical, one of them is redundant and is dropped, leaving only $f = (\overline{A} \cdot B \cdot D)$.

3. Simplify the following equation by combining reducible pairs:

$$f = (\bar{A} \cdot \bar{B} \cdot \bar{C}) + (\bar{A} \cdot B \cdot \bar{C}) + (\bar{A} \cdot \bar{B} \cdot C) + (\bar{A} \cdot B \cdot C)$$
$$\quad\quad 1 \quad\quad\quad\quad 2 \quad\quad\quad\quad 3 \quad\quad\quad\quad 4$$

a. If we combine terms 1 and 2:

$$\left.\begin{array}{c} \bar{A} \cdot \bar{B} \cdot \bar{C} \\[6pt] \bar{A} \cdot B \cdot \bar{C} \end{array}\right\} \bar{A} \cdot \bar{C}$$

b. If we combine terms 3 and 4:

$$\left.\begin{array}{c} \bar{A} \cdot \bar{B} \cdot C \\[6pt] \bar{A} \cdot B \cdot C \end{array}\right\} \bar{A} \cdot C$$

c. If we rewrite the equation using the simplified terms:

$$f = (\bar{A} \cdot \bar{C}) + (\bar{A} \cdot C)$$

d. On inspection we can see that these new terms can be combined to further simplify the equation:

$$\left.\begin{array}{c} \bar{A} \cdot \bar{C} \\[6pt] \bar{A} \cdot C \end{array}\right\} \bar{A}$$

e. The final equation reduces to:

$$f = \bar{A}, \text{ the equivalent of a single inverter for } A.$$

4. An alternate pairing for example 3:

$$f = (\bar{A} \cdot \bar{B} \cdot \bar{C}) + (\bar{A} \cdot B \cdot \bar{C}) + (\bar{A} \cdot \bar{B} \cdot C) + (\bar{A} \cdot B \cdot C)$$
$$\quad\quad 1 \quad\quad\quad\quad 2 \quad\quad\quad\quad 3 \quad\quad\quad\quad 4$$

a. Combining terms 1 and 3 we get:

$$\left.\begin{array}{c} \bar{A} \cdot \bar{B} \cdot \bar{C} \\[6pt] \bar{A} \cdot \bar{B} \cdot C \end{array}\right\} \bar{A} \cdot \bar{B}$$

b. Combining terms 2 and 4:

$$\left.\begin{array}{c} \bar{A} \cdot B \cdot \bar{C} \\[6pt] \bar{A} \cdot B \cdot C \end{array}\right\} \bar{A} \cdot B$$

c. The simplified equation:

$$f = (\bar{A} \cdot \bar{B}) + (\bar{A} \cdot B)$$

d. Combining the two simplified terms:

$$\left.\begin{array}{c} \bar{A} \cdot \bar{B} \\ \\ \bar{A} \cdot B \end{array}\right\}\bar{A}$$

e. The simplified equation:

$$f = \bar{A}$$

In this case the end result is the same whatever our selection of reducible pairs. This is not always true. Sometimes we can come up with two or more equally simple, but different simplified equations.

So far the examples have been trivial and this pairing technique worked well, but as equations get more complex, the method becomes tedious and prone to error.

## THE KARNAUGH MAP

This is a special truth table designed specifically for simplifying equations. There are several variations of this table (sometimes called a *map*), but they are all constructed so that all adjacent entries on the table represent reducible minterm pairs. Although there is more than one way that a Karnaugh map can be labeled and arranged, all versions are used and interpreted in exactly the same way.

Because the Karnaugh map is constructed so that all adjacent squares represent reducible pairs, it is really only an aid in using the pairing technique. The map makes the options obvious and clear because of their highly visual nature. It also allows us to perform multiple pairings in a single operation. Table 3-6 shows the Karnaugh maps for use with two, three, and four variable equations.

A careful examination of all the maps shows that each square represents one of the possible minterms on the standard truth table, and that any pair of adjacent squares represents a reducible pair of minterms. For

**Table 3-6**   Karnaugh Maps

| | $\bar{A}$ | $A$ | | $\bar{A}\bar{B}$ | $\bar{A}B$ | $AB$ | $A\bar{B}$ | | $\bar{A}\bar{B}$ | $\bar{A}B$ | $AB$ | $A\bar{B}$ |
|---|---|---|---|---|---|---|---|---|---|---|---|---|
| $\bar{B}$ | $\bar{A}\cdot\bar{B}$ | $A\cdot\bar{B}$ | $\bar{C}$ | $\bar{A}\bar{B}\bar{C}$ | $\bar{A}B\bar{C}$ | $AB\bar{C}$ | $A\bar{B}\bar{C}$ | $\bar{C}\bar{D}$ | $\bar{A}\bar{B}\bar{C}\bar{D}$ | $\bar{A}B\bar{C}\bar{D}$ | $AB\bar{C}\bar{D}$ | $A\bar{B}\bar{C}\bar{D}$ |
| $B$ | $\bar{A}\cdot B$ | $A\cdot B$ | $C$ | $\bar{A}\bar{B}C$ | $\bar{A}BC$ | $ABC$ | $A\bar{B}C$ | $\bar{C}D$ | $\bar{A}\bar{B}\bar{C}D$ | $\bar{A}B\bar{C}D$ | $AB\bar{C}D$ | $A\bar{B}\bar{C}D$ |
| | a. Two-variable Karnaugh map | | | b. Three-variable Karnaugh map | | | | $CD$ | $\bar{A}\bar{B}CD$ | $\bar{A}BCD$ | $ABCD$ | $A\bar{B}CD$ |
| | | | | | | | | $C\bar{D}$ | $\bar{A}\bar{B}C\bar{D}$ | $\bar{A}BC\bar{D}$ | $ABC\bar{D}$ | $A\bar{B}C\bar{D}$ |

c. Four-variable Karnaugh map

the purpose of this discussion, the indicated minterm has been written for each square, but these are not normally included. Instead, 1's taken directly from the *"f"* column on the standard truth table are entered in the appropriate squares. The rest of the squares are left blank. The size of the map is determined by the number of variables involved and will have as many squares as the standard truth table has rows: $2^N$ where $N$ is the number of variables. In your examination of Table 3-6 you may have overlooked the fact that variables on the upper and lower edges and on the left and right edges are also reducible. In addition, the four corners are considered adjacent in all combinations except on the diagonal. No pairs of terms on a diagonal are reducible.

## LOOPING TERMS AND READING OUT SIMPLIFIED EQUATIONS

### Looping Rules

1. Each loop should be drawn around the largest group of 2, 4, 8, and so on—adjacent entries possible. The number of entries in a loop *must* be an integral multiple of 2.
2. An entry may be involved in any number of loops, but a new loop should not be added unless it includes at least one entry not included in any other loops. Typical looping patterns are shown in Table 3-7.

**Table 3-7**   Looping Patterns

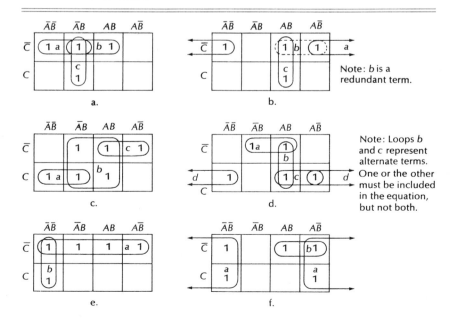

3. After looping, inspect the map for any loop that encloses entries where all of the 1's in the loop are involved in other loops. Remove any such loops.

### Reading Out the Simplified Equation

1. Each loop represents a new simplified minterm for the simplified equation. All simplified minterms will be OR'ed together (connected by the + symbol).
2. Any variable in a given loop which appears in both the complemented and the uncomplemented form drops out.
3. The variables left make up the simplified term for that loop. Individual variables are AND'ed together (joined by the · symbol).

**Example**   Write the simplified terms for each loop in Table 3-7a through f and combine the loops to get the simplified equation for each map.

| Map | Loop | Term | Equation |
|-----|------|------|----------|
| a. | $a$ | $\bar{A} \cdot \bar{C}$ | |
| | $b$ | $B \cdot \bar{C}$ | $f = \bar{A} \cdot \bar{C} + B \cdot \bar{C} + \bar{A} \cdot B$ |
| | $c$ | $\bar{A} \cdot B$ | |
| b. | $a$ | $\bar{B} \cdot \bar{C}$ | |
| | $b$ | $A \cdot \bar{C}$ | $f = \bar{B} \cdot \bar{C} + A \cdot \bar{C} + A \cdot B$ |
| | $c$ | $A \cdot B$ | |
| c. | $a$ | $\bar{A} \cdot C$ | |
| | $b$ | $B$ | $f = \bar{A} \cdot C + B + A \cdot \bar{C}$ |
| | $c$ | $A \cdot \bar{C}$ | |
| d. | $a$ | $B \cdot \bar{C}$ | |
| | $b$ | $A \cdot B$ | $f = B \cdot \bar{C} + A \cdot B + A \cdot C + \bar{B} \cdot C$ |
| | $c$ | $A \cdot C$ | |
| | $d$ | $\bar{B} \cdot C$ | |

Notice that term $b$ is redundant on map $d$. Eliminating that term we get: $f = B \cdot C + A \cdot C + \bar{B} \cdot \bar{C}.$

| | | | |
|-----|------|------|----------|
| e. | $a$ | $\bar{C}$ | $f = \bar{C} + \bar{A} \cdot \bar{B}$ |
| | $b$ | $\bar{A} \cdot \bar{B}$ | |
| f. | $a$ | $\bar{B}$ | $f = \bar{B} + A \cdot \bar{C}$ |
| | $b$ | $A \cdot \bar{C}$ | |

### Don't Cares

In some situations some of the combinations on a truth table are not defined. For example, a binary code for the decimal digits 0 through 9 requires that only ten of the combinations on a sixteen-row truth table be defined. The left over combinations are said to be *don't-care* terms. Because they will never occur as a part of the code, it is academic what the logic circuit would do if they did occur. We "don't care" whether the logic circuit produces a 1 or a 0 output for such will-never-happen combinations.

We can enter either a 0 or a 1 in the *f* column of the truth table for don't-care conditions. However, since the value we assign can make a difference in the simplification process, don't-care terms on the truth table are designated by an uncommitted symbol such as ∅ or X. When loops are being formed on the Karnaugh map, ∅ symbols are included in a loop if they serve to enlarge a loop—in this case the ∅ is treated as a 1 entry. If the ∅ entry cannot be used to enlarge a loop, it is treated as a 0 and ignored.

### Problems

Given the Karnaugh maps in Table 3-8, loop each map and write the simplified equation for each problem.

10. Map A.  11. Map B.  12. Map C.
    Hint: See Table 3-6b.
13. Map D.  14. Map E.  15. Map F.

**Example**  Write the simplified terms for each loop in Table 3-9a and b. Combine the loops to get the simplified equation for each map. Study the table with care.

| *Map* | *Loop* | *Term* | *Equation* |
|---|---|---|---|
| a. | a | $\bar{B} \cdot \bar{D}$ | |
| | b | $\bar{A} \cdot D$ | $f = \bar{B} \cdot \bar{D} + \bar{A} \cdot D + B \cdot \bar{C} \cdot D$ |
| | c | $B \cdot \bar{C} \cdot D$ | |

Note: The loop in the dotted line is tempting but doesn't include any 1 entries that have not already been looped.

**Table 3-8**  Karnaugh Maps for Problems 10 through 15

| | $\bar{A}\bar{B}$ | $\bar{A}B$ | $AB$ | $A\bar{B}$ |
|---|---|---|---|---|
| $\bar{C}$ | 1 | 1 | | 1 |
| $C$ | | 1 | | 1 |

a.

| | $\bar{A}\bar{B}$ | $\bar{A}B$ | $AB$ | $A\bar{B}$ |
|---|---|---|---|---|
| $\bar{C}$ | 1 | | 1 | |
| $C$ | 1 | 1 | 1 | 1 |

b.

| | $\bar{A}\bar{B}$ | $\bar{A}B$ | $AB$ | $A\bar{B}$ |
|---|---|---|---|---|
| $\bar{C}$ | 1 | | 1 | 1 |
| $C$ | 1 | 1 | | 1 |

c.

| | $\bar{A}\bar{B}$ | $\bar{A}B$ | $AB$ | $A\bar{B}$ |
|---|---|---|---|---|
| $\bar{C}$ | 1 | 1 | | 1 |
| $C$ | 1 | 1 | 1 | 1 |

d.

| | $\bar{A}\bar{B}$ | $\bar{A}B$ | $AB$ | $A\bar{B}$ |
|---|---|---|---|---|
| $\bar{C}$ | 1 | | | 1 |
| $C$ | 1 | | | 1 |

e.

| | $\bar{A}\bar{B}$ | $\bar{A}B$ | $AB$ | $A\bar{B}$ |
|---|---|---|---|---|
| $\bar{C}$ | 1 | 1 | | 1 |
| $C$ | | 1 | 1 | |

f.

**Table 3-9**   Simplifying Equations in 4-Variable Karnaugh Maps

A tempting but redundant loop

b.

$$
\left.\begin{array}{ll}
a & B \cdot D \\
b & B \cdot C \\
c & A \cdot D
\end{array}\right\} \quad f = B \cdot D + B \cdot C + A \cdot D
$$

**Problem**

16. Given the Karnaugh maps in Table 3-10, loop each map and write the simplified equation for each problem.

**Example**   Given the following truth table (Table 3-11a), simplify the circuit and draw the logic diagram for both the simplified and unsimplified circuits.

Writing the minterm equation from the truth table:

$$f = (\overline{A} \cdot B \cdot C) + (A \cdot \overline{B} \cdot C) + (A \cdot B \cdot \overline{C}) + (A \cdot B \cdot C)$$

After simplifying with the Karnaugh map in Table 3-11b, we get:

$$f = (A \cdot B) + (A \cdot C) + (B \cdot C)$$

Figure 3-8 shows the unsimplified and simplified logic diagrams.

**Table 3-10**   Karnaugh Maps for Problem 16

|                  | $\overline{A}\overline{B}$ | $\overline{A}B$ | $AB$ | $A\overline{B}$ |
|------------------|:---:|:---:|:---:|:---:|
| $\overline{C}\overline{D}$ | 1 |   |   | 1 |
| $\overline{C}D$            |   |   |   | 1 |
| $CD$                       |   |   | 1 | 1 |
| $C\overline{D}$            | 1 |   | 1 | 1 |

a.

|                  | $\overline{A}\overline{B}$ | $\overline{A}B$ | $AB$ | $A\overline{B}$ |
|------------------|:---:|:---:|:---:|:---:|
| $\overline{C}\overline{D}$ | 1 |   | 1 |   |
| $\overline{C}D$            | 1 |   | 1 | 1 |
| $CD$                       | 1 |   | 1 | 1 |
| $C\overline{D}$            |   |   | 1 |   |

b.

**Table 3-11** Table for the Example in Problem 16

| | 4<br>A | 2<br>B | 1<br>C | f | |
|---|---|---|---|---|---|
| $m_0$ | 0 | 0 | 0 | 0 | |
| $m_1$ | 0 | 0 | 1 | 0 | |
| $m_2$ | 0 | 1 | 0 | 0 | |
| $m_3$ | 0 | 1 | 1 | 1 | $\overline{A}BC$ |
| $m_4$ | 1 | 0 | 0 | 0 | |
| $m_5$ | 1 | 0 | 1 | 1 | $A\overline{B}C$ |
| $m_6$ | 1 | 1 | 0 | 1 | $AB\overline{C}$ |
| $m_7$ | 1 | 1 | 1 | 1 | $ABC$ |

a. Truth table

| | $\overline{A}\,\overline{B}$ | $\overline{A}B$ | $AB$ | $A\overline{B}$ |
|---|---|---|---|---|
| $\overline{C}$ | | | 1 | |
| $C$ | | 1 | 1 | 1 |

b. Karnaugh map

**Problem**

17. Given the simplified equation $f = (A \cdot B) + (A \cdot C) + (B \cdot C)$, plot it in the $f_0$ column of Table 3-12. Hint: The term $(A \cdot B)$ does not define the condition for variable $C$. Therefore, the term $(A \cdot B)$ represents two entries on the table: $(A \cdot B \cdot \overline{C})$ and $(A \cdot B \cdot C)$.

## 3-7 A Case for Simplification

As a general rule, the more complex the specifications are (the more truth table entries involved), the more profitable simplification is likely to be. The following example illustrates the point.

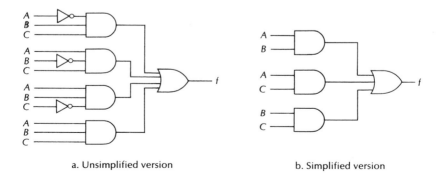

a. Unsimplified version          b. Simplified version

**Figure 3-8** Logic Diagrams

**Table 3-12**  Table for Problem 17

| | 4<br>A | 2<br>B | 1<br>C | f |
|---|---|---|---|---|
| $m_0$ | 0 | 0 | 0 | |
| $m_1$ | 0 | 0 | 1 | |
| $m_2$ | 0 | 1 | 0 | |
| $m_3$ | 0 | 1 | 1 | |
| $m_4$ | 1 | 0 | 0 | |
| $m_5$ | 1 | 0 | 1 | |
| $m_6$ | 1 | 1 | 0 | |
| $m_7$ | 1 | 1 | 1 | |

Truth table

**Example**  Given the following truth table and Karnaugh map (Table 3-13), write the unsimplified and the simplified equations and draw both the simplified and unsimplified logic diagrams.

a. The unsimplified equation:

$$f = (\overline{A} \cdot \overline{B} \cdot \overline{C} \cdot \overline{D}) + (\overline{A} \cdot \overline{B} \cdot \overline{C} \cdot D) +$$
$$(\overline{A} \cdot \overline{B} \cdot C \cdot \overline{D}) + (\overline{A} \cdot B \cdot \overline{C} \cdot \overline{D}) +$$
$$(\overline{A} \cdot B \cdot \overline{C} \cdot D) + (A \cdot \overline{B} \cdot \overline{C} \cdot \overline{D}) +$$
$$(A \cdot \overline{B} \cdot \overline{C} \cdot D) + (A \cdot \overline{B} \cdot C \cdot \overline{D}) +$$
$$(A \cdot B \cdot \overline{C} \cdot \overline{D}) + (A \cdot B \cdot \overline{C} \cdot D)$$

b. The simplified equation:
$$f = \overline{C} + (\overline{B} \cdot \overline{D})$$

The unsimplified logic diagram is shown in Figure 3-9a and the simplified version is shown in part b. Notice that the variable A has dropped out of the system entirely.

**Problem**

18. Given the truth table (Table 3-14) plot the equation: $f = \overline{C} + (\overline{B} \cdot \overline{D})$ in the f column. (Notice that Table 3-14 is a 3 variable table because only the variables B, C, D appear in the equation.

**Table 3-13** A Case for Simplification

| | | 8<br>A | 4<br>B | 2<br>C | 1<br>D | f | Minterms |
|---|---|---|---|---|---|---|---|
| a | $m_0$ | 0 | 0 | 0 | 0 | 1 | $\bar{A}\bar{B}\bar{C}\bar{D}$ |
| e | $m_1$ | 0 | 0 | 0 | 1 | 1 | $\bar{A}\bar{B}\bar{C}D$ |
| i | $m_2$ | 0 | 0 | 1 | 0 | 1 | $\bar{A}\bar{B}C\bar{D}$ |
| | $m_3$ | 0 | 0 | 1 | 1 | 0 | |
| b | $m_4$ | 0 | 1 | 0 | 0 | 1 | $\bar{A}B\bar{C}\bar{D}$ |
| f | $m_5$ | 0 | 1 | 0 | 1 | 1 | $\bar{A}B\bar{C}D$ |
| | $m_6$ | 0 | 1 | 1 | 0 | 0 | |
| | $m_7$ | 0 | 1 | 1 | 1 | 0 | |
| d | $m_8$ | 1 | 0 | 0 | 0 | 1 | $A\bar{B}\bar{C}\bar{D}$ |
| h | $m_9$ | 1 | 0 | 0 | 1 | 1 | $A\bar{B}\bar{C}D$ |
| j | $m_{10}$ | 1 | 0 | 1 | 0 | 1 | $A\bar{B}C\bar{D}$ |
| | $m_{11}$ | 1 | 0 | 1 | 1 | 0 | |
| c | $m_{12}$ | 1 | 1 | 0 | 0 | 1 | $AB\bar{C}\bar{D}$ |
| g | $m_{13}$ | 1 | 1 | 0 | 1 | 1 | $AB\bar{C}D$ |
| | $m_{14}$ | 1 | 1 | 1 | 0 | 0 | |
| | $m_{15}$ | 1 | 1 | 1 | 1 | 0 | |

a. Truth table

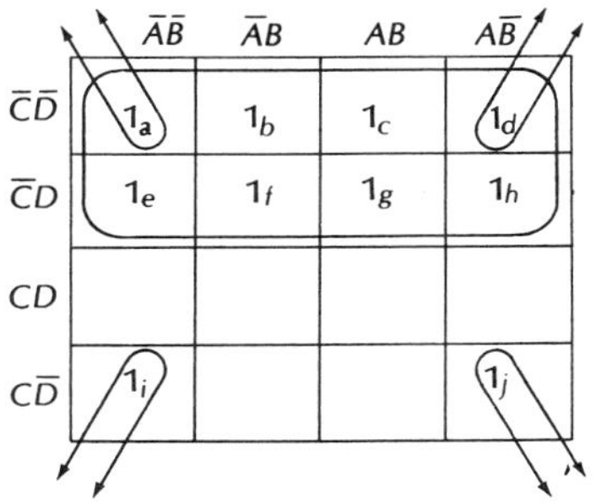

b. Karnaugh map

**Table 3-14** Table for Problem 18

| | 4<br>B | 2<br>C | 1<br>D | f |
|---|---|---|---|---|
| $m_0$ | 0 | 0 | 0 | |
| $m_1$ | 0 | 0 | 1 | |
| $m_2$ | 0 | 1 | 0 | |
| $m_3$ | 0 | 1 | 1 | |
| $m_4$ | 1 | 0 | 0 | |
| $m_5$ | 1 | 0 | 1 | |
| $m_6$ | 1 | 1 | 0 | |
| $m_7$ | 1 | 1 | 1 | |

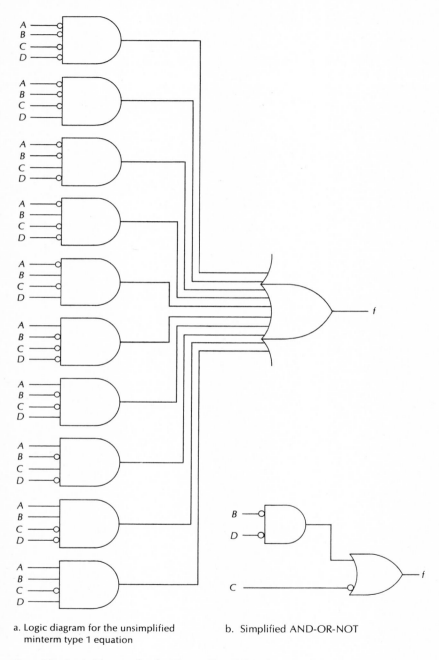

a. Logic diagram for the unsimplified minterm type 1 equation

b. Simplified AND-OR-NOT

**Figure 3-9** Logic Diagrams for the Minterm Type 1 Equation

## 3-8 Additional Methods of Minimizing Hardware

1. When more than one gate input in a logic structure requires a particular inverted variable, a single inverter can be used in place of multiple inverters as long as fan-out rules are observed. (See Figure 3-10.)
2. The distributive laws can sometimes be taken advantage of when differences in gate delay times for the different variables can be tolerated. An example of the first distributive law is shown in Figure 3-11 and the second distributive law in Figure 3-12.

## 3-9 Minterm and Maxterm Forms Using NAND and NOR Logic Gates

### MINTERM CIRCUITS

In Figure 3-1 it was demonstrated that the truth table outputs ($f$) for a positive logic OR and an inverted negative logic AND (NAND) are

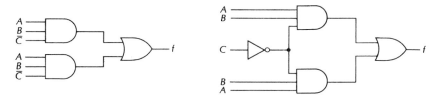

**Figure 3-10**   Combining Inverters

$$A \cdot (B + C) = (A \cdot B) + (A \cdot C)$$

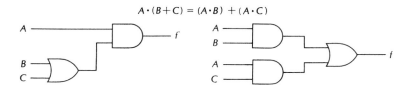

**Figure 3-11**   First Distributive Law

$$A + (B \cdot C) = (A + B) \cdot (A + C)$$

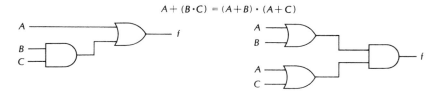

**Figure 3-12**   Second Distributive Law

identical. When NAND logic is used exclusively to form a minterm equation, a NAND gate can replace the OR gate.

In Figure 3-13a, a minterm logic circuit is shown using AND-OR-NOT logic. In part b the NAND gates (1 and 2) produce inverted outputs, so what we need is an inverted negative logic OR gate, which cannot be found in any of the modern logic families. However, the logic dual of a negative logic OR is a positive logic NAND (see Figure 3-1). If we substitute a positive logic NAND for the negative logic OR, we get the circuit shown in Figure 3-13b.

Because the NAND gate is the basic gate in TTL, most minterm circuits using TTL will be implemented as shown in Figure 3-13b instead of in the form shown in part a. In TTL AND and OR gates are more expensive and less available than NAND gates.

## MAXTERM CIRCUITS

The maxterm form using NOR gates is less frequently used than the NAND minterm form, but it does occur. Figure 3-14a shows a max-

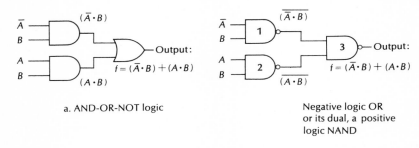

a. AND-OR-NOT logic

Negative logic OR
or its dual, a positive
logic NAND

b. NAND logic equivalent circuit

**Figure 3-13**  Minterm Circuits Using NAND Logic

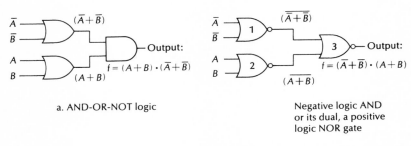

a. AND-OR-NOT logic

Negative logic AND
or its dual, a positive
logic NOR gate

b. NOR logic equivalent circuit

**Figure 3-14**  Maxterm Circuits Using NOR Gates

term circuit using AND-OR-NOT gates, and part b shows the NOR equivalent circuit.

Because the NOR gates (1 and 2) in Figure 3-14b invert the logic gate, 3 must be a negative logic AND gate or its dual (inverted) a positive logic NOR. (See Figure 3-24 for a summary of logic duals.)

**Problems**

Draw the NAND (minterm) logic diagram for each of the following equations:

19. $f = (\bar{A} \cdot B \cdot \bar{C}) + (A \cdot \bar{B} \cdot \bar{C}) + (A \cdot \bar{B} \cdot C)$
20. $f = (A \cdot \bar{B}) + (A \cdot B \cdot \bar{C}) + (B \cdot C) + (\bar{B} \cdot \bar{C})$
21. $f = (A\bar{B}CD) + (\bar{A}\bar{B}C\bar{D}) + (AB\bar{C}\bar{D})$
22. $f = (A \cdot B) + (C \cdot D) + (A \cdot \bar{C})$

## 3-10 The Exclusive-OR Gate

The exclusive-OR is a two-input gate that finds a great many applications in digital systems. The truth table for the exclusive-OR is shown in Table 3-15, and Figure 3-15 is the X-OR (exclusive-OR) logic diagram and symbol.

The TTL 7486 package contains four exclusive-OR circuits that are functionally equivalent to Figure 3-15c. Each circuit is symbolized in Figure 3-15d.

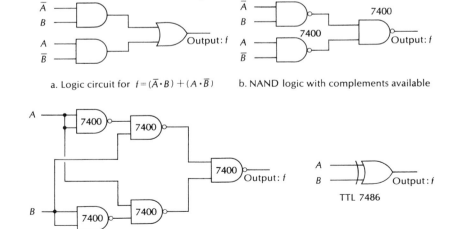

a. Logic circuit for $f = (\bar{A} \cdot B) + (A \cdot \bar{B})$    b. NAND logic with complements available

c. NAND logic when complements are not available    d. X-OR symbol

**Figure 3-15** The X-OR Circuit and Symbol

**Table 3-15** The X-OR Truth Table and Equation

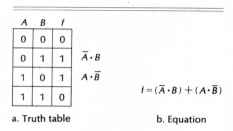

a. Truth table  b. Equation

Among the many applications for exclusive-OR gates, two important examples bear mentioning here.

1. Controlled Complementer

The controllable complement circuit is sometimes called a *controlled inverter* or *true-invert gate*. In this application one input is used as a signal input that produces either a true (non-inverted) output signal or an inverted (complemented) signal, depending upon whether the second input is high or low. Look at truth table 3-15. Let input $B$ be the signal input and put a fixed 0 level on input $A$. A zero on $B$ produces zero out, and one on $B$ produces a one out—the signal out is not inverted. Now, if input $A$ is set to a fixed 1 level, a zero input on $B$ produces a one output, and a one input produces a zero output—the signal is inverted.

An examination of the truth table (3-15) indicates that control and signal inputs can be exchanged with the same results as before.

2. Binary Adder

The truth table for binary addition and the exclusive-OR table are coincidentally identical, which makes the X-OR an ideal circuit element when binary addition is to be performed. We will examine these and other applications in some detail as we encounter them later in the text.

The X-OR gate, like the inverter, is independent of logic definition. It performs the same logic function for both negative and positive logic. X-OR gates are not available with more than two inputs.

**Problem**

23. Draw the NOR (maxterm) logic diagram for an X-OR circuit.

## 3-11    Expanding the Number of Gate Inputs

It is frequently desirable to combine several gates with few inputs each to obtain a larger number of inputs, rather than to purchase a fairly expensive package with the required number of inputs. Figure 3-16 shows how this is accomplished.

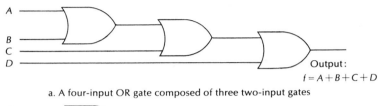

a. A four-input OR gate composed of three two-input gates

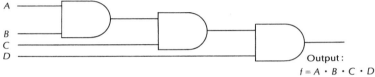

b. A four-input AND gate composed of three two-input gates

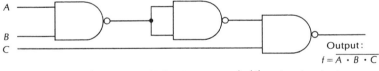

c. A three-input NAND gate composed of three two-input gates

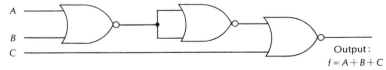

d. A three-input NOR gate composed of three two-input gates

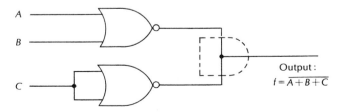

e. "Wired AND" three input NOR gate (open collector)

**Figure 3-16**   Multiple Input Gates

## 3-12  Data Selector Logic

A data selector is a TTL version of a selector switch. In addition to being electronic, it is also unidirectional, but otherwise it is functionally very similar to its mechanical counterpart.

TYPICAL DATA SELECTORS

| Switch Configuration | Data Selector/Multiplexer TTL Type |
|---|---|
| Quad SPDT | 74157 |
| Dual SP 4 position | 74153 |
| Single 8 position | 74152 |
| Single 16 position | 74150* |

\* 24 pin DIP

These devices offer single package solutions to many complex asynchronous logic problems.

The cost of data selector/multiplexer devices is low enough that it is becoming an increasingly common approach when a gates-only circuit cannot be managed with two or three IC packages.

Figure 3-17 shows a NAND gate used as a controlled SPST switch and a logic circuit equivalent of an SPDT switch. Figure 3-17b is a simplified version of a typical data selector. Notice that the basic structure is a minterm logic form.

Figure 3-18 is the logic diagram of the 74151 data selector/ multiplexer. Table 3-16 is the 74151 truth table. The basic circuit again is a standard minterm form logic with inverters added to control the select inputs. An output inverter is provided so that both com-

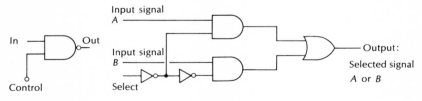

a. SPST switch equivalent    b. SPDT switch equivalent

| Select | Signal out |
|---|---|
| 0 | A |
| 1 | B |

Truth table

**Figure 3-17**  Logic Switch Equivalents

plemented and uncomplemented outputs are available. The strobe (enable) input behaves as a "master switch" to allow (enable) or inhibit the transmission of data to the output. A 0 on this input allows data transmission; a 1 inhibits data transfer. A careful inspection of Table 3-16 reveals that eight possible combinations of $A$, $B$, $C$ on the data-select inputs select each of the eight input lines. Any given combination selects one and only one data input line. By connecting the data input lines to +5V or ground, as dictated by the $f$ column in a truth table, any desired asynchronous logic function involving three variables ($A$, $B$, $C$) can be implemented. The design or analysis is an almost instantaneous process, involving no more than simple inspection. Let us see how it works.

**Example**  Given the truth table (Table 3-17), implement the required logic function using an eight-input data selector. Figure 3-19 shows the completed circuit. To program the desired logic function we simply copied the truth table $f$ column onto the data input lines of the data selector. Then we grounded those lines labeled 0 and connected those

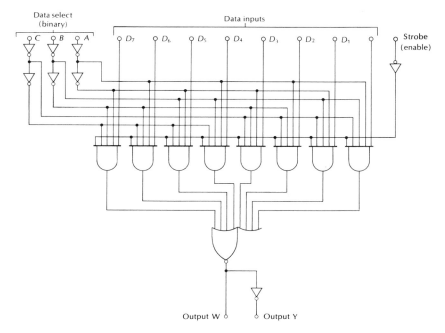

**Figure 3-18**  Logic Diagram of the 74151 Data  Selector/Multiplexer

**Table 3-16**  Truth Table for the 74151 Data Selector/Multiplexer

| C | B | A | Strobe | $D_0$ | $D_1$ | $D_2$ | $D_3$ | $D_4$ | $D_5$ | $D_6$ | $D_7$ | Outputs Y | W |
|---|---|---|--------|-------|-------|-------|-------|-------|-------|-------|-------|-----------|---|
| X | X | X | 1 | X | X | X | X | X | X | X | X | 0 | 1 |
| 0 | 0 | 0 | 0 | 0 | X | X | X | X | X | X | X | 0 | 1 |
| 0 | 0 | 0 | 0 | 1 | X | X | X | X | X | X | X | 1 | 0 |
| 0 | 0 | 1 | 0 | X | 0 | X | X | X | X | X | X | 0 | 1 |
| 0 | 0 | 1 | 0 | X | 1 | X | X | X | X | X | X | 1 | 0 |
| 0 | 1 | 0 | 0 | X | X | 0 | X | X | X | X | X | 0 | 1 |
| 0 | 1 | 0 | 0 | X | X | 1 | X | X | X | X | X | 1 | 0 |
| 0 | 1 | 1 | 0 | X | X | X | 0 | X | X | X | X | 0 | 1 |
| 0 | 1 | 1 | 0 | X | X | X | 1 | X | X | X | X | 1 | 0 |
| 1 | 0 | 0 | 0 | X | X | X | X | 0 | X | X | X | 0 | 1 |
| 1 | 0 | 0 | 0 | X | X | X | X | 1 | X | X | X | 1 | 0 |
| 1 | 0 | 1 | 0 | X | X | X | X | X | 0 | X | X | 0 | 1 |
| 1 | 0 | 1 | 0 | X | X | X | X | X | 1 | X | X | 1 | 0 |
| 1 | 1 | 0 | 0 | X | X | X | X | X | X | 0 | X | 0 | 1 |
| 1 | 1 | 0 | 0 | X | X | X | X | X | X | 1 | X | 1 | 0 |
| 1 | 1 | 1 | 0 | X | X | X | X | X | X | X | 0 | 0 | 1 |
| 1 | 1 | 1 | 0 | X | X | X | X | X | X | X | 1 | 1 | 0 |

**Table 3-17**  Truth Table

|  | C | B | A | f |
|--|---|---|---|---|
| $m_0$ | 0 | 0 | 0 | 1 |
| $m_1$ | 0 | 0 | 1 | 0 |
| $m_2$ | 0 | 1 | 0 | 1 |
| $m_3$ | 0 | 1 | 1 | 1 |
| $m_4$ | 1 | 0 | 0 | 1 |
| $m_5$ | 1 | 0 | 1 | 0 |
| $m_6$ | 1 | 1 | 0 | 0 |
| $m_7$ | 1 | 1 | 1 | 1 |

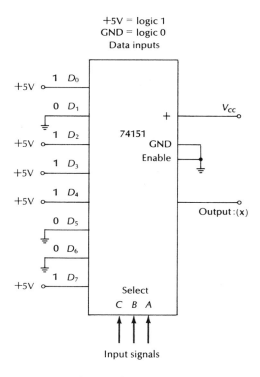

**Figure 3-19**  The Complete Circuit

labeled 1 to +5 volts. It was not necessary to write an equation or to go through the simplification procedure.

There is a great deal of redundancy in data selector logic, but it is of no concern because, unlike gate-only logic, the redundancies don't cost anything extra.

**Problem**

24. Given the data selector logic circuit in Figure 3-20, construct a truth table for it.

## 3-13  Folded Data Selector Logic

With only a little extra effort a folded design can be used to reduce the size of the data selector to half the size required by the previous method. A four-variable truth table would normally require a sixteen-input data selector, but by using the folding technique we can use an eight-input data selector.

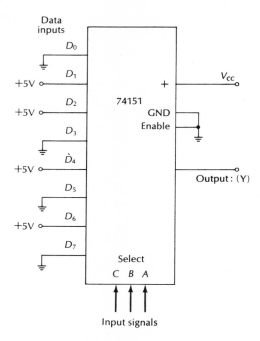

Data inputs

**Figure 3-20** Circuit for Problem 24

A four-variable truth table is shown in Table 3-18 (ignore the $f$ column for now). An examination of the table reveals that there is a repeating pattern of zeros and ones under the $A$, $B$, and $C$ headings. Ignore the entries under $D$ for the time being. The entries under $A$, $B$, and $C$ start with 000,001, . . . ending with 111 at $m_7$ and starting again at $m_8$ with 000. The entire pattern is repeated. Now examine the $D$ column. You will notice that the $D$ entries are all zeros through $m_7$ and all ones from $m_8$ through $m_{15}$. We can take advantage of this situation by considering pairs in which the $A$, $B$, and $C$ entries are identical.

**Example**  Given truth table 3-18, design a folded data selector logic circuit to implement the function.

The procedure is to examine each pair of identical pairs in $A$, $B$, and $C$ (one for $D = 0$ and one for $D = 1$).

The first pair:

$$
\begin{array}{c|ccc}
D & C & B & A \\
\hline
0 & 0 & 0 & 0 & (m_0) \\
1 & 0 & 0 & 0 & (m_8)
\end{array}
$$

We need an output of 1 when $D = 1$ and an output of 0 when $D = 0$. The required output is 0 when $D = 0$, and 1 when $D = 1$. We connect $D$

**Table 3-18**  Truth Table for
Folded Data
Selector Example

|        | D | C | B | A | f |
|--------|---|---|---|---|---|
| $m_0$  | 0 | 0 | 0 | 0 | 0 |
| $m_1$  | 0 | 0 | 0 | 1 | 1 |
| $m_2$  | 0 | 0 | 1 | 0 | 1 |
| $m_3$  | 0 | 0 | 1 | 1 | 0 |
| $m_4$  | 0 | 1 | 0 | 0 | 0 |
| $m_5$  | 0 | 1 | 0 | 1 | 1 |
| $m_6$  | 0 | 1 | 1 | 0 | 1 |
| $m_7$  | 0 | 1 | 1 | 1 | 0 |
| $m_8$  | 1 | 0 | 0 | 0 | 1 |
| $m_9$  | 1 | 0 | 0 | 1 | 0 |
| $m_{10}$ | 1 | 0 | 1 | 0 | 1 |
| $m_{11}$ | 1 | 0 | 1 | 1 | 0 |
| $m_{12}$ | 1 | 1 | 0 | 0 | 1 |
| $m_{13}$ | 1 | 1 | 0 | 1 | 1 |
| $m_{14}$ | 1 | 1 | 1 | 0 | 0 |
| $m_{15}$ | 1 | 1 | 1 | 1 | 0 |

to data input $D_0$ on the data selector in Figure 3-21. Truth table entries
$m_0$ and $m_8$ are now accounted for.

The second pair:

$$
\begin{array}{c|ccc}
D & C & B & A \\
0 & 0 & 0 & 1 & (m_1) \\
1 & 0 & 0 & 1 & (m_9)
\end{array}
$$

The truth table requires a 1 output for $m_1$ (where $D = 0$), and a 0
output for $m_9$, where $D = 1$. We need a 1 out when $D = 0$ and a 0 out
when $D = 1$. These are complementary, so we need to have the complement of $D$ ($\bar{D}$) connected to input $D_1$ of the data selector. (See Figure
3-21.) The truth table entries $m_1$ and $m_9$ are now accounted for.

The third pair:

$$
\begin{array}{c|ccc}
D & C & B & A \\
0 & 0 & 1 & 0 & (m_2) \\
1 & 0 & 1 & 0 & (m_{10})
\end{array}
$$

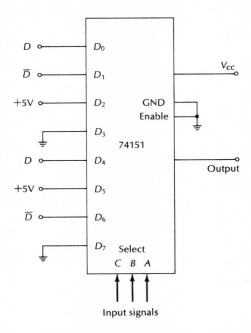

**Figure 3-21**  Folded Data Selector Logic Circuit

In this case both $m_2$ and $m_{10}$ on the truth table produce a 1 output. The output is independent of $D$, so $D_2$ on the data selector is connected to a 1 (+5 volts), so truth table entries $m_0$, $m_8$, $m_1$, $m_9$, $m_2$, $m_{10}$ have been satisfied.

The fourth pair:

$$
\begin{array}{c|ccc}
D & C & B & A \\
0 & 0 & 1 & 1 & (m_3) \\
1 & 0 & 1 & 1 & (m_{11})
\end{array}
$$

The truth table calls for a 0 output for $m_3$ and $m_{11}$, and is independent of the state of $D$. Therefore, a 0 is placed on data selector input $D_3$. Entries $m_3$ and $m_{11}$ are now satisfied.

If we follow this line of reasoning for the balance of the truth table we get the complete circuit as shown in Figure 3-21.

**Problems**

25. Given the following equation, implement it with data selector logic using the direct and then the folded method:

$$
\begin{aligned}
f = &(ABCD) + (A\bar{B}CD) + (A\bar{B}\bar{C}D) + (A\bar{B}\bar{C}\bar{D}) \\
&+ (\bar{A}BCD) + (\bar{A}\bar{B}CD)
\end{aligned}
$$

(Hint: Make a truth table.)

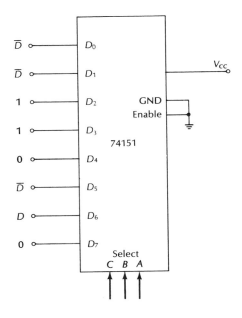

**Figure 3-22**    Folded Data Selector Circuit for Problem 26

26. Given the folded data selector logic circuit in Figure 3-22, write the truth table for it.

## 3-14    Expanding Data Selectors

Data selectors can be connected together to handle larger truth tables than can be accommodated by a single package. The *select* inputs are connected in parallel and *enable* (sometimes called *inhibit*) inputs are used to select one or the other data selector, selecting a different package for each segment of the truth table. Figure 3-23a shows two data

DATA SELECTOR SIZE

| Number of Input Variables | Selector Inputs | Packages Required |
|---|---|---|
| 2 | 2 | $\frac{1}{4}$ |
| 3 | 4 | $\frac{1}{2}$ |
| 4 | 8 | 1 |
| 5 | 16 | 1 |
| 6 | 32 | 2* |
| 7 | 64 | 4* |

* 24 pin packages

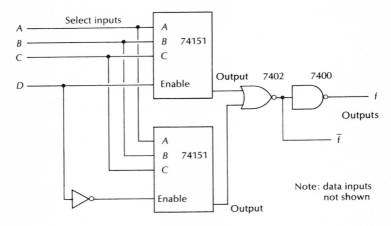

a. Two data selectors connected

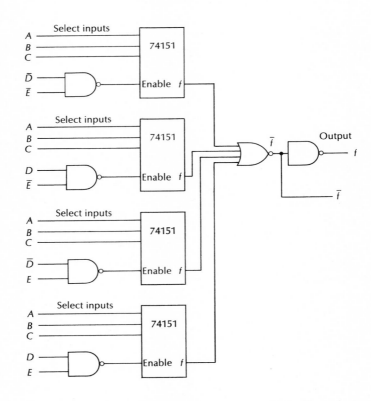

b. Using four data selectors for a thirty-two row truth table

**Figure 3-23**   Data Selectors

selectors connected together and part b shows four data selectors connected together to accommodate a thirty-two-row truth table (without folding). An examination of truth tables of any size will indicate that (in theory at least) any number of data selectors can be combined to handle a truth table of any size. In practice when sixty-four or more combinations are involved, ROM logic generally becomes cheaper and hence the preferred form. We will examine ROM logic in the next section.

## 3-15    ROM Logic

A ROM is a read-only-memory device designed primarily for look-up tables and permanent data or instruction storage. However, it can be used as an extremely powerful tool for large asynchronous logic circuits as well. The devices are programmed by blowing internal fuses, or by using a custom mask in one of the final manufacturing steps. Once programmed, ROM's cannot be altered. There is one (more expensive) kind of ROM that is field programmable and erasable by exposure to ultraviolet light. Logic arrays that satisfy truth tables with from 64 to 4096 rows can be made from ROM's. Designing the logic circuit consists of merely supplying the manufacturer with a truth table of the desired function in conventional form or in the form of computer punch cards. No logic diagrams are generally available and all trouble-shooting or circuit analysis is accomplished by using the truth table. Equations are also too complex at this level to be practical.

There are a number of standard ROM's available for frequently encountered jobs. They may be called decoders, character generators, and so forth, with no indication that they are actually ROM devices. Before the decision is made to use a ROM for an asynchronous logic task, it is important to find out if an off-the-shelf pre-programmed device is available that will do the job. Custom devices are not as expensive as you would expect, but a standard-program device is far cheaper and delivery times much shorter.

We will examine the internal structure and other ROM applications in subsequent chapters.

### THE PROGRAMMABLE LOGIC ARRAY

The PLA is another approach to asynchronous logic design. The concept is similar to data selector logic. PLA devices are currently more expensive than the other methods presented in this chapter, but are becoming more popular.

## SUMMARY

The five gate structures that are of importance in logic are the one-input inverter, two- (or more) input OR, AND, NAND, NOR gates, and the two-input exclusive-OR gate. All logic circuits are made up of combinations of these basic gates.

There are two standard arrangements for logic gates—the minterm form, called the sum-of-products form, and the maxterm form, called

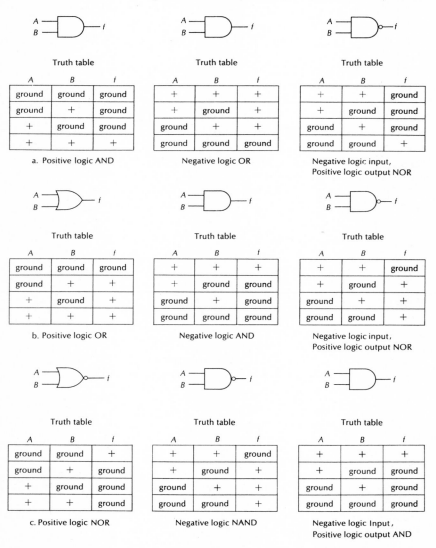

**Figure 3-24**  Summary of Logic Duals

the product-of-sums. The minterm form is the more common because it is the natural form for NAND gate logic, the basic gate in TTL.

## LOGIC DEFINITIONS

| Positive Logic | Negative Logic |
|---|---|
| + = logic 1 | Ground = logic 1 |
| Ground = logic 0 | + = logic 0 |

Simplification is required for gate-only logic circuits to minimize the number of packages. The Karnaugh map is the principal aid.

The logic duals in Figure 3-24 form the basis for NAND-only and NOR-only logic circuits, and can serve as a useful reference.

Asynchronous logic circuits involving more than 4 variables (16 combinations) is a likely candidate for data selector logic. With data selector logic no equations or logic diagrams are involved and no simplification is necessary. Circuit design and analysis is very easy with the aid of a truth table. Folded data selector logic permits the use of a data selector half the size of that required by the direct approach. Data selectors may be combined to implement truth tables that are too large for a single package.

ROM random access memory logic is a reasonable choice when $2^6$, $2^7$, or more combinations exist (6, 7 or more variables involved).

ROM circuits must be right the first time because ROM's are not generally reprogrammable. A ROM would probably not be used even for a fairly complex logic circuit if frequent modifications are required.

### Problems 27 through 30

Write the equations and make logic diagrams for the truth tables in Tables 3-19 through 3-22.

**Table 3-19**

| A | B | C | f |
|---|---|---|---|
| 0 | 0 | 0 | 1 |
| 0 | 0 | 1 | 0 |
| 0 | 1 | 0 | 0 |
| 0 | 1 | 1 | 1 |
| 1 | 0 | 0 | 0 |
| 1 | 0 | 1 | 0 |
| 1 | 1 | 0 | 0 |
| 1 | 1 | 1 | 0 |

Problem 27

**Table 3-20**

| A | B | C | f |
|---|---|---|---|
| 0 | 0 | 0 | 0 |
| 0 | 0 | 1 | 0 |
| 0 | 1 | 0 | 0 |
| 0 | 1 | 1 | 1 |
| 1 | 0 | 0 | 1 |
| 1 | 0 | 1 | 1 |
| 1 | 1 | 0 | 0 |
| 1 | 1 | 1 | 0 |

Problem 28

**Table 3-21**

| A | B | f |
|---|---|---|
| 0 | 0 | 1 |
| 0 | 1 | 0 |
| 1 | 0 | 0 |
| 1 | 1 | 1 |

Problem 29

**Table 3-22**

| A | B | C | f |
|---|---|---|---|
| 0 | 0 | 0 | 0 |
| 0 | 0 | 1 | 1 |
| 0 | 1 | 0 | 1 |
| 0 | 1 | 1 | 0 |
| 1 | 0 | 0 | 1 |
| 1 | 0 | 1 | 0 |
| 1 | 1 | 0 | 1 |
| 1 | 1 | 1 | 0 |

Problem 30

# CHAPTER 4

# FLIP-FLOPS AND LATCHES

*Learning Objectives.   Upon completion of the chapter you should:*
1. *Be able to identify*
   a. *an R-S flip-flop*
   b. *a type T f-f*
   c. *a type D f-f*
   d. *a J-K f-f*
2. *Know clock and input conditions for each type.*
3. *Know how a flip-flop works.*
4. *Know how edge triggering works and where it is used.*
5. *Know how the master-slave circuit works.*
6. *Know how to use a J-K as an R-S, a type T, or a type D.*
7. *Be familiar with the terms direct inputs, set, preset, reset, clear, and toggle.*
8. *Know how direct inputs are used.*
9. *Be familiar with the most important flip-flop IC packages.*
10. *Be able to follow and understand the timing diagram for the edge-triggered type D flip-flop.*
11. *Understand and be able to reproduce the sequence diagram for the J-K master-slave flip-flop.*
12. *Know the purpose of each f-f input configuration.*
13. *Be able to draw the logic diagram and explain the operation of:*
    a. *NAND latch*
    b. *NOR latch*
    c. *clocked NAND latch*
    d. *clocked NOR latch*
    e. *Basic type T*
    f. *Basic type D*
    g. *master-slave J-K f-f*
    h. *edge-triggered D f-f*

Basic memory elements come in two forms, static and dynamic. Static forms consist of two logic gates with the output of the first connected to the input of the second gate. The output of the second gate is in turn coupled back into the input of the first. The result is a regenerative circuit with two stable conditions (two stable states). Additional gating permits switching from one state to another. Once switched to a given state, the circuit—called a *flip-flop*—remains in that state as long as power is applied and no additional switching command pulse is provided.

There are two basic kinds of flip-flops: the type $D$ and the $J$-$K$. Some flip-flops are operated in an asynchronous mode, without clock control, but most of them are operated under the control of a clock pulse in a synchronous system.

There are three distinct kinds of flip-flop memory arrays: rectangular coordinate memories, counting arrays, and shift register systems. These three kinds of memory arrays will be discussed in separate chapters. In this chapter we will concentrate on the operation and properties of the flip-flop elements themselves.

The dynamic memory element involves the control and transfer of a stored charge, and is based on the MOS dynamic logic form discussed in Chapter 2. There is no dynamic logic using bipolar technology. Dynamic memory cells are primarily used in rectangular coordinate memories and shift register memory systems. These will be discussed in Chapter 10.

## 4-1 Basic Memory Latches

The term *latch* refers to a circuit's ability to remain at a particular logic level after having been driven to that state by some externally provided signal. The circuit must remain in that state even after the command or control pulse no longer exists. In a very real sense the latch* *remembers* that that command pulse once existed.

A very simple but limited memory latch circuit is shown in Figure 4-1. This circuit can be latched, but it is necessary to break the circuit or remove the power to reset it. Still, it is the basis of all of the more complex latches and flip-flops, and in some cases it can be a useful circuit in itself.

Figure 4-1a shows the initial conditions with a *low* output and a low on the latch command line, $B$. The feedback line, $A$, is connected to the output so that its condition will always be the same as the output level. By convention we will say that the *latch* is storing (remembering) a logic zero. The output $Q$ is low. We will use the symbol $Q$ instead of $f$ as the output indicator for memory elements so that we can tell whether a Boolean expression represents simply asynchronous logic or memory elements. Now, if we want to store a 1, we change the *low* (0) latch command signal on leg $B$ of the OR gate to a *high* (1) and leave it in that condition long enough for the gate to respond and drive the output $Q$ to a *high* (1) state. This takes 10–50 nanoseconds. As soon as $Q$ goes *high*, the feedback line feeds that *high* level back to the $A$ input of the OR gate.

---

* *Latch* may be used as either a verb or a noun.

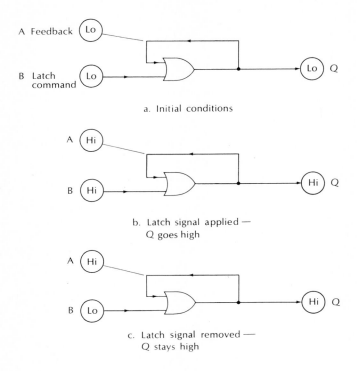

a. Initial conditions

b. Latch signal applied —
Q goes high

c. Latch signal removed —
Q stays high

**Figure 4-1** The Simple OR Gate Latch

The output $Q$ stays *high* and holds the $A$ input *high*, which latches the output at *high*. We can now allow the latch command input $B$ to go *low* (Figure 4-1c) and the output $Q$ remains *high*. The latch is now latched and the latch command input $B$ has no further influence.

It is important to consider the time required to *set* the latch because this *set-up* time (delay), as short as it is, forces us to use some fairly complex latch and flip-flop circuits for most practical applications. Such increased complexity does not, however, significantly add to the cost of integrated circuits.

## 4-2    The NOR Latch

The OR latch in Figure 4-1 can be implemented using NOR gates as shown in Figure 4-2.

The rightmost NOR gate serves as an inverter which performs a double complement for the output $Q$ and the feedback line to leg $A$ of the lefthand (input) NOR gate. The result is the exact equivalent of the OR

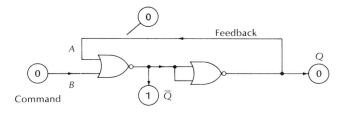

a. Initial conditions

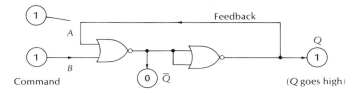

b. Set command applied

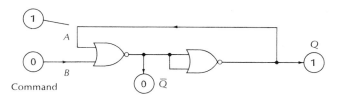

c. Circuit still latched at high

**Figure 4-2**   Simple Latch Using NOR Gates

gate version. One significant difference between the two circuits is the fact that we now have a second output available which is the complement of the $Q$ output. We will call that output $\bar{Q}$. If you will follow Figure 4-2 through, you will see that it operates in exactly the same fashion as the basic OR latch in Figure 4-1. The sequence of events is important because of the gate delay times. The process begins with the initial conditions of a *low* on the set command line $B$, a condition assumed to be stable and to have existed for as long as necessary for the circuit to *settle* down. The set command line is then raised to a *high* and held there until both gates have responded and a valid 1 *(high)* logic level rests on the feedback input $A$. The latch is now *set* and the command input line can go back to 0 *(low)* without affecting the *high* output (1) on $Q$. From this time on, the set command line may change states indefinitely without changing the output of the latch.

## ADDING RESET CAPABILITY TO THE NOR LATCH

It is a simple matter to modify the NOR latch in Figure 4-2 to make it into a full-fledged *set-reset* latch. All that is necessary is to disconnect one of the legs on the NOR gate that was used as an inverter in the simple latch and to use that free gate leg as a *reset* input. Figure 4-3 shows the modified NOR latch with reset capability.

Follow the events in Figure 4-3 to see how the process works.

a. The initial condition requires a *low* (0) on the set command input. $\overline{Q}$ is *high* and $Q$ is *low*. The reset input is *low*. The latch is *reset*.

b. The set line goes to *high* and the reset line remains *low*. The leftmost gate outputs a *low*, and $\overline{Q}$ goes *low*. The righthand gate outputs a 1 (*high*) which brings $Q$ to a 1 and feeds a 1 (*high*) back to the lefthand gate.

c. After feedback input reaches a stable *high* logic level, the set line can return to *low* and the output $Q$ will still remain *high*.

d. After the set line has settled to a logic *low*, the circuit is ready to receive a *reset* command pulse at the reset input. The reset line goes *high*, driving $Q$ *low* and feeding a *low* back to the feedback input of the lefthand gate, which outputs a 1 and drives $\overline{Q}$ to *high*.

e. After $\overline{Q}$ has established a stable *high* logic level, the reset level may drop to *low*. The circuit is now reset and ready to accept a set command whenever we are ready to send it to the set line. Notice that there is a forbidden case where both the set and reset lines are *high* at the same time. If we hit both inputs (set and reset) with a 1 at the same time, both $Q$ and $\overline{Q}$ will be *high*—a forbidden condition. Also you will notice that the only time we have a *low* on both set and reset inputs is after a *high* has remained on one of the lines long enough for the latch to settle. We can have a *low* sitting on both inputs at the same time but initially we cannot deliver them at the same time. If we do, there will be a race, with the final state unpredictable. Most of the refinements we will examine involve methods of avoiding indeterminate states and race problems.

The latch, or flip-flop, circuit is not generally drawn as it has been here. It was drawn this way to make the explanation easier to follow, but it will almost always be drawn as shown in Figure 4-4. A careful examination will prove that Figures 4-3 and 4-4 are actually identical.

Sometimes the circuit is drawn as shown in Figure 4-5, which is based on DeMorgan's law: $\overline{A + B} = \overline{A} \cdot \overline{B}$. Both gates are converted to AND's with inverted inputs.

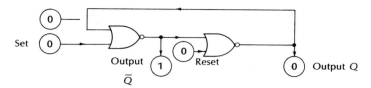

a. Initial conditions

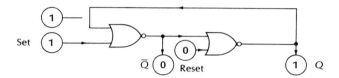

b. Set command pulse applied

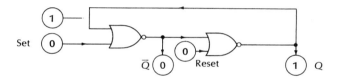

c. Set command pulse removed

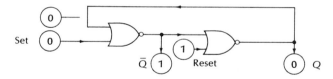

d. Reset command pulse applied

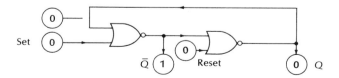

e. Reset command pulse removed

**Figure 4-3** Basic NOR Latch with Reset Capability

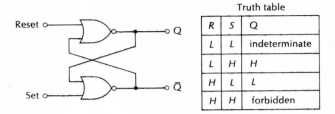

| Truth table | | |
|---|---|---|
| R | S | Q |
| L | L | indeterminate |
| L | H | H |
| H | L | L |
| H | H | forbidden |

**Figure 4-4** R-S Latch Drawn in Conventional Fashion

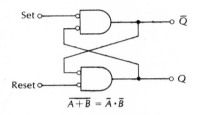

$$\overline{A+B} = \overline{A} \cdot \overline{B}$$

**Figure 4-5** AND Gate Version of the NOR Latch

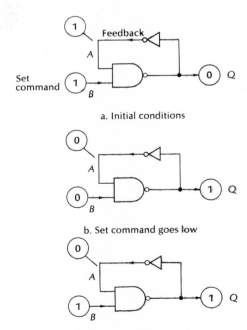

a. Initial conditions

b. Set command goes low

c. Set command returns to high

**Figure 4-6** Simplest Form of the NAND Latch

## 4-3   Basic NAND Latches

NAND latches may be fabricated using standard NAND gates. Figure 4-6 shows the circuit for a simple NAND latch without reset capability. Follow Figures 4-6 and 4-7 through. Figure 4-7 shows the same latch circuit with the inverter replaced by another NAND gate functioning as an inverter. This circuit provides two outputs $\overline{Q}$ and $Q$. Notice particularly that the NAND latches require a *low* for a set command. Also notice the $Q$ output is taken from the lefthand gate and the $\overline{Q}$ is taken from the righthand gate. This is just the opposite of the NOR latch.

Figure 4-8 shows the NAND latch as it is customarily drawn. Figure 4-9 shows an alternate form based on DeMorgan's law: $\overline{A \cdot B} = \overline{A} + \overline{B}$.

### Problem

1. Given the drawing (Figure 4-10), complete the entries (circles) to show how the circuit works.

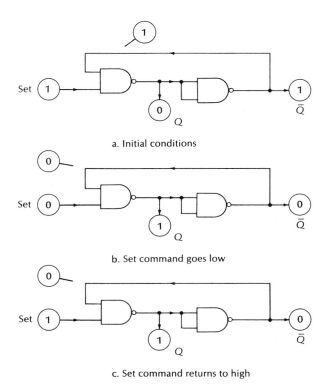

**Figure 4-7**   NAND Latch Circuit Using a NAND Gate to Replace the Inverter

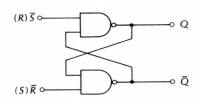

Truth table

| R | S | Q |
|---|---|---|
| L | L | forbidden |
| L | H | H |
| H | L | L |
| H | H | indeterminate |

**Figure 4-8** NAND Set-Reset Latch as Customarily Drawn

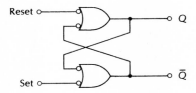

**Figure 4-9** Alternate Representation of the NAND R-S Latch, Based on the Equality $\overline{A \cdot B} = \overline{A} + \overline{B}$

## CONTACT CONDITIONING

Mechanical contacts almost invariably bounce when contact is made. Ordinarily the bounce and multiple make-and-break action that results is no problem. However, when mechanical contacts are used with high-speed logic, the bounce is seen by the gate as multiple pulses. A simple NAND or NOR latch is often used as a switch debouncer (or bounceless pushbutton).

The set (or reset) action is initiated by the first contact closure pulse. Because of the regenerative behavior of the circuit, the switching action once initiated continues even with loss of switch closure.

The only pulse that counts is the first one—the rest are ineffective. NAND and NOR latches for contact conditioning are shown in Figure 4-11.

## 4-4 The D Latch

The simple NOR *R-S* (set-reset) latch we have examined has two potentially unpredictable conditions: *low's* on both set and reset lines at the same time and *high's* on both set and reset lines at the same time. A *low* state on both inputs at the same time is allowed, but only if the two

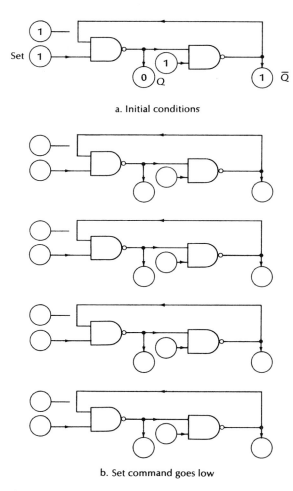

a. Initial conditions

b. Set command goes low

**Figure 4-10**  NAND Latch with Reset Capability

inputs ($R$ and $S$) did not start to go low at the same instant. The end result of *low*-going pulses arriving at both inputs simultaneously is indeterminate.

If both set and reset command pulses exist at the same time, both outputs of the latch will output a 1, a forbidden condition. When the input command pulses drop to 0 (theoretically at the same time), the result is again unpredictable.

One obvious way of preventing command pulses from arriving at both inputs at the same time (1, 1) or (0, 0) is simply to prevent these two conditions from ever coexisting at any time. This is easily ac-

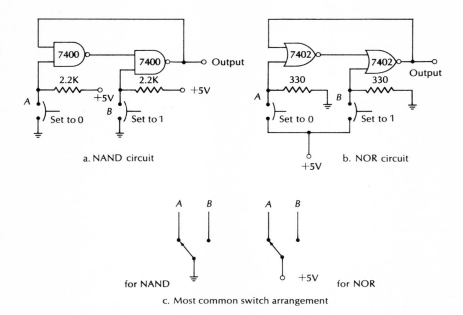

a. NAND circuit

b. NOR circuit

for NAND

for NOR

c. Most common switch arrangement

**Figure 4-11**    Contact Debouncers

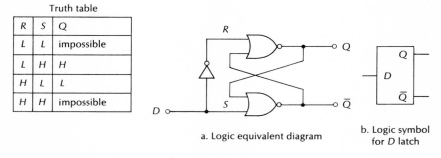

Truth table

| R | S | Q |
|---|---|---|
| L | L | impossible |
| L | H | H |
| H | L | L |
| H | H | impossible |

a. Logic equivalent diagram

b. Logic symbol for $D$ latch

**Figure 4-12**    NOR $D$ Input R-S Latch

complished by using a single inverter in an input arrangement called the $D$ input configuration. Figure 4-12 shows a $D$ input $R$-$S$ latch circuit.

In Figure 4-12 the inverter makes it impossible for both inputs $R$ and $S$ to be at the same logic level at any time. The simple $D$ latch can also be implemented in NAND form. Figures 4-13 and 4-14 show two versions of the NAND $D$ latch, one with a *high-active* $D$ input and one with a *low-active* $D$ input. For a high-active input $Q$ goes *high* when $D$ goes

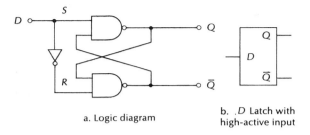

a. Logic diagram

b. *D* Latch with high-active input

**Figure 4-13** NAND Active High *D* Latch

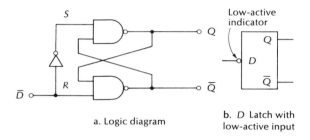

a. Logic diagram

b. *D* Latch with low-active input

**Figure 4-14** NAND Active Low *D* Latch

*high,* and for a low-active input $Q$ goes *high* when $D$ goes *low*. Because the circuit is symmetrical, we could use either variation for either active-high or active-low, simply by changing the labels on the $Q$ and $\overline{Q}$ lines. However when the latch symbol (4-13b and 4-14b) is used, we have no way of knowing how the circuit is configured inside the package without some additional notation. The bubble on the $D$ line of Figure 4-14b is a state indicator that tells us that Q will go *high* when $D$ goes *low*. Some flip-flops and latches have several inputs, some of which are active-high and some active-low. The bubble identifies the active-low inputs.

## 4-5  The R-S Flip-Flop Summary

The *R-S* flip-flop can be constructed with either NAND or NOR gates. The basic circuits are the same as the contact conditioning circuits except that the *R-S* F-F is switched (triggered) by pulses rather than by mechanical contacts. Figure 4-15 shows the NAND circuit, symbol, and truth table for the *R-S* flip-flop.

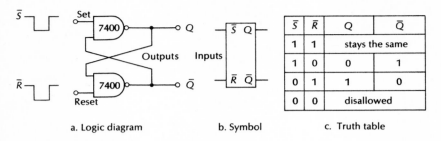

| a. Logic diagram | b. Symbol | c. Truth table |

**Figure 4-15** NAND R-S Flip-Flop

## NAND R-S FLIP-FLOP OPERATION SUMMARY

1. Both inputs left positive: no change in state.
2. *Set* input momentarily grounded: $Q$ goes positive, $\bar{Q}$ goes to ground.
3. *Reset* momentarily grounded: $\bar{Q}$ goes positive, $Q$ goes to ground.
4. Both *set* and *reset* simultaneously grounded: Disallowed state with both $Q$ and $\bar{Q}$ positive. If one input goes to ground slightly before the other, the last input to go positive determines final state. This condition is avoided.

Figure 4-16 shows the NOR gate *R-S* flip-flop, symbol, and its truth table.

## NOR R-S FLIP-FLOP OPERATION SUMMARY

1. Both inputs grounded: no change in state.
2. *Set* input momentarily positive: $Q$ output goes positive, $\bar{Q}$ goes to ground.
3. *Reset* momentarily made positive: $\bar{Q}$ goes positive, $Q$ goes ground.
4. Both *set* and *reset:* Disallowed state with $Q$ and $\bar{Q}$ grounded. In the event that one input goes positive before the other, the final state is determined by the last input to go to ground. This condition is avoided.

### Problems

2. Can the NAND gate *R-S* flip-flop in Figure 4-15 be considered to operate as a negative logic element? Explain.
3. Is the output of the NAND *R-S* positive or negative logic? Can it be either? How?

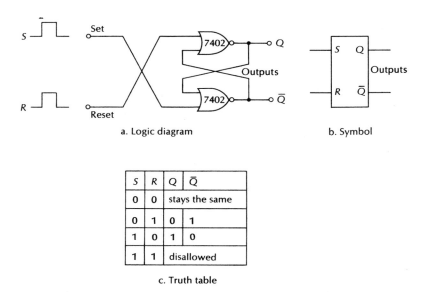

a. Logic diagram

b. Symbol

| S | R | Q | $\bar{Q}$ |
|---|---|---|---|
| 0 | 0 | stays the same | |
| 0 | 1 | 0 | 1 |
| 1 | 0 | 1 | 0 |
| 1 | 1 | disallowed | |

c. Truth table

**Figure 4-16**   NOR *R-S* Flip Flop

## 4-6  Clocked Flip-Flops

In the majority of applications, flip-flops are required not only to store data (0 or 1) but also to pass stored data on to another flip-flop and to receive data from a previous f-f. Chains of flip-flops are connected in two special configurations called *counters* and *shift registers*.

A counter accepts a train of input pulses and stores a count that represents the total number of pulses entering the system. The action is similar to that of the odometer in a car that keeps track of total miles traveled. A transfer of carries from each flip-flop to the next highest order flip-flop is required, as the total is accumulated (as from 'the "units" odometer wheel to the "tens" wheel and so on).

A register is a group of memory elements used for temporary storage. It differs from a *memory* array in that it usually has a much smaller storage capacity and generally is required to hold data for relatively short periods of time because of its location in the system's organization. The most common kind of register is capable of shifting data on command from one element to the next within the register, a capability not usually found in other memory arrays. These shifting registers or *shift registers* do not keep a running total of incoming pulses as do counters. However, in both cases data transfer from flip-flop to flip-flop—involving from 2 to 4000 flip-flops in a chain—is required.

In these two flip-flop applications the simple latch we have previously examined is completely inadequate to the task. Because of system gate delays and flip-flop transition and settling times, timing becomes critical particularly at high data-shift or counting rates.

If the state of flip-flop $A$ is to be transferred to flip-flop $B$, it is essential that both flip-flops have completed any previous state change and have had time to *settle in* before a transfer from $A$ to $B$ is made. Entering an input pulse commanding a change of state while a flip-flop is between states or in an unsettled condition invariably results in unreliable operation. There are two specific timing problems in counters and shift registers.

Every gate in the system has a delay time. These delays are variable from gate to gate—even of a given type number—and are cumulative. In addition, the time required for flip-flops to change states and settle in is quite variable. These delays give rise to the first timing problem.

The second timing problem is called the *race* problem. When a string of flip-flops is direct coupled, a change of state in one flip-flop can race down the entire length of the string, resulting in a completely useless system.

Because of these two problems, flip-flops used in counters and shift registers cannot be of the simple *R-S* type. In order to make counters and shift registers possible, the basic *R-S* circuit is modified into clocked, or synchronous, circuits. In clocked circuits outputs do not change as soon as input conditions change but must wait for a *clock* command pulse before they can respond.

## 4-7   The Clocked R-S Flip-Flop

Figure 4-17 shows the necessary gates added to the *R-S* flip-flop to provide for clock control. The two additional NAND gates allow either the set or reset pulse to trigger the flip-flop only if the clock input is positive. The circuit in Figure 4-17 does not solve the basic timing problems, but it is the first step toward their solution.

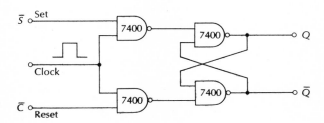

**Figure 4-17**   Clocked *R-S* Flip Flop

## 4-8 The Type T Flip-Flop

The *T* modification in Figure 4-18 provides the *toggle* action required when flip-flops are connected in a counting arrangement. Cross-coupled feedback takes one input of gate *A* to $\overline{Q}$ while a second feedback path ties *Q* to one input of gate *B*. If the flip-flop (gates *C* and *D*) is in the reset state $\overline{Q}$ *high*, there is a *high* on the upper input of steering gate *A*. This feedback signal constitutes a *set* command. Upon the arrival of a clock pulse the flip-flop *sets* to *Q high*. Now, the feedback places a *high* on the lower input of gate *B* and ground on the feedback input to gate *A*. The flip-flop is now conditioned to toggle to reset *(*$\overline{Q}$ *high)* with the arrival of the next clock pulse.

Notice that it takes two clock pulses to cause the flip-flop to make one complete transition from *Q low* to *Q high* and back to *Q low*.

If a train of clock pulses is applied to the input at frequency *f*, the output of *Q* would be a pulse train with a frequency of *f*/2. The circuit is often called a divide-by-2 or binary. Any number of toggle flip-flops

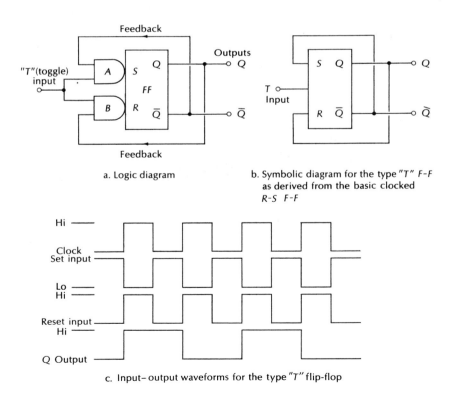

a. Logic diagram

b. Symbolic diagram for the type "*T*" F-F as derived from the basic clocked R-S F-F

c. Input–output waveforms for the type "*T*" flip-flop

**Figure 4-18** Type "*T*" Flip-Flop

can be cascaded for division by successive powers of 2 as shown in Figure 4-19. The circuit is counting by twos.

**Problems**

4. Make a truth table for the type $T$ flip-flop.
5. Given the type $T$ flip-flop in Figure 4-20, draw the waveforms at the outputs $Q$ and $\overline{Q}$.
6. Why does the disallowed state ($Q$ and $\overline{Q}$ both *high*) not occur in the $T$ flip-flop?
7. Does the toggle action occur when the clock goes positive or when it goes to ground?

## 4-9   The J-K Flip-Flop

The circuit configuration in Figure 4-21 is the most versatile flip-flop circuit available. It can function as a clocked $R$-$S$ flip-flop or a toggle flip-flop, as well as performing a number of more specialized functions. In addition to clock provisions and input flexibility, the $J$-$K$ has the advantage that all four possibilities on its truth table are valid—none are forbidden conditions.

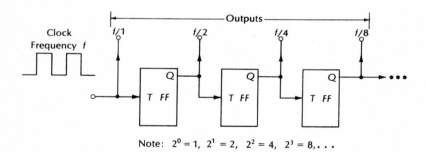

Note:  $2^0 = 1$,  $2^1 = 2$,  $2^2 = 4$,  $2^3 = 8$, . . .

**Figure 4-19**   "*T*" Type Flip-Flops as a Frequency Divider by Powers of Two

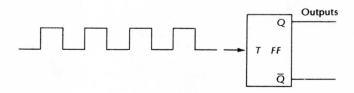

**Figure 4-20**   Figure for Problem 5

## J-K OPERATING CHARACTERISTICS

1. *J* input grounded, *K* input grounded: when the clock goes *low*, nothing happens.

2. *J* input goes positive, *K* input grounded: when the clock goes *low*, *Q* goes (or stays) positive. $\overline{Q}$ is grounded. The 1 on the *J* input is "passed" directly to the *Q* output.

3. *K* input goes positive, *J* input grounded: when the clock goes *low*, $\overline{Q}$ goes *high* and *Q* goes to ground. The 0 on *J* input is transferred directly to the *Q* output.

4. *J* held positive, *K* held positive: the circuit toggles on each clock pulse. The circuit now behaves as a type *T* binary divider or counter stage.

These operating rules are summarized in Table 4-1. The *J-K* can be used as a type *D* flip-flop by adding an inverter, as shown in Figure 4-22. This is a usable circuit, although a packaged type *D* with special characteristics is more frequently used.

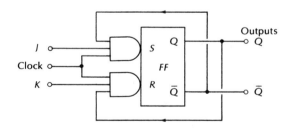

**Figure 4-21** *J-K* Flip-Flop Reconfigured for Clock Input

**Table 4-1** Truth Table for *J-K* Flip-Flop

| Truth table | | |
|---|---|---|
| *J* | *K* | Q, after clock |
| 0 | 0 | no change |
| 0 | 1 | F-F resets |
| 1 | 0 | F-F sets |
| 1 | 1 | F-F toggles |

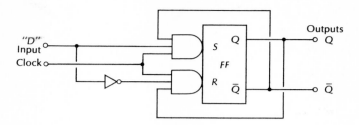

**Figure 4-22** *J-K* Modified with a Type *"D"* Input

## 4-10   The Master-Slave J-K Flip-Flop

So far the flip-flops presented have represented stages in the evolution of the workhorse of flip-flops, the master-slave *J-K*. The master-slave circuit shown in Figure 4-23 has the versatility of the simple *J-K* but effectively eliminates all timing problems including the race problem. The circuit consists of two flip-flops in series, with their clock inputs driven in complementary fashion. The slave stage serves as a kind of holding tank for data to be transferred to the next flip-flop in a counter or shift register chain. Data is buffered and held by the slave until all delays have been allowed for and all circuits have settled in. The master-slave circuit can be considered as having a two-phase clock because of the inverter (see Section 5-5).

### HOW IT WORKS

On the leading edge of the clock pulse, data enters the *J* and *K* inputs on the master flip-flop. On the up-clock the inverter provides a down (*low*) clock for the slave flip-flop, locking out any data input. During the clock *on* time the master has plenty of time to set up (pulse widths are much greater than necessary for set-up). The slave waits during the clock *on* time and cannot change states because the inverter holds its clock input *low*. When the clock pulse first arrives at the master, only the *J* or the *K* input (but not both) is *primed* to cause the master to change state. This priming is accomplished by the feedback lines from the outputs of the slave. The master can only *set* if the slave is in the *reset* state—the reset input is disabled. Or, it can only *reset* if the slave is in the *set* condition—the master reset input is locked out.

Assume that the slave is in the *reset* condition. Before the up ↑ clock and during the clock *on* time, the master flip-flop can only respond to a set command. Even though the master changes state early in the clock *on* period, the slave stays as it was and the master can respond only to a *set* command during the clock *on* period. If a *reset* command should come down the reset line during the clock *on* time (the forbidden condi-

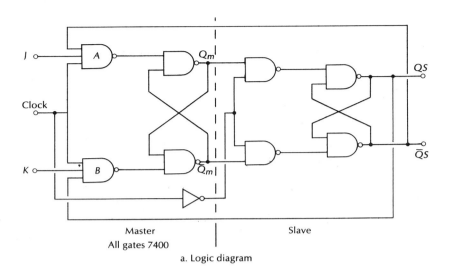

a. Logic diagram

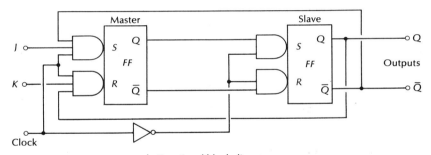

b. Functional block diagram

Clocked inputs

| J | K | Clock → | Output, Q |
|---|---|---------|-----------|
| 0 | 0 | | no change |
| 0 | 1 | | 0 |
| 1 | 0 | | 1 |
| 1 | 1 | | toggles to opposite state |

c. J–K master–slave truth table

Clocking occurs when clock goes low.
Data on J and K can only be changed
immediately after clock goes low. Only
one change of J and K conditions is
allowed per clock cycle.

**Figure 4-23**  Master-Slave J-K Flip-Flop

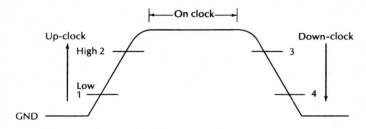

**Figure 4-24**  Clock Waveform for the *J-K* Master-Slave

tion in the *R-S* F-F), that reset pulse is ignored, so the $Q = 1$, $\bar{Q} = 1$ condition doesn't exist for this circuit. At the end of the clock pulse *on* time, the clock pulse to the master falls. For the slave, because of the inverter, the clock is now rising and data from the master can be sampled. During the slave's clock *on* time the master's clock line is *off* and it cannot accept data at either of its inputs. This sequence of events is exactly what we assumed in the operational description of the *R-S* flip-flop. The sequence of events in the master-slave flip-flop can be graphically illustrated by a sequence drawing. (See Figure 4-24.) If we follow the clock waveform drawing in Figure 4-24 through, the sequence goes like this:

1. Primed input of master initiated change of state. Slave locked out by inverted (*down*) clock.
2. By 2 or a little later, master changes state and settles down. Slave still locked out by inverted clock pulse.
3. More than adequate set-up time has been allowed for the master. Slave clock pulse now rising and the slave begins to change states if the master has changed states between 1 and 3.
4. By 4 or a little later the slave has settled into new state. Master stays put during *off* time of clock and waits until the next *up* clock to sample any new data at its inputs.

The master slave concept can be applied to any flip-flop type, but the *J-K* is easily the most versatile. The master-slave circuit is the most nearly foolproof flip-flop configuration.

**Problem**

8. Draw a *J-K* master slave flip-flop based on NOR gates.

## 4-11  Direct Set and Clear

In Figure 4-25 direct *set* and *clear* lines have been added in the slave flip-flop stage. These inputs are override functions independent of the

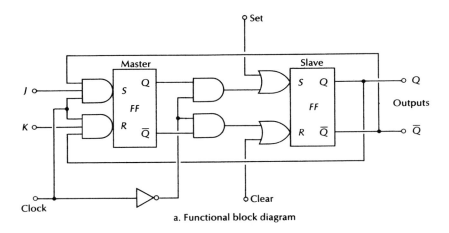

a. Functional block diagram

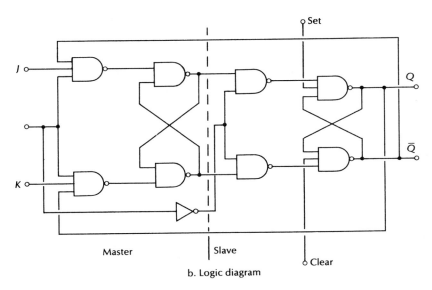

b. Logic diagram

| Set | Clear | Output, Q |
|-----|-------|-----------|
| 0 | 0 | disallowed |
| 0 | 1 | 1 |
| 1 | 0 | 0 |
| 1 | 1 | Normal clocked operation using J and K inputs |

c. Truth table for direct set and clear inputs

**Figure 4-25**   Master-Slave *J-K* Flip-Flop with Direct Set and Clear

clock and other input signals. These inputs are used to clear a shift register or to reset a counter to 0 (or some predetermined count). Only one input may be used at a time. These direct inputs are normally used at the beginning or end of an operation and are not normally used as auxiliary data inputs.

The terms *set* and *preset* are often used interchangeably, as are the terms *reset, clear,* and *preclear.*

## 4-12  Commercial J-K Master-Slave IC's

The most common TTL *J-K* master-slave flip-flops are the 7473, 7476, and the 74107.

### THE 7473

The 7473 is a dual *J-K* master-slave flip-flop with *clear* but no *set* direct input. The most popular and common *J-K* M-S has a nonstandard pin-out.

The clock goes *low* to toggle the flip-flop (level sensitive). The maximum toggle frequency is 20 megahertz and the power supply current per package is 20 mA. The package is a 14 pin DIP.

### THE 7476

This is a dual *J-K* master-slave with both *clear* and *set* direct inputs. The clock goes *low* to toggle the F-F (level sensitive). The maximum toggle frequency is 20 megahertz and the supply current per package is 20 mA. The package is a 16 pin DIP.

### THE 74107

This is identical to the 7473 but with standard pin-out and is preferred for new designs.

### C-MOS: THE 4027 AD, AE, AK

The 4027 is a dual *J-K* M-S with both *clear* and *set* direct inputs. It has two *J* and two *K* inputs plus a clock input. The clock goes to *high* to toggle the flip-flop. Maximum toggle frequency is 8 megahertz. Current per package (quiescent) is 60 $\mu$A., 16 pin.

## 4-13  Level and Edge Triggering

The *J-K* flip-flops are designed to trigger when the clock pulse reaches a specific voltage level. Level triggering is suitable for synchronous operation but when incoming data is not synchronized to the clock, another form of triggering is required.

Edge triggering uses only the trailing or leading edge of the clock (or data) pulse. Triggering occurs only during the appropriate clock transition. Steady state conditions are ignored by edge-triggered circuits. The *D*-type input is required in the bulk of applications where input data are likely to be random or otherwise out of step with the system clock. As a result, standard TTL *D*-type flip-flops are edge triggered.

## 4-14 The Type D Edge-Triggered Flip-Flop

The 7474 is a typical edge-triggered type *D* flip-flop. The logic diagram for one unit in the package is shown in Figure 4-26. The 7474 is a master-slave arrangement that achieves edge sensitivity without *R-C* differentiating circuits. *R-C* circuits are not satisfactory because the edge-triggered flip-flop must be capable of handling input signals from near 0 Hz to the maximum toggle frequency of the device. In some applications it must also handle completely random input data. The master circuit appears on the left and the slave on the right in Figure 4-26.

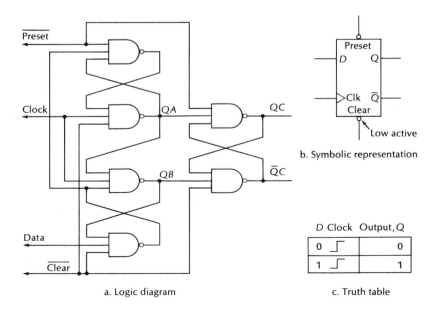

a. Logic diagram

b. Symbolic representation

c. Truth table

**Figure 4-26** Type "*D*" Edge-Triggered Flip-Flop

## OPERATING RULES FOR THE 7474

1. *D* input positive: The *Q* output goes positive (or stays positive) when the clock makes the transition from ground to positive.
2. *D* input grounded: The *Q* output goes to ground (or stays at ground) when the clock makes the transition from ground to positive. Figure 4-27 is a timing diagram illustrating the edge-triggered behavior of the *D* edge-triggered flip-flop.

The following events occur in the process of setting and resetting the flip-flop. Note that events are numbered on the timing diagram to correspond with the following outline of events.

1. *Initial conditions (start to set)* (6) which occurred at the end of the previous reset part of the cycle.
   a. Data  0 *(low)*
   b. Clock  0
   c. $Q_A$  1
   d. $Q_B$  1
   e. $Q_C$  0

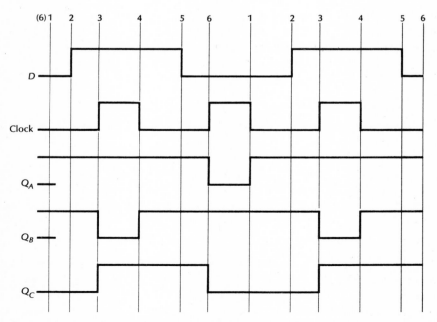

**Figure 4-27**  Timing Diagram for the Edge-Triggered Type "*D*" Flip-Flop

2. *Data line goes high* (1)—set command.
   - a. Data    1
   - b. Clock   0
   - c. $Q_A$      1–no change
   - d. $Q_B$      1–no change
   - e. $Q_C$      0–no change
3. *Clock goes high* (1)—time to set $Q_C$.
   - a. Data    1
   - b. Clock   1
   - c. $Q_A$      1–no change
   - d. $Q_B$      goes *low* (0)
   - e. $Q_C$      goes *high*—latch sets to $Q_C = 1$
4. *Clock goes low* (0).
   - a. Data    1–no change
   - b. Clock   0–goes *low*
   - c. $Q_A$      1–no change
   - d. $Q_B$      1–goes *high*
   - e. $Q_C$      1–remains *high*—no change
5. *Data goes low*—start of reset phase–but no change in $Q_C$ until after clock.
   - a. Data    0 goes *low*—reset command
   - b. Clock   0 still *low*
   - c. $Q_A$      1–no change
   - d. $Q_B$      1–still *high*
   - e. $Q_C$      1–still *set*—must wait for next clock—*high*
6. *Clock goes high*—driving $Q_A$ *low* and resetting $Q_C$ to 0.
   - a. Data    0–still *low*
   - b. Clock   1–goes *high*
   - c. $Q_A$      0–goes *low*
   - d. $Q_B$      1–no change
   - e. $Q_C$      0–goes to 0—reset
1. *Begin new set phase* . . .

Notice on the timing diagram that $Q_C$ (and $\overline{Q}_C$) changes state only on the positive going edge of the clock pulse. The circuit is edge triggered.

### PRESET AND CLEAR INPUTS

Preset and clear inputs for the edge-triggered $D$ flip-flop are level sensitive, independent of clock and $D$ inputs, and override any other existing input conditions. The direct inputs are not used for data but only to establish initial conditions for the system. Table 4-2 is the truth table for the direct inputs.

**Table 4-2**    Truth Table for the
Edge-Triggered Type
"D" Flip-Flop

| Set | Clear | Output |
|-----|-------|--------|
| 0 | 0 | forbidden state |
| 0 | 1 | 1 |
| 1 | 0 | 0 |
| 1 | 1 | normal clocked operation ("D") |

## 4-15   Commercial Type D Flip-Flops

### TTL

The most popular SSI TTL type is the 7474, a dual edge clocked $D$ flip-flop. It is triggered on the *positive*-going edge of the $D$ input (or clock) pulse. Maximum toggle frequency is 25 megahertz and current per package is 17 mA., 14 pin package. Individual clock, set, and clear inputs are provided for each flip-flop.

The 74175 is a quad positive edge-triggered device. All four flip-flops have common clock and common clear inputs. It is intended for service as a memory buffer in counter systems and similar applications. The clear line is normally held *high* and dropped momentarily to *low* to clear (reset) the flip-flop. Because the quad $D$ is generally used as a buffer memory, its frequency is called update frequency rather than toggle frequency. It is the maximum rate at which data can be changed. Maximum update frequency is 35 megahertz and current per package is 30 mA., 14 pin package.

The 74174 is a hex positive edge-triggered type $D$. Except for the number of devices in the package and the current drain, it has the same specifications as the 74175.

All six flip-flops share the same clock and clear inputs. Current per package is 30 mA., 16 pin package.

### C-MOS

The CD 4013 is a dual C-MOS positive edge-triggered type $D$ flip-flop. The two flip-flops feature separate *set* and *clear* and *clock* inputs. Direct inputs (set and clear) are held at ground for normal operation and momentarily taken *high* to set or reset the flip-flop. Maximum update (or toggle) frequency is 10 megahertz and current per package is 60 to 120 $\mu$A., 14 pin package.

The CD 4042 A is a quad positive edge-triggered $D$ latch (flip-flop). The four flip-flops share the same clock-reset lines. Maximum frequency is 2 megahertz. Current per package is 60 to 120 $\mu$A., 16 pin package. Tri-state output C-MOS $D$ latches are also available.

**Important note:** Practically all C-MOS flip-flops are edge-triggered devices, including the $J\text{-}K$ versions.

### 4-16   The Quad D Level-Triggered Flip-Flop

One commercial $D$ level-triggered flip-flop type should be mentioned, the 7475. It is a special device intended for use as a buffer memory between counters and indicator units. There are two enable lines, one for each pair of flip-flops. These simple devices cannot be cascaded, so they cannot be used for shift register or counter service.

### 4-17   Other Flip-Flop Considerations

a. When edge-triggered $D$ and level-triggered $J\text{-}K$ devices are used in the same system, a clock line inverter must be provided. The edge-triggered $D$ is triggered on the positive going (leading edge) part of the pulse, while the $J\text{-}K$ transfers final data out on the negative going (trailing edge) part of the pulse. If the two clock signals are not opposites (180° difference), there will be a serious timing difference between their outputs.

b. Because of its ability to accept random (unequally spaced) data, the type $D$ is often the choice for the first stage in counters and shift registers. It can be converted into a toggle (type $T$) for counter or frequency divider applications. Figure 4-28 shows the configuration.

c. Common reset (clear) or preset (set) lines should not leave a circuit board or go through a connector without being buffered by a gate or inverter.

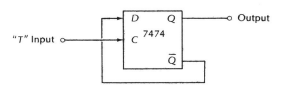

**Figure 4-28**   Edge-Triggered Type "$D$" Reconfigured as a Type "$T$"

    d. Common *clear* and *set* lines should never be allowed to float. Noise pick-up can lead to erratic flip-flop operation. If these lines are not connected to the output of another gate, they should be tied +5 volts through a pull-up resistor of 330 ohms or less (for TTL).

    e. Reset pulses should last for at *least* 10 microseconds to insure the proper reset of all flip-flops on a common reset line.

## SUMMARY

Flip-flops are memory elements that can be used to store data, pass it on, or to divide by 2 for counting operations. Unclocked flip-flops are rarely used in practice because they cannot be used to transfer data from one flip-flop to another. The clocked $R$-$S$ flip-flop is used only occasionally as part of a more complex IC circuit.

The $J$-$K$ level-triggered flip-flop and the edge-triggered $D$ flip-flop are the two most important flip-flop circuits. Both circuits use the master-slave principle to eliminate timing problems when flip-flops are cascaded.

The TTL edge-triggered $D$ is triggered on the positive going edge of the input (clock) pulse. The TTL level-triggered $J$-$K$ is triggered (slave output) on the negative going transition of the input signal (clock). If both types are used in the same system, the two clock signals must generally be 180° out of phase with each other.

The $J$-$K$ is more versatile than the type $D$ but less suitable when input signals are unsynchronized or random. It can be converted into a $D$ by adding an inverter. The $D$ can be modified to toggle for counting applications by connecting the $\bar{Q}$ output back to the $D$ input.

### Problems

  9. Match the following to items (1) through (7) below (more than one answer is possible):

    a. $J$-$K$ master-slave        c. $R$-$S$ (NAND)

    b. Type $D$               d. Clocked $R$-$S$ (NAND)

    (1) Triggers on positive transition.

    (2) Triggers on negative transition.

    (3) Edge triggered.

    (4) Can be used as an $R$-$S$ or type $T$ or modified for type $D$ service.

    (5) The best choice for unequally spaced input pulses.

    (6) Infrequently used.

    (7) The most popular of the four types.

 10. Draw the symbol for each of the following flip-flops:

a. Type *T*      e. *J-K*
b. *R-S*      f. Edge-triggered *D*
c. Clocked *R-S*      g. Master-slave *J-K*
d. Clocked *D*

11. Examine the frequency divider in Figure 4-19. Now show how it can be constructed using *D* flip-flops.
12. Describe the sequence of events in a master-slave flip-flop.
13. What makes clocking and master-slave arrangements necessary?
14. Find two tri-state output flip-flops in the data manual. List the numbers and types.
15. Figure 4-19 shows a frequency divider using type *T* flip-flops. Draw a diagram of a similar one using *J-K* flip-flops.
16. In your own words, describe the operating sequence of a *J-K* master-slave flip-flop.
17. Under what conditions is the type *D* edge-triggered device preferred to the *J-K* master-slave flip-flop?
18. Using a manufacturer's TTL data manual, look under flip-flops to determine whether edge-triggered *J-K* flip-flops are available. Also, see if you can find any level-triggered *D* latches other than the 7475.
19. Are latches listed separately from flip-flops in the data manual? Read the spec sheets and see if you can find a reason why latches could be listed under a separate heading.
20. Look up IC numbers 7494, 74100, 74109, 7493, 7490 in the TTL data manual and answer the questions below.
    a. What type of circuit is it?
    b. What types of flip-flops are used?
    c. Is clear available?
    d. Is preset available?
    e. Is the input positive or negative going for trigger?
    f. Is the clock negative going or positive going for clocking?
21. In your own words describe each of the following input configurations:
    a. *R-S*      b. *J-K*      c. *T*      d. *D*
22. Draw a diagram showing how a *J-K* M-S can be configured into each of the following:
    a. *R-S*      b. *T*      c. *D*
23. Draw the logic diagram for each of the following:
    a. NAND latch
    b. NOR latch
    c. Basic type *T* flip-flop
    d. Clocked NOR latch
    e. Clocked NAND latch
    f. Master-slave *J-K* flip-flop
    g. Edge-triggered type *D*
    h. Basic type *D* (clocked) level-triggered flip-flop

# CHAPTER 5

# CLOCKS AND GATE INTERFACING

*Learning objectives. Upon completion of this chapter you should:*

1. *Be able to define the term interface.*
2. *Be able to draw the interface circuits for each of the following situations (and their converse):*
   a. *DTL to TTL*
   b. *TTL to high threshold T-MOS*
   c. *TTL to silicon-gate P-MOS*
   d. *TTL to N-MOS*
   e. *TTL to C-MOS*
   f. *TTL to ECL*
3. *Be able to define master clock and subordinate clock.*
4. *Be able to define standard parameters for pulse measurements.*
5. *Be able to draw an ideal pulse and properly dimension it.*
6. *Know the cause of undershoot, overshoot, and ringing.*
7. *Be able to draw and explain the operation of the:*
   a. *transistor astable multivibrator*
   b. *logic gate astable (ring oscillator)*
   c. *logic gate crystal-controlled oscillator*
8. *Understand the function and applications of Schmitt-trigger circuit.*
9. *Be able to draw the schematic diagram for practical R-C differentiation circuits.*
10. *Be able to list the characteristics and applications of the monostable multivibrator (one-shot).*
11. *Be able to describe the 555 timer and list typical applications.*
12. *Know the characteristics and applications of the 74121 IC monostable.*

Interfacing is a broad term that implies a bridging of the gap between the various operating characteristics of devices or systems. It can involve methods of cascading gates that have different logic levels, load, or drive characteristics. It can also apply methods of converting the internal code of one system into the internal code required by another. Serial data may be converted into a parallel form (or the other way around) to meet the differing methods of moving data in two systems where one must drive the other. Interface circuits are also generally required between the logic circuits and the outside world of indicator lamps, relays, printers, and such. This chapter will examine the most common interface problems, methods, and circuits as applied to levels, loading, pulse shaping, and other aspects of pulse modification generation and control.

Digital systems are almost invariably provided with a master pulse generator called a *clock*. The clock synchronizes all of the counting and data transfers in the system and provides *enable* (clock) signals for flip-flop, latches, and other memory elements.

Often it becomes necessary to lengthen (stretch) or shorten a pulse or to delay it by a given amount of time. It may also be necessary to be able to separate the leading or trailing edge of a pulse from the remainder and to shape *slow* waveforms into the fast rising pulses required by high-speed logic circuits. The power line is sometimes a pulse source but it must be conditioned into an acceptable form for high-speed logic, and external signals must sometimes be synchronized to the internal system clock.

In the second part of this chapter we will examine ways of generating, synchronizing, delaying, shaping, stretching, and shortening pulses.

## 5-1 Interfacing between Logic Families

A few simple circuits solve most of the problems involved in interfacing gates of different logic families.

### TTL TO DTL

TTL and DTL logic gates are generally directly compatible with the exception of fan-out considerations. The data manuals should be consulted for each particular case. No additional interface circuitry is required.

### TTL to P-MOS (High Threshold)

TTL is interfaced to the older high threshold P-MOS by using either the 7406, 30 volt open collector hex inverter driver or the 7416, 15 volt open collector inverter driver. The required 12 volt pull-up voltage is too high for standard TTL. The P-MOS requires +12 volt and −12 volt power supplies.

### TTL to Silicon Gate P-MOS

The newer silicon gate P-MOS can be directly interfaced with TTL, but an added pull-up resistor improves the noise immunity of the circuit and is usually provided. The same +5 volt power supply should be used for both TTL and MOS. Figure 5-1 shows typical circuits to interface TTL to MOS.

### N-MOS

N-MOS uses the same +5 volt power supply and is directly compatible with TTL.

### C-MOS

TTL can drive C-MOS directly but, again, the pull-up resistor is used to improve noise immunity.

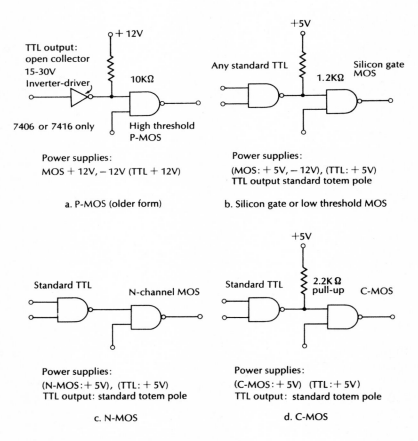

**Figure 5-1** MOS to TTL Interface Circuits

## MOS TO TTL

### High Threshold P-MOS

The older P-MOS requires power supplies of + 12 volts and − 12 volts. The MOS gate can drive only one standard TTL input. An open drain P-MOS gate is used to drive TTL, and a 1 kΩ resistor limits the TTL input current.

### Silicon Gate MOS

The silicon gate MOS requires power supplies of +5 volts and − 12 volts. It can drive one standard TTL load. The +5 volt supply should be the same one for both devices. An open drain MOS device is used.

### N-MOS

N-MOS is directly compatible with TTL. It can drive one standard TTL input.

### C-MOS

C-MOS can directly drive a single low-power TTL input. If two C-MOS gate inputs can be connected together (see Figure 5-2*d*), the parallel transistors in the gate can drive one standard TTL load. When several TTL inputs must be driven, a C-MOS buffer can be used. The CD 4049 is a suitable non-inverting buffer and the CD 4050 is a satisfactory inverting buffer. Both devices contain six buffers in a sixteen pin DIP package. Figure 5-2 shows MOS-to-TTL interface methods.

### INTERFACING TO ECL

Because of the unusual voltage levels used in emitter-coupled logic families, special logic level translators must be used. Figure 5-3 shows MC1067 and MC1068 logic level translator circuits for interfacing ECL and TTL.

## 5-2   Interfacing Logic to Other Devices

An LED (light-emitting diode) can be driven directly by TTL if a suitable current-limiting resistor is provided (see Figure 5-4).

When there are large differences in levels, an optical isolator can often solve the problem. This device contains an LED that illuminates a phototransistor. All four leads are separate, and the only coupling between LED and phototransistor is by way of a beam of light. Figure 5-5 shows a typical incandescent lamp driver.

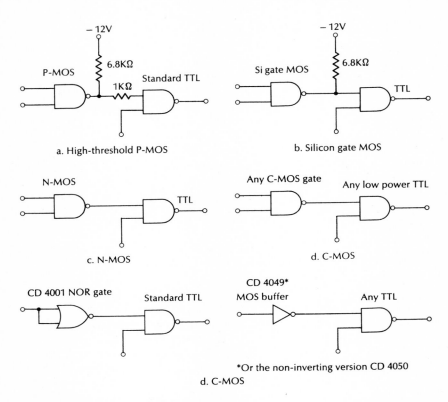

a. High-threshold P-MOS

b. Silicon gate MOS

c. N-MOS

d. C-MOS

*Or the non-inverting version CD 4050

d. C-MOS

**Figure 5-2**   MOS to TTL Interface Circuits

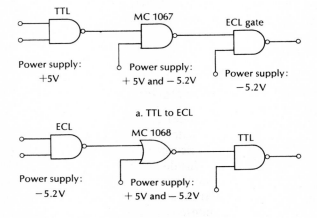

a. TTL to ECL

**Figure 5-3**   TTL to ECL Interface

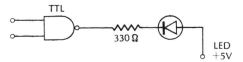

Note: Gate output low 330 Ω resistor grounded. Output high + 5 volts opposes +5 LED supply and LED goes out.

**Figure 5-4** LED Driver

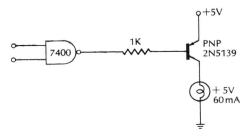

**Figure 5-5** Incandescent Lamp Driver

## 5-3 The Clock

The clock is basically a pulse generator, but it can take on a number of circuit forms. The circuit can be a shaped sine wave derived from the AC power line (as it often is in digital timekeeping clocks), a waveform produced by a free-running multivibrator, or the shaped waveform from a crystal-controlled oscillator.

### MASTER AND SUBORDINATE CLOCKS

Whatever the source, the master clock provides a train of pulses that controls all of the operations in the system, determines the speed at which the system operates, and determines how long it takes to perform an operation—for example, addition.

Clock pulses are often required that are shifted in phase from the master clock or have pulse widths or repetition rates that differ from the basic pulse train. The circuits that provide these master clock-related pulses are called *subordinate clocks*. As the name implies, subordinate clocks derive their output pulses by performing some operation on the pulses generated by the master clock. They are *not* independent pulse generators.

## 5-4 Pulse Parameters

### FREQUENCY AND PERIOD

Clock signals (and other pulses) have certain defined parameters to describe their dimensions in amplitude and time.

### Frequency

The frequency of pulses is a measure of how many pulses occur in a given time period. The measurement is generally given in megahertz (MHz).

### Period

The period is defined as the *time* between two adjacent pulses, and its base unit is the *second*. It is dependent upon the frequency and bears the mathematical relationship: $T = 1/F$, where $T$ = time between pulses and $f$ = the frequency of pulses. If we rearrange the equation in terms of $F$, we get $F = 1/T$. If we know the period, we can always find the frequency by taking the reciprocal; conversely, if we know the frequency, we can take the reciprocal to determine the period.

### Rise and Fall Times

Rise time is generally defined as the time required for a pulse voltage to rise from 10 percent above the (*ideal* pulse) zero volt state, to 90 percent of the ideal pulse maximum amplitude. The 10 percent at the beginning of the pulse's rise and the 10 percent at the end of the rise are practical considerations, allowing for measurements in spite of *ringing, overshoot,* and *undershoot.* Therefore, 10 percent above the zero volts base line and 10 percent below the maximum pulse amplitude has been allowed to insure meaningful measurements. Fall time is the time (ns) required for the pulse voltage to *fall* from 90 percent of its maximum steady-state voltage to 10 percent of maximum amplitude.

### Pulse Width

Pulse width is the time interval, measured at 50 percent above the ideal baseline—zero. Some companies may have different in-house standards.

### Ringing, Undershoot, and Overshoot

At the end of a sudden transition (from *low* to *high* or from *high* to *low*), distributed capacitances and inductances form a resonant circuit that produces a decaying sinusoidal oscillation, which lasts for a time from less than half a cycle to several cycles. The added amplitude is called *overshoot* on the upward transition (see Figure 5-6). At the bottom of the transition, from high to low, ringing may occur again. When the tank circuit energy is dissipated in approximately half a cycle, it is said to be critically damped, and the portion of the first half (ringing) cycle is called *undershoot*. Undershoot and overshoot are measured as a fraction of the maximum steady-state pulse amplitude. Ringing may also be classified by its *self-resonant* frequency. The frequency of the ringing is important only in the sense that it may offer some clue as to the elements causing it.

### Pulse Amplitude

Pulse amplitude is the maximum steady-state pulse height. The actual measurement is taken by projecting the leading edge baseline to the trailing edge of the pulse and measuring from the projected baseline to the top of the trailing edge of the pulse. The measurement is taken in this way because any overshoot (or ringing) will occur at the end of the leading edge *high*-going transition. This tends to obscure the actual pulse amplitude at the top of the leading edge. By the beginning of the pulse downward transition (trailing edge), overshoot and ringing energy should have been dissipated and the steady-state pulse amplitude established. At the end of the pulse fall to zero, undershoot (or ringing) can obscure the baseline for the trailing edge of the pulse. Figure 5-6 shows a dimensioned non-ideal pulse. Logic circuits can tolerate a reasonable amount of pulse imperfection and still operate properly. As a result, we are usually not too concerned about the absolute values of these pulse

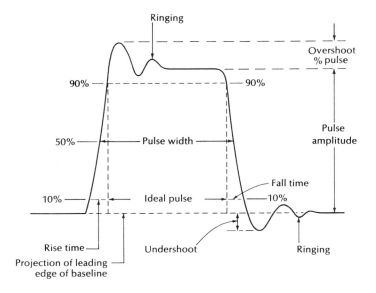

**Figure 5-6**   Non-Ideal Pulse

parameters. However, in difficult troubleshooting problems these parameters can be crucial. The system manufacturer will generally provide information about maximum allowable overshoot, ringing, undershoot, rise time, and so on.

## 5-5 The Inverted Subordinate Clock

The inverted subordinate clock is one of the simplest and most common subordinate clock pulses. Assume, for example, that a system contains a *J-K* master-slave F-F and a leading edge triggered *D* F-F and that they must both be synchronized to the *master* clock. The *D* F-F will transfer data on the *up* clock (leading edge) while the *J-K* master-slave F-F will transfer data on the *down* clock (trailing edge). By inverting the *master* clock signal, we get a subordinate clock signal that provides a *down* clock at the leading edge (*up* clock) of the master clock. With the master clock controlling the *D* latch and the 180° phase inverted subordinate clock controlling the *J-K*, the data transfer from both F-F's occurs at the same time (see Figure 5-7). A clock system with an inverted subordinate clock pulse is often referred to as a two-phase clock.

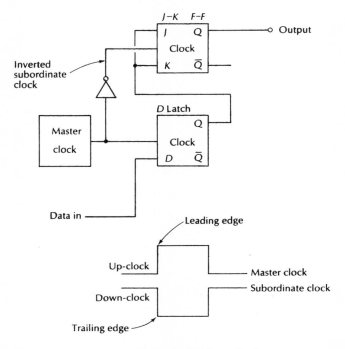

**Figure 5-7** Example Using Inverted Subordinate Clock

## 5-6 The Astable Multivibrator

The astable multivibrator is a free-running $RC$ oscillator. It consists of two common emitter inverting amplifiers connected in a regenerative loop. The free-running frequency is determined by values of $R$ and $C$. Figure 5-8a shows the circuit.

### THEORY OF OPERATION

Assume the following initial conditions:

$$Q_1 \text{ in cutoff}$$
$$Q_2 \text{ in saturation}$$

Operating potentials would then be as follows:

$$\frac{Q_1}{V_{BE1} \text{ less than } +0.6 \text{V}}$$
$$V_{CE1} \approx -V_{cc}$$

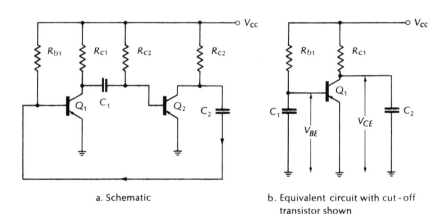

a. Schematic

b. Equivalent circuit with cut-off transistor shown

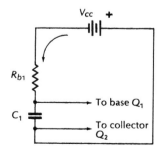

c. Equivalent circuit with cut-off transistor omitted

**Figure 5-8** Astable Multivibrator

$$\frac{Q_2}{V_{BE2}} \approx -0.6\text{V}$$
$$V_{CE2} \approx 0\text{V}$$

Figure 5-8b shows the equivalent circuit for $Q_1$. Assuming that $Q_2$ is in saturation, we can also assume that both base and collector of $Q_2$ are approximately at ground potential. With $Q_1$ in cutoff we can assume that both base and collector represent very high impedances. With these assumptions in mind, we can draw Figure 5-8c. In this figure capacitor $C_1$ charges through $R_{b1}$ toward $V_{cc}$. When $V_{c1}$ reaches approximately 0.6V, base current begins to flow in $Q1$.

In Figure 5-8a base current means collector current. The increased collector causes the collector voltage of $Q_1$ to fall. Because of the capacitive coupling from the collector of $Q_1$ to $Q_2$'s base, $V_{BE}$ of $Q_2$ also falls and $Q_2$'s collector voltage rises accordingly. Because the collector of $Q_2$ is capacitively coupled to the base of $Q_1$, $V_{BE}$ of $Q_1$ increases, causing an increased $Q_1$ base current, increased $Q_1$ collector current, and a diminishing of $Q_1$'s collector voltage. Thus, the regenerative action has begun. $Q_1$'s collector voltage will continue to decrease, driving $Q_2$'s base voltage down and its collector voltage up. $Q_2$'s increasing collector voltage increases $Q_2$'s base voltage, driving its collector voltage down still more. The regenerative action continues until $Q_1$ is in saturation and $Q_2$ is in cutoff. Half the cycle is complete.

The same events take place again but this time with $Q_1$ coming out of saturation and $Q_2$ being driven into saturation for the second half of the cycle. The action continues as long as power is applied.

Figure 5-9 shows the circuit as it is conventionally drawn. To make the previous explanation more meaningful, Figure 5-10 illustrates the

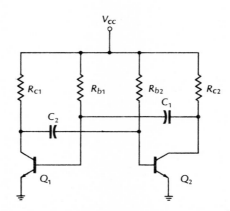

**Figure 5-9** Transistor Astable Multivibrator Schematic

charging circuit for either of the coupling capacitors. The voltage at point $A$ must go from $-V$ to $+V$. Zero volts is halfway between.

The classical equation for finding the charge voltage at the end of time $T$ is:

$$V_c = V(1 - e^{-t/RC})$$

where
$t$ = time
$R$ = resistance
$C$ = capacitance
$e$ = the base of the natural log system
$V_c$ = charge in volts

Solving for $t$ when $V_c = 0.5V$

$$t = 0.69\,RC$$

Because the transistors must be driven into saturation in the full-on (closed switch) condition, the following conditions must be met:

(1)
$$\frac{R_{B1}}{R_{C1}} < hFE\ (Q_1)$$

(2)
$$\frac{R_{B2}}{R_{C2}} < hFE\ (Q_2)$$

A common rule of thumb is:

(1)
$$\frac{R_{B1}}{R_{C1}} \approx 0.5hFE\ (Q_1)$$

(2)
$$\frac{R_{B2}}{R_{C2}} \approx 0.5hFE\ (Q_2)$$

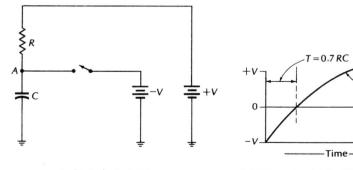

a. Equivalent circuit      b. Voltage at point $A$ with respect to time

**Figure 5-10**   Capacitor Charging Circuit

This provides approximately twice the estimated base current required to drive the transistors into saturation and allows for variations in the actual hFE of the transistors and other component tolerances.

The total time for one cycle is:

$$T = 0.69 \, (R_{B1} \, C_1 + R_{B2} \, C_2)$$

The output waveform of the transistor astable often has a comparatively slow rise/fall time. This can frequently be corrected by cascading two inverters in series with the output of the transistor astable multivibrator.

### FREE-RUNNING OSCILLATORS USING TTL GATES

Figure 5-11 shows the transistor astable circuit of Figure 5-8a redrawn in a cascaded form. It would seem by analogy that the circuit in Figure 5-11 could be implemented using cascaded inverting gates as shown in Figure 5-12. However, the TTL gate, unlike the transistor, is full on

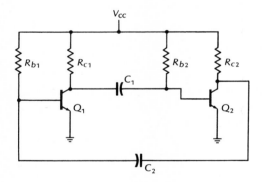

**Figure 5-11**  Transistor Astable Circuit Drawn in Cascaded Form

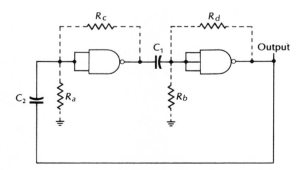

**Figure 5-12**  NAND Gate Astable Multivibrator

and must be driven off. The circuit as shown (with the dotted line resistors omitted) would end up with both gates *on* where no regeneration could occur. Resistors $R_a$ and $R_b$ or $R_c$ and $R_d$ can be added to make the circuit work, but at best it is unpredictable and unstable. The circuit is possible but not very practical.

## 5-7 Logic Gate Oscillator (The Ring Oscillator)

There are a number of practical clock generators based on logic gates. Any odd number of inverting gates will oscillate when connected in a ring, as shown in Figure 5-13. The principle of operation differs, however, from conventional oscillators that use positive feedback at some frequency ($f_0$) that produces a 180° phase shift. In the case of logic gate oscillators, the transition of a gate through its linear region requires a very short time. As a result, conventional phase shift explanations become difficult. A better viewpoint is to consider the gates as ideal switches with built-in delays. The oscillator then can be viewed as logic 1 following itself around the ring. Each time the 1 arrives and leaves at the gate connected to the output, an output pulse appears.

Frequency is a function of the total delay time. Additional elements such as $RC$ time constant circuits can be used to increase the delay and lower the frequency. The maximum frequency is determined by the intrinsic gate delays. Figure 5-14 shows a practical version of a logic gate ring oscillator using TTL 7403 open collector N A N D gates. The circuit is moderately stable and the frequency is controlled by the values of $R$ and $C$. Figure 5-15 shows a C-MOS version using 74C04 C-MOS inverters. The equation for the approximate frequency of the C-MOS circuit is:

$$f \approx \frac{1}{2C(0.405R_{eq} + 0.693R_1)}$$

where

$$R_{eq} = \frac{R_1 R_2}{R_1 + R_2}$$

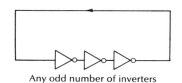

Any odd number of inverters

**Figure 5-13** Basic Ring Oscillator

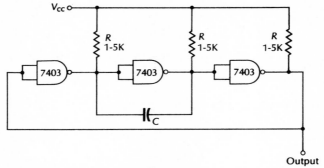

**Figure 5-14**  Practical Ring Oscillator

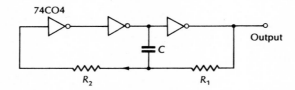

**Figure 5-15**  C-MOS Ring Oscillator

For the special case in which $R_1 = R_2$, the following simplified equation can be written:

$$f \approx \frac{0.559}{RC}$$

In the case of the TTL version, similar equations are less satisfactory because of TTL's low and variable input impedance.

The frequency of any ring oscillator made up of gates only is:

$$f = \frac{1}{2nt_p}$$

where

$\quad\quad f$ = frequency of oscillation
$\quad\quad t_p$ = propagation delay per gate
$\quad\quad n$ = number of gates in the ring

## 5-8  C-MOS Crystal Oscillator

A logic gate oscillator with crystal control can easily be constructed from a C-MOS gate. TTL gates are not as practical for use in crystal

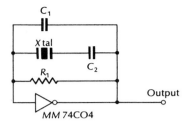

**Figure 5-16**  C-MOS Crystal Controlled
Logic Gate Oscillator

controlled logic gate oscillators because their low input impedance loads the crystal, lowers the $Q$, and impairs stability. The high input impedance of C-MOS makes it ideal for crystal controlled (or $LC$) oscillators. Figure 5-16 shows a simple but practical C-MOS crystal controlled logic oscillator. $R_1$ is a bias resistor on the order of 1–5 megohms. Capacitor $C_1$ pulls the crystal down and $C_2$ pulls it up. The oscillator will oscillate up to 9 MHz. Above that, the gate delay time prevents the system from keeping up with the crystal. The result is instability and, at slightly higher frequencies, failure to oscillate.

## OVERTONE PROTECTION

Third harmonic overtones can be a problem in any design. In the circuit of Figure 5-16 it occurs at about 4 MHz. The problem can be solved by deliberately adding additional gate delay to prevent the circuit from oscillating at the third harmonic. As many gates as required to provide sufficient delay can be added; however, there must always be an odd number of gates in the ring. Figure 5-17 shows the circuit modified for

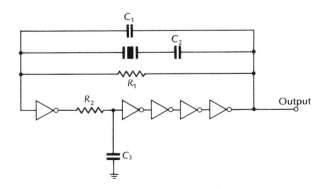

**Figure 5-17**  The C-MOS Oscillator Modified for Overtone Protection

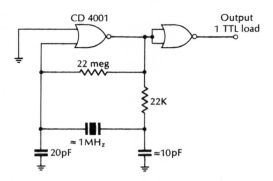

**Figure 5-18**   Another C-MOS Logic Gate Crystal Oscillator

overtone protection. Figure 5-18 shows a popular and slightly different configuration of the C-MOS crystal oscillator with the output interfaced to one standard TTL load.

## 5-9   The Schmitt Trigger

The Schmitt trigger is a threshold-controlled regenerative switch. It is particularly useful when a slowly changing waveform, such as a sinewave or sawtooth, must be reshaped into a fast-rising pulse to be compatible with high-speed logic systems. The important characteristics of the Schmitt trigger are the lower-trip-level (LTL), the upper-trip-level (UTL), and the difference between the LTL and UTL voltages, called the *hysteresis* voltage.

An ordinary (TTL) gate has a conduction threshold level of about 0.8V at which point the transistor begins operating in its linear region where the gain is high. During the transistor's transition through the linear region, it is very sensitive to noise or signal amplitude variations.

The normal logic pulse drives the transistor through the sensitive region in a very short time and provides a constantly rising drive signal. A slow-rising signal tends to remain for a comparatively long time in this sensitive high gain condition where even small noise levels or signal amplitude variations can cause the gate to jitter—to fall in and out of the *on* state. The system could well interpret these variations as several input pulses instead of one or reject the input signal as no pulse at all.

The Schmitt trigger provides a regenerative action that drives the transistor rapidly through the linear region, once the action has been initiated by the input signal. In addition, it provides two threshold levels—one to initiate the trigger's *turn-on* condition and the other, a significantly lower level, to initiate the regenerative *turn-off* action. The

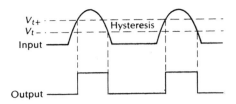

a. Schmitt input and output waveforms

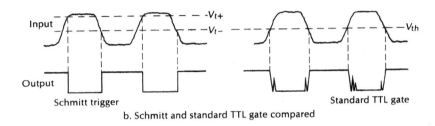

Schmitt trigger                                    Standard TTL gate

b. Schmitt and standard TTL gate compared

**Figure 5-19**   Schmitt Trigger Waveforms

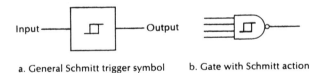

a. General Schmitt trigger symbol          b. Gate with Schmitt action

**Figure 5-20**   Schmitt Trigger Symbols

regenerative action causes a fast-rising (or falling) drive that simulates the rise of a normal digital pulse. The hysteresis makes the system insensitive to noise and small signal amplitude variations that could otherwise cause false triggering. Figure 5-19 shows typical Schmitt trigger waveforms. In this case we will use $V_{T+}$ for the positive-going trip level and $V_{T-}$ for the negative or downward-going trip level. This convention is becoming more common in TTL systems than the notation UTL and LTL.

Figure 5-20 shows the symbolic representations for a Schmitt trigger input. In Figure 5-20b the Schmitt trigger symbol is shown in conjunction with a NAND gate, indicating a gate with a built-in Schmitt trigger. The 7413 is a dual four-input NAND gate with Schmitt action. It will respond to very low rates of change but not to a discrete DC level. Typical TTL Schmitt devices have a hysteresis voltage of about 0.8V.

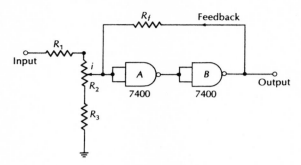

**Figure 5-21**  Two-Gate, Two-State Multivibrator

The Schmitt trigger is essentially a two-gate, two-state multivibrator of the general form shown in Figure 5-21.

The circuit operates as follows: Assume (as initial conditions) that gate *A* is outputting a *high* as a result of 0 volts input signal at point *i* and that gate *B* is outputting a zero. Let the signal voltage rise to the input threshold of gate *A*. Gate *A* switches to an output *low*, switching gate *B* to a *high* output. Because the two gates are inverting gates, the feedback through $R_f$ to the input of gate *A* is positive and the action is regenerative, simulating the fast rise/fall time of the normal digital pulse.

Let the input signal start its negative-going transition toward 0V. Because the feedback resistor has a *high* at the end connected to gate *B*, it pulls the input (point *i*) up toward $V_{cc}$. Therefore the input signal must drop considerably lower than the turn-on threshold before gate *A* can switch to a *high*, initiating the regenerative turn-off action. The voltage divider ($R_2 - R_3$) divides the signal setting the effective threshold voltage. $R_1$ isolates the signal source from point *i*, allowing it to *float* to prevent excessive loading of the feedback resistor $R_f$.

## 5-10  Schmitt Trigger Oscillator

Figure 5-22 shows a simple square-wave oscillator utilizing the Schmitt trigger characteristics of the 74C14 C-MOS inverter.

Assume that the gate output is *high*. The capacitor begins to charge through $R$ with the polarity shown in Figure 5-22. When the voltage across the capacitor reaches $V_{T+}$, the gate output goes *low*. The capacitor now discharges back through $R$ until it reaches $V_{T-}$, and the gate output again goes *high*. The cycle repeats as long as power is applied.

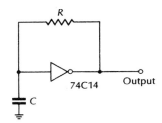

**Figure 5-22** Schmitt Trigger Oscillator

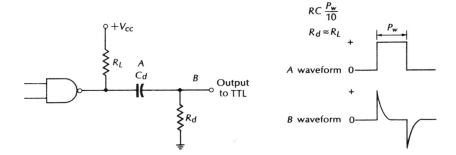

**Figure 5-23** The Differentiator

## 5-11 Differentiating a Pulse to Get a Narrow-Edge Pulse

Figure 5-23 shows how the edges of a pulse can be separated from the rest of the pulse. The pulse width can be found by classical $RC$ time constant equations when all factors are known. For most practical situations, making the $RC$ product $1/10$ to $1/20$ of the pulse width will be adequate, with the added precaution that $R$ cannot be made too small or the differentiated pulse voltage will fall below the approximate level of 2.5 volts required to properly turn on a TTL gate. A diode can be used to eliminate either the negative-going pulse or the positive-going pulse. An inverter can be used to place the positive-going pulse on the trailing edge of the original pulse if desired. $R_d$ and $R_L$ form a voltage divider. With 5 volts for $V_{cc}$ and $R_d \approx R_L$, the voltage across $R_d \approx 2.5V$. This is adequate for a TTL *high* level. Figure 5-24 shows some practical differentiating circuits for producing narrow-edge pulse.

## 5-12 The Monostable Multivibrator (One-Shot or Single Shot)

One of the circuits commonly used for pulse stretching and shortening is the monostable multivibrator (often called the *one-shot*). The one-shot is characterized by having two states—one state stable (preferred)

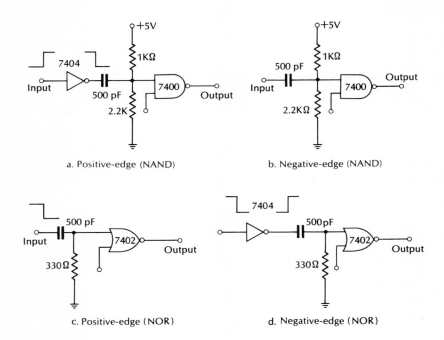

**Figure 5-24** Edge-Triggering Pulses Using Differentiator Circuit

and one semi-stable. When the one-shot receives a trigger pulse, it switches from the stable state into the semi-stable (on either the leading or trailing edge of the pulse) where it stays for a period of time determined by a combination of internal gate delays and an external *RC* timing circuit. The length of time spent in the semi-stable state is independent of the input pulse width. It can be configured to generate either a longer pulse (stretching) or a shorter pulse (shortening) than the input pulse. The one-shot is a regenerative circuit which helps insure sufficiently short *rise* and *fall* times.

Monostable circuits can be constructed from gates, but because of the availability of inexpensive IC monostable packages, it is not often done.

### THE HALF-MONOSTABLE

The half-monostable, so called because it lacks the regenerative action of the true monostable, can be used to shorten a pulse. The command pulse must always last longer than the output pulse. The circuit can be used wherever leading edge or trailing edge pulses of limited accuracy are required. Rise and fall times of the half-monostable are

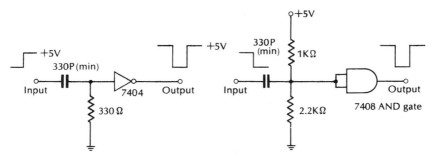

a. Positive-edge input, negative output pulse    b. Negative-edge input, negative output pulse

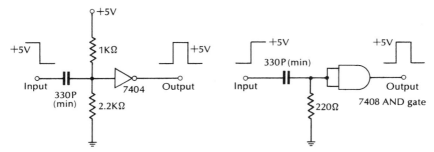

c. Negative-edge input, positive output pulse    d. Positive-edge input, negative output pulse

**Figure 5-25**    Half-Monostable Circuits

much slower than those of the true monostable. Figure 5-25 shows four variations of the half-monostable.

## 5-13    The 555 Timer

The 555 timer is one of several highly stable timing-circuit devices. It can be used as a timer with trigger and reset provisions, as a monostable multivibrator, or as an astable multivibrator.

The timer is capable of producing time periods ranging from microseconds to hours, depending on the value of external timing components. The supply voltage can be from +4.5 to +18 volts. Figure 5-26 shows the functional block diagram of the 555 timer.

### MONOSTABLE OPERATION

Figure 5-27 shows the 555 connected as a monostable. At the beginning of the cycle, transistor $Q_1$ (see Figure 5-26) holds capacitor $C$ at zero volts and the output (pin 3) *low*. The arrival of a negative trigger pulse

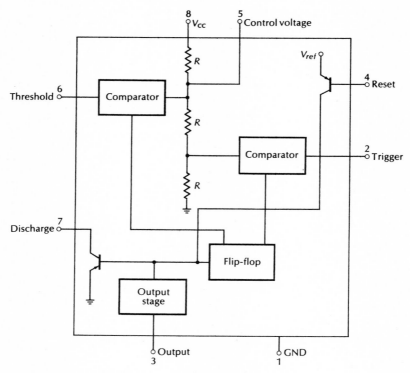

**Figure 5-26** Block Diagram of the 555 Timer

at pin 2 sets the flip-flop. When the flip-flop is set, the transistor $Q_1$ is turned off and the output (pin 3) goes *high*. The capacitor $C$ starts charging toward $2/3\ V_{cc}$, at which point the comparator resets the flip-flop. Transistor $Q_1$ is again turned full-on and rapidly discharges $C$. The output (pin 3) goes low.

The comparator is a high gain differential amplifier. One differential input is connected to a voltage of $1/3\ V_{cc}$ and the other to the trigger input. A comparator provides an abrupt transition in its output voltage at the point where the voltages to its two inputs are equal.

The device triggers on a negative-going input signal when the level reaches $1/3\ V_{cc}$. Once triggered, the circuit will remain in this state until the set time is elapsed, even if it is triggered again during this interval. The time that the output remains in the high state can be determined by the nomogram in Figure 5-28. The charge rate and the threshold level of the comparator are both directly proportional to supply voltage, and

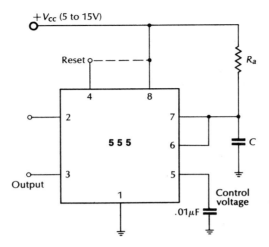

**Figure 5-27**    555 Timer Configured as a Monostable

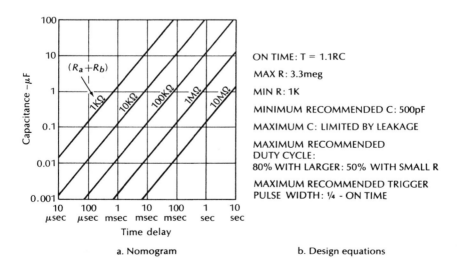

ON TIME: $T = 1.1RC$

MAX R: 3.3meg

MIN R: 1K

MINIMUM RECOMMENDED C: 500pF

MAXIMUM C: LIMITED BY LEAKAGE

MAXIMUM RECOMMENDED
DUTY CYCLE:
80% WITH LARGER: 50% WITH SMALL R

MAXIMUM RECOMMENDED TRIGGER
PULSE WIDTH: ¼ - ON TIME

a. Nomogram                              b. Design equations

**Figure 5-28**    Time-Delay Nomogram and Design Equations for
the Monostable Mode

the timing interval is independent of slow variations in power supply voltage. However, the circuit is sensitive to supply voltage variations that are faster than the timing period. $V_{cc}$ decoupling is frequently required. Figure 5-27 shows the frequency modulation input (pin 5) connected to ground through a .01 $\mu$F capacitor. When this input is not needed, it is good practice to use this capacitor to decouple the $V_{cc}$ line.

Applying a negative pulse simultaneously to the reset terminal (pin 4) and the trigger terminal (pin 2) during the timing cycle discharges the external capacitor and causes the cycle to start over again. The timing cycle will now begin on the positive edge of the reset pulse. During the time the reset pulse is applied, the output is driven low.

When the reset function is not in use, it should be connected to $V_{cc}$ to avoid the possibility of false triggering.

### ASTABLE OPERATION

Figure 5-29 shows the timer connected to operate in an astable mode. In this mode the timer will trigger itself and operate as a free-running multivibrator.

The external capacitor $C$ charges through $R_A$ and $R_B$ and discharges through $R_B$ alone. As a result, the duty cycle (ratio of on-to-off time) is controlled by the ratio of resistors $R_A$ and $R_B$. When the timer is connected as an astable oscillator, this capacitor $C$ charges and discharges between ⅓ and ⅔ $V_{cc}$ as it is in the triggered mode. Because the charge

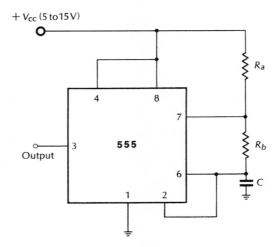

**Figure 5-29**   555 Timer Connected in an Astable Configuration

and discharge points are at specific fractions of $V_{cc}$, the timing is independent of slow variations in $V_{cc}$.

The following equations define the timing and frequency relationships. Figure 5-30 shows a free-running frequency nomogram for the astable configuration.

## TIMING AND FREQUENCY EQUATIONS

1. Charge time (output *high*)

$$t_1 = 0.693 \, (R_A + R_B) \, C$$

2. Discharge time (output *low*)

$$t_2 = 0.693 \, (R_B) \, C$$

3. Total period

$$T = t_1 + t_2 = 0.693 \, (R_A + 2R_B) \, C$$

4. Frequency of oscillation

$$f = \frac{1}{T} = \frac{1.44}{(R_A + 2R_B)} \, C$$

5. Duty cycle

$$D = \frac{R_B}{R_A + 2R_B}$$

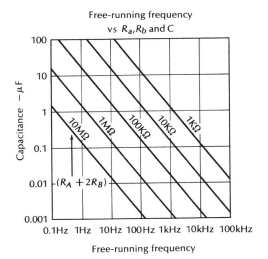

Free-running frequency
vs $R_a, R_b$ and C

**Figure 5-30** Free-Running Frequency Nomogram for the 555
Astable Circuit

## FREQUENCY DIVIDER

The timer can be used as a frequency divider by connecting the circuit as a monostable and adjusting the timing. The timer is triggered by the first incoming pulse and starts its timing cycle. Because it cannot be retriggered during the timing cycle, it is immune to further pulses until the cycle is complete. Thus it can be set to time-out every 2, 3, or 4 pulses, and so on. Synchronization with the input signal results from the fact that the timer begins each new cycle only when initiated by the input frequency signal.

## MISSING-PULSE OR BURST DETECTOR

The configuration shown in Figure 5-31 provides for the detection of a missing pulse in a continuous train or it can detect the start and end of a burst of pulses.

The timing cycle is continuously reset by the pulse train. A change in frequency, a missing pulse, or the termination of the train (end of a burst) allows the timer to time-out causing a change in output level. The time delay is set to be slightly longer than the normal time between pulses.

## PULSE WIDTH MODULATOR

Figure 5-32 shows how the monostable configuration can be used for pulse width modulation. The timer is triggered by a continuous pulse

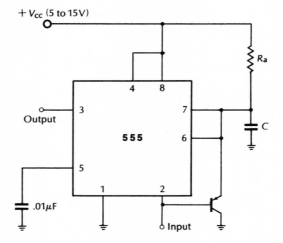

**Figure 5-31**   555 Timer Used as a Missing Pulse Detector

train and the threshold voltage of the comparator is modulated by the signal applied to the control-voltage terminal (pin 5). The pulse width is modulated by varying control voltage. Figure 5-32b shows typical waveforms.

### PULSE POSITION MODULATION

In the circuit in Figure 5-33 the timer is used as a pulse position modulator. The modulation signal is applied to the control-voltage terminal as in the pulse width modulator. In this case, however, the timer is configured for an astable mode instead of a monostable mode.

The 555 is completely compatible with TTL when used with a 5 volt power supply. The practical upper frequency limit is about 500 kHz.

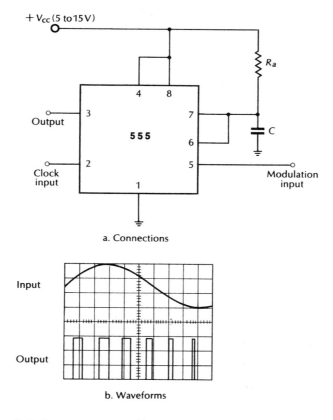

a. Connections

b. Waveforms

**Figure 5-32**   555 Timer as a Pulse Width Modulator

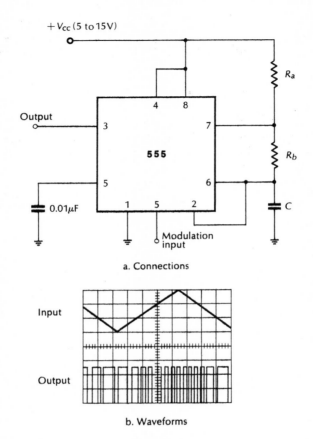

a. Connections

Input

Output

b. Waveforms

**Figure 5-33** Pulse Position Modulation with the 555 Timer

## RETRIGGERABLE (NEGATIVE RECOVERY) MONOSTABLE OPERATION

Normal monostable circuits require time to recover after triggering. Insufficient recovery time results in inaccuracy in the next timing period. Recovery time is frequently longer than the *on* time. Monostable circuits that can be retriggered at any time are called *retriggerable*, or negative recovery, monostable circuits. The 555 is normally nonretriggerable. However, the 555 can be made to function as a retriggerable monostable by adding an external transistor as shown in Figure 5-31.

## 5-14 The IC One-Shot

The 74121 in Figure 5-34 is a complete monostable multivibrator except for an external timing resistor and capacitor. It is a highly stable,

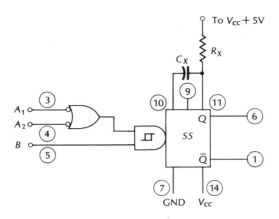

**Figure 5-34**   74121 Monostable (One-Shot)

temperature-compensated circuit. There are three gated inputs: $A_1$, $A_2$ and $B$. The input gate equation for triggering is $T = (\bar{A}_1 + \bar{A}_2)B$, where $B$ is a Schmitt trigger gate input.

This allows the $B$ input to respond to a slowly going positive input voltage, for example a low-frequency sine-wave input. The $B$ input will respond to voltage changes as slow as 1 volt per second. (The $A$ inputs require rates of change in voltage greater than $1V/\mu s$.) The $B$ input fires at between 1.5 and 2 volts. The hysteresis voltage is about 0.8V. The pulse out of the one-shot is initiated by the Schmitt trigger, but the pulse width is determined by the one-shot time constant. The $B$ input is enabled when either $A_1$ or $A_2$ is low. Possible stable output pulse widths range from 40 ns to 40 seconds. The minimum delay of $\approx$ 40 ns uses no external capacitance and only the internal timing resistor. To use the internal timing resistor, pin 11 must be connected to $V_{cc}$. Figure 5-35 shows graphs for selecting external timing components.

## 5-15   74121 One-Shot Applications

### SHORTENING AND DELAYING A PULSE

The circuit in Figure 5-36 can be used to shorten a pulse and delay it.

### NONRETRIGGERABLE OPERATION

Nonretriggerable operation is useful when it is desired to block multiple pulses. The first negative transition initiates the one-shot output pulse. The zero output of the one-shot is fed back to the inverted input OR

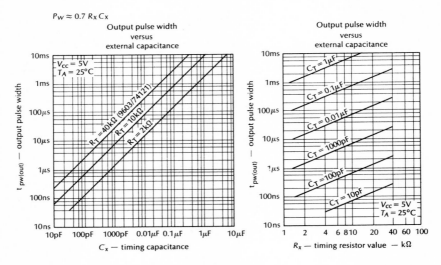

$P_W \approx 0.7\, R_X C_X$

© 1974 Signetics Inc. From *Digital Linear and MOS Data Book*, pp. 2-137.
Used by permission of Signetics Inc., P.O. Box 3004, Menlo Park, Ca. 94025.

**Figure 5-35** External Timing Component Graphs for the 74121

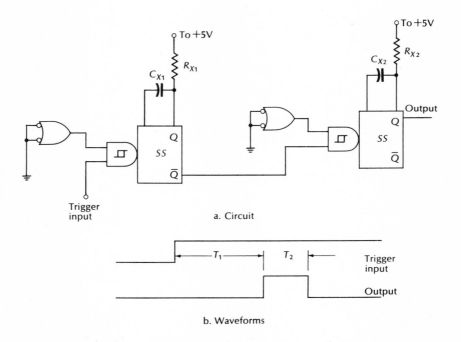

a. Circuit

b. Waveforms

**Figure 5-36** Delaying and Shortening a Pulse with 74121 One-Shots

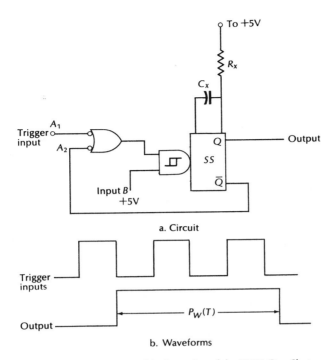

a. Circuit

b. Waveforms

**Figure 5-37**   Non-retriggerable Operation of the 74121 One-Shot

gate, which inhibits any further triggering until the one-shot's timing period has elapsed (see Figure 5-37).

### ASTABLE MULTIVIBRATOR USING ONE-SHOTS

The circuit in Figure 5-38 can be used when a stable predictable astable multivibrator is required. One single-shot fires after its delay; it in turn triggers the other. After its delay period it triggers the first and the cycle begins again.

## SUMMARY

Clock pulses are generated by oscillators that produce output pulses that are logic circuit compatible. Clock generators may be of the logic gate oscillator type, either $R$-$C$ or crystal controlled. Transistor astable multivibrators, 555 timers, and monostable devices operated in an astable mode are also used.

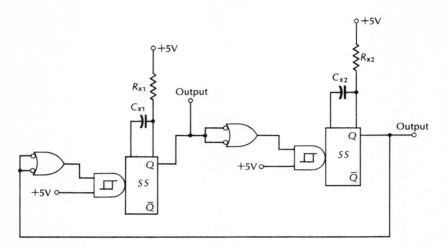

**Figure 5-38** Astable Multivibrator Using 74121 One-Shots

The Schmitt trigger is a regenerative device that can be used to shape slowly changing waveforms, such as sine waves, into logic circuit compatible pulses.

The 555 timer is a popular and versatile device that finds frequent service as a clock generator.

MOS (particularly C-MOS) devices are preferred over bipolar devices for crystal oscillator service. The high input impedance of MOS prevents loading the crystal. Crystal loading reduces the $Q$ of the crystal, making the frequency less stable.

Pulses can be shortened, lengthened, or delayed by using monostable multivibrators (one-shots). Differentiating circuits can be used to provide pulse edges for edge-triggering applications.

**Problems**

1. Define the term *interface*.
2. What must be done to interface TTL to DTL?
3. Draw the schematic for interfacing TTL to silicon-gate P-MOS and for interfacing silicon-gate P-MOS to TTL.
4. Draw the schematic for interfacing N-MOS to TTL and TTL to N-MOS.
5. What is required to interface high-threshold P-MOS to TTL?
6. What is required to interface C-MOS to low-power TTL? To standard TTL?
7. Suggest a device for interfacing TTL and ECL.
8. Define *subordinate clock*.
9. Define the *period* of a clock pulse.

10. Draw an ideal pulse, showing all of the appropriate pulse dimensions.
11. Explain the cause of undershoot, overshoot, and ringing.
12. Why are rise and fall times measured between 10 and 90 percent of the ideal pulse amplitude?
13. Draw the schematic diagram of a transistor astable multivibrator.
14. Draw and explain the operation of a logic gate ring oscillator.
15. Draw the schematic of a C-MOS crystal-controlled logic gate oscillator.
16. Describe the operating characteristics of the Schmitt trigger.
17. Define *hysteresis*.
18. What is meant by UTL and LTL when discussing Schmitt triggers?
19. Suggest some applications for Schmitt triggers.
20. Draw the following differentiator circuits:
    a. positive edge, NAND
    b. negative edge, NAND
    c. positive edge, NOR
    d. negative edge, NOR
21. What is a monostable (one-shot) multivibrator?
22. List some typical applications for the one-shot.
23. What is a 555 timer?
24. List four applications for the 555 timer.
25. What is the range of pulse widths available from the 74121 monostable?
26. What do the terms *retriggerable* and *nonretriggerable* mean with reference to a monostable?
27. List some typical applications of the IC monostable.

# CHAPTER 6

# NUMBER SYSTEMS AND CODES

*Learning Objectives.   Upon completion of this chapter you should:*
1. *Know how to construct a positional number system using any integral radix.*
2. *Be able to write binary numbers in decimal form and decimal numbers in binary form.*
3. *Translate numbers from one radix into another.*
4. *Be familiar with the octal and hexadecimal number systems.*
5. *Be able to write numbers in the BCD and XS-3 coded number systems.*
6. *Be able to define parity and explain its purpose.*
7. *Know the function, applications, and principle of operation of decoders and encoders.*

Digital machines operate in binary, binary-coded numbers, and binary-related number systems such as octal and hexadecimal.

Familiarity with structure and handling of these machine language number systems is essential to the understanding of computer arithmetic systems.

Translation among number systems and among numbers and codes is accomplished electronically by *encoders* and *decoders*. For human translations, there are several human-oriented methods.

This chapter is intended to provide the student with the necessary understanding of number systems and codes and to provide practice in writing computer language numbers and translating among number systems and number codes. Computer methods for translation will also be examined.

## 6-1   Number Systems

Although a positional number system can be constructed around any integral radix (base), we will examine only those most frequently encountered in digital systems—radix 10, radix 2, radix 8, and radix 16.

We will examine radix 10, which is so familiar to us that we rarely think about its structure. All other positional number systems have the

**Table 6-1** Structure of the Decimal System (Radix 10)

| | | Radix column 1 | 0 | Position |
|---|---|---|---|---|
| 3 | 2 | | | |
| Thousands | Hundreds | Tens | Units | Name of position |
| 1000 | 100 | 10 | 1 | Position value in decimal form |
| $10 \times 10 \times 10$ | $10 \times 10$ | 10 | $\frac{10}{10}$ | Use of radix to form value of each position |
| $10^3$ | $10^2$ | $10^1$ | $10^0$ | Position value in exponential form |

Allowable weight digits: 0, 1, 2, 3, 4, 5, 6, 7, 8, 9

Note: The highest allowable weight digit is 9, which is the radix number 10 minus 1.

Base—10 weight digits

| Position 1 (tens) | Position 0 (units) |
|---|---|
| 0 | 0 |
| 1 | 1 |
| 2 | 2 |
| 3 | 3 |
| 4 | 4 |
| 5 | 5 |
| 6 | 6 |
| 7 | 7 |
| 8 | 8 |
| 9 | 9 |

same basic structure as radix 10. Table 6-1 summarizes the decimal system structure.

**Example**

| $10^2$ | $10^1$ | $10^0$ | |
|---|---|---|---|
| 4 | 2 | 5 | $= 4 \times 10^2 + 2 \times 10^1 + 5 \times 10^0 = 400 + 20 + 5$ |

## THE RADIX POINT

In the decimal system, the term *decimal point* is adequate to describe the dot separating the whole numbers from the fractions. In like manner, the dot used in the binary system to separate the group of whole numbers from the group of fractional numbers is a binary point. When it is necessary to discuss this dot without reference to any particular base, we will use the generic term *radix point*.

## THE GENERAL POSITIONAL NUMBER SYSTEM

Positional values are as follows:

| *Whole numbers* | *Units column* |
|---|---|
| $R^n \cdot \cdot \cdot R^3 R^2 R^1$ | $R^0$ |
| *Fractions* | |
| $R^{-1} R^{-2} R^{-3} \cdot \cdot \cdot R^{-n}$ | $R^0$ |

The range of weight digits is zero through $R - 1$, where $R$ is the radix of the system.

## THE STRUCTURE OF THE BINARY SYSTEM

All digital computers on the market use the binary number system. The binary system has the advantage of being the simplest useful positional notation system. It has only two weight digits, 0 and 1. These two symbols may be further symbolized by on-off states in some device. Because of its importance, let us examine the binary system in light of the previous discussion of the positional notation scheme. Table 6-2 shows the structure of the binary system.

**Example**   The subscript identifies the radix and is always written in decimal. Write $43_{10}$ in binary (radix 2). The position values are as follows:

| $2^6$ | $2^5$ | $2^4$ | $2^3$ | $2^2$ | $2^1$ | $2^0$ | Exponent value |
|---|---|---|---|---|---|---|---|
| 64 | 32 | 16 | 8 | 4 | 2 | 1 | Decimal value |
| 0 | 1 | 0 | 1 | 0 | 1 | 1 | Binary number |

$2^6 = 64$. This is larger than 43. We enter a 0 in the $2^6$ column.
$2^5 = 32$. This is less than 43. We enter a 1 in the $2^5$ column.
$2^4 = 16$ and $16 + 32 = 48$. This is larger than 43. We enter a 0 in the $2^4$ column.

**Table 6-2**   Structure of the Binary System (Radix 2)

| 4 | 3 | 2 | 1 | 0 | Position |
|---|---|---|---|---|---|
| Sixteens | Eights | Fours | Twos | Units | Name of position |
| 16 | 8 | 4 | 2 | 1 | Position value in decimal form |
| $2 \times 2 \times 2 \times 2$ | $2 \times 2 \times 2$ | $2 \times 2$ | 2 | $\frac{2}{2}$ | Use of radix to form value of each position |
| $2^4$ | $2^3$ | $2^2$ | $2^1$ | $2^0$ | Position value in exponential form |

$2^3 = 8$ and $32 + 8 = 40$. This is less than 43. We enter a 1 in the $2^3$ column.

$2^2 = 4$. $40 + 4 = 44$. This is more than 43. We enter a 0 in the $2^2$ column.

$2^1 = 2$ and $40 + 2 = 42$. This is less than 43. We enter a 1 in the $2^1$ column.

$2^0 = 1$; $42 + 1 = 43$. We enter a 1 in the $2^0$ column, and the example is complete.

Thus $43_{10} = 101011$ (binary).

**Example** Write 101001 in decimal. Set up the following column headings for the binary system:

| $2^5$ | $2^4$ | $2^3$ | $2^2$ | $2^1$ | $2^0$ | Exponent value |
|-------|-------|-------|-------|-------|-------|----------------|
| 32    | 16    | 8     | 4     | 2     | 1     | Decimal value  |
| 1     | 0     | 1     | 0     | 0     | 1     | Binary number  |

Reading out, we have $32 + 8 + 1 = 41_{10}$.
Thus $101001_2 = 41_{10}$.

**Problems**

Write the following decimal numbers in binary (Hint: See Table 6-2 and expand as necessary):

1. $22_{10}$    4. $37_{10}$    7. $128_{10}$
2. $69_{10}$    5. $144_{10}$   8. $36_{10}$
3. $100_{10}$   6. $41_{10}$    9. $8_{10}$

Write the following binary numbers in decimal:

10. $1000_2$    13. $11001_2$    16. $001101_2$
11. $1001_2$    14. $111010_2$   17. $110101101_2$
12. $11111_2$   15. $101011_2$

**THE DECIMAL FRACTION**

Table 6-3 shows the structure of decimal fractions.

**Table 6-3**  Structure of the Decimal Fraction

| Position | 0 | $-1$ | $-2$ | $-3$ |
|----------|---|------|------|------|
| Decimal fraction | 1 | 0.1 | 0.01 | 0.001 |
| Exponential form | $2^0$ | $2^{-1}$ | $2^{-2}$ | $2^{-3}$ |

## THE STRUCTURE OF THE BINARY FRACTION

Table 6-4 shows the structure of the binary fraction. A comparison of the tables for the decimal system and the binary system shows that the structures are identical except for the radix. We often use radices 8 and 16 because each of these is a power of 2, enabling the machine to still operate in binary. More will be said later in this chapter about these related radices. Table 6-5 shows binary and decimal equivalents.

**Example**  Write $0.11_2$ as its decimal equivalent. Check by common fractions expressed in decimal digits:

| Binary | | Common | | Decimal |
|---|---|---|---|---|
| 0.1 | = | ½ | = | 0.5 |
| +0.01 | = | +¼ | = | +0.25 |
| 0.11 | = | ¾ | = | 0.75 |

**Example**  Write $0.10101_2$ in radix 10.

**Table 6-4**  Structure of Binary Fractions

| Position | 0 | −1 | −2 | −3 | −4 |
|---|---|---|---|---|---|
| Binary fraction | 1 | 0.1 | 0.01 | 0.001 | 0.0001 |
| Use of radix to form value of each position | $\frac{2}{2}$ or $\frac{1}{1}$ | $\frac{2}{4}$ or $\frac{1}{2}$ | $\frac{2}{8}$ or $\frac{1}{4}$ | $\frac{2}{16}$ or $\frac{1}{8}$ | $\frac{2}{32}$ or $\frac{1}{16}$ |
| Basic exponential form | $2^1/2^1$ | $2^1/2^2$ | $2^1/2^3$ | $2^1/2^4$ | $2^1/2^5$ |
| Dividing through for preferred exponential form | $2^0$ | $2^{-1}$ | $2^{-2}$ | $2^{-3}$ | $2^{-4}$ |

**Table 6-5**  Equivalent Fractions

| Binary | Decimal | Common |
|---|---|---|
| 0.1 | 0.5 | $\frac{1}{2}$ |
| 0.01 | 0.25 | $\frac{1}{4}$ |
| 0.001 | 0.125 | $\frac{1}{8}$ |
| 0.0001 | 0.0625 | $\frac{1}{16}$ |
| 0.00001 | 0.03125 | $\frac{1}{32}$ |

| Binary | | Common | | Decimal |
|---|---|---|---|---|
| 0.1 | $=$ | ½ | $=$ | 0.5 |
| 0.001 | $=$ | ⅛ | $=$ | 0.125 |
| $+0.00001$ | $=$ | $+^{1}/_{32}$ | $=$ | 0.03125 |
| 0.10101 | $=$ | $^{21}/_{32}$ | $=$ | 0.65625 |

**Problems**

Write the following binary fractions in decimal notation (Hint: Extend Table 6-4 as necessary):

18. $0.0001_2$      20. $0.101011_2$      22. $0.11011_2$
19. $0.1101_2$      21. $0.01110_2$      23. $0.00001_2$

## THE OCTAL SYSTEM: RADIX 8

Another important number system in digital systems is the octal or radix 8 system. The octal system owes its importance to the fact that it is *related* to radix 2 (binary) in the sense that the radix number 8 can be formed by raising the radix number 2 to the third power ($2^3 = 8$). Table 6-6 shows the structure of the octal system.

**Problems**

Write the following octal numbers in radix 10:

24. $327_8$      26. $6437_8$      28. $001732_8$
25. $71035_8$      27. $48670_8$      29. $7734_8$

**Table 6-6**   The Structure of the Octal System (Radix 8)

| 4 | 3 | 2 | 1 | 0 | Position |
|---|---|---|---|---|---|
| $8^4$ | $8^3$ | $8^2$ | $8^1$ | $8^0$ | Exponential value |
| 4096 | 512 | 64 | 8 | 1 | Decimal value |

Example:   2     1     3     6     7     Number in radix 8

$$8192 + 512 + 192 + 48 + 7 = 8951_{10}$$

Weight digits: 0, 1, 2, 3, 4, 5, 6, 7

Example:

$$21367_8 = 2 \times 8^4 + 1 \times 8^3 + 3 \times 8^2 + 6 \times 8^1 + 7 \times 8^0$$
$$= 2 \times 4096 + 1 \times 512 + 3 \times 64 + 6 \times 8 + 7 \times 1$$
$$= 8192 + 512 + 192 + 48 + 7 = 8951_{10}$$

### THE HEXADECIMAL SYSTEM (RADIX 16)

The hexadecimal system is also related to binary in the sense that the radix number 16 can be formed by raising the binary radix number (2) to the fourth power ($2^4 = 16$).

In the hexadecimal system 16 weight digits are required. We can take digit symbols 0-9 from the decimal system, but there are no *single-position* symbols for the equivalents of decimals 10, 11, 12, 13, 14, and 15. Since practical considerations dictate the use of symbols that are common in printer readouts and the like, the first six letters of the English alphabet have been almost universally adopted for the purpose. Table 6-7 shows the structure of the hexadecimal system and the extra weight digits.

### Problems

Write the following hexadecimal numbers in decimal:

30. $A69_{16}$      32. $429C_{16}$      34. $AF32_{16}$
31. $BFA2_{16}$      33. $2BC_{16}$      35. $4679_{16}$

## 6-2   Binary-Related Radices

In this section we will examine the translations among octal, hexadecimal, and binary. The procedure for translating from one radix into another related one is quite simple.

**Table 6-7**   Additional Symbols for Radix 16

| Decimal equivalent | Symbol |
|:---:|:---:|
| 10 | A |
| 11 | B |
| 12 | C |
| 13 | D |
| 14 | E |
| 15 | F |

Structure of the Hexadecimal (Radix-16) System

| 3 | 2 | 1 | 0 | Position |
|:---:|:---:|:---:|:---:|:---|
| $16^3$ | $16^2$ | $16^1$ | $16^0$ | Exponential form |
| 4096 | 256 | 16 | 1 | Decimal value |

| Example: | 0 | B | A | 3 | Number in radix 16 |
|:---|:---:|:---:|:---:|:---:|:---|
| | 0 | $+ 2816 +$ | $160 +$ | $3 = 2979_{10}$ | |

## TRANSLATION FROM BINARY INTO OCTAL

The procedure is to separate the binary number into groups of three digits and then simply translate each group into its octal equivalent, group by group. The resulting number is the octal equivalent of the original binary number.

The largest decimal digit which can be formed by one binary group (three binary digits) is 111, or decimal 7. The digits 0 through 7 in the units column have exactly the same values in both decimal and octal notation. Thus, if we treat each group of bits as a separate units column, we can translate each group into its decimal equivalent and still have an octal number.

Table 6-8 illustrates how direct translation between binary numbers and numbers written in related radices may be accomplished. The binary number 10110 (decimal 22) is used as an example. The first three rows illustrate a general rule for correct grouping. The last two provide a specific example. The grouping procedure starts at the radix point and proceeds to the left for whole numbers and to the right for fractions. An incomplete group should be completed by adding the appropriate number of zeros. Complete groups are a must in translating from a higher radix number to a lower radix number. It is good practice always to work with complete groups.

**Example**  Translate $10110_2$ into radix 8 (octal). Grouping the binary number and translating into the radix 10 equivalent of each group, we get:

$$\begin{array}{ccl} 010 & 110 & \text{Radix } 2 \\ 2 & 6 & \text{Radix } 8 \end{array}$$

Thus $10110_2 = 26_8$. Note: $26_8 = 22_{10}$.

**Table 6-8**  Binary-Related Radix Translation

|  | Radix 2 | Radix 8 | Radix 16 |
|---|---|---|---|
| Power of 2 | $2^1$ | $2^3$ | $2^4$ |
| Number of digits per group | 1 | 3 | 4 |
| Example: $22_{10} =$ | $0101010_2$ | $26_8$ | $16_{16}$ |
| Binary equivalent (grouped) | 010110 | 2   6<br>010  110 | 1   6<br>0001  0110 |

## TRANSLATING FROM OCTAL INTO BINARY

Translation from octal into binary is accomplished by writing each octal digit as a three-bit binary number and combining the groups.

**Example**   Translate $010011_2$ into octal. Since $2^3 = 8$, the binary number is divided into groups of three. The octal equivalent of each group is

| 010 | 011 | Radix 2 |
|-----|-----|---------|
| 2   | 3   | Radix 8 |

Thus $10011_2 = 23_8$.

**Example**   Translate $26_8$ into radix 2. The number to be translated is separated into the three-bit binary equivalent of each octal digit.

| 2   | 6   | Radix 8 |
|-----|-----|---------|
| 010 | 110 | Radix 2 |

Combining the groups, we have 010110. Thus $26_8 = 010110_2$ or $22_{10}$.

## TRANSLATING FROM HEXADECIMAL INTO BINARY AND VICE VERSA

The following examples will illustrate the procedure:

**Example**   Translate $24C_{16}$ into its equivalent in radix 2. $2^4 = 16$; therefore there will be four bits (binary digits) per group. Writing each hexadecimal digit as a four-bit binary number, we get:

| 2    | 4    | C    | Radix 16 |
|------|------|------|----------|
| 0010 | 0100 | 1100 | Radix 2  |

Combining groups yields $001\ 001\ 001\ 100_2$. Thus $24C_{16} = 001\ 001\ 001\ 100_2$.

**Example**   Translate $00\ 010\ 011_2$ into hexadecimal. Since $2^4 = 16$, we divide the binary number into groups of four. Translating each group into hexadecimal, we get:

| 0001 | 0011 | Radix 2  |
|------|------|----------|
| 1    | 3    | Radix 16 |

Thus $00010011_2 = 13_{16}$.

**Example**   Translate $110\ 001_2$ into hexadecimal.

| 0011 | 0001 | Radix 2  |
|------|------|----------|
| 3    | 1    | Radix 16 |

Thus $110\ 001_2 = 31_{16}$.

**Problems**

Translate the following numbers into binary.

36. $134_8$        39. $4667_8$        42. $9767610_{16}$
37. $136_8$        40. $1233210_8$     43. $3214_8$
38. $14C_{16}$      41. $9B_{16}$

Translate from binary into the indicated radix.

44. 001011101 into radix 8
45. 1011101 into radix 4
46. 111110110101 into radix 16
47. 101011010 into octal
48. 11101011111 into octal
49. 011010000 into hexadecimal

### SHORTCUT TRANSLATION METHODS

#### Translation from Radices 16, 8, 2 into Radix 10

The procedure presented here is valid for translating from *any* radix into radix 10, but we will use only the most common radices (16, 8, 2) as examples. To translate a whole number in any radix into radix 10, we proceed as follows:

1. Multiply the most significant digit (MSD) for the given number by the given radix, and add the next digit.
2. Multiply this result by the given radix, and add the next digit.
3. Repeat the process until every digit in the given number has been used.

The final result will be the translated number in radix 10. The simplified form of this process is as follows:

1. MSD of number $\times$ radix + next digit = result
2. Previous result $\times$ radix + next digit = result
3. Repeat until all digits are used.

**Example**    Translate $101010_2$ into radix 10.

$$(0 \times 2) + 1 \ldots \ldots \ldots = 1$$
$$(1 \times 2) + .0 \ldots \ldots \ldots = 2$$
$$(2 \times 2) + ..1 \ldots \ldots \ldots = 5$$
$$(5 \times 2) + ...0 \ldots \ldots = 10$$
$$(10 \times 2) + ....1 \ldots \ldots = 21$$
$$(21 \times 2) + .....0 \ldots \ldots = 42_{10}$$

(previous result) $\times$ (radix) + (next digit) = result

The same method used in the above example can be used for the following example. The tabular form used in the two previous examples was chosen because it best illustrates the method. A more practical form can be mastered with a little practice. The method is the same; only the form is changed.

**Example** Translate $101010_2$ into radix 10. Note that for easy comparison the number used here is the same as that in the above example. From the simplified rule (for whole numbers only)

(MSD of number or previous result) × (radix) + (next digit) . . .

$$= \text{result in radix 10}$$

| 0 | 1 | 0 | 1 | 0 | 1 | 0 | Number in radix 2 |
|---|---|---|----|----|----|----|-------------------|
|   | 1 | 2 | 5 | 10 | 21 | 42 | Result in radix 10 |

If no confusion results, it is permissible to omit the zero at the beginning of the number in $R_2$.

**Example**

Translate $247_8$ into radix 10.

| 2 | 4 | $7_8$ |
|---|----|--------|
| 2 | 20 | $167_{10}$ |

Answer: $247_8 = 167_{10}$

Translate $5BF_{16}$ into radix 10.

| 5 | B | F |
|---|----|------|
| 5 | 91 | 1471 |

Answer: $5BF_{16} = 1471_{10}$

When the translation is from binary to decimal, it is often more convenient to translate by grouping (related radices), translating $R_2$ into $R_8$ or $R_{16}$, and then, using the method above, translate from $R_8$ or $R_{16}$ into decimal.

**Problems**

Translate the following into radix 10.

50. $237_8$        52. $370_8$        54. $429_{16}$
51. $665_8$        53. $AB3_{16}$        55. $FF3_{16}$

**TRANSLATION FROM RADIX 10 INTO RADICES 2, 8, 16**

The following procedure is valid for translating numbers written in radix 10 into their numerical equivalents in *any* radix. Again, the examples will deal only with the most commonly encountered radices (2, 8, and 16).

**Process**

(*Note:* The following procedure applies to whole numbers only.)

1. Divide the given radix 10 number by the number of the radix into which you wish to translate.
2. If there is no remainder, record a 0 in the remainder row (see the examples). If there is a remainder, record that remainder in the remainder row.
3. Divide the quotient from the preceding step by the radix number and record any remainder.
4. Continue the process until the quotient becomes 0.

**Example**  Translate $96_{10}$ into binary. (*Note:* The operations in the example proceed from right to left. If the process is carried out from left to right, the result will read out in reverse order.)

$$\frac{0}{2\overline{)1}}$$

| | | | | | | | |
|---|---|---|---|---|---|---|---|
| | $\dfrac{1}{2\overline{)3}}$ | $3$ | | | | | |
| $\dfrac{0}{1}$ | $\dfrac{2}{1}$ | $2\overline{)6}$ | $6$ | | | | |
| $\cdot$ | $1$ | $\dfrac{6}{0}$ | $2\overline{)12}$ | $12$ | | | |
| $\cdot$ | $\cdot$ | $0$ | $\dfrac{12}{0}$ | $2\overline{)24}$ | $24$ | | |
| $\cdot$ | $\cdot$ | $\cdot$ | $0$ | $\dfrac{24}{0}$ | $2\overline{)48}$ | $48$ | |
| $\cdot$ | $\cdot$ | $\cdot$ | $\cdot$ | $0$ | $\dfrac{48}{0}$ | $2\overline{)96}$ | start |
| $\cdot$ | $\cdot$ | $\cdot$ | $\cdot$ | $\cdot$ | $0$ | $\dfrac{96}{0}$ | |

| 1 | 1 | 0 | 0 | 0 | 0 | 0 | remainder row |
|---|---|---|---|---|---|---|---|
| MSD | | | | | | LSD | |

Answer: $96_{10} = 1100000_2$

Note: MSD = most significant digit
      LSD = least significant digit

**Example**   Translate $22_{10}$ into octal.

$$
\begin{array}{c}
0 \\
8\overline{)2}
\end{array}
$$

$$
\begin{array}{ccl}
 & 2 & \\
 & 8\overline{)22} & \text{start} \\
 & \underline{16} & \\
 & 6 & \\
\cdot & \cdot & \\
\cdot & \cdot & \\
\cdot & \cdot & \\
2 & 6 & \text{remainder row}
\end{array}
$$

MSD   LSD

Answer: $22_{10} = 26_8$

**Example**   Translate $150_{10}$ into hexadecimal.

$$
\begin{array}{ccl}
0 & 9 & \\
16\overline{)9} & 16\overline{)150} & \text{start} \\
\cdot & \underline{144} & \\
\cdot & 6 & \\
\cdot & \cdot & \\
\cdot & \cdot & \\
9 & 6 & \text{remainder row}
\end{array}
$$

Answer: $150_{10} = 96_{16}$

**Problems**

Translate the following radix 10 numbers into binary.

| | | |
|---|---|---|
| 56. 75 | 58. 76 | 60. 33 |
| 57. 197 | 59. 225 | 61. 44 |

Translate the following radix 10 numbers into octal.

| | | |
|---|---|---|
| 62. 75 | 64. 76 | 66. 27 |
| 63. 197 | 65. 225 | 67. 100 |

Translate the following radix 10 numbers into hexadecimal.

| | | |
|---|---|---|
| 68. 75 | 70. 76 | 72. 4390 |
| 69. 197 | 71. 225 | 73. 1975 |

## 6-3   Coded Number Systems

There are a number of numeric and several alphanumeric codes. Alphabet symbols are encoded into bits, as are special symbols and instructions such as carriage return (for an input-output typewriter, for example). First let us examine numeric codes and their properties.

### THE BINARY-CODED DECIMAL SYSTEM

In a BCD number system the original positional decimal structure is retained, but each decimal digit is represented by a four-bit number:

| 9 | 5 | 4 | Decimal number |
|------|------|------|----------------|
| 1001 | 0101 | 0100 | BCD equivalent |

Four binary digits is the minimum number by which all decimal digits 0 to 9 can be represented. Table 6-9 shows the structure of the BCD system.

**Example**   Write $234_{10}$ in BCD.

| 2 | 3 | 4 | Decimal |
|------|------|------|---------|
| 0010 | 0011 | 0100 | BCD |

Further examples are shown in Table 6-10.

### Problems

Write the following decimal numbers in BCD:
74. 1234      75. 8765      76. 98910        77. 5809

The BCD code we have just examined is the *natural* BCD (NBCD) code and is only one of several BCD codes in use. The reason for

**Table 6-9**   Structure of the BCD System

| 3 | 2 | 1 | 0 | Position |
|---|---|---|---|----------|
| Thousands | Hundreds | Tens | Units | Position value |
| $2^3 2^2 2^1 2^0$ | $2^3 2^2 2^1 2^0$ | $2^3 2^2 2^1 2^0$ | $2^3 2^2 2^1 2^0$ | BCD value in exponential form |

**Table 6-10**   Decimal Numbers and Their BCD Equivalents

| Decimal numbers | BCD equivalent | | |
|-----------------|------|------|------|
| 001 | 0000 | 0000 | 0001 |
| 123 | 0001 | 0010 | 0011 |
| 546 | 0101 | 0100 | 0110 |
| 879 | 1000 | 0111 | 1001 |

having other codes lies in certain properties, such as ease in checking errors or in complementing the code for subtraction, a process we will examine in the chapter on computer arithmetic circuits. Each of the codes has advantages and disadvantages. The selection of a code involves choosing the one with the properties most desired for a particular application.

All basic BCD codes use only 10 of the 16 possible combinations of 4 bits since they must represent only digits 0–9. The unused combinations can be treated as error combinations because they are not a part of the code.

### ERROR-DETECTOR CIRCUIT FOR NBCD

Here we will develop a circuit to detect those combinations that are not part of the NBCD code. This same circuit is used in BCD adders to detect when a correction must be made to the sum. We will look at that application in the chapter on arithmetic circuits.

The error-detector circuit must detect those combinations not used in the NBCD code. These are the combinations of four bits in binary that represent the binary equivalents of decimal digits 10, 11, 12, 13, 14, and 15. Table 6-11 is the truth table for the NBCD error detector.

Plotting the problem on the truth table (see Table 6-11) and writing the type-one minterm equation, we get:

$$f = (A \cdot \overline{B} \cdot C \cdot \overline{D}) + (A \cdot \overline{B} \cdot C \cdot D) + (A \cdot B \cdot \overline{C} \cdot \overline{D})$$
$$+ (A \cdot B \cdot \overline{C} \cdot D) + (A \cdot B \cdot C \cdot \overline{D}) + (A \cdot B \cdot C \cdot D)$$

Plotting the equation on the Karnaugh map (Table 6-12) and reading out the simplified equation from loop $a$, we get $A \cdot C$ and from loop $b$ we get $A \cdot B$. Combining the terms we get $f = (A \cdot B) + (A \cdot C)$ as the final simplified equation. The logic diagram is shown in Figure 6-1.

### THE EXCESS-3 CODE (XS-3)

The excess-3 code is another form of BCD code. It differs from natural BCD in that the 10 combinations required to encode the decimal digits

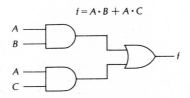

**Figure 6-1** NBCD Error Detector Logic Diagram (Simplified Version)

**Table 6-11** Truth Table for the NBCD Error Detector

| | $2^3$ | $2^2$ | $2^1$ | $2^0$ | |
| | A | B | C | D | f |
|---|---|---|---|---|---|
| 0 | 0 | 0 | 0 | 0 | 0 |
| 1 | 0 | 0 | 0 | 1 | 0 |
| 2 | 0 | 0 | 1 | 0 | 0 |
| 3 | 0 | 0 | 1 | 1 | 0 |
| 4 | 0 | 1 | 0 | 0 | 0 |
| 5 | 0 | 1 | 0 | 1 | 0 |
| 6 | 0 | 1 | 1 | 0 | 0 |
| 7 | 0 | 1 | 1 | 1 | 0 |
| 8 | 1 | 0 | 0 | 0 | 0 |
| 9 | 1 | 0 | 0 | 1 | 0 |
| 10 | 1 | 0 | 1 | 0 | 1 |
| 11 | 1 | 0 | 1 | 1 | 1 |
| 12 | 1 | 1 | 0 | 0 | 1 |
| 13 | 1 | 1 | 0 | 1 | 1 |
| 14 | 1 | 1 | 1 | 0 | 1 |
| 15 | 1 | 1 | 1 | 1 | 1 |

**Table 6-12** Karnaugh Map for the NBCD Error Detector

| | $\bar{A}\cdot\bar{B}$ | $\bar{A}\cdot B$ | $A\cdot B$ | $A\cdot\bar{B}$ |
|---|---|---|---|---|
| $\bar{C}\cdot\bar{D}$ | | | 1 | |
| $\bar{C}\cdot D$ | | | 1 | |
| $C\cdot D$ | | | 1 | 1 |
| $C\cdot\bar{D}$ | | | 1 | 1 |

(0–9) are taken from the middle of the table starting with the binary equivalent of decimal 3. Table 6-13 shows the decimal digits 0–9 and their excess-3 equivalents.

**Examples**

1. $425_{10} = 0111 \quad\quad 0101 \quad\quad 1000_{XS-3}$
2. $379_{10} = 0110 \quad\quad 1010 \quad\quad 1100_{XS-3}$
3. $146_{10} = 0100 \quad\quad 0111 \quad\quad 1001_{XS-3}$
4. $80_{10} = 1011 \quad\quad 0011_{XS-3}$

**Problems**

78. Write the following decimal numbers in XS-3 code.
    a. 6421     b. 5790     c. 386     d. 9700
79. Design an XS-3 error detector.
    a. Make a truth table.
    b. Simplify if possible, using a Karnaugh map.
    c. Draw a logic diagram using NAND logic.

**Table 6-13** Decimal Equivalents in the XS-3 Code

| Decimal number | Excess−3 equivalent |
|----------------|---------------------|
| 0 | 0011 |
| 1 | 0100 |
| 2 | 0101 |
| 3 | 0110 |
| 4 | 0111 |
| 5 | 1000 |
| 6 | 1001 |
| 7 | 1010 |
| 8 | 1011 |
| 9 | 1100 |

### THE BINARY-CODED OCTAL SYSTEM

Because radix 2 and radix 8 are related, we can form a coded structure similar to BCD but composed of binary-coded octal (BCO) groups.

Table 6-14 shows the BCO structure and equivalent weight digits.

**Examples**

$$147_{10} = 001 \quad 100 \quad 111_{BCO}$$
$$760_{10} = 111 \quad 110 \quad 000_{BCO}$$
$$235_{10} = 010 \quad 011 \quad 101_{BCO}$$

**Problem**

80. Write the following BCO numbers in decimal.
   a. $001 \quad 010 \quad 111 \quad 110_{BCO}$
   b. $110 \quad 101 \quad 100 \quad 000_{BCO}$

### SUMMARY OF NATURAL CODES AND VARIATIONS

Two of the most important natural codes are binary-coded octal and binary-coded decimal (and the variations on these two). These are called *natural* codes because the column headings are the natural radix 2 headings. The excess-3 code (sometimes abbreviated XS-3) is a BCD scheme that has been modified to make it possible to generate the complement for subtraction by simple inversion or 0's and 1's.

The hexadecimal (radix 16) system is also popular in modern computers. Hexadecimal numbers are more compatible with human communications than straight binary numbers and, since this system is a *relative* of radix 2, it is also compatible with the computer's basic

**Table 6-14**    The BCO Structure and Equivalent Weight Digits

| 3 | 2 | 1 | 0 | Position |
|---|---|---|---|---|
| 512 | 64 | 8 | 1 | Position value |
| $8^3$ $2^2 2^1 2^0$ | $8^2$ $2^2 2^1 2^0$ | $8^1$ $2^2 2^1 2^0$ | $8^0$ $2^2 2^1 2^0$ | BCO value in exponential form |
| 000 | 001 | 011 | 101 | Number in BCO |
| 0 | 1 | 3 | 5 | Octal equivalent |

Example (to the left of the "Number in BCO" row)

a. Structure of the BCO system

| Octal digit | BCO Equivalents |
|---|---|
| 0 | 000 |
| 1 | 001 |
| 2 | 010 |
| 3 | 011 |
| 4 | 100 |
| 5 | 101 |
| 6 | 110 |
| 7 | 111 |

b. Octal weight digits and their BCO equivalents

binary language. The computer operates in straight binary, but the hexadecimal grouping is more convenient for humans to deal with.

Because arithmetic is performed in straight binary without the need for correction circuits, hexadecimal numbers can be complemented for subtraction by simply changing all 0's to 1's and all 1's to 0's. The translation from decimal into hexadecimal is fairly easy to mechanize.

Many computers are organized into dual hexadecimal groups. Each hexadecimal group consists of four binary bits and each pair of groups (eight bits) is called a *byte*. (A group of four bits is called a nibble.) Such an organization allows considerable flexibility in that the programmer has the option of treating a byte as either a single eight-bit character or as two BCD digits. Within the range of eight bits there is adequate room to encode alphabetic information, special symbols, a sign bit, and extra bits for error-detecting purposes.

## WEIGHTED CODES

Weighted codes are not generally used as a computer internal language. Internal computation is performed in straight binary, octal, or hexadecimal. Some pocket calculators operate in BCD as an internal language, but they are an exception to the general rule. Weighted codes are used primarily in conjunction with input-output devices and numerical displays. These codes are similar to the natural codes in that they follow a sort of positional notation structure, but they differ in that the position values are not ascending powers of some base. In the weighted codes the position values are quite arbitrary; they may be anything the code designer desires.

An example of a weighted code is the four-bit binary code called the 2, 4, 2, 1 code. Table 6-15 illustrates the similarities and differences between it and a natural four-bit BCD system and shows the binary code group 1001 translated from each code into its corresponding decimal value.

Another popular weighted code is the 6, 4, 2, 1 code. Any four-bit BCD system, weighted or natural, has some built-in self-checking properties because there are always six unused combinations. The occurrence of one of these forbidden combinations indicates an error. Unfortunately, these forbidden combinations do not provide an optimum error-detecting situation. To provide more nearly optimum error-detecting facility, five-bit codes of two distinct types have been adopted. In one case a fifth bit is added to an existing four-bit code so that each five-bit group always contains either an odd number (odd parity) or an even number (even parity) of 1's. The added bit is called a *parity bit*. Both odd and even parity codes are used. In the second type of self-checking code a constant number of 1's is built into the structure of the code.

**Table 6-15**  Comparison of Natural BCD and Weighted 2,4,2,1 Codes

Natural BCD

| $2^3$ $2^2$ $2^1$ $2^0$ | Exponential values |
|---|---|
| 8  4  2  1 | Decimal position value |
| 1  0  0  1 | Binary number (code group) |

$(1 \times 8) + (0 \times 4) + (0 \times 2) + (1 \times 1) = 9_{10}$

Weighted 2, 4, 2, 1

| None | Exponential values |
|---|---|
| 2  4  2  1 | Decimal position value |
| 1  0  0  1 | Binary number (code group) |

$(1 \times 2) + (0 \times 4) + (0 \times 2) + (1 \times 1) = 3_{10}$

Table 6-16 shows an odd-parity natural BCD code, an even-parity natural BCD code, and a structured self-checking code. This structured code is a weighted code with position values 7, 4, 2, 1, 0. It is commonly called the *two-out-of-five code* because all valid combinations contain two 1's and three 0's.

## THE BI-QUINARY SYSTEM

The bi-quinary system illustrates an important class of number codes in which two digits are required to indicate the value in each position. In the quinary portion of the two-digit group, the weight digits 0, 1, 2, 3, 4 may represent either the corresponding decimal digits or decimal digits 5 to 9, depending on the digit in the *bi* portion. A 0 in the bi portion means that the quinary digit represents decimals 0 to 4, and a 1 in the bi portion means that the quinary digit represents decimals 5 to 9. Thus decimal 75 written in bi-quinary is

| Bi | Quinary | Bi | Quinary | |
|----|---------|----|---------|---|
| 1  | 2       | 0  | 5       | Bi-quinary number |
|    | 7       |    | 5       | Decimal equivalent |

Table 6-17 shows the bi-quinary structure.

A weighted seven-bit code can be derived from the bi-quinary system. This code, with position values 5, 0 and 4, 3, 2, 1, 0, is illustrated in Table 6-18.

The bi-quinary code is another example of a code with an intrinsic error-detection capability. It is a two-out-of-seven code in which the representation of each decimal digit contains a single 1 in the bi group and a single 1 in the quinary group. There is a similarly constructed code called the qui-binary code, which has position values 8, 6, 4, 2, 0 and 1, 0.

**Table 6-16**  Examples of Error-Detecting Codes

| Decimal number | Odd-parity natural BCD | Even-parity natural BCD | Structured weighted code |
|----------------|------------------------|-------------------------|--------------------------|
|                | P8421                  | P8421                   | 74210                    |
| 0              | 10000                  | 00000                   | 11000                    |
| 1              | 00001                  | 10001                   | 00011                    |
| 2              | 00010                  | 10010                   | 00101                    |
| 3              | 10011                  | 00011                   | 00110                    |
| 4              | 00100                  | 10100                   | 01001                    |
| 5              | 10101                  | 00101                   | 01010                    |
| 6              | 10110                  | 00110                   | 01100                    |
| 7              | 00111                  | 10111                   | 10001                    |
| 8              | 01000                  | 11000                   | 10010                    |
| 9              | 11001                  | 01001                   | 10100                    |

**Table 6-17** Decimal and Bi-Quinary Equivalents

| Decimal | Bi | Quinary |
|---------|-----|---------|
| 0 | 0 | 0 |
| 1 | 0 | 1 |
| 2 | 0 | 2 |
| 3 | 0 | 3 |
| 4 | 0 | 4 |
| 5 | 1 | 0 |
| 6 | 1 | 1 |
| 7 | 1 | 2 |
| 8 | 1 | 3 |
| 9 | 1 | 4 |

**Table 6-18** Bi-Quinary Code

| Decimal number | Bi | Quinary |
|----------------|-----|---------|
|  | 50 | 43210 |
| 0 | 01 | 00001 |
| 1 | 01 | 00010 |
| 2 | 01 | 00100 |
| 3 | 01 | 01000 |
| 4 | 01 | 10000 |
| 5 | 10 | 00001 |
| 6 | 10 | 00010 |
| 7 | 10 | 00100 |
| 8 | 10 | 01000 |
| 9 | 10 | 10000 |

Table 6-19 shows three additional codes that have distinctive *patterns* that make error checking relatively easy and certain. Table 6-20 shows the Gray code which is used for digital encoding or rotating shaft positions and other mechanical positioning applications. Because of its unweighted structure, it is difficult to manipulate and must usually be translated into some other code for processing.

## 6-4 Parity Checkers and Generators

Exclusive-OR gates can be used to check for parity. The circuit is a modulo 2 adder, which is the same as a binary adder except that no carries are generated. An even number of *ones* added together always yields a sum function of zero while an odd number of *ones* added together produces a sum function of 1. Because the exclusive-OR truth table is the same as the truth table for binary addition, it makes an ideal

**Table 6-19** Some Additional Codes

| Decimal | 51111 | Shift-counter | Ring-counter 9876543210 |
|---------|-------|---------------|-------------------------|
| 0 | 00000 | 00000 | 0000000001 |
| 1 | 00001 | 00001 | 0000000010 |
| 2 | 00011 | 00011 | 0000000100 |
| 3 | 00111 | 00111 | 0000001000 |
| 4 | 01111 | 01111 | 0000010000 |
| 5 | 10000 | 11111 | 0000100000 |
| 6 | 11000 | 11110 | 0001000000 |
| 7 | 11100 | 11100 | 0010000000 |
| 8 | 11110 | 11000 | 0100000000 |
| 9 | 11111 | 10000 | 1000000000 |

**Table 6-20** Gray Code

| Decimal | Gray code |
|---------|-----------|
| 0 | 0000 |
| 1 | 0001 |
| 2 | 0011 |
| 3 | 0010 |
| 4 | 0110 |
| 5 | 0111 |
| 6 | 0101 |
| 7 | 0100 |
| 8 | 1100 |
| 9 | 1101 |
| 10 | 1111 |
| 11 | 1110 |
| 12 | 1010 |
| 13 | 1011 |
| 14 | 1001 |
| 15 | 1000 |

adder element for the parity detector. The parity detector can also be used as a parity generator by arranging it so that the existing parity is determined and the appropriate output from the detector is used to add a parity bit as needed.

Figure 6-2 shows a four-bit parity detector. Figure 6-3 shows a nine-bit (eight bits plus a parity bit) parity detector generator. The appropriate output is applied to the ninth bit position to achieve parity.

## 6-5 Encoders and Decoders

The encoding matrix is a group of gate circuits arranged to provide a coded output from a discrete input. An example is the encoding of a decimal key on a keyboard into a binary code (such as BCD) that a

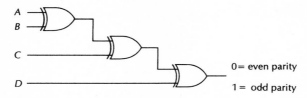

**Figure 6-2**    Four-Bit Parity Detector

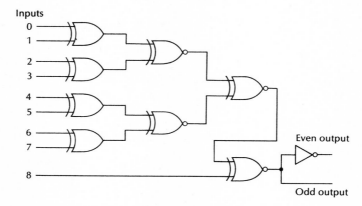

**Figure 6-3**    Nine-Bit Parity Detector-Generator

calculator can process. Figure 6-4 shows the encoding circuit to encode decimal into BCD.

### DECODERS

Most common decoding functions can be implemented with standard off-the-shelf IC's. The decoder samples a combination of bits and puts out a discrete single pulse for each desired combination. Decoders are used either for translating from a binary code into decimal or for providing a discrete output pulse to interrogate a memory location or route data or to perform some other discrete activity. Figure 6-5 shows a two-line to four-line decoder and truth table.

The truth table indicates that the two inputs provide four possible combinations for outputs. The circuit can have as many AND gates as there are possible combinations. Thus, three input lines could provide eight outputs (from eight AND gates), four lines in could produce sixteen output lines, and so on. In general, $N$ inputs can provide $2^N$ outputs. Figure 6-6 shows a four-line to sixteen-line decoder.

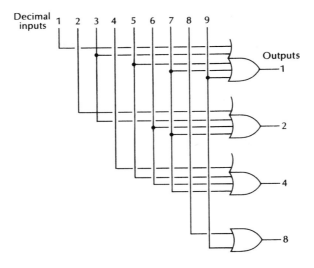

**Figure 6-4**   Decimal-to-Binary Encoder Logic Diagram

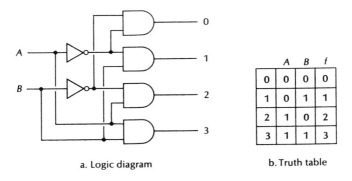

| a. Logic diagram | | b. Truth table |

| A | B | f |
|---|---|---|
| 0 | 0 | 0 | 0 |
| 1 | 0 | 1 | 1 |
| 2 | 1 | 0 | 2 |
| 3 | 1 | 1 | 3 |

**Figure 6-5**   Two-Line to Four-Line Decoder

**Problem**

81. Write the equation for each of the AND gates (0, 1, 2, 3) in Figure 6-5.

**SIMPLIFICATION**

The equations for the BCD-to-decimal decoder (the first ten combinations) are as follows:

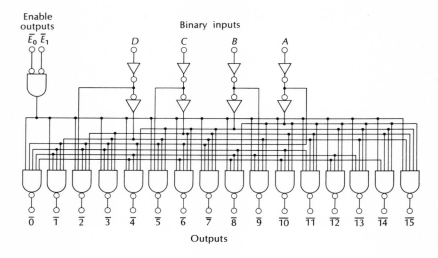

**Figure 6-6** Logic Diagram for a Four-Line to Sixteen-Line Decoder

| | |
|---|---|
| 0 | $\bar{A} \cdot \bar{B} \cdot \bar{C} \cdot \bar{D}$ |
| 1 | $A \cdot \bar{B} \cdot \bar{C} \cdot \bar{D}$ |
| 2 | $\bar{A} \cdot B \cdot \bar{C} \cdot D$ |
| 3 | $A \cdot B \cdot \bar{C} \cdot D$ |
| 4 | $\bar{A} \cdot \bar{B} \cdot C \cdot \bar{D}$ |
| 5 | $A \cdot \bar{B} \cdot C \cdot \bar{D}$ |
| 6 | $\bar{A} \cdot B \cdot C \cdot \bar{D}$ |
| 7 | $A \cdot B \cdot C \cdot \bar{D}$ |
| 8 | $\bar{A} \cdot \bar{B} \cdot \bar{C} \cdot D$ |
| 9 | $A \cdot \bar{B} \cdot \bar{C} \cdot D$ |

If false data rejection is not required, the circuit can be simplified by plotting it on a Karnaugh map and assuming that combinations (on a truth table) from 9 through 15 will never occur in BCD. In theory at least, this is a valid assumption because these combinations represent error or false data combinations. False data are always a possibility but there are more economical ways of eliminating them. Those combinations from 10–15 do not exist in the BCD code and, as a result of assuming that they will never occur, they are called *don't care* combinations. Whenever *don't care* combinations appear on a Karnaugh map, they are designated by the symbol ∅ (or X) and may be considered to be 1 entries on the Karnaugh map if they can be used to enlarge a loop around a group of ones resulting in a simplification. If they cannot

**Table 6-21**  Karnaugh Map with Don't Cares for
BCD-to-Decimal Decoder

|  | $\bar{A}\bar{B}$ | $\bar{A}B$ | $AB$ | $A\bar{B}$ |
|---|---|---|---|---|
| $\bar{C}\bar{D}$ | 0 | 1 | 3 | 2 |
| $\bar{C}D$ | 4 | 5 | 7 | 6 |
| $CD$ | ∅ | ∅ | ∅ | ∅ |
| $C\bar{D}$ | 8 | 9 | ∅ | ∅ |

∅ = Don't care

be used to enlarge a loop around one or more 1's, the *don't care* entries are treated as zeros and *not* looped. Table 6-21 shows the Karnaugh map for the BCD-to-decimal decoder using *don't cares*.

The equations for the ten outputs without false data rejection are as follows:

$$
\begin{array}{ll}
0 & \bar{A} \cdot \bar{B} \cdot \bar{C} \cdot \bar{D} \\
1 & A \cdot \bar{B} \cdot \bar{C} \cdot \bar{D} \\
2 & \bar{A} \cdot B \cdot \bar{C} \\
3 & A \cdot B \cdot \bar{C} \\
4 & \bar{A} \cdot \bar{B} \cdot C \\
5 & A \cdot \bar{B} \cdot C \\
6 & \bar{A} \cdot B \cdot C \\
7 & A \cdot B \cdot C \\
8 & \bar{A} \cdot D \\
9 & A \cdot D
\end{array}
$$

The circuit for a commercial BCD-to-decimal decoder is shown in Figure 6-7.

### ADDING A STROBE INPUT

There are several ways in which a strobe input can be added to the decoder in Figure 6-7. The most obvious is to add an extra input to each NAND gate and connect them all together to function as a strobe input. This input could then be connected to a BCD error-detector

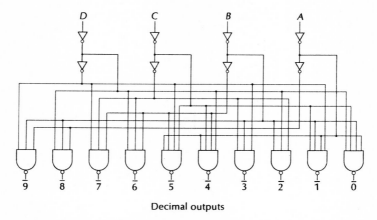

**Figure 6-7**   Simplified BCD-to-Decimal Decoder

circuit such as is shown in Figure 6-1 (with an extra inverter) to inhibit the entire decoder whenever false data are generated.

A second method of adding a strobe is to use the circuit shown in Figure 6-8 for decoders that reject false data. It operates by deliberately introducing the *false* combination 1111, which inhibits the decoder. A strobe can be used whenever data must be *sampled* only at some *specified time*.

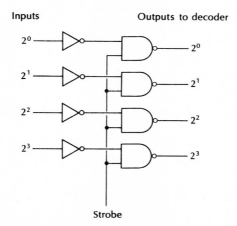

**Figure 6-8**   Strobe Circuit for Decoders with False
Data Rejection

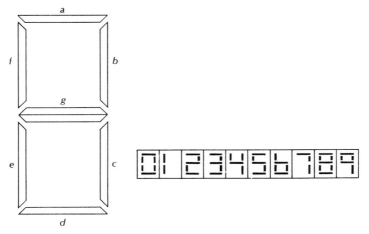

**Figure 6-9**   Seven-Segment Numerical Display

## 6-6   The Seven-Segment Numerical Display and Decoder

One of the most common numerical display systems uses seven segments to display digits 0–9. Figure 6-9 shows the arrangement and how the digits are formed. The decoder is a complex circuit, but considerable simplification is possible. Table 6-22 demonstrates the elaborate simplification process for the seven-segment decoder.

## SUMMARY

Computers perform arithmetic in straight binary or in one of several binary-related number systems and binary codes. The most important

**Table 6-22**   Karnaugh Maps for the BCD–to–7 Segment Decoder

| | $\bar{A}\bar{B}$ | $\bar{A}B$ | $AB$ | $A\bar{B}$ | | | $\bar{A}\bar{B}$ | $\bar{A}B$ | $AB$ | $A\bar{B}$ |
|---|---|---|---|---|---|---|---|---|---|---|
| $\bar{C}\bar{D}$ | 1 | 1 | 1 | 0 | | $\bar{C}\bar{D}$ | 1 | 1 | 1 | 1 |
| $\bar{C}D$ | 1 | ∅ | ∅ | 1 | | $\bar{C}D$ | 1 | ∅ | ∅ | 1 |
| $CD$ | ∅ | ∅ | ∅ | ∅ | | $CD$ | ∅ | ∅ | ∅ | ∅ |
| $C\bar{D}$ | 0 | 0 | 1 | 1 | | $C\bar{D}$ | 1 | 0 | 1 | 0 |

$$\bar{a} = \bar{A}\cdot C + A\cdot\bar{B}\cdot\bar{C}\cdot\bar{D}$$

Segment a

$$\bar{b} = A\cdot\bar{B}\cdot C + \bar{A}\cdot B\cdot C$$

Segment b

Table 6–22 continued

|        | $\overline{A}\overline{B}$ | $\overline{A}B$ | $AB$ | $A\overline{B}$ |
|--------|------|------|------|------|
| $\overline{C}\overline{D}$ | 1 | 0 | 1 | 1 |
| $\overline{C}D$ | 1 | ∅ | ∅ | 1 |
| $CD$ | ∅ | ∅ | ∅ | ∅ |
| $C\overline{D}$ | 1 | 1 | 1 | 1 |

$$\overline{c} = \overline{A}\cdot B\cdot \overline{C}$$
Segment c

|        | $\overline{A}\overline{B}$ | $\overline{A}B$ | $AB$ | $A\overline{B}$ |
|--------|------|------|------|------|
| $\overline{C}D$ | 1 | 1 | 1 | 0 |
| $\overline{C}D$ | 1 | ∅ | ∅ | 0 |
| $CD$ | ∅ | ∅ | ∅ | ∅ |
| $C\overline{D}$ | 0 | 1 | 0 | 1 |

$$\overline{d} = \overline{A}\cdot \overline{B}\cdot C + A\cdot B\cdot C + A\cdot \overline{B}\cdot \overline{C}$$
Segment d

|        | $\overline{A}\overline{B}$ | $\overline{A}B$ | $AB$ | $A\overline{B}$ |
|--------|------|------|------|------|
| $\overline{C}\overline{D}$ | 1 | 1 | 0 | 0 |
| $\overline{C}D$ | 1 | ∅ | ∅ | 0 |
| $CD$ | ∅ | ∅ | ∅ | ∅ |
| $C\overline{D}$ | 0 | 1 | 0 | 0 |

$$\overline{e} = \overline{B}\cdot C + A$$
Segment e

|        | $\overline{A}\overline{B}$ | $\overline{A}B$ | $AB$ | $A\overline{B}$ |
|--------|------|------|------|------|
| $\overline{C}\overline{D}$ | 1 | 0 | 0 | 0 |
| $\overline{C}D$ | 1 | ∅ | ∅ | 1 |
| $CD$ | ∅ | ∅ | ∅ | ∅ |
| $C\overline{D}$ | 1 | 1 | 0 | 1 |

$$\overline{f} = B\cdot \overline{C} + A\cdot B + A\cdot \overline{C}\cdot \overline{D}$$
Segment f

|        | $\overline{A}\,\overline{B}$ | $\overline{A}B$ | $AB$ | $A\overline{B}$ |
|--------|------|------|------|------|
| $\overline{C}\overline{D}$ | 0 | 1 | 1 | 0 |
| $\overline{C}D$ | 1 | ∅ | ∅ | 1 |
| $CD$ | ∅ | ∅ | ∅ | ∅ |
| $C\overline{D}$ | 1 | 1 | 0 | 1 |

$$\overline{g} = \overline{B}\cdot \overline{C}\cdot \overline{D} + A\cdot B\cdot C$$
Segment g

computer language number systems are straight binary, octal, and hexadecimal. BCD and XS-3 are used primarily in pocket calculators and small instruments.

Decoders and encoders perform electronic translation among number systems and coded number systems. Human translation requires methods that are more suited to human computational capabilities.

CHAPTER 7

# COUNTERS

*Learning Objectives.   Upon completion of this chapter you should:*
  *1. Be able to draw logic diagrams for the following counters:*
     *a. Binary ripple up-counter*
     *b. Binary ripple down-counter*
     *c. Binary ripple up/down counter*
     *d. Synchronous up-counter*
     *e. Synchronous down-counter*
     *f. 5 × 2 decimal counter*
     *g. 6, 2, 3 mod 12 counter*
  *2. Be able to recognize and explain the following circuits:*
     *a. Clock synchronizing circuit*
     *b. One-and-only-one synchronizing circuit*
     *c. N-and-only-N synchronizing circuit*
     *d. D flip-flop counter circuit*
  *3. Know when to use a D flip-flop and when a J-K is more appropriate.*
  *4. Be able to explain the operation of:*
     *a. The binary ripple up-counter*
     *b. The binary ripple down-counter*
     *c. The binary ripple up/down counter*
     *d. The synchronous up/down counter*
     *e. Presettable counters*
  *5. Be able to compute the maximum operating frequency for a ripple counter.*
  *6. Know what modulus counters are and the methods for obtaining a modulus that is not an integral multiple of 2.*
  *7. Be able to explain uses of synchronizing circuits.*
  *8. Be able to explain the operation of programmable counters.*
  *9. Be able to program a programmable counter.*
  *10. Be familiar with typical decoder circuits.*

Counters are among the most common digital circuits. They can be used to count people, items, pulses, and events. They are also used to count program steps in computers and to advance the program to the next step. Frequency can be measured by counting cycles referenced to a precise time period. There is an almost unlimited variety of counter applications. In this chapter we will examine the basic counter circuits and configurations.

## 7-1  Ripple Counters

The ripple counter is the simplest and most basic counter. It is easily implemented with *J-K* flip-flops. The term *ripple* is derived from the fact that the output of each flip-flop is connected to the input of the following flip-flop, so that the count must propagate down the line, activating each flip-flop in sequential order. The count seems to *ripple* down the chain. Figure 7-1 shows a four-stage binary ripple counter.

Initially all flip-flops are reset to 0 (*Q-low*). The clock input to F-F *A* sets the F-F to 1 on the negative-going transition of the clock pulse. F-F *B* does not change states (assuming master-slave F-F's) until its clock input goes to 0, which happens on the second clock pulse when $Q_A$ goes to zero. $Q_A$ changes states at every second clock pulse, $Q_B$ changes states every fourth clock pulse, F-F *C* changes states every eighth clock pulse, and so on (see Figure 7-1b). At the end of the fifteenth clock pulse, all F-F's are at $Q = 1$. On the sixteenth pulse $Q_A$ is reset to zero, and this command ripples down the string to bring all of the F-F's back to the $Q = 0$ state. The circuit is said to be asynchronous because only one of the F-F's is under the direct control of the clock. The rest of them are clocked by the output of the preceding F-F.

The maximum operating frequency of a simple ripple counter of the form shown in Figure 7-1 is determined at the fifteenth to sixteenth transition where the counter must go from 1111 to 0000. In this case all of the counters must change states and the clock pulse must ripple through all four F-F's. This particular transition is selected because it requires the longest time of any count in the sequence and involves the cumulative delays of *all* of the F-F's in the chain. In longer chains the condition in which the counter changes from *all* ones to *all* zeros is used to determine the maximum speed.

Maximum counting frequency is given by:

$$\frac{1}{f}(\text{max}) = N(T_p) + T_s$$

where

$$f = \text{frequency} \left(\frac{1}{f} = \text{period}\right)$$

$N$ = number of F-F's in the string
$T_p$ = propagation delay of one F-F
$T_s$ = strobe time − pulse width of decoded output

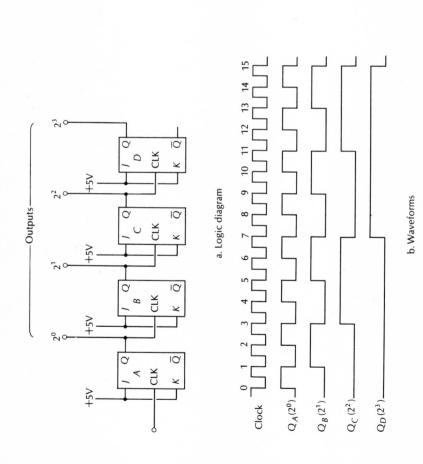

a. Logic diagram

b. Waveforms

| Count | D | C | B | A |
|---|---|---|---|---|
| 0 | 0 | 0 | 0 | 0 |
| 1 | 0 | 0 | 0 | 1 |
| 2 | 0 | 0 | 1 | 0 |
| 3 | 0 | 0 | 1 | 1 |
| 4 | 0 | 1 | 0 | 0 |
| 5 | 0 | 1 | 0 | 1 |
| 6 | 0 | 1 | 1 | 0 |
| 7 | 0 | 1 | 1 | 1 |
| 8 | 1 | 0 | 0 | 0 |
| 9 | 1 | 0 | 0 | 1 |
| 10 | 1 | 0 | 1 | 0 |
| 11 | 1 | 0 | 1 | 1 |
| 12 | 1 | 1 | 0 | 0 |
| 13 | 1 | 1 | 0 | 1 |
| 14 | 1 | 1 | 1 | 0 |
| 15 | 1 | 1 | 1 | 1 |
| 16 | 0 | 0 | 0 | 0 |

c. Truth table

**Figure 7-1** Binary Ripple Counter (Up-Counter, Asynchronous)

**Example**   If four F-F's are arranged as in Figure 7-1, assume a propagation delay of 50 ns per F-F and a decoding time (strobe time) of 50 ns.

$$\frac{1}{f}(\text{max}) = 4(50) + 50 = 250 \text{ ns}$$

$$f \text{ max} = 4 \text{ MHz}$$

The binary ripple counter in Figure 7-1 is also a frequency divider because F-F $A$ requires two master-clock pulses for one complete $(\bar{Q}\text{-}Q\text{-}\bar{Q})$ output transition, thus producing a subordinate clock pulse with a frequency of half the master-clock frequency. F-F $B$ produces a second subordinate clock frequency (one-fourth the master clock frequency and one-half the first subordinate clock frequency; see the timing diagram in Figure 7-1.) Two F-F's is a divide-by-4 circuit, three F-F's is a divide-by-8 circuit, and so on. The frequency division is given by $2^n$, where $n$ is the number of cascaded F-F's. Keep in mind that the longer the chain, the lower the maximum master-clock frequency must be. The primary deficiency of the simple ripple counter is the low speed due to cumulative propagation delays and the frequency limitation imposed by the number of flip-flops in the chain. Later in this chapter we will examine the faster synchronous counter that requires only one F-F propagation delay regardless of how many F-F's are in the chain.

## 7-2   Synchronizing Circuits

There are a number of situations in which data must be synchronized with the system clock. In some ripple counter chains it is desirable to resynchronize the output with the clock. The ripple form of propagation causes delays that put the output pulses out of synchronization with the original input signal. Outside-world data generally bear no time relationship to the internal clock.

The circuit in Figure 7-2 produces a string of clock pulses that begins with the first clock pulse following a *high* on the $D$ input. The output stays *high* until the first clock pulse following the $D$ input's *high*-to-*low* transition (see the timing diagram in Figure 7-2). The output *high* duration is nearly the same width as the $D$ input pulse and will begin and end with a clock pulse.

A variation of the synchronizing circuit in Figure 7-2 produces an integral number of clock pulses for the duration of the input pulse. The circuit is shown in Figure 7-3. Notice that both inputs to the NOR gate are inverted. The negative logic NOR is the dual of a positive logic AND gate. A steady stream of clock pulses is delivered to the gate and to the clock input of the flip-flip. When an unsynchronized pulse arrives at the $D$ input, the next clock pulse sets the flip-flop to $Q$ *high* and $\bar{Q}$

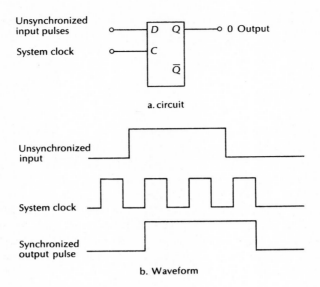

a. circuit

b. Waveform

**Figure 7-2** Synchronizing Circuit

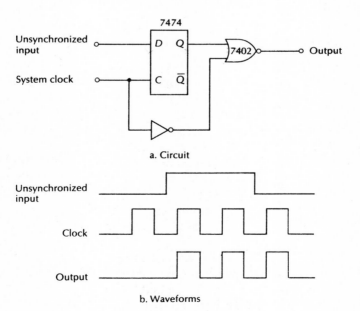

a. Circuit

b. Waveforms

**Figure 7-3** Modified Synchronizing Circuit

*low*. The 7402 now allows the clock pulses through. The double inversion yields a positive-going train of output pulses. When the *D* input goes *low*, the flip-flop must wait for the next clock pulse before it can reset. When the F-F is reset, the gate inhibits the clock pulses and the output stays *low*.

### THE N-AND-ONLY-N CIRCUIT

When we want to produce only a given number of pulses for each input pulse, we can use the circuit in Figure 7-4. The *N*-and-only-*N* circuit is a modification of Figure 7-3 with an added feedback path. The counter counts a predetermined number of pulses and then resets the flip-flop. The type *D* flip-flop in the first stage is used as an *R-S* flip-flop, taking advantage of an existing *D* flip-flop in the package. Both reset and set pulses are differentiated for edge triggering.

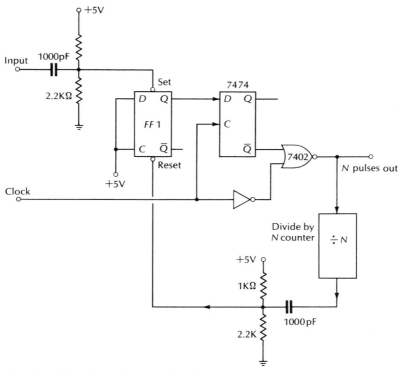

**Figure 7-4** *N*-and-Only-*N* Synchronizing Circuit

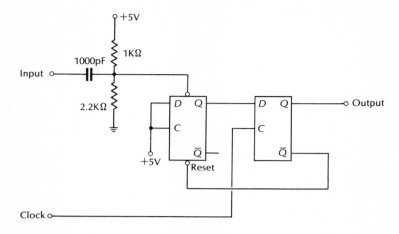

**Figure 7-5** One-and-Only-One Synchronizer Circuit

**Operation**

1. Input pulse sets F-F 1, starting a train of output pulses.
2. The divide-by-$N$ counter counts the number of pulses until it reaches its maximum count. Its output then resets F-F 1, stopping the pulse train after exactly $N$ pulses.

Because the input pulse is edge triggered, it has no effect on the circuit after the initial setting of F-F 1, which will be reset by the counter whatever the input state.

**THE ONE-AND-ONLY-ONE CIRCUIT**

If only a single, perfectly timed clock pulse for each input pulse is required, the $N$-and-only-$N$ circuit can be considerably simplified as shown in Figure 7-5. The circuit will produce a single standard clock pulse regardless of the timing or width of the input pulse.

**A RESYNCHRONIZING AND DEGLITCHING\* CIRCUIT**

A long ripple counter ends up with enough delays due to the ripple propagation times that the outputs become increasingly out of synchronization with the clock. The longer the counter chain, the more the outputs get out of step with the clock. As long as the outputs are not out of step by more than one entire clock pulse, the circuit in Figure 7-6 can be used to resynchronize the outputs. The circuit has the added

---

\* *Glitch* is jargon for an undesirable and sometimes unexplainable transient.

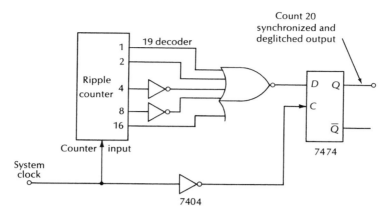

**Figure 7-6** Resynchronizing and Deglitching Circuit

advantage of eliminating the switching transient (glitch) that always occurs when TTL changes states. The NOR gate decodes 19, one count less than the desired count. The resynchronizing circuit delays the output until it coincides exactly with clock pulse 20. There are special TTL devices such as the 74120 that can be used for synchronizing purposes, but they are not common or readily available.

## 7-3  Ripple Counters Using the D Flip-Flop

The type $D$ flip-flop can be configured as a toggle flip-flop by connecting $\overline{Q}$ back to the $D$ input as shown in Figure 7-7a. Figure 7-7b shows $D$ flip-flops connected as a ripple *up*-counter and part c shows a *down*-counter using $D$ flip-flops.

## 7-4  Decoding Counters

Binary counters produce a binary output sequence which follows the standard truth table. They produce the binary equivalents of decimals 0, 1, 2, 3, 4, 5, 6, and so on. In most counter applications these binary combinations must be decoded either into decimal or sixteen individual unique states for a four-stage counter or into the proper code for activating seven-segment display devices. Although decoders were explained in Chapter 6, standard IC decoders were not examined.

### IC DECODERS

The 7442 is a TTL binary-to-decimal decoder. It decodes from ordinary binary 1, 2, 4, 8 to 10 unique output states. In the 7442 the

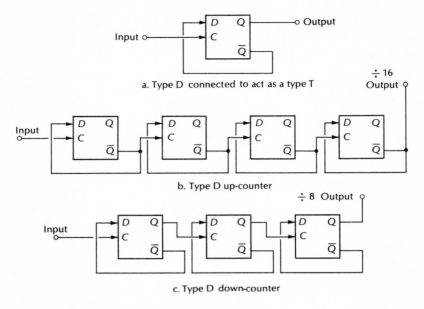

a. Type D connected to act as a type T

b. Type D up-counter

c. Type D down-counter

**Figure 7-7**   Type D Flip-Flop as Counter/Divider

decoded output goes *low* while all of the other output lines remain *high*. As a decimal decoder the input must be in the 1, 2, 4, 8 form. For 8 (or fewer) unique states, the outputs can be relabeled to accommodate any code. Figure 7-8 shows the 7442 connected to a BCD (1, 2, 4, 8) counter.

### Two-Line to Four-Line Decoders

The 74155 and 74156 decoders are dual two-line to four-line decoders that can decode two two-stage counters, using a single package. The 74155 uses a totem pole output and the 74156 is an open collector version.

### DECODER/DATA DISTRIBUTORS

The 74154 is a universal four-line to sixteen-line decoder or sixteen-position data distributor. It is the electronic analog of a single-pole sixteen-position switch when used as a data distributor. When it is used as a decoder, it is considered to be a universal decoder because it decodes all of the sixteen possible 1, 2, 4, 8 combinations. To use a different code (any code), it is necessary only to change the labels on the output line and route them to other circuitry according to the altered designations.

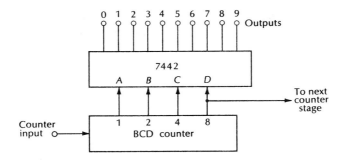

**Figure 7-8** 7442 Decoder

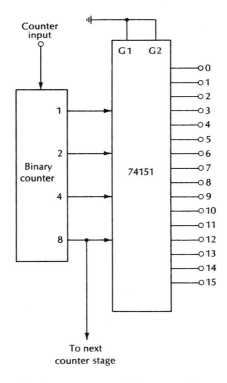

**Figure 7-9** 74154 Decoder/Data Distributor

Figure 7-9 is a block diagram of the 74154 as it would be connected as a 1, 2, 4, 8 decoder. The circuit shows $G_1$ and $G_2$ grounded. With enable lines $G_1$ and $G_2$ grounded, all outputs will be *high* except for the selected output. With one enable line at ground and the other connected to a source of data, the input data can be distributed to any of the sixteen output lines. With the counter doing the selecting, the circuit becomes a sixteen-position automatic stepping switch or commutator. The 74159 is an open collector version of the 74154.

### MATRIX DECODING

When a large number of stages must be decoded, the data distributor can be used in a matrix configuration as shown in Figure 7-10. The technique is based on the same idea used with folded data selector logic in Chapter 3. The truth table for a four-variable system (four-stage counter in this case) consists of two identical sets of eight combinations. The two sets are distinguished by 0's in the 16's column for the first set and 1's in the 16's column for the second set. (If this is not clear, refer to Table 3-18.) The circuit in Figure 7-10 takes advantage of the truth table pattern by using one decoder to decode the first half of the table and a second decoder to decode the second half. Because of stray current paths, output loads must be connected through series diodes. LED's may be used (since they are diodes themselves) without series diodes.

### Problem

1. Design a matrix decoder using 74154's to decode a five-stage binary counter. *Challenge:* Try it for a six-stage counter.

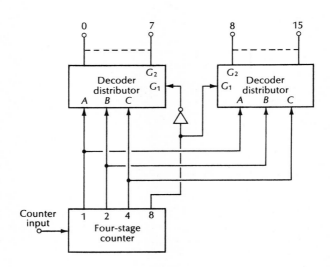

**Figure 7-10** Two Data Distributors

## 7-5 Decoder-Drivers

There are several special decoders intended for driving numerical display devices. The decoders previously discussed have outputs that are TTL compatible. Decoder-drivers have outputs compatible with whatever kind of display they are intended to drive. Table 7-1 describes common decoder-drivers, and Figure 7-11 shows the circuit for driving various kinds of display devices.

The resistors with the Nixie and LED circuits are used to limit current. Both devices have steep voltage current curves, indicating that a small increase in applied voltage can cause a very large and possibly destructive increase in current. Individual resistors are used for each cathode in the LED display to avoid the problem of current hogging by

**Table 7-1**   Decoder Drivers

| Type Number | Type of Display | Display Voltage | Display Current |
|---|---|---|---|
| 7445 | 10 individual incandescent lamps | 5 volts | 80 mA |
| 7447 | 7 segment common anode LED | 5 volts | 10 mA per segment typical |
| 7447 | 7 segment RCA numitron incandescent | 5 volts | 10—15 mA per segment |
| 74141 | Nixie gas discharge display | 60 volts | 7 mA |

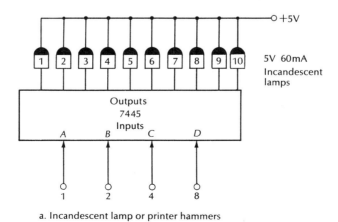

a. Incandescent lamp or printer hammers

**Figure 7-11**   Circuit for Driving Various Display Devices

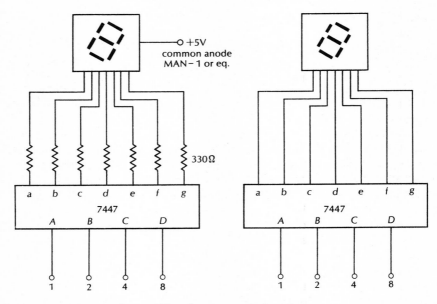

b. 7474 LED and seven-segment incandescent

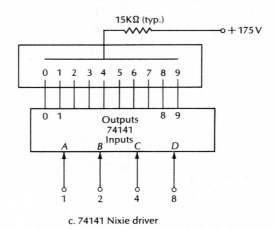

c. 74141 Nixie driver

**Figure 7-11**  continued

one segment at the expense of others, which can cause unequal brightness of the various segments when several are activated at the same time.

All outputs of these decoders are *high* except for the selected outputs. Opposing voltages in the *high* state hold the indicators or segments off. The selected output goes *low*, taking one end of the display element(s) to ground.

Recall that TTL can sink a fairly large current in the *low* condition, but is not able to handle much current in the *high* state. C-MOS decoders are available but can generally drive only two low-power TTL loads.

### DISPLAY MEMORY

Very often in counter display systems a memory in the form of a latch is employed to hold a display value while the counter is working on a new count. Without the latch the display would be a distracting blur during the counting period. The 7475 *level clocking* (and 74100) quad latch is one popular IC for this task. Note that this latch is level clocking, not edge clocking as some data sheets seem to imply.

For edge clocking devices, the 74175 quad *D* and 74174 hex *D* latches are available. To use the level-triggered latches, a *high* is placed on the enable lines and the latches follow the inputs. The enable lines are taken to ground to hold the count on the display. To use the 74175 and 74174 edge-triggered latches, the clear is normally held *high*. The positive-going edge of a pulse enters data into the latch and holds it. The *clear* line is momentarily taken to ground to clear the latches. Latches are placed between the counter and the decoder.

## 7-6  Down-Counters

*Down*-counters count backwards from some predetermined value toward zero. They are subtracting counters, reducing the count by one unit per input pulse. An ordinary *up*-counter can be converted to a *down*-counter by simply taking the outputs from the $\bar{Q}$ outputs of the flip-flops. If the $\bar{Q}$ outputs are not available, the $Q$ outputs can be inverted with the same results. Assume that the circuit in Figure 7-12 has been cleared to all $Q$'s = 0. Compare the truth tables in parts b and c. Notice that, while $Q$ outputs represent an upward count, the $\bar{Q}$ outputs are counting down.

The outputs for a *down*-counter can be taken from the $Q$ outputs if the circuit in Figure 7-12 is modified as shown in Figure 7-13.

If gate circuits are added that can effectively route the circuit paths as shown in either Figure 7-12 or 7-13 on command, the result is a reversible counter called an *up/down* counter. Figure 7-14a shows how this can be done. Figure 7-14b shows a complete *up/down* counter circuit. *Up/down* counters are more expensive than *up*-counters, more because of small demand rather than the increased complexity.

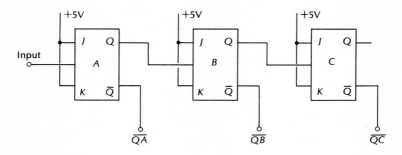

a. Outputs

| Count | QA | QB | QC |
|-------|----|----|----|
| 0 | 0 | 0 | 0 |
| 1 | 0 | 0 | 1 |
| 2 | 0 | 1 | 0 |
| 3 | 0 | 1 | 1 |
| 4 | 1 | 0 | 0 |
| 5 | 1 | 0 | 1 |
| 6 | 1 | 1 | 0 |
| 7 | 1 | 1 | 1 |

| Count | $\overline{QA}$ | $\overline{QB}$ | $\overline{QC}$ | Decimal equivalent |
|-------|-----------------|-----------------|-----------------|--------------------|
| 0 | 1 | 1 | 1 | 7 |
| 1 | 1 | 1 | 0 | 6 |
| 2 | 1 | 0 | 1 | 5 |
| 3 | 1 | 0 | 0 | 4 |
| 4 | 0 | 1 | 1 | 3 |
| 5 | 0 | 1 | 0 | 2 |
| 6 | 0 | 0 | 1 | 1 |
| 7 | 0 | 0 | 0 | 0 |

b. Q outputs                    c. $\overline{Q}$ outputs

**Figure 7-12**   Binary Ripple Down-Counter (Asynchronous) with Outputs Taken from $\overline{Q}$

## 7-7   Synchronous Counters

Fully synchronous counters eliminate the problem of cumulative F-F delays because all data transfers are clocked at the same time. The propagation delay is only one flip-flop delay regardless of the number of flip-flops in the counter chain. In addition to one flip-flop delay, there is also a gate delay and generally a decoder delay, but these are fairly constant and not a function of counter length.

The maximum clock frequency is given by:

$$\frac{1}{f} = T_p + T_g$$

where

$$T_p = 1 \text{ flip-flop delay and}$$
$$T_g = 1 \text{ gate structure delay}$$

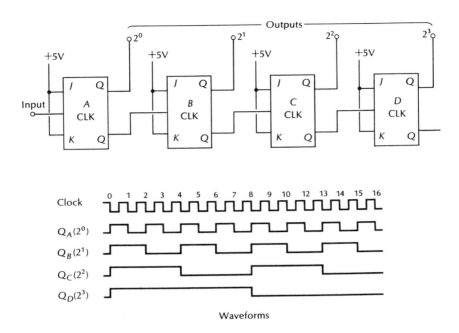

**Figure 7-13**   Binary Ripple Down-Counter (Asynchronous) Using Q Outputs

**Example**   Assume a flip-flop delay of 50 ns and a gate delay of 30 ns.

$$\frac{1}{f} = 50 + 30 = 80 \text{ ns}$$

$$f = \frac{1}{80} \text{ ns} = 12.5 \text{ MHz}$$

Figure 7-15 shows the simplest synchronous counter. Notice that both flip-flops are clocked at exactly the same time since the second flip-flop does not have to wait for the first to pass along the clock pulse.

In order to extend the length of the counter and maintain synchronous clocking, additional gates are required which make the counter more complex. A four-stage synchronous counter is shown in Figure 7-16.

## 7-8   Synchronous Up/Down Counters

A synchronous *down*-counter can be constructed by using the $\overline{Q}$ outputs in the same fashion as in the ripple counter, and using the same

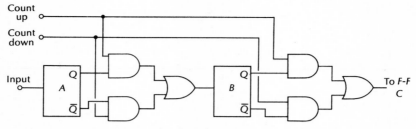

Note: Outputs are taken from the Q outputs of the flip-flops.

a. Gating structure

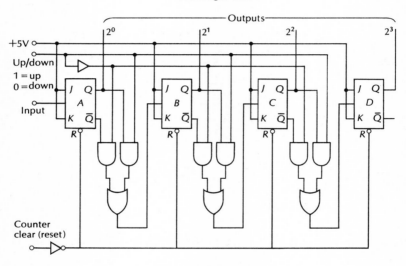

b. Complete logic diagram

**Figure 7-14** Binary Up/Down Counter (Ripple Asynchronous)

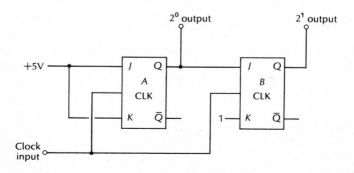

**Figure 7-15** Parallel Clocked Synchronous Counter

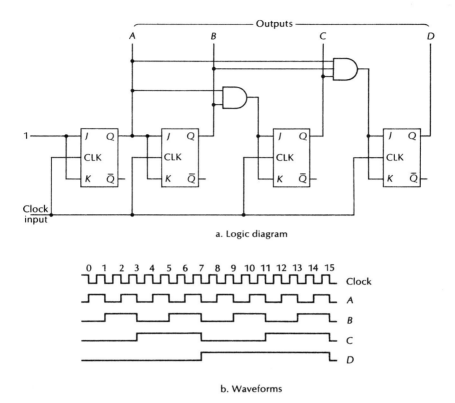

a. Logic diagram

b. Waveforms

**Figure 7-16** Fully Synchronous (Up) Counter

gating structure as in the *up*-counter in Figure 7-16. The synchronous *down*-counter circuit is shown in Figure 7-17. By adding gates to transfer data out of the $Q$ or the $\bar{Q}$ outputs on command, we arrive at the reversible *(up/down)* synchronous counter shown in Figure 7-18.

### RIPPLE-CARRY SYNCHRONOUS COUNTERS

An examination of the logic circuit for the fully synchronous counter reveals that each additional F-F requires an additional gate and that each successive gate requires one more input than the gate for the preceding stage. A compromise configuration that retains the synchronous operation of the flip-flops with a simpler gate structure is called the *ripple-carry synchronous counter*.

Though flip-flop delay is not cumulative, ripple-carry gate delays are. Thus, the circuit is faster than the simple ripple counter but slower than the fully synchronous parallel-carry counter. The logic diagram for a synchronous ripple-carry *up/down* counter is shown in Figure 7-19.

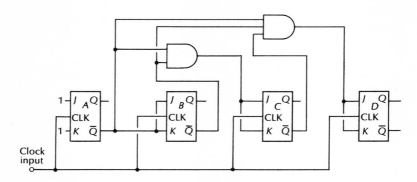

**Figure 7-17** Synchronous Down-Counter

## 7-9 Modulus Counters

The modulus (mod) of a counter is simply the number of counting states before it begins to repeat itself. A four-stage counter has a natural modulus of 16, a three-stage counter has a modulus of 8, and so on.

So far the counters we have examined have all operated at their natural modulus, using their full count length. A counter can, however, be made to count to any desired modulus by selecting a counter with a natural modulus that is the next step higher than the desired modulus and then causing it to skip the proper number of steps. Counts can be skipped anywhere in the natural sequence.

Usually some form of feedback is used to force the counter one or more extra counts ahead or to clear the counter before the end of the natural count sequence.

When we want to have a ripple counter operate in some modulus that is not a power of 2, the following procedure can be used (for preset mode counters):

1. Find $n$, the number of flip-flops required, that is, find the nearest power of 2 that yields a higher count than the modulus number, $N$. If we assume a modulus (mod) of 5, $2^2 = 4$ is not enough, but $2^3 = 8$ is sufficient. The exponent is the number of flip-flops, so three flip-flops are required. Note that three F-F's can count up to 111, or $7_{10}$, before resetting naturally to 000. Because 5 (the modulus) is less than 7, three F-F's are required.
2. Connect all flip-flops as a ripple counter, as shown in Figure 7-20.
3. Find the binary number $N-1$.
4. Connect all flip-flop outputs ($Q$) that are 1 at count $N - 1$ to one of the inputs on a NAND gate. Use one NAND gate input for the clock.

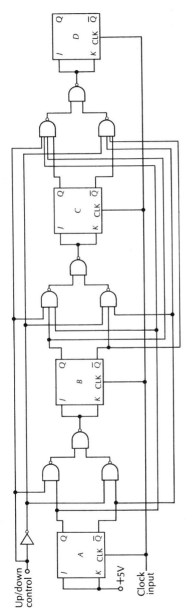

**Figure 7-18** Synchronous Up/Down Counter

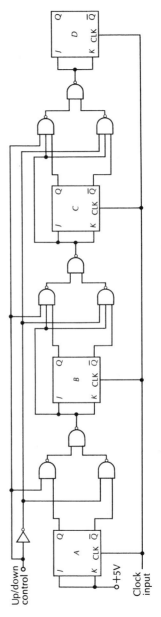

**Figure 7-19** Synchronous Up/Down Counter with Ripple Carry

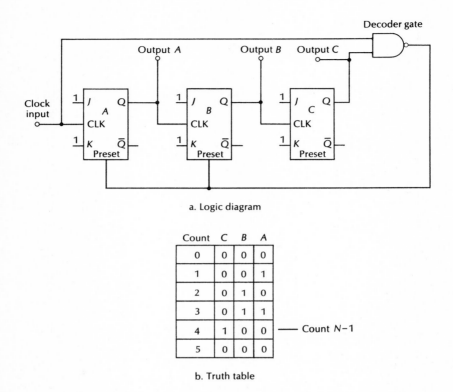

a. Logic diagram

| Count | C | B | A |
|-------|---|---|---|
| 0 | 0 | 0 | 0 |
| 1 | 0 | 0 | 1 |
| 2 | 0 | 1 | 0 |
| 3 | 0 | 1 | 1 |
| 4 | 1 | 0 | 0 |
| 5 | 0 | 0 | 0 |

—— Count $N-1$

b. Truth table

**Figure 7-20**    Logic Diagram for a Mod 5 Counter Using F-F's with Preset Capability

5. Connect the NAND gate output to the *preset* input of all flip-flops that are at $Q = 0$ at count $N - 1$.

**Example**    Draw the logic diagram of a modulus 5 ripple counter using presets.

1. The number of F-F's required is 3.
2. $N - 1 = 5 - 1 = 4$

   $\qquad\qquad\qquad$ CBA
3. $4_{10}$ in binary = 1 0 0

(Figure 7-20 shows the logic diagram and truth table for this device.)

## MODULUS COUNTERS USING FLIP-FLOPS WITHOUT PRESET CAPABILITY

Many IC flip-flops do not have preset inputs. When such flip-flops are used, they can be configured as follows:

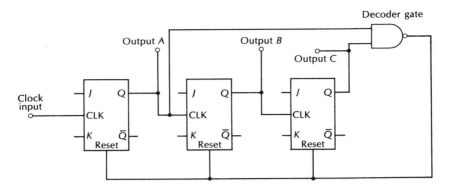

**Figure 7-21**  Mod 5 Ripple Counter Using the Reset Method

1. Find the number of flip-flops required. Find the nearest power of 2 larger than the mod number. Assuming a modulus of 20, $2^4 = 16$, $2^5 = 32$; five flip-flops are required.
2. Connect all flip-flops as a ripple counter.
3. Find the binary number $N$ (the modulus number).
4. Find the flip-flops that have 1's on $Q$ at the $N$th count. In this example it would be flip-flops $A$ and $C$.
5. Connect a NAND gate with inputs connected to $Q$ of the flip-flops that have $Q = 1$ at count $N$ (the highest count in the sequence). Connect the output of the NAND gate to the clear (reset) inputs on *all* flip-flops.

The circuit will count up to $N - 1$ and on the $N$th count will go to the number $N$ momentarily—long enough for the NAND gate to detect the presence of the number $N$ and reset the counter to all zeros. Figure 7-21 shows the logic diagram.

One problem with this scheme is that a fairly broad range of reset times exists among the various flip-flops in a string. Because of different loading conditions from one flip-flop to another and because of normal tolerances in circuitry, the reset time may vary. The negative-going pulse may not always be long enough to reset all counters.

There are two basic methods of overcoming this difficulty. One involves the use of a latch with clock reset and the other uses some form of monostable. Figure 7-22 shows a mod 5 counter with latch reset, and Figure 7-23 shows a mod 5 counter with monostable reset. Notice that *all* F-F's are reset at count $N$, including those that were naturally in a $Q = 0$ state at count $N$. This is done to insure that the new cycle begins

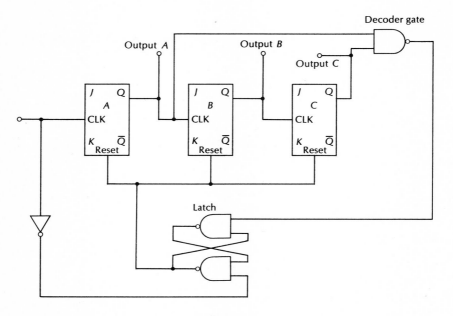

**Figure 7-22** Mod 5 Ripple Counter Using a Latch Reset

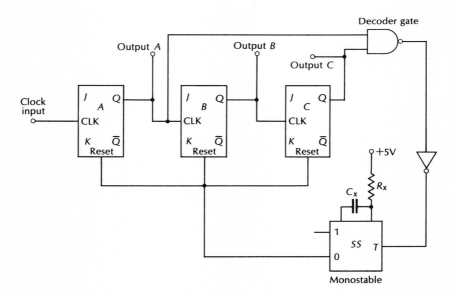

**Figure 7-23** Mod 5 Ripple Using Monostable Reset

at zero and to prevent any miscount from the previous cycle from carrying over into the next. Some counter circuits include the 0 states of the flip-flops not in the 1 state at count $N$ as inputs to the NAND gate. In that case, they are taken from the $\overline{Q}$ outputs of the flip-flops involved. The NAND gate used in preset and clear mode counters is a single condition decoder.

## 7-10   IC Counter Techniques

Modern IC counters often combine several counter techniques in an IC package. Combinations of synchronous and asynchronous techniques combined with gateless feedback and inhibit circuits are common. Many of these counters provide a great deal of flexibility coupled with simplicity and standardization by using combinations of two or more different modulus counters. For example, a mod 2 and a mod 3 counter can be combined as a divide-by-3-by-2 combination, providing two versions of a mod 6 counter.

A divide-by-3, divide-by-2 pair can be combined with another divide-by-2 counter to get a mod 12 counter. Two versions of decimal counters can be formed using a divide-by-2, divide-by-5 or a divide-by-5, divide-by-2 configuration.

In addition, each modulus counter in a given package can be arranged for external connections that allow the individual modulus counters to be used separately or configured for two or more different counting modes.

### DIVIDE-BY-4 HYBRID PARALLEL-CLOCKED GATELESS COUNTER

Figure 7-24 shows the logic diagram of a mod 4 (binary two-stage) counter using a parallel (synchronous) clock and ripple count propaga-

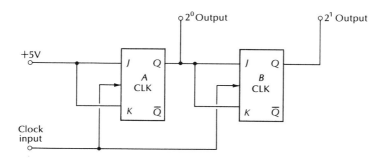

**Figure 7-24**   Parallel-Clocked Gateless Counter

tion. This configuration provides the flexibility necessary for most of the hybrid counter forms.

**Problem**

2. Using what you know about *J-K* flip-flops, analyze the operation of the circuit in Figure 7-24. (Hint: see the operation of the divide-by-3 counter.)

### DIVIDE-BY-3 COUNTER

Figure 7-25 shows a divide-by-3 (mod 3) counter. The following shows how it operates (see Table 7-2):

1. Initial Conditions (Count 0)
   a. F-F *A* is reset to 0.
   b. F-F *B* is reset to 0.
   c. $\bar{Q}$ of F-F *B* is at a logical 1 and is connected to the *J* input of F-F *A*. F-F *A* will operate in a toggle mode as long as $\bar{Q}$ of F-F *B* is at 1.

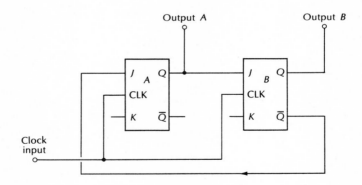

**Figure 7-25**   Mod 3 Counter

**Table 7-2**   Mod 3 Hybrid Counter Truth Table

| Count Number | $Q_b$ | $Q_a$ |
|:---:|:---:|:---:|
| 0 | 0 | 0 |
| 1 | 0 | 1 |
| 2 | 1 | 0 |
| 3 | 0 | 0 |

2. Count 1
   a. F-F $A$ toggles to $Q = 1$, F-F $B$ no change
3. Count 2
   a. F-F $A$ toggles to $Q = 0$, F-F $B$ toggles to $Q = 1$
   b. $\bar{Q}$ of F-F $B$ goes to logical zero, preventing F-F $A$ from setting to $Q = 1$.
4. Count 3
   a. $QB$ goes to 0
   b. $QA$ locked out—stays at 0

## DIVIDE-BY-5 COUNTER

Figure 7-26 shows the logic diagram of a mod 5 counter with two feedback control paths. Table 7-3 shows the truth table for the mod 5 hybrid counter. Notice particularly the two feedback control paths:

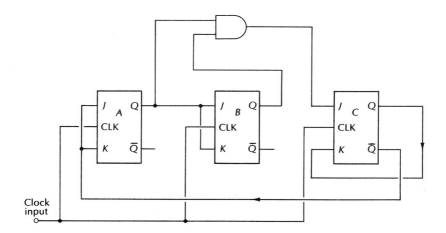

**Figure 7-26** Synchronous Mod 5 Counter

**Table 7-3** Truth Table for Mod 5 Counter

| Count | C | B | A |
|-------|---|---|---|
| 0 | 0 | 0 | 0 |
| 1 | 0 | 0 | 1 |
| 2 | 0 | 1 | 0 |
| 3 | 0 | 1 | 1 |
| 4 | 1 | 0 | 0 |
| 5 | 0 | 0 | 0 |

from $Q_c$ to $K_c$ and $\overline{Q}_c$ back to $J\text{-}K_a$. The counting sequence goes as follows:

1. Count 0
   Initial conditions: F-F's $A$, $B$, and $C$ reset to $Q = 0$
2. Count 1
   a.  F-F $A$ toggles to 1 ($Q = 1$)
   b.  F-F's $B$ and $C$ remain at $Q = 0$
   c.  $\overline{Q}$ of F-F $C = 1$ and places $J\text{-}K$ of F-F $A$ at logical 1
3. Count 2
   a.  F-F $A$ toggles to $Q = 0$
   b.  F-F $B$ toggles to $Q = 1$
   c.  F-F $C$ remains at $Q = 0$ ($\overline{Q} = 1$)
4. Count 3
   a.  F-F $A$ toggles to $Q = 1$
   b.  F-F $B$ remains at $Q = 1$
   c.  F-F $C$ remains at $Q = 0$
5. Count 4
   a.  F-F $A$ toggles to $Q = 0$
   b.  F-F $B$ toggles to $Q = 0$
   c.  F-F $C$ toggles to $Q = 1$
   d.  F-F $C$ returns a logical 0 from $\overline{Q}_c$ back to F-F $A$. This will prevent F-F $A$ from toggling to $Q = 1$ on the fifth clock pulse (count 5)
   e.  $Q$ on F-F $C$ places a logical 1 on $K$ of F-F $C$. This will force F-F $C$ to rest to 0 on count 5
6. Count 5
   a.  F-F $A$ remains at $Q = 0$ because of the logical 0 fed back from $\overline{Q}$ of F-F $C$
   b.  F-F $B$ remains at $Q = 0$           CBA
       The next natural count would be 1 0 1, and nothing need be done to insure a $Qb = 0$ for count 5. It would not have toggled in any event
   c.  F-F $C$ has a logical 1 on the $K$ input causing it to reset to $Q = 0$ on count 5

## MOD 6 COUNTERS

### Divide-by-2, Divide-by-3 Counter

Mod 6 counters can be formed by combining the mod 3 counter from Figure 7-25 with a single F-F (divide-by-2). If the binary (divide-by-2) is used as the input stage, each two clock pulses will provide one subordinate clock pulse to the divide-by-3 circuit. The binary stage will toggle on each clock pulse. The divide-by-3 stage will follow the count

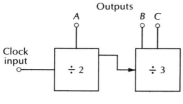

| Count | C | B | A |
|---|---|---|---|
| 0 | 0 | 0 | 0 |
| 1 | 0 | 0 | 1 |
| 2 | 0 | 1 | 0 |
| 3 | 0 | 1 | 1 |
| 4 | 1 | 0 | 0 |
| 5 | 1 | 0 | 1 |
| 6 | 1 | 1 | 0 |

a. Block diagram

b. Truth table

**Figure 7-27**   Divide-by-2, Divide-by-3 Mod 6 Counter and Truth Table

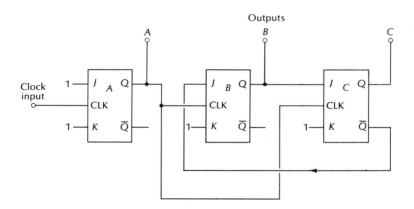

**Figure 7-28**   Mod 6 Divide-by-2, Divide-by-3 Counter

pattern for the mod 3 circuit in Figure 7-25, except that it will remain in each count state for two counts instead of making some change at every count as it does when used alone. Figure 7-27 shows a block diagram of the divide-by-2, divide-by-3 arrangement and its corresponding mod 6 truth table. An examination of the truth table in this figure indicates that the count for this configuration is a normal binary series count. Figure 7-28 shows the complete logic diagram for the divide-by-2, divide-by-3 mod 6 counter.

### Divide-by-3, Divide-by-2 Counter

By placing the divide-by-3 section at the input of the chain, a mod 6 counter is obtained but the counting sequence is 0, 1, 2, 4, 5, 6, 0

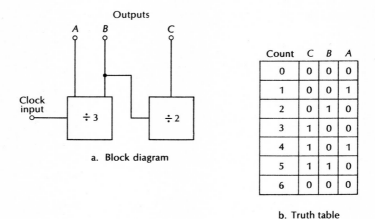

| Count | C | B | A |
|-------|---|---|---|
| 0 | 0 | 0 | 0 |
| 1 | 0 | 0 | 1 |
| 2 | 0 | 1 | 0 |
| 3 | 1 | 0 | 0 |
| 4 | 1 | 0 | 1 |
| 5 | 1 | 1 | 0 |
| 6 | 0 | 0 | 0 |

a. Block diagram

b. Truth table

**Figure 7-29** Divide-by-3, Divide-by-2 Mod 6 Counter and Truth Table

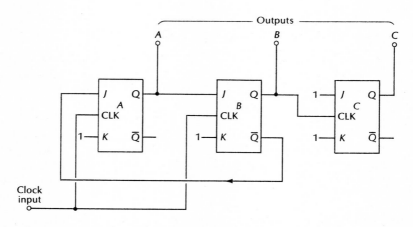

**Figure 7-30** Logic Diagram for the Divide-by-3, Divide-by-2 Mod 6 Counter

(decimal equivalents) rather than the natural 0, 1, 2, 3, 4, 5, 0, binary sequence count. The block diagram and truth table are shown in Figure 7-29 and the logic diagram is shown in Figure 7-30.

In the case of the divide-by-3, divide-by-2 configuration, the divide-by-3 counter goes through its complete counting sequence before the divide-by-2 is toggled. At the end of the second divide-by-3 cycle, the divide-by-2 circuit resets to zero. (See the truth table in Figure 7-29.)

**Table 7-4**  MSI Counters

Non-Presettable

| Type | Mod. | Count Direction | Synchronous Max. Clock Rate MHz | Ripple Max. Clock Rate MHz | Configuration | Clock | Unit Cascadable |
|------|------|-----------------|--------------------------------|----------------------------|---------------|-------|-----------------|
| 7490 | 10 | up | | 18 | 2 × 5 | neg. edge | no |
| 7492 | 12 | up | | 18 | 2 × 6 | neg. edge | no |
| 7493 | 16 | up | | 18 | 2 × 8 | neg. edge | no |

Presettable

| Type | Mod. | Count Direction | Synchronous Max. Clock Rate MHz | Ripple Max. Clock Rate MHz | Configuration | Clock | Unit Cascadable |
|------|------|-----------------|--------------------------------|----------------------------|---------------|-------|-----------------|
| 74160 | 10 | up | 32 | | 1 × 10 | pos. edge | yes |
| 74161 | 16 | up | 32 | | 1 × 16 | pos. edge | yes |
| 74190 | 10 | up/down | 25 | | 1 × 10 | pos. edge | yes |
| 74191 | 16 | up/down | 25 | | 1 × 16 | pos. edge | yes |
| 74192 | 10 | up/down | 32 | | 1 × 10 | pos. edge | yes |
| 8280 | 10 | up | | 35 | 2 × 5 | neg. edge | no |
| 74177 | 16 | up | | 35 | 2 × 8 | neg. edge | no |
| 8288 | 12 | up | | 35 | 2 × 6 | neg. edge | no |

## TTL MSI COUNTERS

The 54/74 (and the 8200) series provides a small but versatile collection of off-the-shelf counters to satisfy many common counting circuit requirements. Table 7-4 summarizes the common available types.

## 7-11   The 7493 Binary Counter

Figure 7-31 shows the logic diagram of the 7493 binary counter, a divide-by-2, divide-by-8 ripple counter. They may be used separately or connected externally to form a divide-by-16 counter. The counter has a gated reset-to-0 input. Either or both (set to 0) inputs to $R_0$ and $R_n$ must be at ground for normal counting. Both set-to-0 inputs are taken *high* (+5V) to reset the counter to zero.

The counter advances on the negative-going edge of the clock. The clock waveform must be TTL compatible and can have a maximum frequency of 20 MHz. To make it a mod 16 counter, the clock is connectecd to input $A$ and an external jumper is connected from $Q_A$ (pin 12) to clock $A$ (pin 1). The 7493 counts *up* only.

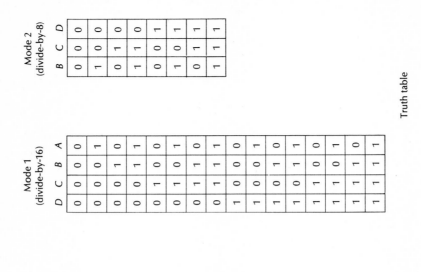

**Mode 1 (divide-by-16)**

| D | C | B | A |
|---|---|---|---|
| 0 | 0 | 0 | 0 |
| 0 | 0 | 0 | 1 |
| 0 | 0 | 1 | 0 |
| 0 | 0 | 1 | 1 |
| 0 | 1 | 0 | 0 |
| 0 | 1 | 0 | 1 |
| 0 | 1 | 1 | 0 |
| 0 | 1 | 1 | 1 |
| 1 | 0 | 0 | 0 |
| 1 | 0 | 0 | 1 |
| 1 | 0 | 1 | 0 |
| 1 | 0 | 1 | 1 |
| 1 | 1 | 0 | 0 |
| 1 | 1 | 0 | 1 |
| 1 | 1 | 1 | 0 |
| 1 | 1 | 1 | 1 |

**Mode 2 (divide-by-8)**

| B | C | D |
|---|---|---|
| 0 | 0 | 0 |
| 1 | 0 | 0 |
| 0 | 1 | 0 |
| 1 | 1 | 0 |
| 0 | 0 | 1 |
| 1 | 0 | 1 |
| 0 | 1 | 1 |
| 1 | 1 | 1 |

Truth table

DIP (top view)

| 1 | $CP_b$ | $CP_a$ | 14 |
| 2 | $R_{0(1)}$ | NC | 13 |
| 3 | $R_{0(2)}$ | $Q_a$ | 12 |
| 4 | NC | $Q_d$ | 11 |
| 5 | $V_{cc}$ | GND | 10 |
| 6 | NC | $Q_b$ | 9 |
| 7 | NC | $Q_c$ | 8 |

Logic symbol

5493, 7493

$V_{cc}$ = Pin 5
GND = Pin 10
NC = Pins 4, 6, 7, 13

**Figure 7-31**  Logic Diagram for the 7493 Binary Counter

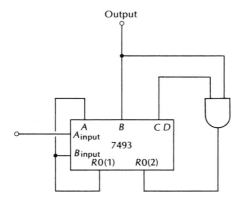

**Figure 7-32**  Divide-by-7 Counter Using the 7493

### 7493 CONFIGURATIONS

1. Divide-by-7 (7493)

    Operation: Decodes 6 and resets to zero.

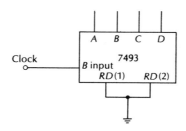

**Figure 7-33**  Divide-by-8 Counter Using
the 7493

2. Divide-by-8 (7493)

    Operation: Input to divide-by-8 section only.

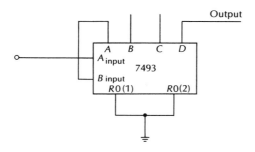

**Figure 7-34**  Divide-by-16 Ripple Counter Using the
54/7493

3. Divide-by-16 (7493)

Operation: Jumper from the divide-by-2 output to the divide-by-8 input.

**Problems**

3. Explain the operation of the divide-by-9 circuit in Figure 7-35.
4. Explain the operation of the divide-by-10 counter in Figure 7-36. Use a count truth table.

## 7-12 The 7490 Decade Counter

The 7490 decade counter contains separate divide-by-2 and divide-by-5 counters composed of a total of four master-slave flip-flops. Gated inputs are provided to reset all outputs to 0 or to preset to BCD 9 ($1001_{BCD}$).

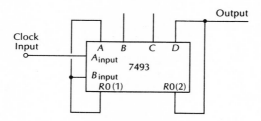

**Figure 7-35** Divide-by-9 Ripple Counter Using the 54/7493

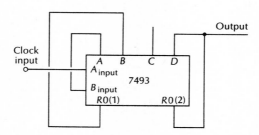

**Figure 7-36** Divide-by-10 Ripple Counter Using the 54/7493

The 7490 is a ripple counter, with a maximum clock rate of 18 MHz. The count is advanced on the negative-going clock edge. The clock signal must be TTL compatible. The counter requires normal TTL rise and fall times for proper operation. For normal counting operation the two set-to-0 and the two set-to-9 inputs must be grounded.

To set to 0, one or both of the set-to-0 inputs must go positive (*high*). To set to 9, one or both of the set-to-9 inputs must go positive. Reset/ set pulses should be as wide as possible—10 microseconds or wider.

There are three *basic* counting modes: mod 5 and mod 2 separately, a divide-by-2, a divide-by-5, and a divide-by-2/divide-by-5 decade counter. It may also be easily configured for divide-by-6 and divide-by-7 counting modes. Figure 7-37 shows the complete logic diagram for the 54/7490 decade counter. Figure 7-38 shows external configurations and truth tables for the three primary counting modes.

The BCD mode is natural BCD, the most commonly used mode for decimal counting, and can be decoded by several off-the-shelf decoders. The symmetrical divide-by-10 mode provides a symmetrical output waveform and must be divided by a power of 10.

### Problems

5. Draw a timing diagram for each of the two decimal counting modes.
6. Describe how the count progresses starting with a set-to-9 condition followed by grounding the set-to-9 input and starting the count.

## 7-13   The 54/7492

The 7492 is a divide-by-2, divide-by-6 pair of ripple (*up*) counters. Figure 7-39 shows the block diagram. The count advances on the negative transition of the clock, and the maximum clock rate is 18 MHz. Both set-to-0 lines are grounded for normal counting operation. One (or both) set lines is taken *high* to set-to-0 (reset). The preferred mod 12 count requires a jumper from $Q_A$ to $\overline{CP}_{BC}$. The clock input is on $\overline{CP}_A$. The other possibility, a jumper from $Q_D$ to $\overline{CP}_A$ with input to $\overline{CP}_A$, yields a different sequence that is not (normal) binary related.

### Problem

7. Draw a timing diagram for the preferred counting mode and another for the alternate connection for the divide-by-12 7492.

## 7-14   The 7492 and 7493 as Various Modulus Counters

Modulus counters using 7492 and 7493 configured for modulus 7, 9, 11, 12, 13, 14, and 15 are shown in Figure 7-40.

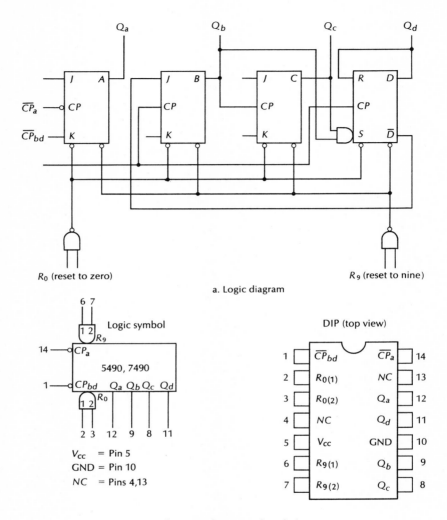

a. Logic diagram

b. Basing diagram and symbol

**Figure 7-37**  Logic Diagram for the 54/7490 Decade Counter

## 7-15  Programmable Counters

The most popular kind of programmable counters is typified by the 74161 mod 16 and the 74160 mod 10 presettable counters. These units can be programmed to operate in any modulus by using enough packages and programming. Programming consists of connecting program inputs to +5V or ground as required by the desired count. This can be

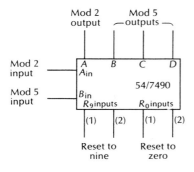

a. Mod 2 and Mod 5 counter

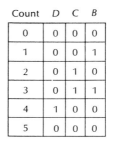

| Count | D | C | B |
|-------|---|---|---|
| 0 | 0 | 0 | 0 |
| 1 | 0 | 0 | 1 |
| 2 | 0 | 1 | 0 |
| 3 | 0 | 1 | 1 |
| 4 | 1 | 0 | 0 |
| 5 | 0 | 0 | 0 |

b. Divide-by-5 truth table

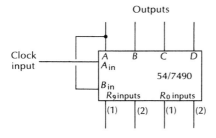

c. Binary coded decimal count

| Count | D | C | B | A |
|-------|---|---|---|---|
| 0 | 0 | 0 | 0 | 0 |
| 1 | 0 | 0 | 0 | 1 |
| 2 | 0 | 0 | 1 | 0 |
| 3 | 0 | 0 | 1 | 1 |
| 4 | 0 | 1 | 0 | 0 |
| 5 | 0 | 1 | 0 | 1 |
| 6 | 0 | 1 | 1 | 0 |
| 7 | 0 | 1 | 1 | 1 |
| 8 | 1 | 0 | 0 | 0 |
| 9 | 1 | 0 | 0 | 1 |
| 10 | 0 | 0 | 0 | 0 |

d. Truth table for BCD mode

| Count | D | C | B | A |
|-------|---|---|---|---|
| 0 | 0 | 0 | 0 | 0 |
| 1 | 0 | 0 | 1 | 0 |
| 2 | 0 | 1 | 0 | 0 |
| 3 | 0 | 1 | 1 | 0 |
| 4 | 1 | 0 | 0 | 0 |
| 5 | 0 | 0 | 0 | 1 |
| 6 | 0 | 0 | 1 | 1 |
| 7 | 0 | 1 | 0 | 1 |
| 8 | 0 | 1 | 1 | 1 |
| 9 | 1 | 0 | 0 | 1 |
| 10 | 0 | 0 | 0 | 0 |

f. Truth table for the symmetrical divide-by-10 mode

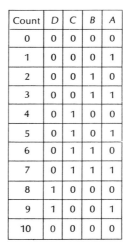

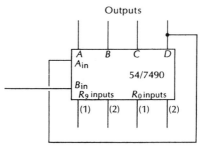

e. Symmetrical divide-by-10 mode using the 54/7490

**Figure 7-38**    Configurations and Truth Tables for the Three  Primary Counting Modes of the 54/7490

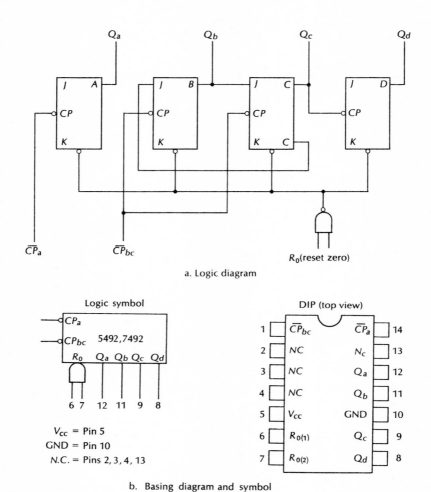

a. Logic diagram

b. Basing diagram and symbol

**Figure 7-39** The 54/7492 Divide-by-Twelve Counter (Divide-by-2, Divide-by-6)

accomplished by using BCD switches to vary the count at will. Figure 7-41 shows the input, output, and control terminals for the 74161.
Functions:

1. $Q_A$, $Q_B$, $Q_C$, $Q_D$: outputs
2. $P_1$, $P_2$, $P_4$, $P_8$: presetting inputs
3. Held at +5V for normal counting. Taken to ground to enter preset values.
4. *Clear*, set-to-0: Normally held +5V for counting. Taken to ground to clear-to-0.

| Mode 1 (Divide-by-12) | | | | | Mode 2 (Divide-by-6) | | | | Mode 3 (Divide-by-12) | | | |
|---|---|---|---|---|---|---|---|---|---|---|---|---|
| A | B | C | D | | B | C | D | | A | B | C | D |
| 0 | 0 | 0 | 0 | | 0 | 0 | 0 | | 0 | 0 | 0 | 0 |
| 1 | 0 | 0 | 0 | | 1 | 0 | 0 | | 0 | 1 | 0 | 0 |
| 0 | 1 | 0 | 0 | | 0 | 1 | 0 | | 0 | 0 | 1 | 0 |
| 1 | 1 | 0 | 0 | | 0 | 0 | 1 | | 0 | 0 | 0 | 1 |
| 0 | 0 | 1 | 0 | | 1 | 0 | 1 | | 0 | 1 | 0 | 1 |
| 1 | 0 | 1 | 0 | | 0 | 1 | 1 | | 0 | 0 | 1 | 1 |
| 0 | 0 | 0 | 1 | | | | | | 1 | 0 | 0 | 0 |
| 1 | 0 | 0 | 1 | | | | | | 1 | 1 | 0 | 0 |
| 0 | 1 | 0 | 1 | | | | | | 1 | 0 | 1 | 0 |
| 1 | 1 | 0 | 1 | | | | | | 1 | 0 | 0 | 1 |
| 0 | 0 | 1 | 1 | | | | | | 1 | 1 | 0 | 1 |
| 1 | 0 | 1 | 1 | | | | | | 1 | 0 | 1 | 1 |

c. Truth tables

**Figure 7-39**  continued

5. *T* connected to the *carry-out* of the previous stage for cascaded synchronous operation.
6. *Carry-out:* Goes *high* at the maximum count: $Q_A = 1$, $Q_B = 1$, $Q_C = 1$, $Q_D = 1$. Produces *low* output for all other counts.
7. *P*: Enable; held positive for normal counting.

## PROGRAMMING THE COUNTER

The counter is programmed by setting the counter to an initial count using the preset inputs $P_1$, $P_2$, $P_4$, $P_8$. When the load control goes to +5V, the counter begins to advance on the positive edge of each clock pulse. The counter starts its counting at the preset number and continues counting until it reaches the highest possible count. At the end of the count, the counter goes back to 0000. The 1111 condition is decoded and the *carry-out* line goes high on the maximum count. This carry output level can be fed back (through an inverter) to the load input, enabling the preset values to be loaded again.

The counter counts from preset count to the maximum count, resets to the preset value, and begins counting a new cycle. The modulus is: $N - n_p$, where $N$ is the natural modulus (maximum count) of the counter and $n_p$ is the preset count. For example:

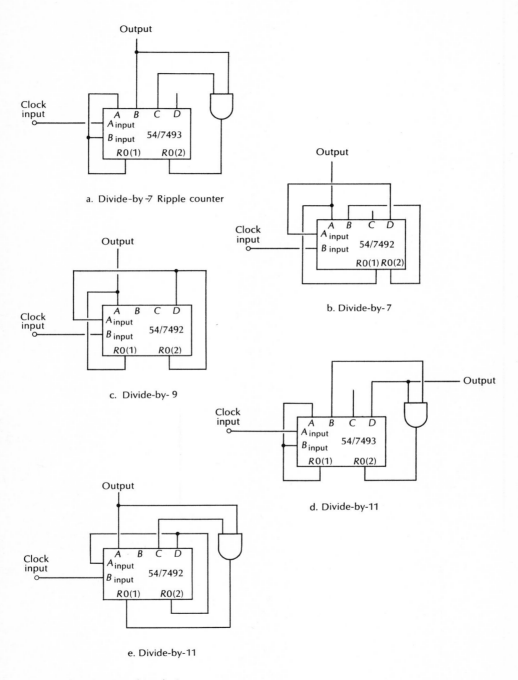

a. Divide-by-7 Ripple counter

b. Divide-by-7

c. Divide-by-9

d. Divide-by-11

e. Divide-by-11

**Figure 7-40** Various Mod Ripple Counters

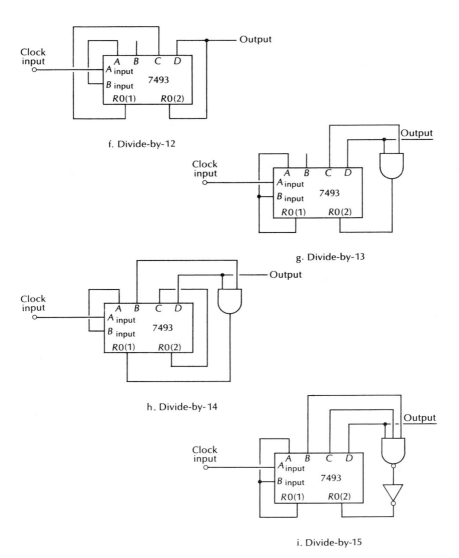

f. Divide-by-12

g. Divide-by-13

h. Divide-by-14

i. Divide-by-15

Figure 7-40 continued

1. Preset counter to count 5 modulus: $n_p = 5$
   Natural modulus: $N = 16$
   Programmed modulus: $N - n_p = 16 - 5 = 11$
2. Preset counter to count 3 modulus: $16 - 3 = 13$

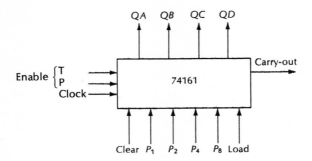

**Figure 7-41** 74161 Presettable Counter

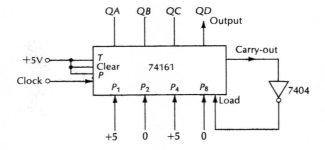

**Figure 7-42** 74161 Configured for a Mod 11

Figure 7-42 shows the 74161 programmed for modulus 11. The preset inputs are set to the difference between the natural modulus (16) $N$ and the desired modulus (11). The presets must be set to $+5$ or gnd. $P_8 = 0$, $P_4 = 1, P_2 = 0, P_1 = 1$; where $+5V = 1$.

The fact that 0000 is not available except at the natural modulus can sometimes be a problem. These counters can be cascaded for larger counts as shown in Figure 7-43.

### Problems

8. Program a 74161 counter for modulus 9, 10, and 12. List the missing binary combinations for each case.
9. The 74160 is a mod 10 version of the 74161. Look it up in the data book and show how to program it for a modulus of 6.
10. Make a drawing showing how to cascade two 74160 counters programmed for a modulus of 88.

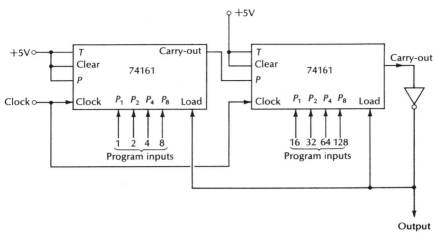

**Figure 7-43** Divide-by-1-through-256 Counter.

11. Make a drawing showing a 74160 and a 74161 cascaded and programmed for a modulus of 225.
12. Make a table of all of the presettable counters you can find in the data manual. Look in both TTL and C-MOS manuals (see Table 7-4, for example).

## 7-16 Other Programmable Counter Schemes

There are older presettable counters (the Signetics 8200 series, for example) that require additional external logic to decode the 1111 condition. These devices are still in use but they are not as convenient as the newer types. C-MOS versions are also available, some of which are bidirectional. Bidirectional TTL units are also available.

Another method of presetting counters involves presetting to some count and then counting *down* to zero. The MC 4018 is a typical example.

### Problem

13. Special challenge: Draw a circuit using the MC 4018 counter using whatever extra gates might be needed. The counter should produce binary output combinations that follow the standard truth table (in order 0000, 0001, and so on). Program the counter for a modulus of 12.

## 7-17 Application

Figure 7-44a shows a typical basic single-stage counter arrangement. The circuit is extended to three stages in part b. The signal conditioner is a Schmitt trigger or some other device for conditioning the signal.

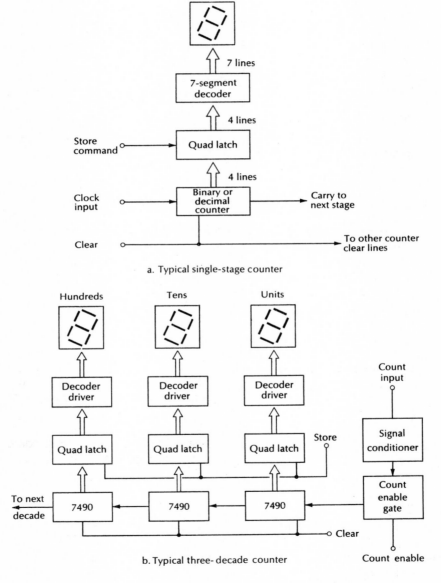

a. Typical single-stage counter

b. Typical three-decade counter

**Figure 7-44** Typical Single-Stage Counter Arrangement and Three-Decade Counter

This process is necessary if anything but a TTL compatible square wave is to be the counter. Figure 7-45a shows a typical arrangement of these elements. A typical counter gate circuit is shown in part b of this figure.

## SUMMARY

IC counters are available in a variety of forms and with a variety of capabilities.

Counters are either ripple or synchronous (or hybrid). Synchronous counters are faster but more complex. Bidirectional (*up/down*) counters are available in both synchronous and asynchronous (ripple) forms.

A counter can be made to count with any modulus by shortening the natural count. Programmable counters are variable modulus devices. The modulus is determined by setting conditions on the programming inputs.

Synchronizers are used to bring outside-world signals into synchronization with the system clock or to resynchronize the output of a counter where the ripple operation has forced the outputs out of synchronization.

In many applications, counters must be decoded to perform the desired function. A variety of IC decoders are available for this purpose.

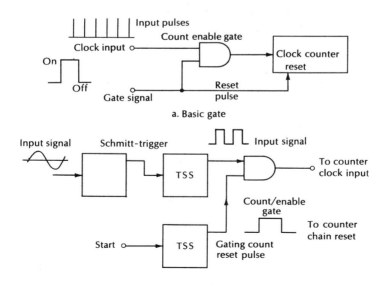

a. Basic gate

b. Conditioning and gating circuit

**Figure 7-45**  Signal Conditioning and Counter Gating

**Problems**

14. Draw the logic block diagram for a three-stage binary ripple *up*-counter. What is its natural modulus?
15. Draw the logic block diagram for a binary ripple *up/down* counter.
16. Given a six-stage binary ripple counter using flip-flops with a delay of 30 nanoseconds per flip-flop, compute the maximum operating frequency for the counter.
17. Describe the basic techniques for obtaining a counter modulus that is not an integral multiple of 2.
18. How many equivalent propagation delays are there in a five-stage synchronous counter?
19. When are synchronizing circuits necessary?
20. What kind of flip-flop should generally be used for stage one in the counter system in Figure 7-44?
21. What is an *N*-and-only-*N* circuit? What purpose does it serve?
22. Draw the logic block diagram for a four-stage binary ripple *up*-counter using type *D* flip-flops.
23. Draw the logic block diagram for a four-stage binary ripple *down*-counter using type *D* flip-flops.
24. What is the purpose of a display memory? What is its most common form?
25. Define *modulus counter*.
26. Why must reset (clear) pulses be ten microseconds (or more) wide?
27. What is a programmable counter?
28. What is a presettable counter?
29. Why are current limiting resistors required in LED display lines? (Give two reasons.)
30. What is the drive capability of a typical C-MOS decoder-driver?

# CHAPTER 8

# SHIFT REGISTERS
# AND SHIFT REGISTER COUNTERS

*Learning Objectives. Upon completion of this chapter you should:*
 1. *Be able to describe the shift register.*
 2. *Know how flip-flop counters and shift registers differ.*
 3. *Define: SISO, SIPO, PIPO, PISO.*
 4. *Be able to explain the difference between true parallel loading and preset-only loading.*
 5. *Be able to describe the characteristics of a left/right shift register.*
 6. *Be able to draw the several functional external connections for the left/right shift registers.*
 7. *Be able to describe the operating characteristics of the universal shift register.*
 8. *Be able to draw and explain the operation of a shift register ring counter.*
 9. *Be able to identify the modulus of the ring counter by the number of stages.*
 10. *Be able to draw the functional block diagram for a Johnson counter of length N.*
 11. *Be able to draw the decoding circuitry for any Johnson counter.*
 12. *Be able to define these terms: disallowed state, disallowed subroutine, self-start circuitry, self-correcting circuitry, modulus.*
 13. *Be aware of the Johnson counter's use in C-MOS.*

The shift register is a memory system consisting of flip-flops or MOS dynamic memory cells. The special feature of the shift register is that data can be transferred on command from cell to adjacent cell as many times as desired.

In the simplest type of shift register, data are entered serially one bit at a time until the desired number of bits have been entered and stored. Before each new bit enters the input, all of the previously entered bits are moved one stage (or cell) down the line to make room for the new bit. The data are shifted one stage at a time until all bits have arrived in turn at the output of the register. More complex registers provide outputs for each stage so that the entire contents of the register can be sampled in a single clock time. Parallel loading is also available on some shift registers where the entire register can be loaded in a single clock time.

The *universal* shift register is capable of right or left shift, both serial and parallel data entry and output. Because of the number of output pins required for universal operation, it is generally restricted to shift registers with only a few stages.

Shift register packages are available with a wide variety of combinations of features and lengths. TTL shift registers are available with up to about 10 cells, and MOS devices with 2000 to 4000 stages are common.

In this chapter we will be primarily concerned with basic shift register operation and the application of small registers to special counting circuits. In Chapter 10 we will study some larger shift registers and their applications.

## 8-1 The Shift Register

Shift registers are synchronous systems using $J$-$K$ flip-flops or type $D$ flip-flops. Large MOS devices use either MOS flip-flops or dynamic MOS cells.

Figure 8-1 shows a basic shift register using $J$-$K$ flip-flops. Unlike the ripple counter circuit, both $Q$ and $\bar{Q}$ outputs are used and the circuit is *not* a frequency divider.

If there is a 1 in the first stage, $Q_1$ will be *high*. On the next clock pulse the *high* on $Q_1$ will transfer to $Q_2$. The first stage will either remain as it was before the clock or change states depending on the status of its $J$ and $K$ lines. If the first stage is in condition $\bar{Q}_1 = 1$, the next clock pulse will transfer that to stage 2 and make $\bar{Q}_2 = 1$.

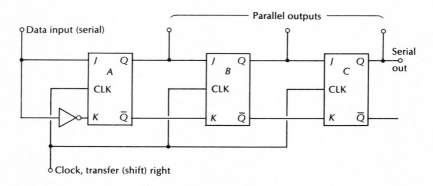

**Figure 8-1** Using J-K Flip-Flops in a Shift Register

In summary, the input conditions of each flip-flop at clock time $T$ will be transferred to the next stage at clock time $T + 1$. Notice that the first stage in Figure 8-1 uses a type $D$ input circuit, a common configuration in shift registers. It is possible to construct an entire shift register using type $D$ flip-flops as shown in Figure 8-2. Most of the latest shift registers use edge-triggered $D$ flip-flops.

The $J$-$K$ version in Figure 8-1 has a single data input in a $D$ arrangement, called a *single-rail* input. If both $J$ and $K$ were available as separate data inputs, we would have a *double-rail* input. When both $Q$ and $\bar{Q}$ are available as output, it becomes a double-rail output. If only $Q$ is used as an output, it is a single-rail output.

Single-rail inputs and outputs are more of a packaging consideration than a logical one. Assume that an eight F-F shift register is to have all $Q$'s and $\bar{Q}$'s available—this would require sixteen leads on the package with no leads available for inputs, clock, reset, GND, or $V_{cc}$. The register could only fit in a sixteen-lead package if fewer F-F's were used or the $\bar{Q}$ lines were simply not brought out of the package. In many applications the $\bar{Q}$ outputs can easily be left out or can be *derived* by using an inverter and the $Q$ output.

Shift registers are also classified as serial or parallel *in* and serial or parallel *out*. Any shift register can be used in the serial-*in*/serial-*out* mode, but not all have parallel *in* or parallel *out* capability. Parallel *in* means that the data can be loaded into all flip-flops at the same time, while for a serial *in*, each bit (0 or 1) must be loaded into the input F-F and shifted over to make room for the next bit. The process continues until the register is loaded. When parallel *out* capability exists, all $Q$'s are brought out of the package and the state of all flip-flops can be *read* at the same time. In a serial-*out* mode, the bits must be shifted out of the register one at a time to be used. The circuit in Figure 8-1 is a serial-*in* shift register with either parallel or serial *out* capability.

Shift register classifications:

a. SISO: Serial-in/serial-out     c. PISO: Parallel-in/serial-out
b. SIPO: Serial-in/parallel-out     d. PIPO: Parallel-in/parallel-out

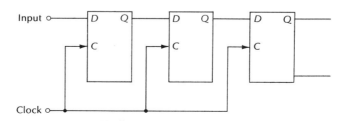

**Figure 8-2** Type D Shift Register

Table 8-1 Common TTL and C-MOS Shift Registers

| Length (Stages) | Type Number | TTL or C-MOS | Parallel Outputs | Direction | Parallel Load | Clear |
|---|---|---|---|---|---|---|
| 8 | 7491 | TTL | no | right | no | no |
| 4 | 7494 | TTL | no | right | preset only | yes |
| 4 | 7495 | TTL | yes | right/left | synchronous | no |
| 4 | 74C95 | C-MOS | yes | right/left | synchronous | no |
| 5 | 7596 | TTL | yes | right | preset only | yes |
| 8 | 74164 | TTL | yes | right | no | yes |
| 8 | 74C164 | C-MOS | yes | right | no | yes |
| 8 | 74165 | TTL | no | right | asynchronous | yes |
| 8 | 74C165 | C-MOS | no | right | asynchronous | yes |
| 8 | 74166 | TTL | no | right | synchronous | yes |
| 4 | 74194 | TTL | yes | right/left | synchronous | yes |
| 4 | 74195 | TTL | yes | right | synchronous | yes |
| 4 | 74C195 | C-MOS | yes | right | synchronous | yes |

All parallel-out registers are also capable of serial-out, and all parallel-in registers are capable of serial-in operation. The reverse of these two cases is not true.

### PARALLEL LOADING CONSIDERATIONS

Some parallel load shift registers have preset-only capability. This means that an individual 1 in a given stage cannot be changed to a 0. The entire register must first be cleared to all zeros and reloaded with altered data.

True parallel load registers allow updating at any time without clearing first. Table 8-1 lists some common TTL shift registers and, among other information, states whether the register is a true parallel load or preset-only device.

Loading may be either asynchronous or clocked. In synchronous (clocked) load devices, loading always occurs with or at the fall of the clock pulse. Most TTL shift registers clock on the positive-going transition of the clock pulse.

## 8-2 The Right/Left Shift Register

One very useful capability in shift registers is that of bidirectional shifting—right shift or left shift. This mode generally requires that both parallel inputs and parallel outputs be available along with some added gates to control the shift direction. A shift register with all of these capabilities, with a few minor additions to increase the flexibility, yields a configuration known as the *universal shift register*. See the functional block diagram for the 7495 left/right shift register in Figure 8-3.

The PE (parallel enable) controls the data entry mode (serial or parallel) and is frequently labeled *mode control*. A 0 input on PE enables all of the AND gates labeled 1. Both parallel and serial outputs are available but when the parallel inputs are disabled by the AND gates labeled 2, it is in a serial shift right circuit in this mode. A 1 on the PE (mode control) input allows parallel data to enter and load the register.

After loading, the mode control can be switched back to serial-right shift and the data shifted *right*, through the register. In this way parallel data can be converted into serial form, one bit at a time. Conversely, data can be converted from serial into parallel form by shifting the data into the register serially and taking the data from parallel outputs. The mode input should not be allowed to change states during clocking. Two clock inputs are provided so that parallel and serial entries can be made at different clock phases or rates. Proper timing of the two clocks can insure that the mode does not change too near the clocking edge of a clock pulse. A 10 ns delay is required for standard TTL after the clock pulse before mode switching can take place (although no delay is required between a mode change and next clock pulse). A 100 ns delay is required for the low-power TTL version of the left/right shift register.

The left/right shift register can be configured for a left/right serial input mode by wiring it as shown in Figure 8-4d.

### UNIVERSAL SHIFT REGISTER

The universal shift register is similar to the right/left shift register just discussed except that extra gating circuits are provided so that all modes can be obtained upon command. No external wiring is required to get the right/left shift mode. A *load* input allows the parallel loading when the input is at logical 1, and returns the register to a right/left shift mode with a logical 0 on the *load* input. The logic diagram of the 74194 universal shift register is shown in Figure 8-5.

### Problems

1. Define single-rail and double-rail inputs and outputs.
2. What can be done to obtain a $\bar{Q}$ when $\bar{Q}$'s are not brought out of the IC package?
3. Define *serial in, serial out, parallel in,* and *parallel out.*
4. Answer the following with regard to shift registers with parallel-*out* capabilities:
   a. Are $\bar{Q}$'s always available?
   b. Can a parallel-*out* register always be used for serial-*out*?
5. Describe the capabilities of the universal shift register.

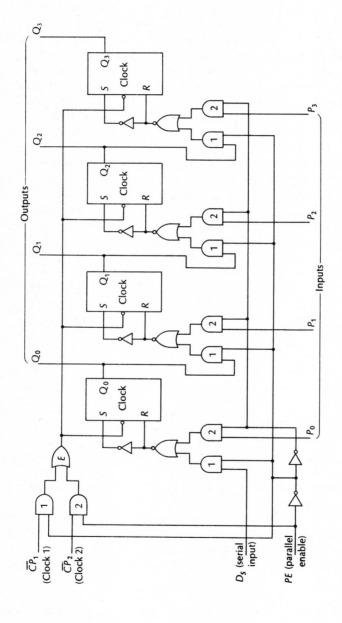

© 1974 Signetics Inc. From *Digital Linear and MOS Data Book*, pp. 2-137.
Used by permission of Signetics Inc., P.O. Box 3004, Menlo Park, Ca. 94025.

**Figure 8-3**  The 54/7495 Left/Right Shift Register

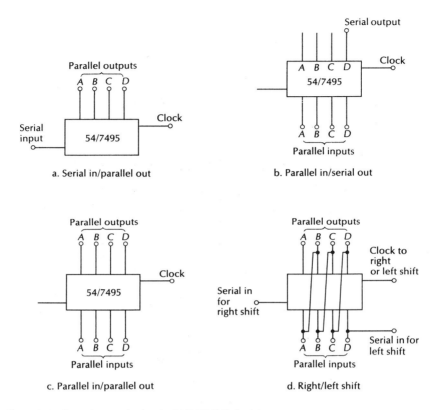

a. Serial in/parallel out

b. Parallel in/serial out

c. Parallel in/parallel out

d. Right/left shift

**Figure 8-4**   Operating Modes for the 54/7495 Shift Register

## 8-3   Other Common Shift Register Configurations

Shift registers come in a variety of forms: serial-*in*/serial-*out*, parallel-*in*/parallel-*out*, serial-*in*/parallel-*out*, parallel-*in*/serial-*out* and configurations capable of any of these combinations. In addition, there are right-shift registers, left-shift registers, and bidirectional registers. Most of these varieties are available with several bit lengths, with four-, five-, and eight-bit lengths being the most common. Table 8-1 can be used as a shift register selection guide for 54/7400 series and C-MOS shift registers.

Figures 8-6 through 8-9 show the logic diagram for typical examples from each row of the selection guide. The 54/74194 universal shift register from row 2 and the 54/7495 parallel-*in*/parallel-*out* register from row 1 (Table 8-1) have already been covered.

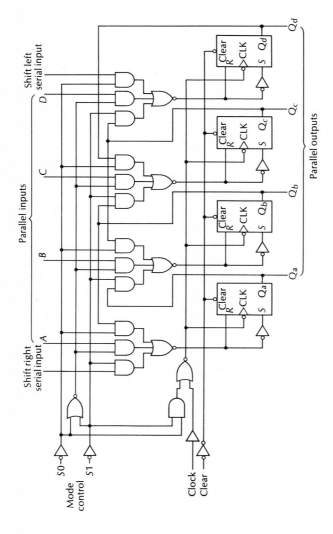

© 1974 Signetics Inc. From *Digital Linear and MOS Data Book*, pp. 2-137.
Used by permission of Signetics Inc., P.O. Box 3004, Menlo Park, Ca. 94025.

**Figure 8-5**   54/74194 Universal Shift Register

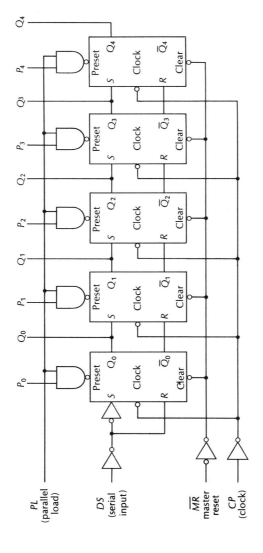

© 1974 Signetics Inc. From *Digital Linear and MOS Data Book*, pp. 2-137.
Used by permission of Signetics Inc., P.O. Box 3004, Menlo Park, Ca: 94025.

**Figure 8-6**  54/7496 Five-Bit Shift Register with Serial/Parallel In and Serial/Parallel Out (Right Shift Only)

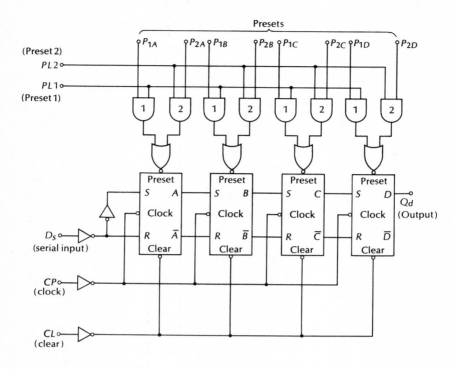

**Figure 8-7**   The 7494 Four-Bit Shift Register

Some shift registers, such as the 74165, are designed primarily for parallel-to-serial conversion. When the register is used for this purpose, data are loaded in parallel (all F-F's are set to 1 or 0 simultaneously), and the data are clocked out of their serial output, one bit at a time. The data are marched in abreast and clocked out in single file.

## 8-4   Four-Bit Data Selector/Storage Register

The 54/74L98 is not actually a shift register in the strictest sense, but it is very similar to one. As you will see by the logic diagram shown in Figure 8-10, it can be used as a shift register if properly connected. The *selected* word data are transferred to the F-F outputs on the negative-

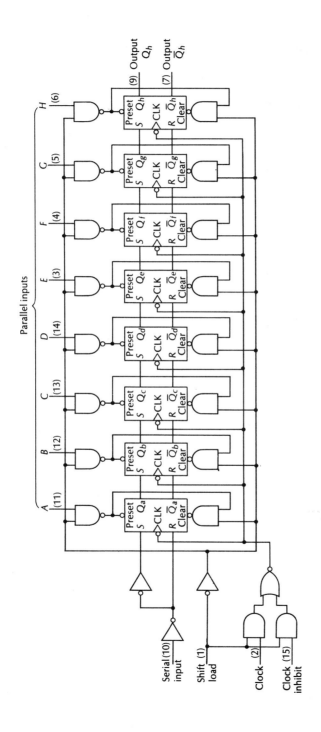

**Figure 8-8** 54/74165 Eight-Bit Shift Register

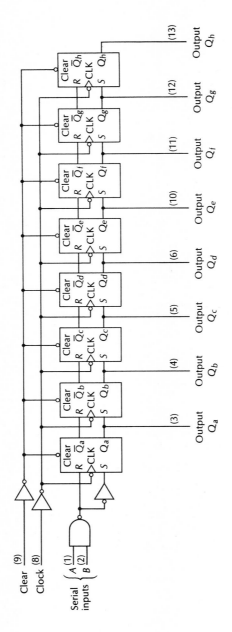

© 1974 Signetics Inc. From *Digital Linear and MOS Data Book*, pp. 2-137.
Used by permission of Signetics Inc., P.O. Box 3004, Menlo Park, Ca. 94025.

**Figure 8-9** 54/74164 Eight-Bit, Serial In-Parallel Out Shift Register

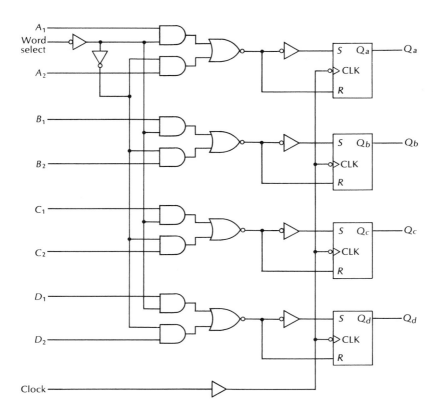

**Figure 8-10**    54/74L98 Data Selector/Storage Register

going edge of the clock pulse. Word one is *selected* by applying a logical 0 to the word-select input. A 0 on the word-select input selects word two. Two clock inputs are provided for different phases or clock rates for the two sets of data.

## 8-5    The Shift Register Ring Counter

A ring counter can be formed by loading a 1 into the leftmost F-F of a shift register, with the serial-*out* connected to the serial input, and clocking the 1 down the chain. After as many counts as there are F-F's, the 1 will have propagated out the end of the rightmost F-F and will have been returned to the one where it started. The ring counter is very inefficient in its use of flip-flops. For example, four flip-flops used in an ordinary binary counter can provide sixteen discrete outputs when decoded, while a ring counter can produce only four discrete states with four flip-flops. The key word here is *decoded*. The ring counter requires no decoding hardware, as opposed to the fairly complex decoding structures required for binary counters.

The binary counter gets $2^N$ counts, where $N$ is the number of flip-flops, where the ring counter has a maximum count of $N$. Counters with a modulus that is not a power of 2 utilize flip-flops *less* efficiently than those with a power of 2, and *more* efficiently than the ring counter. However, the ring counter is the only common one that requires no decoding. Modulus counters may skip certain possible binary combinations, often by returning to zero before the natural maximum count has been reached. The combinations skipped are called *invalid* or *disallowed* states because, if the counter is working properly, they will never occur in the counting sequence. For example, in a decimal counter the binary equivalents of 10, 11, 12, 13, 14, 15 (base 10) will never occur because the counter uses only 10 states (0–9).

In the ring counter there are always $2^N - N$ disallowed states ($N$ = the number of flip-flops). Figure 8-11 shows the functional block diagram and truth table of a four F-F ring counter. The *initiate* line resets all flip-flops but $A$ to 0 and presets $A$ to 1.

The ring counter must be cleared and loaded with a *single* 1. If noise, power supply shutdown, or some other factor causes more than a single 1 to be loaded (or no 1's at all), the counter will be loaded with a disallowed state and will start counting (when clocking begins) in a disallowed subroutine. For a four F-F ring counter there are five disallowed subroutines possible using the $2^N - N$ disallowed states. If $2^N = 16$ and $N = 4$, then $2^N - N = 16 - 4 = 12$ disallowed (or invalid) states. Once the counter is started with a disallowed state, it falls into a disallowed subroutine and will never count properly until the counter is forced by external influence to get to a state where *one and only one* F-F is at $Q = 1$. Any count sequence that includes a disallowed state is called a disallowed subroutine. In many cases it is necessary that the counter not only have just one $Q = 1$ in the chain, but also that the count begin with a specified F-F each time.

The circuit in Figure 8-11 provides an *initiate* input that sets all F-F's to 0 except $A$. $A$ is set to 1 to prevent disallowed conditions. Figure 8-11b shows the disallowed states and possible disallowed subroutines for a four F-F ring counter.

## SELF-CORRECTING FEEDBACK

The gate structure shown in Figure 8-12 can be used to automatically correct the counter when it gets locked into a disallowed subroutine. To

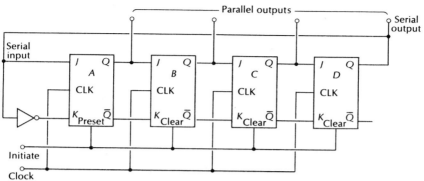

a. Logic diagram

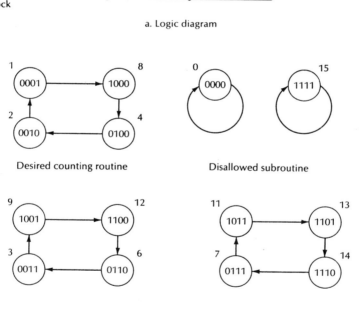

Desired counting routine          Disallowed subroutine

Disallowed subroutines

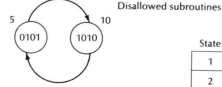

| State | 1 | 2 | 3 | 4 | |
|-------|---|---|---|---|-----------|
| 1 | 1 | 0 | 0 | 0 | Preloaded |
| 2 | 0 | 1 | 0 | 0 | |
| 3 | 0 | 0 | 1 | 0 | |
| 4 | 0 | 0 | 0 | 1 | |
| 5 | 1 | 0 | 0 | 0 | |

b. Disallowed states and disallowed
subroutines for the ring counter

c. Truth table

**Figure 8-11**   4 Flip-Flop Ring Counter

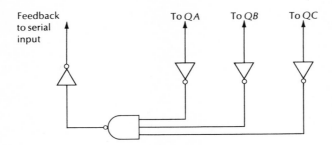

**Figure 8-12**   Feedback Circuit for a Four-Flip-Flop Ring Counter
(Self starting and self correcting)

use this circuit, you must be able to allow enough time (up to four counts) for the counter to make the correction. This configuration is self-starting even from 0000.

### THE ZERO CIRCULATING RING COUNTER

Figure 8-13 shows a self-correcting, self-starting ring counter based on the 54/7496 shift register. The circuit is a five-bit ring counter that circulates a 0 rather than a 1. The NAND gate could be eliminated if the start of each count were preceded by loading 1's into all presets except $A$ after clearing. All allowable combinations contain one 0 and four 1's. The NAND gate prevents disallowed combinations after a maximum of four counts.

## 8-6   The Johnson Counter

The Johnson counter is similar to the ring counter except that the *complement* of the output of the last flip-flop is fed back to the serial input of a shift register, resulting in a total count of $2N$, where $N$ is the number of F-F's. The Johnson counter has $2^N - 2N$ disallowed states and can get locked into disallowed subroutines. The functional block diagram of the basic Johnson counter is shown in Figure 8-14, and the truth table for this device is shown in Table 8-2.

## 8-7   Decoding the Johnson Counter

Decoding the Johnson counter involves a two-input NAND gate for each decoded output. Each flip-flop drives two gate inputs. An evaluation of the truth table (Table 8-2) reveals that only one output changes states with any given clock pulse. Decoding is synchronous because

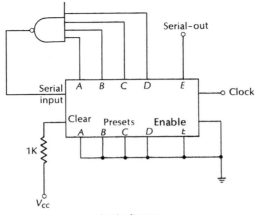

a. Logic diagram

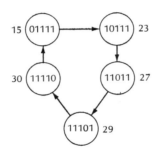

b. Allowed count routine

**Figure 8-13**   Zero-Circulating Ring Counter

only one change occurs at a time and it happens with the clock. The output changes can be more easily visualized with the help of the timing diagram in Figure 8-14. Notice that the $Q$ outputs are shifted in phase by 360° where $M$ is the counter modulus $M$, and that the phase shift continues through the second 180° if we use the $\overline{Q}$ outputs. It is the symmetry shown in the timing diagram and truth table that makes decoding a straightforward procedure. Figure 8-15 shows the decoding circuit for counters of modulus 3, 4, 5, 6, 7, 8, and 10. (Mod 9 is left as a student problem.)

If you study the even modulus decoder circuits in Figure 8-1 and the truth tables, you will observe the following pattern:

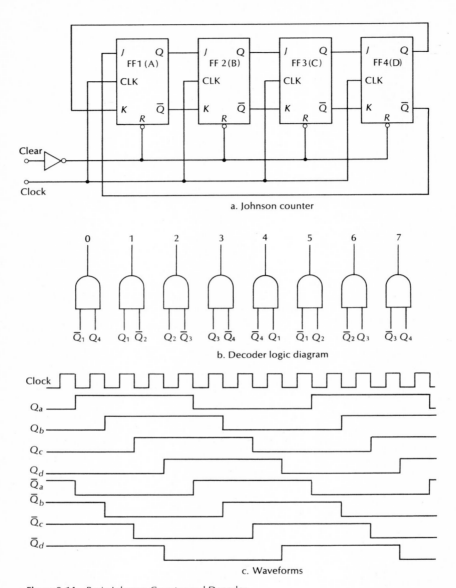

a. Johnson counter

b. Decoder logic diagram

c. Waveforms

**Figure 8-14**   Basic Johnson Counter and Decoder

(1) The $Q$'s of flip-flops $A$ and $N$ are NANDed. $N$ is the last flip-flop in the string.

(2) The $\overline{Q}$'s of flip-flops $A$ and $N$ are NANDed.

(3) In each remaining row in the truth table there is a 1-0 pair adjacent to each other. These two entries define the inputs to the

**Table 8-2** Truth Table for
the Four-Flip-Flop
Johnson Counter

| State | Flip-flop | | | |
|---|---|---|---|---|
| | A | B | C | D |
| 0 | 0 | 0 | 0 | 0 |
| 1 | 1 | 0 | 0 | 0 |
| 2 | 1 | 1 | 0 | 0 |
| 3 | 1 | 1 | 1 | 0 |
| 4 | 1 | 1 | 1 | 1 |
| 5 | 0 | 1 | 1 | 1 |
| 6 | 0 | 0 | 1 | 1 |
| 7 | 0 | 0 | 0 | 1 |
| 0 | 0 | 0 | 0 | 0 |

NAND gate for that row. No other entries in the row are used. Note these examples (see Table 8-2):

Row 1: a 1 under $A = A$ and a 0 under $B = \bar{B}$ results in $f = A \cdot \bar{B}$.
Row 2: a 1 under $B$ is followed by a 0 under $C$. The NAND gate inputs are $B$ and $\bar{C}$.
Row 6: a 0 under $B$ is adjacent to a 1 under $C$. The NAND gate inputs are $\bar{B}$ and $C$.

In the case of odd modulus number counters, one gate will be missing in the decoder as compared to that of the next higher even modulus counter. Otherwise all of the observations previously made are valid.

**Problems**

6. Write the truth table for a modulus 9 Johnson counter.
7. Draw the decoding circuit for a modulus 9 Johnson counter.
8. Write the truth table for a modulus 12 Johnson counter.
9. Draw the decoding circuit for a modulus 12 counter.

## JOHNSON COUNTER USING 7495 SHIFT REGISTER

The Johnson counter can be implemented using the 7495 shift register. An enable pulse on the mode control and clock 2 lines loads the counter with zeros, acting as a reset-to-0 function. The functional block diagram is shown in Figure 8-16. The inverter is required because the Johnson counter demands that the complement of the output be fed back to the input. In the 7495, $\bar{Q}$ outputs are not available so an inverted $Q_D$ is used. Refer to Figure 8-3 for the 7495 logic diagram.

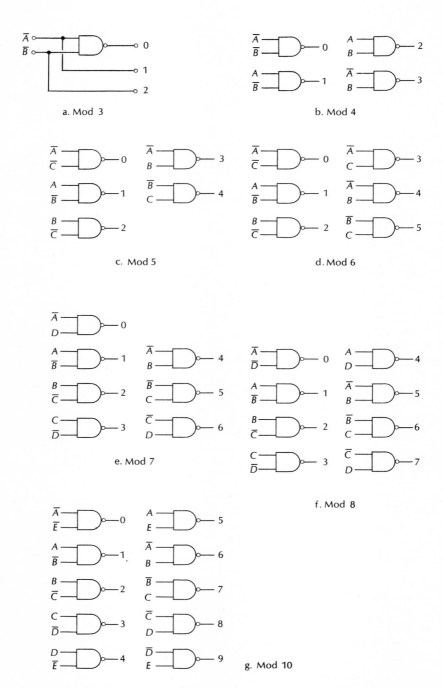

**Figure 8-15**   Johnson Counter Decoding

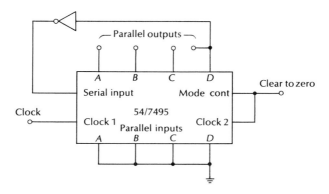

**Figure 8-16**  Johnson Counter Implemented with the 7495 Shift
Register

### SELF-STARTING, SELF-CORRECTING JOHNSON COUNTER

Figure 8-17 shows the functional block diagram of a four-F-F Johnson
counter with additional gating to provide self-correction and self-starting in the desired counting routine.

### ODD-LENGTH JOHNSON COUNTERS

So far we have been concerned with even length (2, 4, 8, and so on)
counters. An odd-length counter can be obtained by deriving the $J$
input feedback from the $\bar{Q}$ of the next-to-last flip-flop in the chain. In
many cases the $\bar{Q}$ outputs are not available and an inverter must be
used in conjunction with the $Q$ output of the next-to-last stage. Figure
8-18 shows the configuration for Johnson counters of modulus 3, 5,
7, and 10.

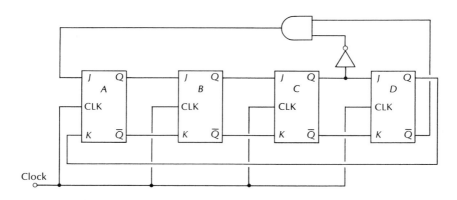

**Figure 8-17**  Four-Flip-Flop Johnson Counter with Self-Starting and Self-Correcting Gate

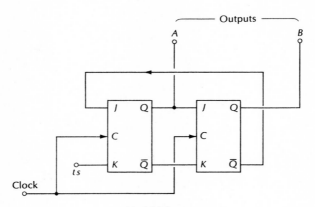

a. Mod 3 Johnson counter

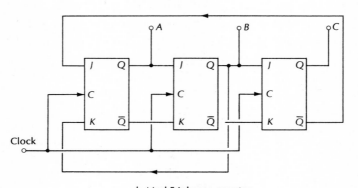

b. Mod 5 Johnson counter

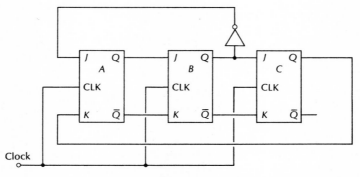

c. Mod 5 odd–length Johnson counter

**Figure 8-18** Johnson Counters

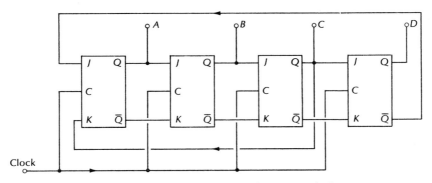

d. Mod 7 counter using 7473 for negative clocking

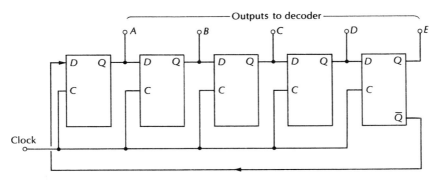

e. Mod 10 (decade) counter using type *D* flip-flops

Figure 8-18 continued

## 8-8  Johnson Counter IC's

Several C-MOS IC's are available that use Johnson counters with on-the-chip decoders. The CD 4017 decimal counter and the 4018 presettable counter are examples. C-MOS designers have found the Johnson counter attractive.

The circuit is synchronous but simpler than some of the synchronous circuits used in TTL. Decoders can be built in easily and pre-existing shift register cell designs can be used by the manufacturer.

In Chapter 10 we will examine MOS registers, recirculating registers, and additional shift register applications.

## SUMMARY

Shift registers come in various lengths, capabilities, and limitations. A particular register is selected to fit an individual job. Shift registers are classified by direction of shift capability: right-shift, left-shift, or right/ left shift. They are also categorized according to parallel or serial data entry and data exit.

Most shift registers have type $D$ inputs to the first stage. All shift registers are capable of serial input and output, but only some are capable of parallel loading (input) and (or) parallel output. Parallel loading is either preset-only, where changes in input data can be made only after clearing the entire register, or true parallel loading, where data can be changed at any time. The right/left shift register can be wired to perform any of the functions SISO, SIPO, PIPO, PISO, and right/left shift. They must, however, be connected according to the desired functions.

The universal shift register can be made to shift from one to another of all of the possibilities above by setting levels on control inputs.

Shift registers can be connected as synchronous counters by using appropriate feedback. Johnson counter decoding is simple and the counter produces clean symmetrical output signals. A number of C-MOS counters use the Johnson counter as the basic counter element with on-the-chip decoding.

### Problems

10. What is meant by parallel-to-serial conversion (shift registers)?
11. What is the natural modulus of a five-bit shift register ring counter?
12. What are the primary advantage and the primary disadvantage of the shift register ring counter?
13. What is meant by an invalid or disallowed state?
14. What is a disallowed subroutine?
15. What must be done to start a ring counter?
16. In a five-bit ring counter, how many disallowed states exist?
17. Describe self-correcting feedback.
18. What is the difference between the 1 circulating and the 0 circulating ring counter? Does either form require decoding?
19. What is the purpose of decoding a counter? In light of your answer, why is it not necessary to decode a ring counter?
20. What is the basic circuit difference between a ring counter and the Johnson counter?
21. Compare the ring and Johnson counters with respect to the number of possible counts for $N$ flip-flops?
22. How many disallowed states exist for a Johnson counter with $N$ flip-flops?

23. Is the decoding circuitry for a Johnson counter more or less complex than for a binary ripple counter?
24. Draw the functional block diagram for a mod 8 Johnson counter using the 54/7495 shift register. (See Figure 8-3.)
25. Draw the functional block diagram for a mod 8 Johnson counter with self-start/self-correction gating using the 54/7495 shift register.
26. Draw the functional block diagram of a decade (mod 10) Johnson counter using the 54/7496 shift register.

# CHAPTER 9

# COMPUTER ARITHMETIC

*Learning Objectives.    Upon completion of this chapter you should be able to:*
  1. *Write numbers in signed magnitude and complement notations.*
  2. *Perform addition and subtraction with signed magnitude and radix-minus-1 and radix complement notation.*
  3. *Perform multiplication and division using computer methods.*
  4. *Trace data through the several kinds of adder circuits.*
  5. *Relate the data flow in adder circuits to the appropriate algorithm.*
  6. *Relate multiplication and division algorithms to the circuits that perform them.*

All mathematical operations from the simplest to the most complex can be reduced to processes of simple addition and subtraction, and subtraction can also be reduced to addition. Addition could even be reduced to the level of simple counting and the manipulation of pebbles.

The adder in most computers performs the full range of mathematical operations. Even a relatively simple problem may involve a sizable number of steps. The computer works so fast that a great many simple steps can be taken in a very short time. The instructions that provide the computer with step-by-step directions for solving a problem are called an *algorithm*. The computer program can be viewed as a very long compound algorithm.

Numbers are represented either in a form called *signed magnitude* or in a form called *complement notation*. These representations have been chosen because they require simpler circuitry to implement than other methods of number representation.

In this chapter we will study the methods of number representation, and how arithmetic is performed in each system. Then we will examine the circuitry that performs addition and subtraction in each system of notation. Finally, we will see how the adder can be used to perform multiplication and division.

## DEFINITIONS OF ARITHMETIC TERMS

*Minuend:* The number from which another is to be subtracted.
*Subtrahend:* The number to be subtracted from the minuend.

*Addend:* A number to which another is to be added.

*Augend:* The number to be added to the addend. Because addition is commutative, the terms *addend* and *augend* are occasionally used interchangeably.

*Commutative:* Because $A + B = B + A$ addition is commutative and since $A \times B = B \times A$, multiplication is commutative. Because $A - B \neq B - A$, subtraction is not commutative. Division is not commutative because $A/B \neq B/A$.

*Multiplicand, Multiplier,* and *Product:*

$$
\begin{array}{r}
5 \text{ multiplicand} \\
\times 4 \text{ multiplier} \\
\hline
20 \text{ product}
\end{array}
$$

*Quotient, Dividend,* and *Remainder:*

$$
\begin{array}{r}
21 \quad \text{quotient} \\
\text{divisor} \quad 7)\overline{150} \quad \text{dividend} \\
\underline{147} \\
3 \quad \text{remainder}
\end{array}
$$

## 9-1 Algorithms

The arithmetic section of a computer is generally little more than a memory and logic system capable of performing binary addition. Subtraction is performed by a procedure known as *complement arithmetic,* in which the subtrahend is complemented and the difference found by addition. Multiplication can be accomplished by successive additions, and division can be performed by successive subtractions.

A computer must have detailed instructions telling it when to add, when to complement, where to store partial and finished results, and where to find numbers and new instructions for the next operation. Such instructions are called a *program.* There are three kinds of programs: hardwired, firmware, and software. Software is the most versatile of the three because it can be anything that can be conceived, within the limitations of the machine. It consists of a written detailed list of all of the operations a computer is to perform and the order in which they must be performed, along with the memory locations of data to be stored and retrieved during the problem.

These instructions are then put on punch cards, tape, or some other medium whereby they can be loaded into the computer's memory. The data to be worked with is also loaded into the memory when the *go* button is pushed; the machine then follows the program stored in its memory, *fetching* new data and further instructions at its own rate without human intervention until the problem is finished.

An algorithm is a special kind of program that instructs the computer in how (step-by-step) to use the adder to perform subtraction, multiplication, and division, to extract roots, and so on. Algorithms were not developed for computers, however. The example that we will study here, known as Newton's method, was developed by Isaac Newton. It is a commonly used algorithm in modern electronic computing.

The difference between an algorithm, or computer program, and most other lists of instructions—a recipe, for example—is that the number of steps in an algorithm is not known in advance. Another important aspect of an algorithm is the concept of varying degrees of correctness. An algorithm may be iterated (repeated a number of times) until the solution reaches the answer that is correct to some predetermined value. The program is complete only when the proper degree of correctness is reached.

Suppose, for example, that we wish to extract an accurate square root using a pocket calculator that is capable of only add, subtract, multiply, and divide functions. Let us assume the problem is to find the square root of 125. Here is the algorithm for extracting the square root (Newton's method):

a. Call the square root $r$.
b. Let $X$ = the number for which the square root is to be found.
c. Let $S$ = 0.00001 (some predetermined small value).

| Algorithm Step | Instruction |
|---|---|
| 1. | Set: $r = 1$ |
| 2. | Compute: $r = \frac{1}{2}(x/r = r)$ |
| 3. | Evaluate: |
| | Is $(r^2 - X) \lessgtr S$? |
| | a. If yes, stop. The problem is finished. |
| | b. If no, return to step 2 and repeat. |

The first step in the algorithm establishes a starting point. Setting $r = 1$ as a first approximation is done because the computer cannot easily make a reasonable rough approximation of the square root of a number. If a fair approximation can be made, it takes fewer steps to get to an answer; where we start is otherwise unimportant. Extra steps are of little consequence at computer speeds, but for our example let us start by setting $r = 10$. $10^2 = 100$, which is not far from 125, but is enough to demonstrate the method.

Considering the limitations of the calculator we are using for the example, suppose we break steps 2 and 3 down into the appropriate substeps. We will retain the notation $n^2$, but we will have to implement it by multiplying $n$ by itself (assuming the calculator has no $n^2$ key). Here is the algorithm for a calculator:

| *Algorithm Step* | *Instruction* |
|---|---|
| Step 1. | Set $r =$ (first approximation of $x$); in this case it is 10. Let $S$ equal 0.0001. |

a. Set $r$ equal to 10.
b. (1) $x/r =$
   (2) $+r =$
   (3) $\div 2 = r$ (the revised approximation)
c. Evaluate
   (1) $r^2 =$
   (2) $-x = S$   stop or reiterate

First iteration

Step 2.
  a. $x/r = 125/10 = 12.5$
  b. $+r = 22.5$
  c. $\div 2 = 11.25$

Step 3.
  a. $r^2 = 11.25 \times 11.25 = 126.5625$
  b. $-x = 1.5625$
       $1.5625 > S$

Second iteration

Step 2.
  a. $x/r = 125/11.25 = 11.11111$
  b. $+r = 22.36111$
  c. $\div 2 = 11.18056$

Step 3.
  a. $r^2 = 11.18056 \times 11.18056 = 125.00492$
  b. $-x = 0.00492$
       $0.00492 > S$

Third iteration

Step 2.
  a. $x/r = 125/11.18056 = 11.180119$
  b. $+r = 22.360679$
  c. $\div 2 = 11.180339$

Step 3.
  a. Evaluate
   (1) $r^2 = 124.99998$
   (2) $-x = 0.00002$
        $0.00002 < 0.0001$

End.

Newton's method is an excellent example of an algorithm suitable to mechanization because it consists of the repetition of a few very simple steps. From a human standpoint (doing it by hand at any rate), this method is tedious, but it is ideally suited for digital systems.

**Problems**

Using Newton's method, find:
1. $\sqrt{14}$

2. $\sqrt{490}$

Assume $S = 0.0001$.

### BINARY REPRESENTATIONS FOR ARITHMETIC OPERATIONS

There are three common methods used to represent numbers in binary computers. In most cases, both positive and negative numbers must be handled. The choice of either signed magnitude, radix complement, or radix-minus-one complement notation affects the logical design of the system.

## 9-2 Signed Magnitude Representation

In signed magnitude representation part of the computer word is used for the absolute value in binary. Another part of the word is reserved for the sign using 0 to represent + and 1 to represent −. For example, assume an eight-bit word with the leftmost bit reserved for the sign.

a.

| *Sign* | *Number* |
|--------|----------|
| 0 | 0000110 |

| + | 6 |
|---|---|

b.

| *Sign* | *Number* |
|--------|----------|
| 1 | 0000110 |

| − | 6 |
|---|---|

**Problems**

Express the following decimal numbers in signed magnitude binary representation:

3. −64      4. 125      5. −125      6. 14

The algorithms used for arithmetic operations must include rules for dealing with signs:

*Addition algorithm (signed magnitude)*
1. To add numbers with like signs, add the magnitudes and affix the common sign.
2. To add numbers with unlike signs, find the *difference* of the magnitudes and use the sign of the number with the largest magnitude.

*Subtraction algorithm (signed magnitude)*
1. Change the sign of the subtrahend.
2. *Add* the subtrahend, with the changed sign, to the minuend.

## 9-3  The Radix Complement

Because complement arithmetic has many advantages in terms of ease of mechanization, it is the most popular form for representing binary numbers. The radix complement of a computer number is defined as:

$$\text{Radix complement} = R_n - N$$

*where R* is the radix
      *n* is the number of bits in the computer word
      *N* is the number to be complemented

**Example**

If $R = 10$ and $n = 5$, find the radix complement of 976:

$$10^5 - 976$$
$$100000 - 976 = 99024$$

The radix-minus-1 complement is one less than the radix complement and can be found as follows:
Find the radix-minus-1 complement of 976:

$$
\begin{array}{ll}
99999 & \\
-976 & \\
\hline
99023 & \text{radix-minus-1 complement} \\
+1 & \text{adding 1} \\
\hline
99024 & \text{we get the radix complement}
\end{array}
$$

## 9-4  Addition and Subtraction

**BINARY ADDITION**

The following defines the addition of binary digits *A* and *B*:

| $A + B$ | *Sum* | *Carry* |
|---|---|---|
| $0 + 0$ | $= 0$ | 0 |
| $0 + 1$ | $= 1$ | 0 |
| $1 + 0$ | $= 1$ | 0 |
| $1 + 1$ | $= 0$ | 1 |
| $1 + 1 + 1$ | $= 1$ | 1 |

The last case includes a carry from the previous column.

**Examples**

1.  1
    +1
    ──
    10

3.  0
    +1
    ──
    1

5.  111   carry
    1101
    +0111
    ─────
    10100

2.  1
    +0
    ──
    1

4.  0
    +0
    ──
    0

6.  1010
    +1101
    ─────
    10111

## BINARY SUBTRACTION

Subtraction follows the same pattern as that used in decimal subtraction except that a *borrow* involves borrowing a 2 from the next higher order column instead of a 10 as in decimal subtraction.

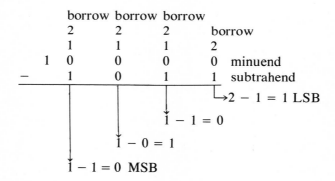

**Problems**

Add the following binary numbers:

7.   10110
     +11101
     ──────

9.   00111
     +10101
     ──────

8.   100110
     +010100
     ───────

10.  010111
     +111001
     ───────

## 9-5  Binary Complement Arithmetic

In the binary system complementing is easily mechanized using an inverter or an exclusive-OR true complement gate. The radix-minus-1 complement requires only that all ones be changed to zeros and all zeros to ones.

The radix complement can then be obtained by simply adding 1. The add 1 operation can be performed by the existing adder hardware, and no subtraction operation is required to get either the one's or two's complement.

Find the one's and the two's complement of each of the following binary numbers:

1. 010110 the number
101001 the one's complement
   +1 adding 1

101010 the two's complement

2. 1011000 the number
0100111 the one's complement
   +1 adding 1

0101000 the two's complement

## Problems

Find the one's complement and the two's complement of the following binary numbers:

| | | |
|---|---|---|
| 11. 10101101 | 13. 110101011 | 15. 0100011 |
| 12. 11100011 | 14. 000111 | 16. 001000 |

## FINDING THE TWO'S COMPLEMENT BY INSPECTION

The following shortcut procedure can make finding the two's complement easier.

$$2^6 \cdots 2^0$$
1 0 1 1 0 0 0  − LSB (least significant bit)

MSB ⎯⎯⎯⎯⎯⎯⏌
(most significant bit)

1. Start at the LSB and inspect each bit in turn, moving toward the MSB.
2. For each 0 in the number, change it to a 1.
3. When you encounter the first 1 in the number, retain that 1 in the complement.
4. Thereafter, replace all 1's by 0's and all 0's by 1's, including the sign bit on the left of the binary point.

The sign is included as a part of the binary number in two's complement notation.

## TWO'S COMPLEMENT NOTATION

In two's complement notation the leftmost bit is reserved as a sign bit. A positive number is written as a normal binary number with a 0 as a sign bit. A negative number is expressed as the two's complement with a 1 for the sign bit. Consider the following examples:

a. One's complement representation of +5 and −5 using an eight-bit register:

b. The two's complement representation of +5 and −5 using an eight-bit word.

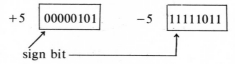

Complement representation is easy to implement in digital hardware, and addition and subtraction can be performed without regard for the sign of the number. The following examples illustrate typical addition operations using two's complement notation. The boxes represent registers.

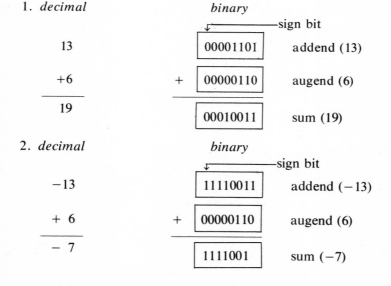

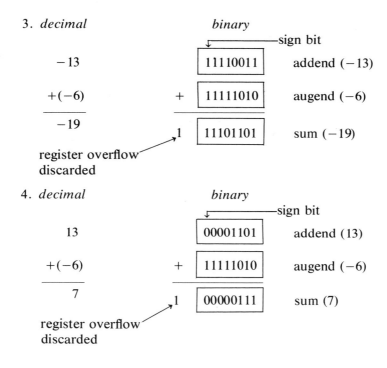

3. *decimal*                  *binary*

                                          ─── sign bit
       −13                   11110011        addend (−13)

     +(−6)               +   11111010        augend (−6)
     ─────                   ─────────
       −19                 1 11101101        sum (−19)

   register overflow
   discarded

4. *decimal*                  *binary*

                                          ─── sign bit
        13                   00001101        addend (13)

     +(−6)               +   11111010        augend (−6)
     ─────                   ─────────
         7                 1 00000111        sum (7)

   register overflow
   discarded

## SUBTRACTION

Subtraction is performed by taking the two's complement of the subtrahend and *adding* it to the minuend. The process is illustrated by the following examples.

1. *decimal*                  *binary*

         6                   00000110        minuend (6)

     −(−13)              −   11110011        subtrahend (−13)
     ─────
        19                   00000110        minuend (6)

                         +   00001101        complement of subtrahend
                             ─────────
                             00010011        difference (19)

2. *decimal*                    *binary*

6                   | 00000110 |         minuend (6)

−13          −    | 00001101 |         subtrahend (13)

− 7               | 00000110 |         minuend (6)

          +      | 11110011 |         complement of subtrahend

                  | 11111001 |         difference (−7)


3. *decimal*                    *binary*

13                 | 00001101 |         minuend (13)

− 6          −    | 00000110 |         subtrahend (6)

7                  | 00001101 |         minuend (13)

          +      | 11111010 |         complement of subtrahend

            1    | 00000111 |         difference (7)

register
overflow discarded


4. *decimal*                    *binary*

−13               | 11110011 |         minuend (−13)

− 6          −    | 00000110 |         subtrahend (−6)

−19               | 11110011 |         minuend (−13)

          +      | 11111010 |         complement of subtrahend

            1    | 11101101 |         difference (−19)

register overflow
discarded

**Problems**

Perform the following additions using two's complement notation:
17. 22 + 11        20. −14 + 29
18. 16 + (−8)       21. (−66) + (−100)
19. −6 + 12        22. 49 + 68
Perform the following subtractions using two's complement notation:
23. (−22) − (−14)     26. (−16) − 64
24. 22 − (−14)      27. 64 − 16
25. (−22) − 14      28. 44 − 72

## 9-6  Floating Point Notation

Floating point notation is the computer representation of numbers written in scientific notation. In fixed point notation the proper positioning of the decimal point requires significant effort on the part of the programmer. Scientific notation (floating point) is easier for the programmer and has the specific advantage that nonsignificant zeros need not be stored. The part that is normally the units part (mantissa) is carried as a fraction. The value $.642136 \times 10^{10}$ could be stored as:

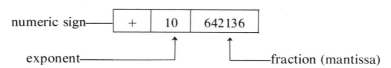

Because the exponent may require a range of from +99 to −99, some way of indicating the sign of the exponent is necessary. The most common approach is to *bias* the exponent by adding to it some large value such as 64. If the exponent part is positive and is less than 64, it is negative. If the bias is 64, the number $0.642136 \times 10^{-3}$ would be represented and stored as:

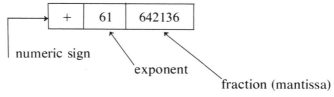

The value −419632 would be represented as:

| − | 70 | . 419632 |

When the representation is in binary, as is normally the case, a sixteen-bit floating point word would be represented and stored as:

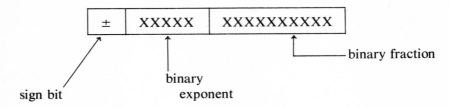

The leftmost digit indicates the bias figure, in this case 10000 (decimal 64). The binary exponent represents a power of 2.

$$\text{for: } 10101.10_2 = .1010110 \times 10^{101},$$

where $10_2^{101} = 2_{10}^5$

The *radix number* in *any* radix is 10. The number would be represented and stored in a register as:

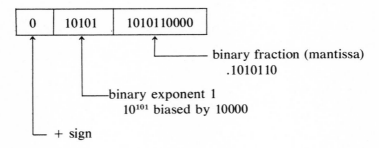

Write each of the following numbers in (a) sign magnitude notation, (b) two's complement notation, and (c) one's complement notation. Write all results in binary.

29. $26_{10}$     32. $-26_{10}$     34. $-11_{10}$
30. $19_{10}$     33. $-19_{10}$     35. $-44_{10}$
31. $11_{10}$

## 9-7   Binary Addition and the Half Adder

The several binary combinations and their sums are:

$$
\begin{array}{cccc}
0 & 0 & 1 & 1 \\
+0 & +1 & +0 & +1 \\
\hline
0 & 1 & 1 & 10
\end{array}
$$

— augend ($A$)
— addend ($B$)
— sum ($S$)
— carry ($C$)

**Table 9-1**  Binary Addition

| $A + B =$ Sum | Carry |  | A | B | Sum | Minterms |  | A | B | Carry | Minterms |
|---|---|---|---|---|---|---|---|---|---|---|---|
| $0 + 0 =$  0 | 0 |  | 0 | 0 | 0 |  |  | 0 | 0 | 0 |  |
| $0 + 1 =$  1 | 0 |  | 0 | 1 | 1 | $(\bar{A}\,B)$ |  | 0 | 1 | 0 |  |
| $1 + 0 =$  1 | 0 |  | 1 | 0 | 1 | $(A\,\bar{B})$ |  | 1 | 0 | 0 |  |
| $1 + 1 =$  0 | 1 |  | 1 | 1 | 0 |  |  | 1 | 1 | 1 | $(A \cdot B)$ |

Sum equation: sum $= \bar{A}B + A\bar{B}$
This is the exclusive-OR function and
and can be written as sum $= A \oplus B$.

a. Addition table              b. Sum truth table              c. Carry truth table

Table 9-1 shows the binary addition table and the same table written in truth table form. An examination of minterms yields the equation $S = \bar{A} \cdot B + A \cdot \bar{B}$. You may recognize this as the exclusive-OR function $S = A \oplus B$.

The truth table for the carry function is identical to the truth table for the AND gate. Figure 9-1 shows two representations for the implementation of a circuit to perform binary addition.

The circuit shown in Figure 9-1 is called a *half adder* because it does not have a provision for adding a carry from a preceding addition. The functional block diagram for the half adder is shown in Figure 9-2.

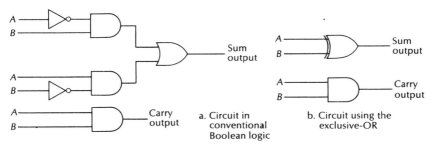

a. Circuit in conventional Boolean logic

b. Circuit using the exclusive-OR

**Figure 9-1**  Logic Circuit to Perform Binary Addition

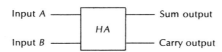

**Figure 9-2**  Half Adder Block Diagram Symbol

**Addition Examples**

1.  $$111 \text{ —— carry}$$
    $$1011 \text{ —— addend}$$
    $$\underline{+0101} \text{ —— augend}$$
    $$10000$$
    carry

2.  $$11 \text{ —— carry}$$
    $$0110 \text{ —— addend}$$
    $$\underline{0010} \text{ —— augend}$$
    $$1000$$

## 9-8 The Full Adder

Consider the following addition problem:

$$111 \text{ —— carry}$$
$$1011 \text{ —— } A$$
$$\underline{+1111} \text{ —— } B$$
$$11010$$

carry

Notice that in the second and fourth columns (from the left) we ended up with three ones to be added as a result of a carry from the preceding addition. A full adder involves three variables: the addend, the augend, and the carry from the previous addition. Because the bits may be added in any order, we can call them $A$, $B$, and $C$ on the truth table in any order. We must now expand our set of addition rules to include the possibility of a carry.

**ADDITION COMBINATIONS WHEN A CARRY IS TO BE ADDED**

| $A$ | $B$ | $C$ | Sum | Carry | |
|---|---|---|---|---|---|
| | | | $2^0$ | $2^1$ | |
| $0 + 0 + 0$ | | $= 0$ | | $0$ | $A$—Addend |
| $0 + 0 + 1$ | | $= 1$ | | $0$ | $B$—Augend |
| $0 + 1 + 0$ | | $= 1$ | | $0$ | $C$—Carry from previous addition |
| $0 + 1 + 1$ | | $= 0$ | | $1$ | |
| $1 + 0 + 0$ | | $= 1$ | | $0$ | |
| $1 + 0 + 1$ | | $= 0$ | | $1$ | |
| $1 + 1 + 0$ | | $= 0$ | | $1$ | |
| $1 + 1 + 1$ | | $= 1$ | | $1$ | |

**Table 9-2**  Full Adder Truth Table

| m | A | B | C | Sum | Carry |
|---|---|---|---|-----|-------|
| 0 | 0 | 0 | 0 | 0 | 0 |
| 1 | 0 | 0 | 1 | 1 | 0 |
| 2 | 0 | 1 | 0 | 1 | 0 |
| 3 | 0 | 1 | 1 | 0 | 1 |
| 4 | 1 | 0 | 0 | 1 | 0 |
| 5 | 1 | 0 | 1 | 0 | 1 |
| 6 | 1 | 1 | 0 | 0 | 1 |
| 7 | 1 | 1 | 1 | 1 | 1 |

The bottom row involves the addition of three units, but there is no three-weight digit in binary so it must be written as 11 ($2^1 + 2^0$). Table 9-2 shows the truth table version of the addition table including the carry from a previous addition. If we combine the minterms for the sum equation we get:

$$S = ABC_{n-1} + A\bar{B}\bar{C}_{n-1} + \bar{A}\bar{B}C_{n-1} + \bar{A}B\bar{C}_{n-1}$$

and for the carry equation we get:

$$C_n = \bar{A}BC_{n-1} + A\bar{B}C_{n-1} + AB\bar{C}_{n-1} + ABC_{n-1}$$

We can plot both equations on the Karnaugh map in Table 9-3 to see if they can be simplified. It is apparent that the sum equation cannot be simplified. The carry equation reduces to:

$$C_n = BC_{n-1} + AC_{n-1} + AB$$

The logic circuits for the full adder sum and carry functions are shown in Figure 9-3.

**Table 9-3**  Karnaugh Maps for the Full Adder

a. Sum map                           b. Carry map

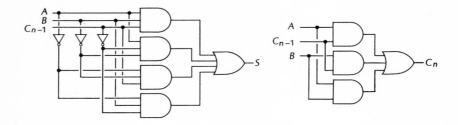

**Figure 9-3** Full Adder Logic Diagram

## 9-9 A Full Adder Composed of Two Half Adders

In this section we will introduce a useful shortcut, practice some important algebraic manipulations, and see how two half adders can be combined to form a full adder (Figure 9-4 shows the circuit for doing so).

We will use the letters $A$, $B$, and $C$ as variables. Table 9-2 shows what is expected from any full adder, including one composed of two half adders. An examination of the diagram in Figure 9-4 shows that the output of half adder 1 forms one input of half adder 2. The minterm equation is:

$$S = (\overline{A} \cdot \overline{B} \cdot C) + (\overline{A} \cdot B \cdot \overline{C}) + (A \cdot \overline{B} \cdot \overline{C}) + (A \cdot B \cdot C)$$

Call one input to the second half adder $R$ (the useful shortcut) and write the sum equation for the second half adder, using $C$ and $R$ to set up the initial equation. The sum equation for the second half adder can be written first in terms of $C$ and $R$. The more complex sum output, which feeds into it, can be substituted after the basic equation has been set up. The equation is as follows:

$$S = (\overline{C} \cdot R) + (C \cdot \overline{R}), \text{ (or } S = C \oplus R)$$

Substituting the output of the first half adder for $R$, where

$$R = (A \cdot \overline{B}) + (\overline{A} \cdot B)$$

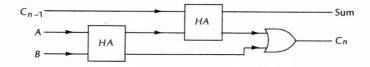

**Figure 9-4** Full Adder Composed of Two Half Adders

we get

$$S = \overline{C} \cdot [(A \cdot \overline{B}) + (\overline{A} \cdot B)] + C \cdot \overline{[(A \cdot \overline{B}) + (\overline{A} \cdot B)]}$$

Multiplying the first complex term through by $\overline{C}$, we get:

$$(\overline{C} \cdot A \cdot \overline{B}) + (\overline{C} \cdot \overline{A} \cdot B)$$

The second term also requires multiplying out by $C$, but first clear the long complement bar.

$$C \cdot [(\overline{A} + B) \cdot (A + \overline{B})]$$

Multiplying through by $C$, we get the following products:

$$C \cdot \overline{A} \cdot A$$
$$C \cdot \overline{A} \cdot \overline{B}$$
$$C \cdot B \cdot A$$
$$C \cdot B \cdot \overline{B}$$

The first (and last) term drops out, because ($A$ and $\overline{A}$ and $B$ and $\overline{B}$) cannot coexist, or, stated another way, $A \cdot \overline{A} = 0$ and $C \cdot 0 = 0$. This leaves us with

$$(C \cdot \overline{A} \cdot B) + (C \cdot B \cdot A)$$

Combining the results of the two simplified sum terms, we get a final equation (1), and by rearranging we get (2).

(1) $S = (\overline{C} \cdot A \cdot \overline{B}) + (\overline{C} \cdot \overline{A} \cdot B) + (C \cdot \overline{A} \cdot \overline{B}) + (C \cdot A \cdot B)$
(2) $S = (\overline{A} \cdot \overline{B} \cdot C) + (\overline{A} \cdot B \cdot \overline{C}) + (A \cdot \overline{B} \cdot \overline{C}) + (A \cdot B \cdot C)$

The second equation (2) is the same equation we derived from Table 9-2.

Now analyze the carry circuit for the full adder composed of two half adders. Table 9-2b is the truth table for the carry circuit of any three-bit binary full adder. The minterm equation is:

$$C_n = (\overline{A} \cdot B \cdot C) + (A \cdot \overline{B} \cdot C) + (A \cdot B \cdot \overline{C}) + (A \cdot B \cdot C)$$

The simplified equation is

$$C_n = (A \cdot B) + (A \cdot C) + (B \cdot C)$$

Examine the circuit in Figure 9-4. The OR gate has $A \cdot B$ as one input. The second input is taken from the number 2 half adder's carry output. The second half adder's inputs are $C$ and $R$, where

$$R = (\overline{A} \cdot B) + (A \cdot \overline{B})$$

The carry equation is

$$C_n = A \cdot B + C \cdot R$$

Substituting $\overline{A} \cdot B + A \cdot \overline{B}$ for $R$, we get

$$C_n = A \cdot B + C \cdot (\overline{A} \cdot B) + (A \cdot \overline{B})$$

Multiplying by C in the second term, we get:

$$C_n = A \cdot B + (\overline{A} \cdot B \cdot C) + (A \cdot \overline{B} \cdot C)$$

Expanding the first term,

$$C_n = A \cdot B \cdot C + A \cdot B \cdot \overline{C} + \overline{A} \cdot B \cdot C + A \cdot \overline{B} \cdot C$$

which, in a slightly different order, is the same equation as derived from Table 9-2b.

### SUBTRACTION USING THE RADIX AND RADIX-MINUS-1 COMPLEMENT

Subtraction in parallel machines is nearly always performed by adding either the radix or the radix-minus-1 complement of the subtrahend to the minuend. The method of subtracting through addition with complements can be illustrated by some examples.

### Radix Complement Example

Subtract $124_{10}$ from $125_{10}$ by means of the radix complement.

1. Generating the complement of $124_{10}$, we have:

$$\begin{array}{r} 1000_{10} \\ -124_{10} \\ \hline 876_{10} \end{array}$$

2. Adding $125_{10}$ to the complement of $124_{10}$, we have:

$$\begin{array}{r} 125_{10} \\ +876_{10} \\ \hline 1\ 001_{10} \end{array}$$

3. The 1 generated at the far left is considered an overflow and is not part of the result. It does, however, provide one important bit of information. The fact that the overflow 1 was generated indicates that the result of the subtraction is a positive number.

**Example**  Subtract $125_{10}$ from $124_{10}$ by means of the radix complement.

1. Generating the radix complement of $125_{10}$, we have

$$\begin{array}{r} 1000 \\ -125 \\ \hline 875 \end{array}$$

2. Adding $124_{10}$ to the radix complement of $125_{10}$ gives us

$$\begin{array}{r} 875 \\ +124 \\ \hline 999 \end{array}$$

3. In this case there is no overflow, which indicates that the answer is a negative number and that the final result will be obtained after this result has been complemented. Complementing the answer for step 2 yields

$$\begin{array}{r} 1000 \\ -999 \\ \hline 0001 \end{array}$$

The absence of an overflow in step 2 indicates a negative sign or a 0. Thus the final result is $-1_{10}$.

In all three previously discussed systems of binary signed number representation, negative numbers are written in complement form and the result would be correct at the end of step 2, and the recomplementing operation would *not* be performed.

### THE RADIX-MINUS-1 COMPLEMENT

If the radix-minus-1 complement is to be used, the computer must "know" when to add 1 to the result and when to withhold it. When the result of a subtraction is a positive number, an overflow is generated. This tells the computer to add 1, and the operation is known as an end-around carry. Since an overflow is not generated when the result of a subtraction is negative, there is no end-around carry. The absence of the overflow is, in a sense, an instruction to complement again and to affix a negative sign to the result.

Let us repeat the two previous examples using the $R - 1$ complement. Subtract $124_{10}$ from $125_{10}$ using the $R - 1$ complement.

1. Finding the $R - 1$ complement of 124:

$$\begin{array}{r} 999 \\ -124 \\ \hline 875 \end{array}$$

2. Adding 125 to the complement of 124:

$$\begin{array}{r} 125 \\ +875 \\ \hline 1000 \end{array}$$

$\llcorner\!\!\longrightarrow 1$    end-around carry

$$\begin{array}{r} \hline +001 \end{array}$$    result

The fact that an end-around carry was generated indicates that the result is a positive number.

Now subtract $125_{10}$ from $124_{10}$ using the $R - 1$ complement.

1. Finding the $R - 1$ complement of 125:

$$\begin{array}{r} 999 \\ -125 \\ \hline 874 \end{array}$$

2. Adding 124 to the complement of 125:

$$\begin{array}{r} 124 \\ +874 \\ \hline 998 \qquad \text{result} \end{array}$$

No end-around carry is generated; the sign is negative and the result must be recomplemented to get the absolute value.

3. Taking the $R - 1$ complement of 998:

$$\begin{array}{r} 999 \\ -998 \\ \hline -001 \end{array}$$

The result is $-1$.

**Problems**

Using the radix complement, carry out the following subtractions (all radix 10 numbers):

36. $1257 - 1134$     38. $4293 - 3971$

37. $59 - 67$     39. $3971 - 4293$

Perform the following subtractions using the diminished radix complement (all radix 10 numbers):

40. $1257 - 1134$     42. $4293 - 3971$

41. $59 - 67$     43. $3971 - 4293$

## 9-10 Addition and Subtraction Using Sign and Magnitude Binary Representation

The following examples illustrate addition and subtraction procedures for binary numbers represented in sign and magnitude notation.

a. Adding two positive numbers

$+11_{10} = \boxed{0 \quad 01011}$    sign / magnitude

$+13_{10} = \boxed{0 \quad 01101}$

$+24 \;\; = \boxed{0 \quad 11000}$

To add two positive numbers, add the magnitudes and use the common sign $(0 = +, 1 = -)$.

b. Adding two negative numbers

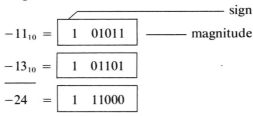

To add two negative numbers, add the magnitudes and use the common sign.

c. Adding two numbers with unlike signs
(1) Augend magnitude larger

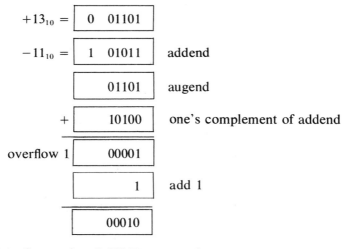

To add two numbers with unlike signs, add the augend to the complement of the addend. Then add the end-around carry to the sum. Affix the sign of the augend to the final sum (the sign of the number with the largest magnitude).

(2) Addend magnitude larger or equal

$+11_{10} = $ | 0   01011

$-13_{10} = $ | 1   01101

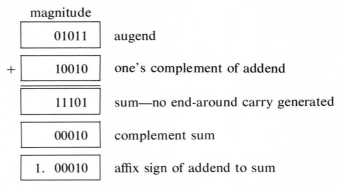

magnitude

|        |         |                                          |
|--------|---------|------------------------------------------|
|        | 01011   | augend                                   |
| +      | 10010   | one's complement of addend               |
|        | 11101   | sum—no end-around carry generated        |
|        | 00010   | complement sum                           |
|        | 1. 00010 | affix sign of addend to sum             |

To add two numbers with unlike signs, add the augend to the complement of the addend. There is no end-around carry, so the sum must be complemented. Affix the sign of addend (the sign of the number with the largest magnitude).

### SUMMARY OF SIGNED MAGNITUDE ALGORITHMS

a. Adding two positive or two negative numbers
   (1) Add magnitudes.
   (2) Affix the common sign to the sum.

b. Adding two numbers with unlike signs and with the *augend* having the *larger* magnitude
   (1) Add the augend magnitude to the complement of the addend magnitude.
   (2) Add the end-around carry to the sum (magnitude part).
   (3) Affix the sign of the number with the larger magnitude, in this case the sign of the augend.

c. Adding two numbers with unlike signs and with the *addend* having the *larger* magnitude
   (1) Add the augend magnitude to the complement of the addend magnitude.
   (2) No end-around carry is generated; complement the sum.
   (3) Affix the sign of the number with the larger magnitude, in this case the sign of the *addend*.

## 9-11   The Logical Implementation of Signed Magnitude Addition/Subtraction

The 7483 is a typical TTL IC adder package. It uses ripple-through (serial) carry internally wired through the four full adders in the package.

The circuit uses DTL logic for inputs and high fan-out TTL logic with a high-speed Darlington pair output circuit. The use of DTL and

Darlington output circuitry reduces the carry delay and minimizes the need for more complex look-ahead carry circuitry. The logic diagram for the 7483 is shown in Figure 9-5. It should be noted that the actual logic circuit for the 7483 may differ from one manufacturer to another.

### LOOK-AHEAD CARRY CIRCUITS

Faster adder circuits have a feature called *look-ahead carry,* which eliminates the speed limitations caused by the cumulative carry propagation time as it ripples through the adders. The look-ahead carry adder has additional gates to sample the input and decode the condition for each stage that will produce a carry so that the carry does not have to ripple through a string of adders. The look-ahead gates deliver the carries to all stages at the same time. In this system the carries are handled in parallel, while they are serial in ripple carry adders. Figure 9-6 shows the logical implementation of a signed magnitude adder/subtracter. The exclusive-OR gates on input and output lines function as controlled inverters.

With a constant 0 on input $A$, a 1 on $B$ produces a 1 output, and a 0 on $B$ produces a 0 output. This is the non-inverted condition. With a constant 1 on input $A$, a 0 on input $B$ produces a 1 output, and a 1 on $B$ produces a 0 output. This is the inverting mode. See the truth table in Figure 9-7a and b. Figure 9-7c shows a four-bit true/invert (true complement) circuit. If only four bits are required (including the sign bit), $A4$ is connected to $V_{cc}$ and $B4$ is connected to GND to enable carry propagation.

### Problems

Write the following decimal numbers in sign-magnitude binary form and then add them.

| 44. | +49 | 45. | −64 | 46. | −39 | 47. | +64 |
|---|---|---|---|---|---|---|---|
| | +37 | | +28 | | −42 | | −28 |

## 9-12   One's Complement Addition/Subtraction

The following examples illustrate the addition of signed numbers in one's complement notation:

a. Adding two numbers that have the same sign:
   (1) two positive numbers

$$\begin{array}{rl}
+13_{10} = & 0.01101 \\
+11_{10} = & 0.01011 \\
\hline
24 \quad = & 0.11000
\end{array}$$

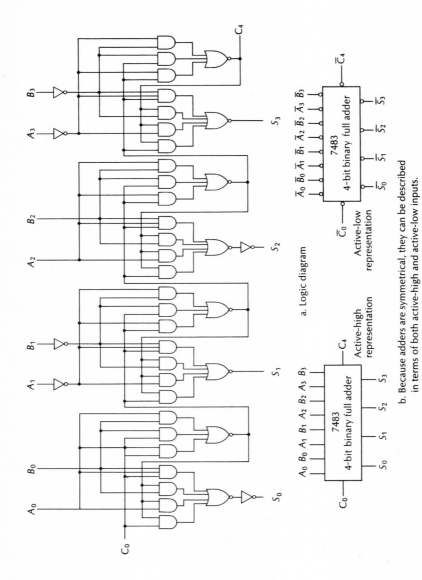

a. Logic diagram

Active-high representation

Active-low representation

b. Because adders are symmetrical, they can be described in terms of both active-high and active-low inputs.

**Figure 9-5**   Logic Diagram for the 7483 Four-Bit Ripple Carry Adder

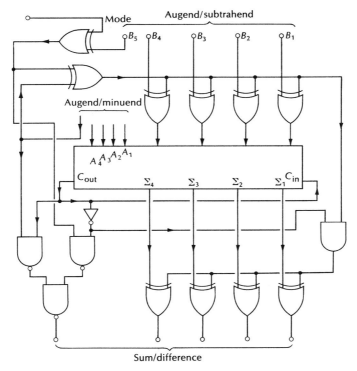

**Figure 9-6** Logical Implementation of Sign and Magnitude Addition/Subtraction
Addend/Subtrahend

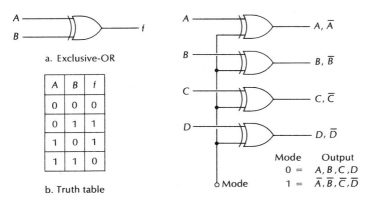

a. Exclusive-OR

| A | B | f |
|---|---|---|
| 0 | 0 | 0 |
| 0 | 1 | 1 |
| 1 | 0 | 1 |
| 1 | 1 | 0 |

b. Truth table

| Mode | Output |
|------|--------|
| 0 = | $A, B, C, D$ |
| 1 = | $\overline{A}, \overline{B}, \overline{C}, \overline{D}$ |

c. Four-bit true/complement generator

**Figure 9-7**   True/Complement Generator

Add numbers, including the sign bit.
(2) two negative numbers

$$
\begin{array}{rlll}
& & 1 \text{ carry} & \\
-13 & = & 1.10010 & \text{augend} \\
-11 & = & 1.10100 & \text{addend} \\
\hline
-24 & & \longrightarrow 1 & \text{add end-around carry} \\
\hline
& & 1.00111 & \text{sum}
\end{array}
$$

Add the two numbers including sign bit and then add the end-around carry. Note that both numbers are written in one's complement form.

b. Adding two numbers with opposite signs:
(1) positive answer

$$
\begin{array}{rlll}
& & 1\ 1\ 1 & \\
-11 & = & 1.10100 & \text{augend} \\
+13 & = & 0.01101 & \text{addend} \\
\hline
+\ 2 & = & 0.00001 & \\
& & \longrightarrow 1 & \\
\hline
& & 0.00010 &
\end{array}
$$

(2) negative answer

$$
\begin{array}{rlll}
-13 & = & 1.10010 & \text{augend} \\
+11 & = & 0.01011 & \text{addend} \\
\hline
-\ 2 & = & 1.11101 & \text{no end-around carry}
\end{array}
$$

Add the two numbers including sign bit. If the numbers are written in proper one's complement form, the result is in proper one's complement form.

c. Subtraction:

For subtraction in one's complement notation, complement the subtrahend, including the sign bit, and follow addition procedures.

**Problems**

48. Summarize the algorithms for addition in one's complement notation.

Write the following decimal numbers in one's complement notation and then add them.

| 49. $+14$ | 50. $-14$ | 51. $+23$ | 52. $-69$ |
|-----------|-----------|-----------|-----------|
| $+\ 6$ | $-\ 6$ | $-19$ | $+49$ |

53. $-72$
    $-53$

54. $-23$
    $+19$

55. $+54$
    $-72$

Write the following decimal numbers in one's complement notation and then subtract them.

56. $+46$
    $+22$

58. $-14$
    $-47$

60. $+23$
    $+19$

57. $-63$
    $+39$

59. $-22$
    $-37$

## LOGIC FOR IMPLEMENTING ONE'S COMPLEMENT ADDITION AND SUBTRACTION

The logic diagram of a system for performing one's complement addition and subtraction is shown in Figure 9-8. Figure 9-9 shows the 74H87 true/complement (1/0) element and its truth table.

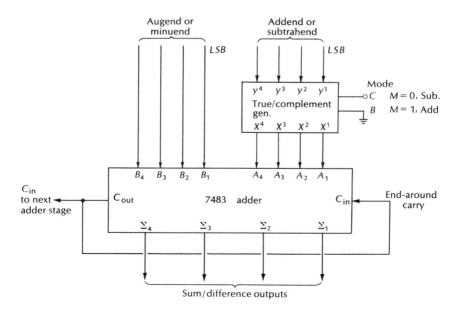

**Figure 9-8** Typical One's Complement Adder/Subtracter

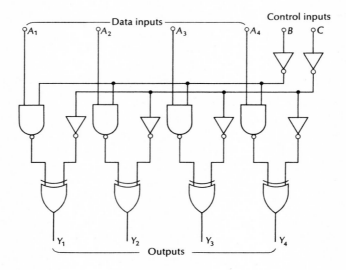

a. Logic diagram

| Control inputs | | Outputs | | | |
|:---:|:---:|:---:|:---:|:---:|:---:|
| *B* | *C* | $Y_1$ | $Y_2$ | $Y_3$ | $Y_4$ |
| *L* | *L* | $\bar{A}_1$ | $\bar{A}_2$ | $\bar{A}_3$ | $\bar{A}_4$ |
| *L* | *H* | $A_1$ | $A_2$ | $A_3$ | $A_4$ |
| *H* | *L* | *H* | *H* | *H* | *H* |
| *H* | *H* | *L* | *L* | *L* | *L* |

b. Truth table

**Figure 9-9**   Logic Diagram and Truth Table for the True/Complement (1/0) Element

## 9-13   Two's Complement Addition and Subtraction

The following examples illustrate the algorithms for adding and subtracting in two's complement notation.

a. Addition
   (1) Adding two positive numbers:

$$
\begin{array}{rll}
& 1111 & \text{carry} \\
+13 = & 0.01101 & \text{augend} \\
+11 = & \underline{0.01011} & \text{addend} \\
+24 = & 0.11000 & \text{sum}
\end{array}
$$

Add the two numbers including sign bit.

(2) Adding two negative numbers:

$$
\begin{array}{rll}
& 1\ 111 & \text{carry} \\
-13 = & 1.10011 & \text{augend} \\
-11 = & 1.10101 & \text{addend} \\
\hline
-24 = & 1.01000 & \text{sum}
\end{array}
$$

carry
discarded $\rightarrow 1$

Add the two numbers including the sign bit, ignoring the carry from the addition of the sign bit column. Numbers are written in proper two's complement form.

(3) Adding numbers with opposite signs:

$$
\begin{array}{rll}
& 1\ 11 & \text{carry} \\
-11 = & 1.10101 & \text{augend} \\
+13 = & 0.01101 & \text{addend} \\
\hline
+\ 2 = & 0.00010 & \text{sum}
\end{array}
$$

carry
discarded $\rightarrow 1$

$$
\begin{array}{rll}
& 1\ 11\ 1 & \text{carry} \\
+13_{10} = & 0.01101 & \text{augend} \\
-11_{10} = & 1.10101 & \text{addend} \\
\hline
+\ 2\quad & 0.00010 & \text{sum}
\end{array}
$$

carry
discarded $\longrightarrow 1$

Add the two numbers and ignore all carry outputs from the sign bit column.

b. Subtraction

(1)
$$
\begin{array}{rl}
+13 = & 0.01101 \quad \text{minuend} \\
-(+11) = & 0.01011 \quad \text{subtrahend} \\
\hline
+\ 2 &
\end{array}
$$

$$
\begin{array}{rl}
1\ 11 & \text{carry} \\
0.01101 & \text{minuend} \\
1.10100 & \text{complement of subtrahend} \\
1 & \text{add 1} \\
\hline
\end{array}
$$
carry discarded $\rightarrow 1$ $\ 0.00010$ difference

(2)
$$
\begin{array}{rl}
+13 = & 0.01101 \quad \text{minuend} \\
-(-11) = & 1.10101 \quad \text{subtrahend} \\
\hline
+24 &
\end{array}
$$

$$
\begin{array}{ll}
111 & \text{carry} \\
0.01101 & \text{minuend} \\
0.01010 & \text{complement of subtrahend} \\
\underline{\phantom{0.0101}1} & \text{add 1} \\
0.11000 & \text{difference}
\end{array}
$$

Add the one's complement of the subtrahend to the minuend. Add 1 to the result to restore the sum of the two's complement form. Ignore any carry from the sign bit column.

## 9-14   Implementing Two's Complement Addition and Subtraction

The functional block diagram for a two's complement addition and subtraction circuit is shown in Figure 9-10. The circuit has no end-around carry provision because the carry from the sign bit column is always discarded. In the subtract mode the subtract command is inverted and fed into the carry input ($C_n^- - 1$), effectively adding a 1 to the result, to restore the *difference* to the proper two's complement form. The two's complement can always be formed by adding 1 to the one's complement.

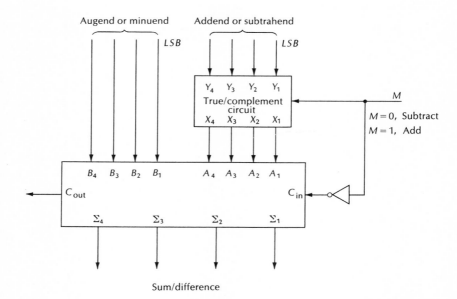

**Figure 9-10**   Typical Two's Complement Adder/Subtracter

## 9-15 Binary-Coded-Decimal (BCD) Addition and Subtraction

Many calculators and other small-scale digital systems display the results directly on numerical readouts. For this kind of system a decimal code, generally the natural BCD (8421) or the excess-3 code, is often the most practical implementation of the necessary computing hardware.

### BINARY-CODED-DECIMAL SYSTEM

In a BCD number system the original positional decimal structure is retained, but each decimal digit is represented by a four-bit binary number:

| 9 | 5 | 4 | Decimal number |
|------|------|------|----------------|
| 1001 | 0101 | 0100 | BCD equivalent |

Four binary digits is the minimum number by which all decimal digits 0 to 9 can be represented. Table 9-4 shows the structure of the BCD system. Look at the following example:

Write $234_{10}$ in BCD.

| 2 | 3 | 4 | Decimal |
|------|------|------|---------|
| 0010 | 0011 | 0100 | BCD |

Further examples are shown in Table 9-5.

**Table 9-4**  Structure of the BCD System

| 3 | 2 | 1 | 0 | Position |
|---|---|---|---|----------|
| Thousands | Hundreds | Tens | Units | Position value |
| $2^3 2^2 2^1 2^0$ | $2^3 2^2 2^1 2^0$ | $2^3 2^2 2^1 2^0$ | $2^3 2^2 2^1 2^0$ | BCD value in exponent form |

**Table 9-5**  Decimal Numbers and Their BCD Equivalents

| Decimal numbers | BCD equivalent |
|-----------------|----------------|
| 001 | 0000  0000  0001 |
| 123 | 0001  0010  0011 |
| 546 | 0101  0100  0110 |
| 879 | 1000  0111  1001 |

When BCD numbers are used, conversion to display becomes simple, since it can be done one digit at a time where no digit is ever larger than 9. Arithmetic is actually done within the machine in binary, and therein lies a problem. Since radix 2 and radix 10 are not related, the carry generated by adding two digits will not occur under the same conditions for decimal digits and BCD digits. The following example will illustrate this problem:

| *Decimal* | *BCD* | | |
|---|---|---|---|
| | 1 | 0 | |
| 26 | 0010 | 0110 | position |
| +38 | +0011 | 1000 | |
| 64 | 0101 | 1110 | |

Note that in adding $26_{10} + 38_{10}$ a carry is produced in position 0 $(1110_2 = 14_{10})$. In a sense the result in BCD is correct $(0101 + 1110 = 50 + 14)$, but the maximum allowable weight number for position 0 has been exceeded. If the decimal-position notation scheme is to be preserved, the result must be expressed as $60 + 4$ $(0110 - 0100)$. The following will help to illustrate the point:

| *Decimal* | | *BCD* | |
|---|---|---|---|
| 1 | | 0001 | |
| +2 | | +0010 | |
| 3 | no carry required | 0011 | result correct |
| 3 | | 0011 | |
| +4 | | +0100 | |
| 7 | no carry required | 0111 | result correct |
| 5 | | 0101 | |
| +5 | | +0101 | |
| 10 | carry required | 1010 | result not correct, no carry generated |
| 6 | | 0110 | |
| +5 | | +0101 | |
| 11 | carry required | 1011 | result not correct, no carry generated |
| 9 | | 1001 | |
| +7 | | +0111 | |
| 16 | carry required | 1 0000 | carry generated, but result not correct |

In this last case a carry is generated in the BCD addition, but position 0 is incorrect. In the decimal system the first carry occurs at 10. In the BCD system the first carry occurs at 16; that is, 15 is the largest decimal number that can be expressed in four binary digits. The difference between 10 and 16 is 6, and notice that 6 is the number required to make the BCD sum correct.

A brief study of the system will indicate that 6 must be added to any sum $10_{10}$ or greater to maintain the decimal structure. This implies that the machine must be able to recognize when a number $10_{10}$ or larger has been generated.

For sums between 10 and 15 the NBCD error detector examined in Chapter 6 can be used. For sums larger than 16 a *natural* carry is generated. The outputs from the error detector and from the adder-carry output can be used to activate a separate add-6 or 0 (only) circuit.

**Example**  BCD Addition

Add $259_{10}$ and $378_{10}$

| *Decimal* | | *BCD* | | | |
|---|---|---|---|---|---|
| | | 1 | 1 | carries | |
| 259 | | 0010 | 0101 | 1001 | |
| +378 | | +0011 | 0111 | 1000 | |
| 637 | | 0110 | 1101 | 0001 | sum |
| | + | | 0110 | 0110 | add |
| | | 0110 | 0011 | 0111 | BCD result |
| | | 6 | 3 | 7 | decimal equivalent of BCD results |

**SUMMARY**

1. Add each BCD group as an ordinary pair of binary numbers.
2. If the decimal equivalent of the sum produced is less than 10, the result is correct.
3. If the decimal equivalent of the sum is 10 or greater, add binary 6 and add any overflow beyond four binary digits to the LSB column of the next BCD group to the left.

**Problems**

Write each of the following decimal numbers in BCD and then add them.

61.  398 + 297
62.  525 + 425
63.  2081 − 1097
64.  5700 + 479

## BCD ADDER CIRCUIT

The BCD adder circuit is shown in Figure 9-11. The two adders are four-bit binary full adders of the same kind used in the previous adder circuits. The two AND and one OR gates form the BCD error detector (decoder) that instructs the correction adder to add 0000 for sums less than 10 and to add 0110 for sums between 10 and 15. The carry output from the adder is also connected to the input of the OR gate to implement the add-6 correction adder for sums larger than 10. The output of the add-6.decoder gate also provides the proper *decimal* carry to the next BCD adder decade. The correction adder can be the same device type as the primary adder. To add 0110, $A1$ and $A4$ can be kept at a constant 0 logic level.

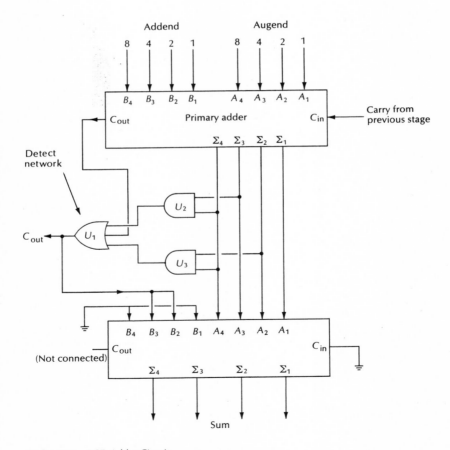

**Figure 9-11** BCD Adder Circuit

## BINARY-CODED-DECIMAL SUBTRACTION

Figure 9-12 shows a BCD subtracter circuit that uses the one's complement method. The minuend and the one's complement of the subtrahend are added by the primary adder. The result is transferred through a true/complement circuit (four exclusive-OR gates or a 74H87 or similar true/complement circuit) to the correction adder. The correction adder then either adds 0000 or 1010 depending upon the sign of that particular decade and the sign of the total result.

## ALGORITHMS

1. True/complement circuit
   a. If the end-around carry is 1, the sign is +. *Transfer true results* to the correcting adder.

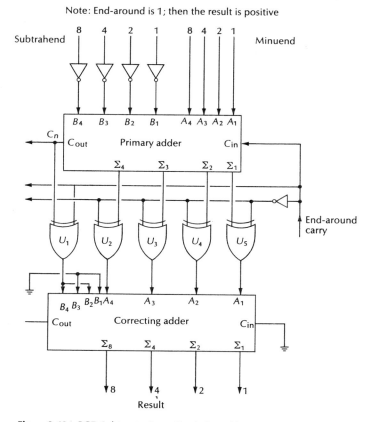

**Figure 9-12**   BCD Subtracter Stage One's Complement Type.

b. If the end-around carry is 0, the sign is $-$. *Transfer the complement* of the output of the primary adder to the correcting adder.
2. The correcting adder
   a. End-around carry $= 1$
      $C_n = 1$ correcting adder adds 0000
      $C_n = 0$ correcting adder adds 1010
   b. End-around carry $= 0$
      $C_n = 1$ correcting adder adds 1010
      $C_n = 0$ correcting adder adds 0000
   c. All carries from the correcting adder are ignored.
      These rules can be summarized in Boolean notation as:

$$\text{Add } 1010 = C_{eac} \cdot \overline{C}_n + C_{eac} \cdot C_n$$
$$\text{where } C_{eac} \text{ is the end-around carry.}$$

This proves upon inspection to be the exclusive-OR function and can be written as:

$$\text{Add } 1010 = C_{eac} \oplus C_n$$

An examination of Figure 9-12 indicates that an exclusive-OR gate is used to control the correcting adder.

## BCD SUBTRACTION USING THE NINE'S COMPLEMENT

Because the BCD system is a coded decimal system, subtraction can be carried out using the nine's complement. Figure 9-13 shows a spe-

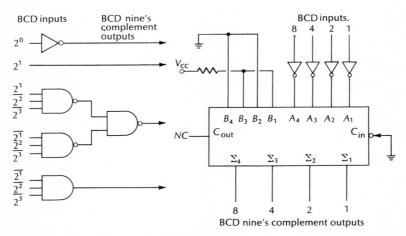

a. Logic method          b. Using a 7483 adder to generate the BCD nine's complement

**Figure 9-13** Two Nine's Complement Generators

cial nine's complement circuit and Figure 9-14 shows a complete BCD nine's complement subtraction functional block diagram. An adder can be used to extract the nine's complement. The adder nine's complement generator adds 0101 (the complement of 1010) to the subtrahend.

## 9-16 Excess-3 Addition and Subtraction

The excess-3 code is the most popular of several self-complementing codes. In this context self-complementing means that the one's complement is identical to generating the nine's complement of the decimal number.

The simple inversion of each bit in the XS-3 code yields the nine's complement. For subtraction the subtrahend can be complemented by a true/complement circuit instead of a special nine's complement generator. The functional block diagram of an XS-3 adder is shown in Figure 9-15. Table 9-6 provides XS-3 equivalents for decimal digits and nine's complement values.

The addition algorithm for XS-3 addition is shown below. Add the two numbers.

a. If an end-around carry is produced, add 0011 ($3_{10}$)
b. If *no* end-around carry is produced, subtract 0011 or add its complement, 1100.

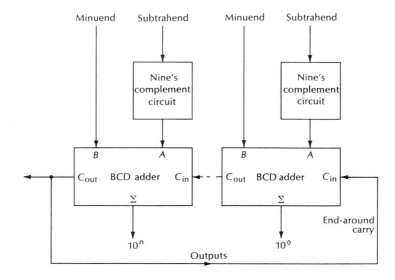

**Figure 9-14**  Typical Nine's Complement BCD Subtracter

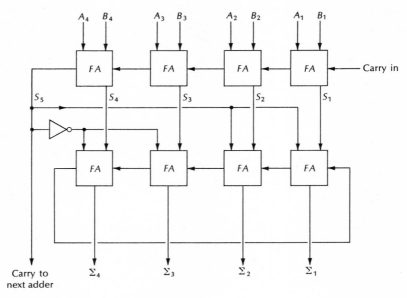

**Figure 9-15**   Four-Bit Excess-Three Adder

**Table 9-6**   Decimal Equivalents in the XS-3 Code

| Decimal number | Excess–3 Equivalent | Nine's Complement |
|:---:|:---:|:---:|
| 0 | 0011 | 1100 |
| 1 | 0100 | 1011 |
| 2 | 0101 | 1010 |
| 3 | 0110 | 1001 |
| 4 | 0111 | 1000 |
| 5 | 1000 | 0111 |
| 6 | 1001 | 0110 |
| 7 | 1010 | 0101 |
| 8 | 1011 | 0100 |
| 9 | 1100 | 0011 |

**Examples**

a.  Add $879_{10}$ and $132_{10}$.

| *Decimal* | *Excess-3 BCD* | | |
|:---:|:---:|:---:|:---:|
| | 1 | 1 | carry |
| 879 | 1011 | 1010 | 1100 |
| +132 | +0100 | 0110 | 0101 |
| 1011 | 1 0000 | 0001 | 0001  uncorrected sum |

This result is correct for BCD, but 3 must be added to each column to restore the number to the excess-3 code.

| 0001 | 0000 | 0001 | 0001 | uncorrected sum |
|------|------|------|------|-----------------|
| 0011 | 0011 | 0011 | 0011 | add 3 |
| 0100 | 0011 | 0100 | 0100 | corrected sum |

b. Add $321_{10}$ and $122_{10}$ in excess-3.

| *Decimal* | | *Excess-3 BCD* | | |
|-----------|------|------|------|--|
| 231 | 0101 | 0110 | 0100 | |
| +122 | +0100 | 0101 | 0101 | |
| 353 | 1001 | 1011 | 1001 | uncorrected sum |

There was no overflow so 3 must be subtracted. This is accomplished by adding the complement of 0011, 1100.

| 11 | 1111 | carry | |
|------|------|------|--|
| 1001 | 1011 | 1001 | uncorrected sum |
| 1100 | 1100 | 1100 | add 1100 |
| 0110 | 1000 | 0101 | |
| | | 1 | end-around carry |
| 0110 | 1000 | 0110 | corrected sum |

## 9-17 Half and Full Subtracters

Although subtraction through the use of complement notation is the most widely used method, some machines use a subtracter circuit that is very similar to the common adder circuit. Table 9-7 is the truth table for binary subtraction. The *difference* equation written from Table 9-7 is $D = \bar{A} \cdot B + A \cdot \bar{B}$. This is the exclusive-OR function and can be written as $D = A \oplus B$. The *borrow* equation as written from the truth table is $B = \bar{A} \cdot B$. These two equations differ but little from the half adder equations:

$$\text{Sum} = A \oplus B$$
$$\text{Carry} = A \cdot B$$

The difference is simply an inverted $A$ for the subtracter and *not* inverted for addition. Figure 9-16 shows a half subtracter circuit, a combined adder/subtracter circuit using an exclusive-OR gate as a *controlled* inverter, and the method of combining two half subtracters to form a full subtracter. Figure 9-17 shows a four-bit subtracter functional block diagram.

**Table 9-7** Subtraction Truth Tables

| A | B | Difference | Minterms |
|---|---|------------|----------|
| 0 | 0 | 0 | |
| 0 | 1 | 1 | $(\overline{A}\,B)$ |
| 1 | 0 | 1 | $(A\,\overline{B})$ |
| 1 | 1 | 0 | |

a. Subtraction difference truth table

b. Difference equation: $D = \overline{A}\,B + A\,\overline{B}$
This is also the exclusive-OR function: $D = A \oplus B$
The sum and difference equations are identical

d. Borrow equation: $B = \overline{A} \cdot B$
Summary of equations
Addition:
  Sum $= A \oplus B$
  Carry $= A \cdot B$

| A | B | Borrow | Minterms |
|---|---|--------|----------|
| 0 | 0 | 0 | |
| 0 | 1 | 1 | $\overline{A}\,B$ |
| 1 | 1 | 0 | |
| 1 | 1 | 0 | |

c. Subtraction borrow truth table

Subtraction rules

| $A-B$ = | Difference | Borrow |
|---------|------------|--------|
| 0−0 = | 0 | 0 |
| 0−1 = | 1 | 1 |
| 1−0 = | 1 | 0 |
| 1−1 = | 0 | 0 |

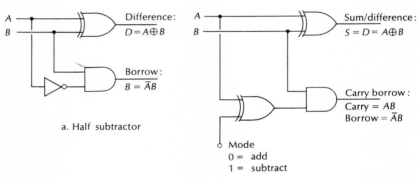

a. Half subtractor

b. Combined half adder/subtractor

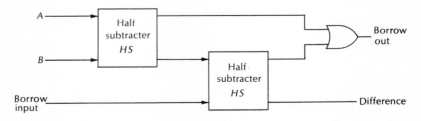

c. Two half subtractors connected as a full subtractor

**Figure 9-16** Half Subtracter, Half Adder/Subtracter and Full Subtracter

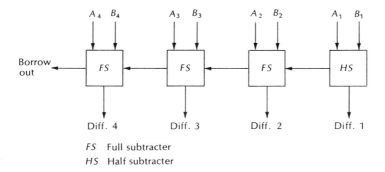

Figure 9-17 A Four-bit Binary Subtracter

## 9-18 Serial Addition

Figure 9-18 shows a serial adder scheme where a full adder and flip-flop perform serial binary addition. For active-*high* operands, the carry flip-flop must be set when the least significant bit is applied. For active-*low* operands, the flip-flop must be reset when the least significant bit is applied.

Serial addition/subtraction can easily be accomplished using two full adders and a flip-flop. The upper adder in Figure 9-19a serves as a conditional inverter. Exclusive-OR gates could be used. This scheme requires either a second pass for end-around carry or that the carry

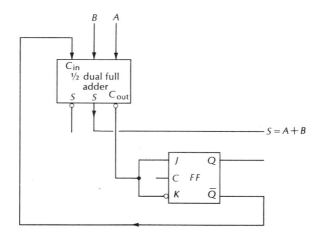

Figure 9-18 Serial Adder

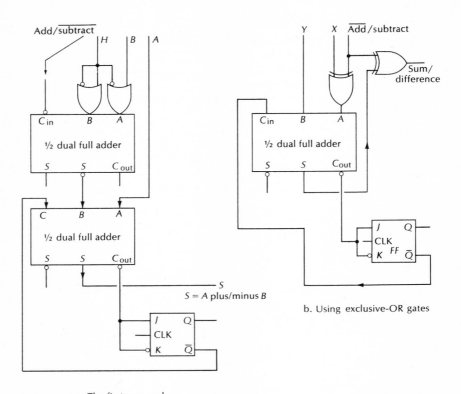

a. The first approach

**Figure 9-19** Serial Addition and Subtraction

flip-flop starts out set for add, reset for subtract (with active-*high* operands, but the opposite with active-*low* operands). This second pass can be avoided by using two exclusive-OR gates in the data path, thereby effectively using the adder with active-*high* operands in one mode and active-*low* operands in the other.

For both addition and subtraction, the carry flip-flop must start out set for active-*high* operands, reset for active-*low* operands (see Figure 9-19b).

## 9-19  Binary Multiplication

Multiplication is performed as successive additions. The notation $5 \times 7$ implies a shortcut method of adding seven fives:

$$5 \times 7 = 5 + 5 + 5 + 5 + 5 + 5 + 5 = 35$$

The algorithm used in human calculation involves multiplying the multiplicand by each digit in the multiplier and adding the partial products.

We also use the device of shifting the partial product one position to the left, which in the decimal system is equivalent to multiplying by 10 (conversely a shift of one position to the right would be the equivalent to dividing by 10).

In binary notation shifting one position to the left is equivalent to multiplying by 2. Binary multiplication can be mechanized using an approach similar to the longhand method because binary multiplication (one pair of bits at a time) is such a simple process. In binary there are only two possible results for the multiplication of any pair of bits. Note the following examples:

$$
\begin{array}{lll}
(1)\quad 0 & (2)\quad 1 & (3)\quad 1 \\
\quad\ \ \times 0 & \quad\ \ \times 0 & \quad\ \ \times 1 \\
\quad\ \ \ \overline{\phantom{x}0} & \quad\ \ \ \overline{\phantom{x}0} & \quad\ \ \ \overline{\phantom{x}1}
\end{array}
$$

and for multibit numbers:

$$
\begin{array}{lll}
1101 & 1101 & \text{multiplicand} \\
\underline{\times 0\phantom{00}} & \underline{\times 1\phantom{00}} & \text{multiplier} \\
0000 & 1101 &
\end{array}
$$

The rules are as follows:

a. When a binary number is multiplied by 0, the result is 0.
b. When a binary number (multiplicand) is multiplied by 1, the result is the original number (the multiplicand).

The following example illustrates the procedure that is likely to seem most obvious because it is very much like the way we normally do multiplication. In this example, all of the partial products are found and then added simultaneously. Successive addition of each partial product is as follows:

$$
\begin{array}{ll}
\quad\ 111 & \text{If the least significant bit of the multiplier} \\
\quad\underline{101} & \text{is a 1, the multiplicand is transferred to the} \\
\quad\ 111 & \text{output as a partial product.} \\
\\
\ \ 0111 & \text{If the next least significant bit is a 0,} \\
\ \ 0111 & \text{the product is shifted right one position.} \\
\ \ \underline{111\phantom{0}} & \text{If MSB is a 1, the product is shifted right} \\
100011 & \text{one position and added to the multiplicand.}
\end{array}
$$

We will use this example to illustrate the mechanics of the process in Figure 9-20, parts a through f.

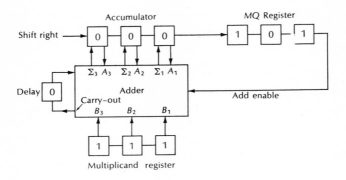

a. First step

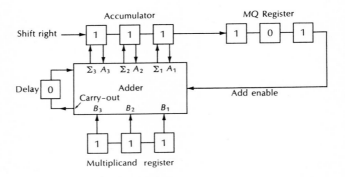

b. Second step

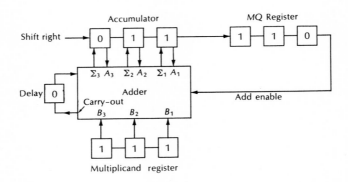

c. Third step

**Figure 9-20**   Binary Multiplication

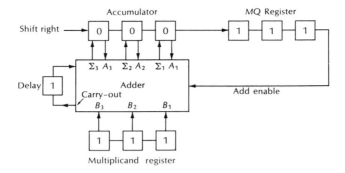

d. Fourth step

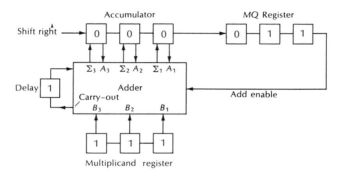

e. Fifth step

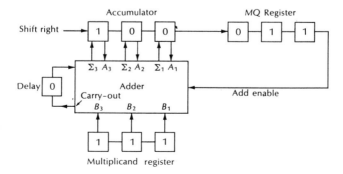

f. Sixth step

**Figure 9-20**   continued

a. This part shows the initial problem loaded into the appropriate registers. The multiplicand register will not change during the operation. The multiplier is loaded into the MQ register. The output of the MQ register is connected to the adder, but it does *not* supply bits to be added. Its output state is actually an instruction that tells the adder either to add or not to add (1 = add, 0 = don't add). This particular input on the adder is simply an add enable input.

b. The 1 on the add enable input enables the adder to add the contents of the accumulator to the multiplicand.

$$
\begin{array}{ll}
000 & \text{accumulator} \\
+111 & \text{multiplicand} \\
\hline
111 & \text{new accumulator contents}
\end{array}
$$

Part b shows the status of the registers after the addition.

c. Shift the accumulator and MQ registers right one position. This puts a zero in the rightmost cell of the MQ register, which instructs the adder *not* to add, thereby inhibiting addition. Part c shows the contents of all registers at this stage of the process.

d. Again, the accumulator and MQ registers are shifted right. The 1 in the rightmost cell of the MQ register enables the adder, and the contents of the accumulator are added to the multiplicand.

$$
\begin{array}{ll}
11 & \text{carry} \\
001 & \text{accumulator} \\
+111 & \text{multiplicand} \\
\hline
1\ \ 000 & \text{new accumulator contents}
\end{array}
$$

Notice that a carry-out of the adder is produced. This is stored in the delay element for use after the next shift right.

e. Shift right. This part shows the contents of all registers after the shift. The 1 in the rightmost cell of the MQ register enables the adder. However, in this case there is a 1 stored in the carry delay cell. Gating circuitry, not shown in Figure 9-20, inhibits the transfer of data from the multiplicand register so that only the carry is added to the contents of the MQ register.

f. This part shows the final contents of all registers.

## BCD MULTIPLICATION

BCD multiplication is handled very much like binary multiplication except that BCD groups are carefully arranged in the registers to maintain their essentially decimal character. This method of listing partial products is slightly different from the usual longhand procedure in order to keep down the number of registers.

**Example**

a. *Conventional*

$$
\begin{array}{r}
4 \quad 7 \quad 5 \\
\times 4 \\
\hline
2 \quad 0 \\
2 \quad 8 \quad \\
1 \quad 6 \quad \quad \\
\hline
1 \quad 9 \quad 0 \quad 0
\end{array}
$$

b. *Diagonal*

$$
\begin{array}{r}
4 \quad 7 \quad 5 \\
\times 4 \\
\hline
\end{array}
$$

$$
1 \quad 9 \quad 0 \quad 0
$$

The diagonal arrangement requires only two registers.

**LOOK-UP TABLES**

As read-only memories (ROM) go down in price, the use of look-up tables becomes increasingly attractive. Individual digit products can be placed permanently in memory and retrieved when needed. This eliminates the need for multiplication and reduces the multiplication process to one of simply looking up the partial products and adding them as shown in example b.

## 9-20 Binary Division

Division is the opposite of multiplication and can therefore be accomplished by a series of repeated subtractions, as illustrated below:

**Example**

a. *Conventional*

$$
\begin{array}{r}
5 \quad \text{quotient} \\
\text{divisor } 10\overline{)50} \quad \text{dividend}
\end{array}
$$

b. *By subtraction*

$$
\begin{array}{rl}
50 & \\
-10 & \\
\hline
40 & \text{first subtraction} \\
-10 & \\
\hline
30 & \text{second subtraction} \\
-10 & \\
\hline
20 & \text{third subtraction} \\
-10 & \\
\hline
10 & \text{fourth subtraction} \\
-10 & \\
\hline
00 & \text{fifth subtraction} - \text{quotient} = 5
\end{array}
$$

The process can be extended to a larger figure but the number of steps becomes so large that the division operation becomes quite slow. To divide 1800 by 6 would require 300 subtractions. The shifting process can be used to drastically reduce the number of subtractions. The following example approximates one common computer method. It differs only in the fact that we can determine the proper number of zeros behind the 6 by inspection, where the computer must use a trial-and-error procedure to make the determination. The quantity added to the quotient at each step is the equivalent of a computer register left shift (10 = one-place shift, 100 = two-place shift, and so on, as shown below:

| | *Add to quotient* | *Quotient total* |
|---|---|---|
| 300 | | *Quotient* |
| 6$\overline{)1800}$ | *Add to quotient* | *total* |
| −600 | | |
| 1200 | 100 | 100 |
| −600 | | |
| 600 | 100 | 200 |
| 000 | 100 | 300 quotient |

**BINARY DIVISION ALGORITHM (RESTORING METHOD)**

a. Subtract divisor from dividend. If result is a positive number, put 1 in rightmost bit of quotient register; if result is a negative number, add divisor back to dividend.
b. Shift quotient left by one bit and shift divisor right by one bit (or dividend left).

c. Repeat steps a and b.

d. Continue steps a through c until a subtraction yields a difference of all 0 bits, until required accuracy is obtained, or until all available bit positions in quotient register are filled.

### Example in Applying the Division Algorithm*

1. Subtract
2. Shift and subtract
3. Add
4. Shift and subtract
5. Shift and subtract

*Contents of*
*quotient register*

```
            1011
 1010 |1101110
       1010               0000
      ──────
      001111             0001
       1010              0010
      ──────
      11011
      1010
      ──────
      01111             0010
      1010              0100
      ──────
      01010             0101
      1010              1010
      ──────
      0000              1011   final quotient
```

### Problems

Write the following in BCD and add:

65.   49          66.   546         67.   421        68.   997
     +63               +194              +315              +894

Write the following in binary signed magnitude, radix complement, and radix-minus-1 complement notations, and perform the indicated operations:

69. $(-42) - 36$          73. $(-64) + (-29)$          76. $(-64) + (-64)$
70. $(-36) - 42$          74. $(-64) - (-29)$          77. $43 - 96$
71. $(-64) + 29$          75. $64 - 64$                78. $43 - (-96)$
72. $(-29) + 64$

---

* For a comprehensive discussion of division processes see Flores, *The Logic of Computer Arithmetic,* Prentice-Hall, 1963.

## SUMMARY OF ALGORITHMS

1. Addition by sign and magnitude

    *Two numbers of same sign*

    To magnitude of augend, add magnitude of addend. Use common sign.

    *Two numbers of opposite sign—augend magnitude larger*

    To magnitude of augend, add one's complement of addend magnitude. End-around carry. Affix sign of augend.

    *Two numbers of opposite sign—addend magnitude larger (or equal)*

    To magnitude of augend add one's complement of addend magnitude. There is no end-around carry. Complement result and affix sign of addend.

2. Addition using one's complement notation

    *Two numbers of same sign*

    To augend magnitude, add addend magnitude. Use common sign. To one's complement of augend magnitude, add one's complement of addend magnitude. Add end-around carry. Affix common sign (answer in one's complement form).

    *Two numbers of opposite sign*

    To magnitude of augend (in one's complement form, if negative), add magnitude of addend (in one's complement form, if negative). Add end-around carry.

3. Addition using the two's complement

    *Two numbers of same sign*

    To augend magnitude, add addend magnitude. Use common sign. To two's complement of augend magnitude, add two's complement of addend magnitude and ignore carry. Affix common sign.

    *Two numbers of opposite sign—augend magnitude larger*

    To magnitude of augend, add two's complement of addend including sign bits. Ignore carry from sign bits. To two's complement of augend magnitude, add magnitude of addend; add sign bits also. Ignore carry from sign bits.

    *Two numbers of opposite sign—addend magnitude larger (or equal)*

    To two's complement of augend magnitude, add magnitude of addend including sign bits. Ignore carry from sign bits.

# CHAPTER 10

# MEMORY SYSTEMS

*Learning Objectives.* *Upon completion of this chapter you should:*
1. *Be able to classify (according to use and access time) the following memory types:*
   a. *Core*
   b. *MOS LSI Memories*
   c. *MOS LSI Shift Register Memories*
   d. *Bipolar Scratch Pad and Buffer Memories*
   e. *Cassette Drives*
   f. *Core Memories*
   g. *Punched Paper Tape and Cards*
   h. *Computer Tape*
   i. *ROM*
   j. *RAM*
2. *Be able to describe core memory construction and principle of operation.*
3. *Be able to draw the schematic diagrams for: a static MOS, a dynamic MOS, and a bipolar typical memory cell.*
4. *Be able to explain the operation of each of the memory cells (in 3).*
5. *Be able to define DRO and know where it applies.*
6. *Be able to describe both bit and word organization in RAM's.*
7. *Know the output drive capabilities of typical MOS memories.*
8. *Know the kinds of ROM's commercially available and the special characteristics of each.*
9. *Know what kinds of (recirculating MOS) shift registers are typically available.*
10. *Know what kinds of output configurations are available in MOS memory chips.*
11. *Be familiar with MOS timing problems and their relationship to troubleshooting.*
12. *Know ROM programming and erasing techniques.*

Automatic processing of data in a computer depends upon being able to store a list of operational commands called the *program,* along with the numerical or other data to be operated on. The computer must have access to instructions and data at computer speeds.

Any computer contains several kinds of memories, each of which is generally allocated the kind of memory task best suited to it. The use of several memory forms is dictated by a trade-off in cost per bit of memory and memory speed. As a general rule, the faster the access to a memory type, the higher the cost per bit.

## MAIN MEMORY

The computer main memory is random-access, which means that the time required to retrieve data from the memory is the same regardless of the memory location. This is in contrast to magnetic tape, for example, where many unwanted memory locations may have to be passed through before arriving at the desired location. In the case of magnetic tape, the number of unwanted locations that have to pass under the head before the desired data could be retrievable can vary considerably depending on its relative location on the tape. Consequently, the time required to retrieve a given set of data is variable. For main memory purposes, constant access time is important to the overall computer timing cycle. Access time must be predictable and constant. Random-access memories are generally magnetic core or semiconductor arrays. Main memories are moderately fast but generally much slower than some of the smaller semiconductor support memories.

## REGISTERS AND BUFFER MEMORIES

Register memories are support memories often dedicated to specific tasks such as storing immediate data for input to an arithmetic logic unit (ALU) or for retaining the output results of an ALU. Registers are generally flip-flop arrays, often in shift register form. Small but fast buffer memories, often called *scratch pad,* are coming into increasing use. These are often random-access memories where blocks of data can be transferred from the main memory just prior to the time that the machine requires the data. This allows the computer to access data at the faster rate of the scratch pad instead of the slower rate of the main memory.

## MASS MEMORIES

Mass memories are capable of storing a very large quantity of data inexpensively, but with very slow access times. Mass memories include magnetic tape, punched paper tape, punched cards, and magnetic disc and drum memories. Mass memories are not accessed directly. Data are transferred from mass storage into main memory where they are directly accessed during processing or transferred to buffer storage for access.

Main memories have two important registers: the memory address register (MAR) and the memory data or buffer register. The memory address register stores the address of the word in memory on which the computer is currently working. The memory buffer register stores the contents of that main memory location.

### RANDOM-ACCESS MEMORIES

Until fairly recently the magnetic core memory was the overwhelming choice for main memory applications. However, semiconductor memories promise to at least partially displace core memories. The cost per bit of core memory has stabilized and, barring some breakthrough, is not likely to become less expensive. Semiconductor memories have already become cheaper for medium-sized memories and are generally faster than core memories.

## 10-1 Memory Mediums

### PUNCHED PAPER CARDS

Punched paper cards were used by Joseph Marie Jacquard as early as 1801 for controlling the weaving of textile patterns on an automated loom. By computer standards, the punched card is a very slow access memory, but it is capable of a theoretically infinite storage capacity at a very low cost per bit of storage.

The most common punched card format has 80 columns. Each column can represent either the decimal digits 0–9, letters of the alphabet, or special symbols depending upon the arrangement of punches in three special zones. The punched card format is shown in Figure 10-1, and Table 10-1 shows the punched card code. Figure 10-2 shows a card punched to contain the following: DIGITAL TECHNOLOGY-647 SMITH, SHAKESPEARE. #46975 & L310@$23.00/UNIT.

### PUNCHED PAPER TAPE

Punched paper tape is commonly used in conjunction with teletype (TTY) systems. Many modern machines use the American Standard Code for Information Interchange (ASCII or US ASCII), but there are several other codes in use, including the older five-level Baudot code. The complete ASCII code can be found in Table 11-3. Figure 10-3 shows the ASCII tape format, and Figure 10-4 shows the format of the five-level code. The arrow in Figure 10-3 indicates the direction of tape travel. The tape is read against the arrow.

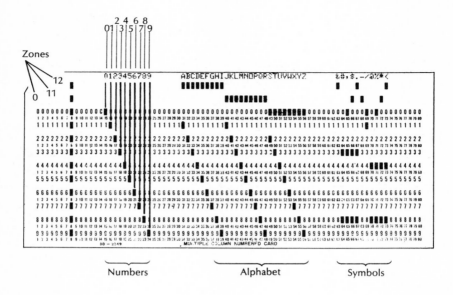

**Figure 10-1** Punched Card Format

**Table 10-1** Punched Card Code

| Numerical Row Only | Zone 12 Plus Numerical Row Below | Zone 11 Plus Numerical Row Below | Zone 12 Plus Numerical Row Below |
|---|---|---|---|
| 0=0 | | | |
| 1=1 | 1=A | 1=J | |
| 2=2 | 2=B | 2=K | 2=S |
| 3=3 | 3=C | 3=L | 3=T |
| 4=4 | 4=D | 4=M | 4=U |
| 5=5 | 5=E | 5=N | 5=V |
| 6=6 | 6=F | 6=O | 6=W |
| 7=7 | 7=G | 7=P | 7=X |
| 8=8 | 8=H | 8=Q | 8=Y |
| 9=9 | 9=I | 9=R | 9=Z |

## MOVING MAGNETIC MEMORY TRACKS

Magnetic track recording methods using reel-to-reel tape, casettes, magnetic discs (both rigid and flexible or "floppy"), and drums have become common methods for storing large volumes of data. Tape is capable of storing indefinitely large amounts of data, but its sequential (serial) nature and mechanical speed limitations make it a slow access storage medium. Sophisticated electronically controlled tape transport

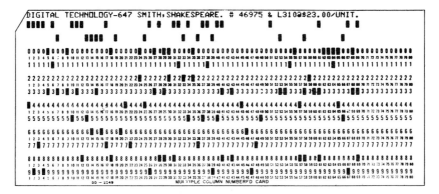

This card is punched for the following data:
DIGITAL TECHNOLOGY-647 SMITH, SHAKESPEARE.
#46975 & L310 @ $23.00/UNIT.

**Figure 10-2** Sample Punched card

machines are used in larger computer systems. Entertainment cassette machines have recently become popular for use with programmable calculators, minicomputers, and remote terminals.

Magnetic discs and drums use the same magnetic recording principle as that of magnetic tape except that the recording track is a specific *band* on the surface of the disc or drum. Each drum or disc contains a number of bands and often has several read and write heads. Multiple heads permit parallel reading or writing of several bands and allow a string of information to be repeated several times around the track to shorten the access time. Many of these drums and discs turn more than 10,000 RPM and require that write and read heads be floated on a cushion of air to minimize friction and wear.

Although a given band on a drum or disc has a short finite length compared with tape, it still can store a considerable amount of data. Because the velocity of the head moving along the track can be so much greater than practical tape velocities, drum and disc storage has a much shorter access time, although this method of storage is still far slower than the internal electronic working speed of even the slowest digital machine. As a result, its principal use is as a speed buffer between keyboard, punched cards, tape, and so on and the high-speed internal main memory.

Figure 10-5 shows the typical organization of a magnetic drum. A drum memory can store from 20 to 20,000 bytes,* with a typical access

---

* A *byte* is a group of bits, usually eight.

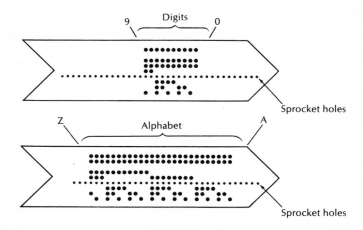

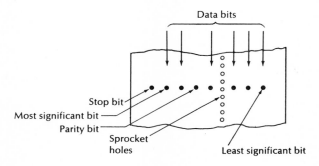

**Figure 10-3**   ASCII Coded Punched Paper Tape

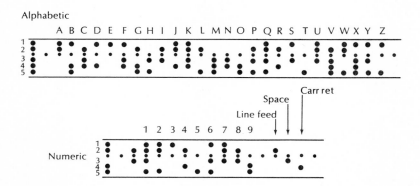

**Figure 10-4**   Five-Level Punched Paper Tape Code

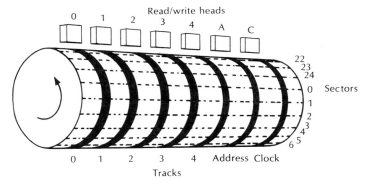

**Figure 10-5**   Magnetic Drum Memory

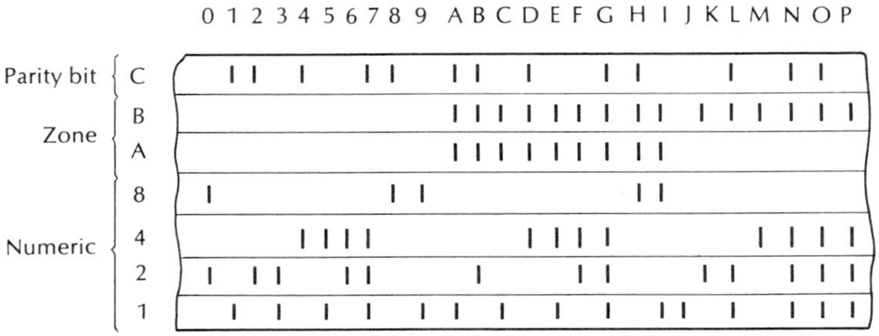

0 1 2 3 4 5 6 7 8 9   A B C D E F G H I J K L M N O P

**Figure 10-6**   Typical Magnetic Tape Format

time of 10 to 100 $\mu$s. (Access time is a measure of how long it takes to locate and read out a given group of data.) Figure 10-6 shows the magnetic tape format.

## DISC MEMORIES

Disc memories using stacks of solid metal discs with an oxide coating have been in use for some time. These machines are fast but bulky and expensive. A slower but very inexpensive disc memory system uses inexpensive, easily stored, flexible plastic discs. The floppy-disc memory is cheap enough to be used with small systems such as microcomputers. Discs can store up to 3 million bytes on a plastic disc. Floppy

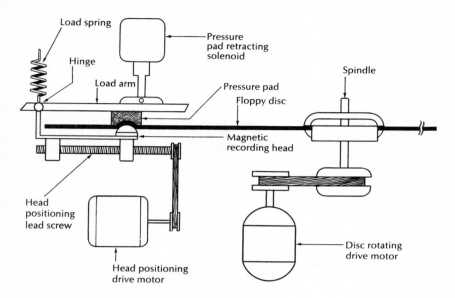

**Figure 10-7**   Mechanism of the Floppy Disc System

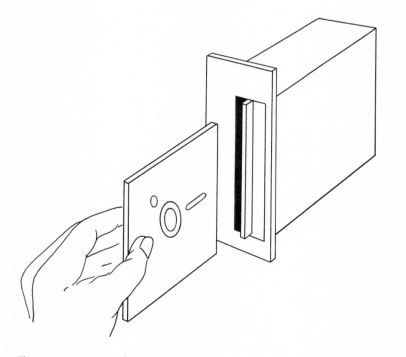

**Figure 10-8**   Inserting Floppy Disc Cartridge into Machine

**Table 10-2**  Comparison of Mechanical Memory Types

| Memory type | Typical Capacity Bytes | Access Time $\mu$ Sec | Use |
|---|---|---|---|
| Magnetic drum | 20-2,000,000 | 10-100 | Medium speed internal storage |
| Floppy disc | 3,000,000 | 300 $\mu$ S | Low speed high density external storage |
| Magnetic tape | 20,000,000* | 1-100  seconds | |
| Punched cards | 80-90 per card | 50-150 | Low speed external storage |
| Punched paper tape | 11 per inch | 600 | |

* Per reel

discs have a rotational speed of 360 RPM and have an average access time of less than 300 ms. There are generally 70 or more tracks which are selected by moving the read/write head across the disc. Figure 10-7 shows the basic features of the floppy-disc drive mechanism. Figure 10-8 shows a floppy disc in its plastic-cartridge carrier being inserted into the memory drive unit. Table 10-2 compares the types of mechanical memory systems.

## NONMECHANICAL MAGNETIC MEMORIES

Several memory schemes use magnetized domains located at fixed spots in a matrix. The movement from one magnetic spot to another is accomplished through electronic switching instead of mechanical motion. The most common form of this class is the *core* memory. It consists of an array of tiny ($\approx$.050″ OD) toroid (doughnut shaped) cores threaded on hairlike wires, forming a rectangular grid. Each core is a memory cell that can store either 0 or 1. Individual cores are either wound as a few turns of ultra-thin magnetic ribbon or made by pressing a magnetic oxide and a binder into a dense toroid (doughnut) shape. The pressed (ferrite) core is the most common. Core memory has been the favored main memory element for several years. It requires power only when writing or reading out data, but read/write currents are quite high—100 mA to 1 A. Core memory cost per bit is fairly low but it is not likely to become appreciably cheaper. In terms of speed, the core's only commonly used competition is semiconductor memory.

Plated wire and magnetic film memories also use fixed position magnetic domains but not discrete cores. These memories have promised denser storage at lower cost than core memories, but have not yet lived up to the projected potential and have proved in practice to be slower than cores. At this moment it is questionable that further improvements in plated wire and magnetic film memories will make them truly popular forms.

Cryogenic memories are still in the research and development stage. These memories are based on the fact that certain materials at critical temperatures a few degrees above absolute zero exhibit zero resistance. A current induced in a tin (or lead) loop at cryogenic temperatures will continue to circulate indefinitely unless the temperature is changed, the current loop is opened, or an additional magnetic field is used to alter the loop's zero resistance threshold. In an experiment at Massachusetts Institute of Technology started in 1956, a current of several hundred amperes was induced in a lead ring immersed in liquid helium. It was still flowing in 1965 when the experiment was terminated. There are still, however, a number of practical problems to be solved in this type of memory.

### SEMICONDUCTOR MEMORIES

Currently the most promising and fastest growing memory technology is semiconductor memories. Both bipolar and MOS memories are available. Bipolar memories are faster with typical access times of 50 to 100 ns as compared to 150 ns for the faster dynamic MOS memory and 500–1000 ns for the slower static MOS memory. Core memories have access times of 300–1000 ns and longer. Table 10-3 compares the three semiconductor memory types. The figures in this table are approxi-

**Table 10-3** Comparison of Current Semiconductor Memories

|  | Bipolar | Static MOS | Dynamic MOS |
|---|---|---|---|
| Bit density gate area/SQ mils | 52.8 | 10.6 | 10.6** |
| Speed access time | 30-100 nS | 250-500 nS | 85-150 nS |
| Power consumption per gate | 1 mW | 0.2 mW | 0.2 mW** |
| Cost: cents/bit        1975 | 5.0 | 0.1 | 0.05 |
| Projected*        1982 | 0.4 | 0.03 | 0.02 |

*This assumes some levelling off in the trend by about 1978. Any cost estimates are likely to be too high. At any rate, they can be considered as only rough estimates.

**Dynamic MOS can be constructed with half as many gates per memory cell as static MOS, depending on cell structure.

mate, but, other than price, they are of the correct order of magnitude. The rapid plummeting in the cost of calculator chips is sobering, in light of the short time involved.

The most exciting recent development in this area is Integrated Injection Logic ($I^2L$). Nearly every major manufacturer is working on some form of it. $I^2L$ logic can be produced in densities twice that of MOS, at the same or lower cost, with speeds similar to TTL bipolar logic and power requirements half that of MOS.

## 10-2 Core Memory

Magnetic core memories consist of many toroidal cores strung in a rectangular grid as illustrated in Figure 10-9.

The cores have a square loop magnetization curve as shown in Figure 10-10. This kind of curve describes the behavior of a magnetic material that has a critical point at which the flux density produced by a secondary field causes the core to become permanently magnetized. At flux densities below this critical value, the magnetic material relaxes to

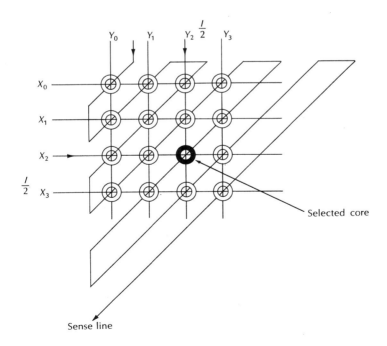

**Figure 10-9** Magnetic Core Memory Plane

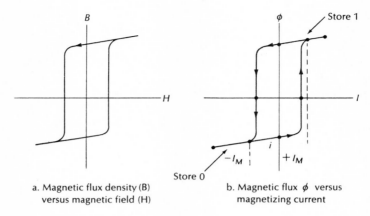

a. Magnetic flux density (B)           b. Magnetic flux $\phi$ versus
   versus magnetic field (H)              magnetizing current

**Figure 10-10**   Ferrite-Core Hysteresis Curves

its original state as soon as the external magnetic field is removed. If the external field is produced by current flowing through a wire, there is some critical current at which the core will remain permanently magnetized after the current ceases to flow through the wire. In Figure 10-9, slightly more than half the critical current is passed down line $Y_2$ and a similar amount through line $X_2$. The two fields combine to magnetize the core at the intersection of $Y_2, X_2$. All other cores receive only about half enough current-produced magnetic field to switch them into a permanently magnetized condition. Thus, one and only one (selected) core is *switched* as a result of the two half-critical currents.

Figure 10-9 shows a sense line threaded through all cores. The line is threaded back and forth to effectively cancel induced currents in the sense line as a result of magnetic domain movement in unselected cores. To read out of the memory, the status of desired cores is determined by selecting each core by passing half-critical currents through the appropriate $X$ and $Y$ lines in a direction opposite that used for writing into the core. As the selected core is switched from one magnetized direction to the opposite direction, its collapsing field induces a voltage in the sense winding. Figure 10-11 illustrates current flow and magnetic field direction for storing either zero or one. This method of core selection is called *coincident current* selection. Notice that only 8 lines are required to select 16 cores (Figure 10-9). 1024 cores can be selected by 64 lines. Two lines, a combination of one $X$ and one $Y$, out of the 64 select one of the 1024 cores.

The output voltage from the sense line is quite small and, because of the way the sense line is routed through the cores, may produce either a positive or a negative pulse when a selected core is sensed. A special

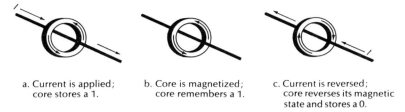

a. Current is applied; core stores a 1.

b. Core is magnetized; core remembers a 1.

c. Current is reversed; core reverses its magnetic state and stores a 0.

**Figure 10-11**    Current Flow and Magnetic Field Directions in Magnetic Cores

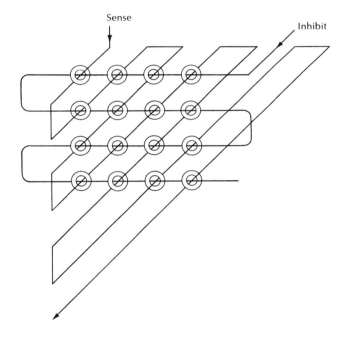

Note: Select lines are omitted for clarity.

**Figure 10-12**    Core Plane with Sense and Inhibit Lines

sense amplifier is used to establish proper levels for the rest of the system.

As a matter of construction convenience, when core assemblies are organized in stacks, the $X$ and $Y$ select lines have their directions alternated as shown in Figure 10-12 to allow for the addition of an inhibit line.

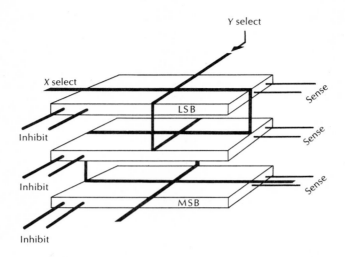

**Figure 10-13** Core Array of Stacked Planes

Computer data is generally organized into groups of bits called a *word*. It is common practice to have a stack of core planes in which there are as many planes as there are bits in the particular computer's word. A stylized sketch of a core plane memory stack is shown in Figure 10-13. This organization permits the same $X$ and $Y$ select lines to address all of the planes in the stack by inhibiting an entire plane when a 1 is not to be written at a particular $X$-$Y$ intersection of a given plane. In planes where a 1 is to be written at that location, the plane is not inhibited. This arrangement greatly reduces the number of select lines required and the associated drive hardware. A memory of 1024 20-bit words (20,480 bits) requires 32 $X$ lines, 32 $Y$ lines, and 20 inhibit lines; thus, 84 lines can address 20,480 bits.

In order to read out of a core, the core's magnetic state must be changed. The readout is said to be destructive because the original data is lost in the process of reading it. (Destructive readout is abbreviated DRO.) The destruction of data in the process of reading it is not generally tolerable. In order to overcome this deficiency in the core memory system, data is stored briefly in flip-flops and written back into the memory. Figure 10-14 shows the scheme for accomplishing nondestructive readout. The read cycle becomes a combined read/write cycle and proceeds as follows:

1. Clear all flip-flops.
2. Select cores to read—all selected cores set to the zero state. Data transferred to flip-flops for temporary storage.

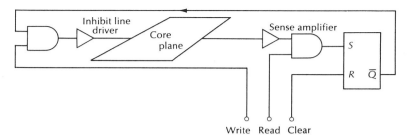

**Figure 10-14**    Core Memory Stack Showing Nondestructive Readout System

3. Write pulse gate flip-flop states into core driver and inhibit amplifiers. The $\bar{Q}$ lines from the flip-flop control the inhibit lines.

## 10-3    Bipolar RAM's

Bipolar random-access memories are high-speed semiconductor memories (20–100 ns access time). They are often used as scratch-pad and buffer memories. Bipolar RAM's consist of an array of 64 to 1000 flip-flops, an address decoder, all necessary driver and sense amplifiers, and chip enable logic.

Two kinds of organization are commonly used: word organization and bit organization. Bit organization requires an $X$ and a $Y$ decoder. Each bit is individually accessible at the unique intersection of a given $X$ and a given $Y$ line. Figure 10-15 shows the block diagram of a sixteen-bit bit-organized bipolar RAM. The single desired flip-flop is addressed as a 1 on one $X$ line and a 1 on one $Y$ line. The addressed cell is then set to a 1 by entering a write 1 command ($W_1$ input), or set to a 0 by entering a write 0 command ($W_0$ input).

To read out of the memory, a specific cell (flip-flop) is addressed as it is for writing and the outputs of the sense amplifiers carry the condition of that cell. Figure 10-16 shows the schematic of a typical bipolar RAM memory cell.

The sixteen-bit memory in Figure 10-15 requires 4 $X$-select lines and 4 $Y$-select lines. It also requires that one and only one $Y$ line and one $X$ line be enabled at a time. More than one cell will be selected if more than one line on each axis is enabled. In a read condition, if two cells are selected at the same time and one is 0 and the other 1, a short between $V_{cc}$ and ground results. In order to avoid this possibility, to reduce the number of pins on the chip, and to make the memory compatible with binary addressing, two decoders are added. The block diagram is shown in Figure 10-17. Most RAM's have the decoders on the chip.

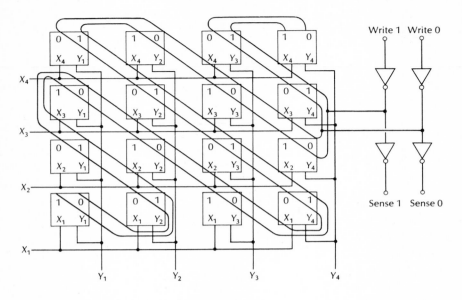

**Figure 10-15**   Logic Diagram of a Sixteen-Bit RAM

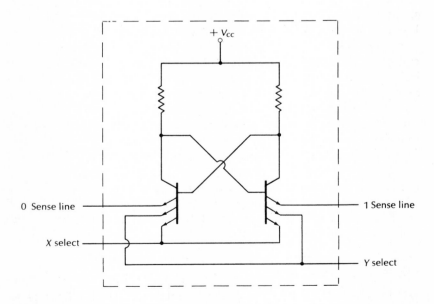

**Figure 10-16**   Basic Bipolar Memory Cell

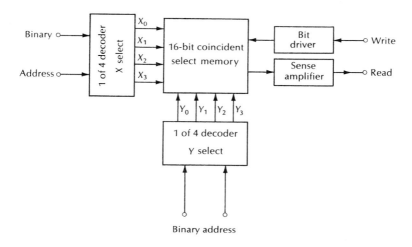

**Figure 10-17**   Decoded RAM

A 1024-bit, bit-organized RAM would require 32 $X$-select and 32 $Y$-select lines. 64 package pins would be required for the select inputs alone. If, however, an $X$ and a $Y$ decoder are included on the chip, the memory can be fully addressed with only 5 $X$-select inputs and 5 $Y$-select inputs. This makes a 16-pin package a possibility.

Modern RAM's can be combined in planes with the outputs of several chips connected to a common bus. Each chip has a chip enable input so that all address lines can be paralleled, greatly expanding the memory size. Up to 100 RAM's with tri-state outputs can be placed on a common bus, but this is rarely done because it is generally more economical to go to MOS devices for memories this large in order to reduce the package count, even though MOS speed is slower. Connecting from two to ten bipolar packages in this fashion is common practice.

Figure 10-18 shows four sixteen-bit decoded RAM's connected in parallel. In the circuit in this figure, 64 locations can be addressed with a total of six bits for the address code. Table 10-4 illustrates how the number of address bits varies with different size memory chips in the plane, or parallel, arrangement.

## 10-4   Word-Organized RAM's

Word-organized RAM's require only one decoder which addresses an entire word consisting of a predetermined number of bits instead of a

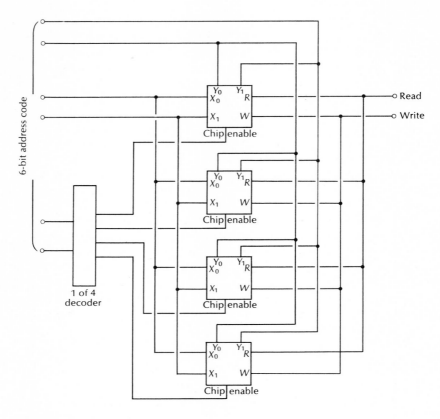

**Figure 10-18** Expanding RAM Memory

**Table 10-4** Numbers of Address Bits Required for Different Configurations

| Each Decoded RAM Number of Bits | Address Bits Per RAM | Number of Stacked RAMS | Total Bits (4 Packages) | Total Address Bits |
|---|---|---|---|---|
| 16 | $2X + 2Y = 4$ | 4 | 64 | 6 |
| 256 | $4X + 4Y = 8$ | 4 | 1024 | 10 |
| 1024 | $5X + 5Y = 10$ | 4 | 4096 | 12 |
| 4096 | $6X + 6Y = 12$ | 4 | 16,384 | 14 |

single bit. The RAM is organized as *W* words of *N* bits. A specific word is selected by the single decoder and all bits in the selected word are either written into or read out simultaneously (in parallel). Some word-organized RAM's provide tri-state bidirectional input/output lines in which the same lines are used both to write into and read out of the memory. Figure 10-19 shows a word-organized RAM.

Memories are classified according to their organization. For example, a memory organized into 16 words of thirty-two bits each would be classified as a $(W \times N)$ $16 \times 32$ memory where *N* is the number of bits per word. Total memory size is also defined in terms of the next lower number of bits, bytes, or words. For example, a 65,536-bit memory would be classified as a 65K memory, a 4,096-byte memory would be called a 4K-byte memory.

The memory cell in a bipolar memory is a simplified TTL flip-flop structure and is called a static memory because the flip-flop, once set, remains set barring power interruption or deliberate resetting. The readout is naturally nondestructive. A basic bipolar memory cell is shown in Figure 10-16. Two outputs are provided to provide overall flexibility. The outputs are taken from one of the emitters (on each transistor) rather than from the collector, providing the low impedance high-drive capabilities of an emitter follower without using an addi-

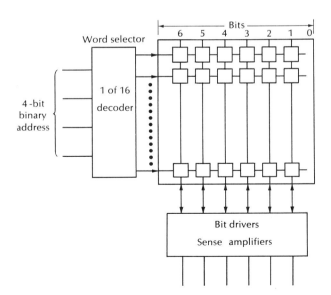

**Figure 10-19**  Word-Organized RAM

tional buffer transistor. The low impedance emitter follower output provides the high-drive current necessary for rapid switching of the output stage (sense amplifier).

## TYPES OF OUTPUT STAGES

Memory chips are very often connected together in arrays to provide longer words (more bits per word) and a larger number of words than can be obtained from any single chip. In order to facilitate ORing the outputs of the several sense amplifiers, two output forms have been generally adopted: open collector and tri-state outputs.

The usual totem pole TTL output circuit is faster than an open collector circuit because of its active pull-up and pull-down capability; however, totem pole outputs cannot be hard wired together. One of a pair of output stages can be conducting at a high logic level, connecting the common output line to the $+V_{cc}$ line through a negligible resistance, while at the same time the other output stage can be at a low logic level, connecting the common output to ground. This condition results in a heavy load across the power supply and an indeterminate output logic state. The open collector approach, however, permits the selection of a common collector resistor to provide proper levels in a wired-OR configuration.

In a tri-state output stage, the third state is not a logic level but a virtual open circuit. This allows inactive chip outputs to "float," neither drawing current nor delivering current to the wired node. The circuit is a modified totem pole and, for valid logic states, provides both active pull-up and active pull-down.

A random-access memory is often called a read/write memory. Some people prefer the read/write terminology because of the possible confusion with read-only memories, some of which can also be addressed at random but cannot be written into as part of the normal computer operation. However, the terms ROM and RAM are generally so well understood that there is little confusion.

## 10-5    A Typical Commercial Bipolar RAM

The Signetics 82516–82517 is a typical 256 × 1 bipolar RAM. It is available in two output versions: tri-state (82516) and open collector (82517). The inputs are internally buffered to provide very low input current requirements, typically 25 microamperes for a logic 1 state and 100 $\mu$A for a logic 0. The relatively high input impedance permits stacking (paralleling) without external drivers.

The memory has on-the-chip decoding and provides three chip enable inputs for flexibility in controlling large groups of bus connected

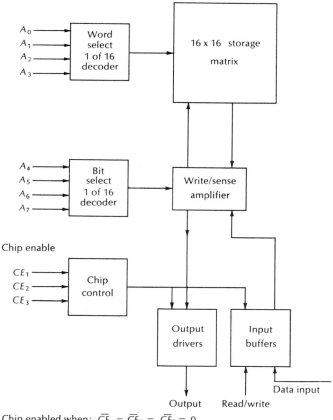

Chip enabled when: $\overline{CE}_1 = \overline{CE}_2 = \overline{CE}_3 = 0$

**Figure 10-20**   The 82516 and 82517 RAM

chips. The typical access time is 30 nanoseconds and the power consumption is 1.5 mW/bit. Figure 10-20 shows the block diagram for this device. Typically, 100 or more chips of the tri-state version can be connected to a common bus. A number of manufacturers make units with similar specifications.

## 10-6   MOS RAM's and Shift Registers

When larger memories are required, MOS (or $I^2L$) is more practical than the TTL kind of bipolar circuitry. Power dissipations of much less than 1 milliwatt per bit are common compared with conventional bipolar devices with their 1.5+ milliwatts per bit. This represents far less chip power for an MOS device. More important, however, is the ease of manufacture and the consequently lower cost of large MOS memories.

There are two kinds of MOS cells used in memory systems: a more or less conventional flip-flop circuit called *static* MOS and a stored charge circuit called *dynamic* MOS. The dynamic MOS is cheaper because it is capable of much larger densities of circuits per chip as a result of its much simpler circuit structure. It also consumes far less power than static MOS. Dynamic MOS is more difficult and less flexible to use, however, because the storage capacitors require periodic refreshing and the multiphase clock timing is fairly critical. Dynamic shift registers are not usable in situations where clock rates below approximately 500 Hz are required because of the small but significant leakage of the storage capacitors.

MOS memories take three basic forms: random-access, read-only, and shift register memories. We will discuss each of these in this chapter.

## 10-7 MOS RAM Memory Cells

### THE STATIC CELL

Figure 10-21 shows a typical MOS flip-flop circuit used in static RAM memories. MOS FET transistors $Q_3$ and $Q_4$ take the place of load resistors. Active load resistors require much less chip space, require no separate processing, and dissipate far less power than ordinary resistors. Transistors $Q_1$ and $Q_6$ serve as data transfer gates. Transistors $Q_2$ and $Q_5$ are connected in an ordinary simple flip-flop configuration. The static cell can *remember* data as long as power is applied; it does not need periodic refreshing.

### DYNAMIC CELLS

The only counterpart of the dynamic cell in bipolar circuitry is the $I^2L$. The operation of dynamic cells depends upon the nearly infinite input impedance and the capacitive nature of the MOS FET transistor. Data is stored as a charge on the input (or an auxiliary capacitor) capacitance. Because any real capacitor has some leakage, the dynamic memory will gradually ''forget,'' and must be periodically refreshed as necessary. A precharge method simplifies the refreshing operation but does not eliminate the problem.

There are several basic random-access memory cell structures used in MOS technology. Figure 10-22 shows three typical RAM cell circuits. In part a, transistor $Q_2$ is the storage cell and $C_1$ is the input

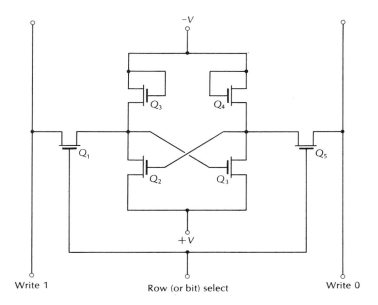

**Figure 10-21** Typical Static Memory Cell

capacitance of $Q_2$. To write in data, $Q_1$ is switched to a low impedance state charging $C_1$ (or discharging $C_1$, if precharge is used). Transistor $Q_3$ is a combination active load resistor and transfer gate that transfers the output of the memory cell ($Q_2$) to the *read data* line upon a command from the read select line.

The circuit in part b is basically the same as that in part a except that read and write lines are combined to reduce the amount of interconnecting wiring on the chip. A two-phase clock controls the read/write cycles in the device. In part c the transistor $Q$ is used as a transfer gate, and a passive on-the-chip capacitor is used as the storage element.

## 10-8 Shift Register Cells

MOS shift registers with one-hundred- to several thousand-bit storage are available for a multitude of tasks. These are generally serial-in/serial-out (SISO) and are available in both static and dynamic forms. TTL registers with lengths of more than 8–16 bits are not common.

### STATIC DEVICES

Static MOS shift register cells are modified MOS flip-flops. Figure 10-23 shows a typical MOS static shift register cell. Basically the circuit

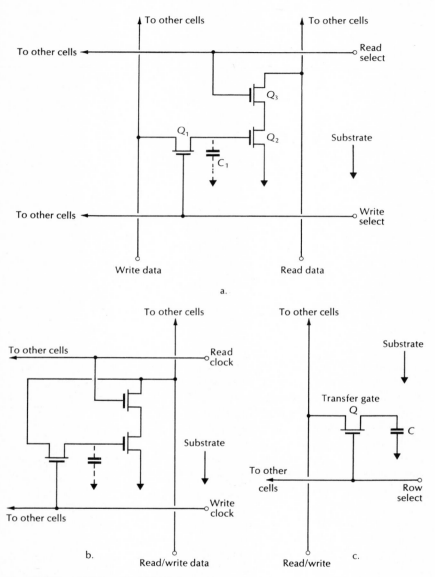

**Figure 10-22**   MOS Dynamic RAM Cells

consists of two MOS inverters, using transfer gates in the feedback circuits. The circuit is basically a flip-flop. The two cells are isolated from each other by the transfer gate transistors $Q_3$ and $Q_5$. Data transfer into the cell and are coordinated from one half of the cell to the other

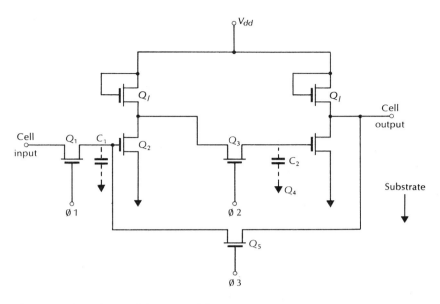

**Figure 10-23**   MOS Static Shift Register Cell

by a three-phase clock. The three-phase clock signals are normally generated by circuitry on the memory chip. The three-phase signals are derived on the chip from a standard TTL single-phase clock signal input. TTL interface input/output and similar circuitry is also included on the memory chip, making it fully TTL compatible.

The circuit in Figure 10-23 operates as follows: when $\emptyset 1$ is *low,* data is transferred through $Q_1$ to $C_1$. At this time $\emptyset 2$ and $\emptyset 3$ are *high* and $C_2$ is isolated from the left half of the cell. When the TTL system clock goes *low* (for active-high units), $\emptyset 1$ goes *high* and $\emptyset 2$ goes *low*. When $\emptyset 1$ is *high,* $C_1$ is isolated from the input terminal. $\emptyset 2$ *low* causes $Q_3$ to conduct, transferring data to $C_2$. Phase 3 requires about 5 microseconds to go *low,* to provide sufficient latch-up time. The feedback signal through $Q_5$ latches up the cell until the next TTL clock pulse arrives and, via the three-phase internal clock, causes new data to shift into the cell, while the cell outputs the previous data for the next cell in line. The system of $\emptyset 1$ and $\emptyset 2$ clocks provides behavior similar to that of a bipolar master-slave flip-flop and, like the master-slave, eliminates the race problem. $\emptyset 3$ is necessary to control the latch-up function. The $\emptyset 3$ clock imposes a limitation on the maximum system clock pulse width, which can be found in the data sheet for the particular device being used.

## DYNAMIC SHIFT REGISTER CELLS

The dynamic shift register cells use the stored charge principle. A two-phase, non-overlapping clock is required, but no third phase is necessary because there is no latch-up feedback. Capacitor refreshing is required, thus imposing a limitation on the minimum clock speed, typically a few hundred hertz. Figure 10-24 shows the schematic diagram of the dynamic shift register cell. The circuit works as follows:

When $\emptyset 1$ (in) is *low*, the data stored as a charge on $C_1$ is transferred through $Q_3$ to $C_2$. When $\emptyset 1$ (in) goes *high*, $\emptyset 2$ (out) goes *low*, transferring data out of the cell. The *high* on $\emptyset 1$ (in) isolates $C_2$ from the input.

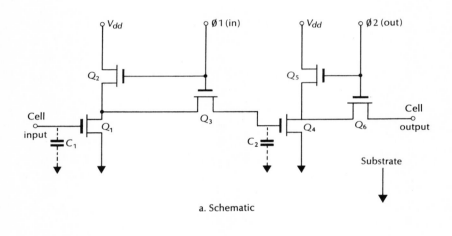

a. Schematic

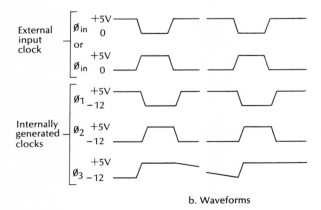

b. Waveforms

**Figure 10-24**   Dynamic Shift Register Cell

Data is transferred from one cell to the next with each pair of clock pulses.

$Q_2$ and $Q_5$ are turned on by the clocks. As a result, power consumption varies with the clock duty cycle. Refreshing is accomplished in this case by simply shifting data frequently enough, which means that there is always a minimum useful clock rate for this kind of shift register.

## 10-9  Clocks and MOS

The clock pulses for MOS constitute a special set of problems. MOS clocks generally must have voltage swing from +5V to −12 or so, and the waveform must be clean. In troubleshooting systems using MOS gates or gate array (such as a memory), one of the first things to check is the clock waveforms, since many problems of erratic behavior can be traced to clock problems. Positive overshoot that tends to forward bias the substrate diode is one particular cause of erratic circuit operation. Figure 10-25 shows an ideal waveform and three unsatisfactory waveforms:

a. This is the ideal waveform.

b. This shows a case of positive overshoot that causes the substrate diode to become forward biased. This condition upsets the output driving levels to the following gate input, resulting in erratic over-

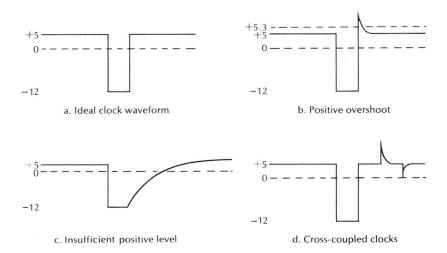

a. Ideal clock waveform

b. Positive overshoot

c. Insufficient positive level

d. Cross-coupled clocks

**Figure 10-25**  Clock Waveform Problems

all circuit behavior. This is most common of all clock problems in MOS systems. Because the substrate diode was never intended to go into forward bias, manufacturers have made no effort to maintain specific parameters for its behavior. As a result, a positive overshoot clock problem may set up a condition in which some MOS units will exhibit varying degrees of erratic performance. This can be a very confusing situation if you don't know what to look for.

c. In this case, the positive-going clock pulse never quite reaches the +5 level (the zero reference level for MOS). With this fault the clock can sometimes seem to be working for some functions but not for others. For example, an MOS shift register may clock data through the register but the register may refuse to accept and store any new data entries.

d. This illustrates a case of cross talk (or cross-coupling) generally caused by clamping problems, high impedance positive-going switching, or power supply decoupling problems. Properly functioning pull-up and pull-down drivers are essential.

Overshoot problems can be overcome by using a clock output buffer (MOS driver) that is optimized for rise and fall times and provides adequate active pull-up and pull-down behavior. Figure 10-26 shows three possible clock output stages for driving MOS:

a. This part shows a single-ended bipolar output stage with resistor pull-up. Such a circuit is generally unacceptable because it has poor noise immunity, a slow rise time, and no active pull-down.

b. This is the conventional totem pole (TTL) output stage. It produces a generally acceptable clock waveform for MOS, although not the best. Because of the frequently added pull-up resistor used to interface TTL to MOS, a failure of the upper transistor converts the circuit to the form in part a, exhibiting poor waveform characteristics similar to those in a.

c. This stage uses complementary output transistors and provides excellent rise and fall times and lack of overshoot as a result of active pull-up and pull-down. Figure 10-27 shows a frequently recommended TTL clock to MOS interface driver. The inputs are capacity coupled to the TTL clock generator. Resistor $R_4$ lengthens the time constant for operation with clock rates below 750 kHz. $R_4$ should be eliminated for clock rates above 750 kHz.

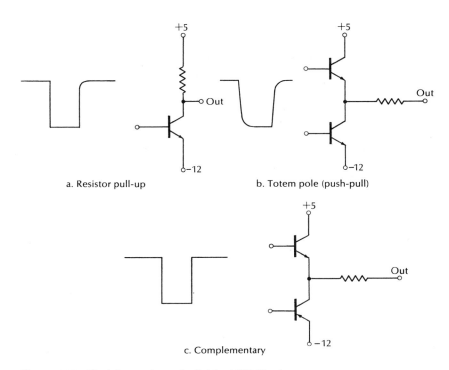

a. Resistor pull-up       b. Totem pole (push-pull)

c. Complementary

**Figure 10-26**    Clock Output Stages for Driving MOS Circuits

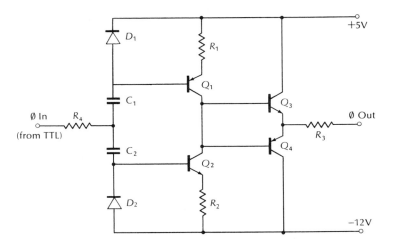

**Figure 10-27**    Recommended TTL-MOS Interface Driver

## MULTIPLE-PHASE CLOCKS

Many of the high-level MOS devices require multiphase clocks. Timing, levels, and waveform control of these clocks constitute a good part of the troubleshooter's and designer's problems when working with $P$-type MOS devices. Figure 10-28 shows a typical two-phase clock generator for MOS memories. Each output requires a buffer driver of the sort shown in Figure 10-27. The two-phase circuit produces alternate pulses of about one-fourth the input clock pulse width.

Figure 10-29a shows the block diagram indicating how a monostable multi can be used to produce two-phase variable-width clock pulses in conjunction with the circuit in Figure 10-27. Figure 10-29b shows one-shots used to provide independent variable two-phase clock pulses. Part c shows two-phase clock waveforms.

## 10-10   MOS Memory Output Stages

Four output configurations are used in MOS: bare drain (analogous to the open collector in bipolar), internal pull-down resistor output (a single-ended configuration), push-pull, and tri-state. P-MOS devices must have their outputs inverted for TTL compatibility.

### BARE DRAIN

Figure 10-30a shows the bare drain configuration. This is the simplest structure and requires an *external* (to the chip) pull-down resistor. This output configuration is used for wired-OR connections as shown in part b. The pull-down resistor is used to sink the 1.6 mA required by a standard TTL input. The bare drain MOS FET exhibits a resistance (source to drain) of about 500 ohms in the *on* condition.

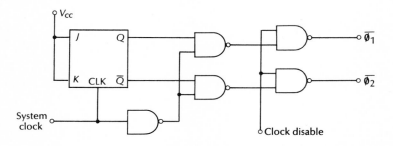

**Figure 10-28**   Two-Phase TTL Clock Generator

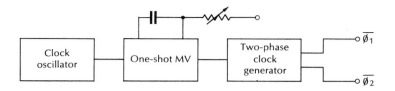

a. Variable clock pulse generator

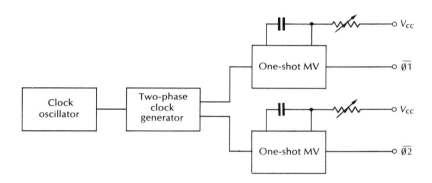

b. Independent pulse with control for each phase.

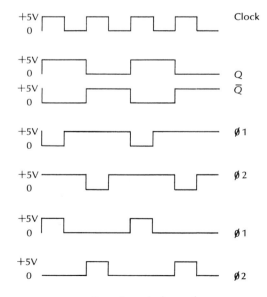

c. Two-phase clock waveforms

**Figure 10-29**   Variable Width Two-Phase Clock Generators and Two-Phase Clock Waveforms

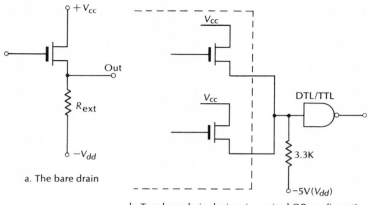

a. The bare drain

b. Two bare drain devices in a wired OR configuration

**Figure 10-30** MOS Output Circuits

## INTERNAL PULL-DOWN RESISTOR CONFIGURATION

Some of the devices with internal pull-down resistors are designed to interface with other MOS units and will not drive a TTL input. Others with a lower value pull-down resistor can be wired as a pair in the wired-OR configuration and will drive a single TTL input. The configuration is the same as that shown in Figure 10-30 except that the resistor is internal.

## PUSH-PULL

The push-pull circuit is analogous to the totem-pole output in TTL (see Figure 10-31). The two transistors are driven with complementary signals. When the upper transistor is on (and the lower one is off), the output line is connected to $V_{cc}$ by an effective resistance of about 500Ω. When the lower transistor is on (and the upper transistor is off), the output line is connected through about 500 Ω t o $V_{DD}$.

## THREE-STATE OUTPUT

The push-pull circuit has the advantage of active pull-up and pull-down, but like the totem-pole configuration in TTL, outputs cannot be paralleled. The tri-state circuit is used to get the best of both worlds in addition to an open circuit state to eliminate the loading of inactive outputs.

The third, open output state is achieved by using an output enable line on both gates in a push-pull output stage. Figure 10-32 shows the

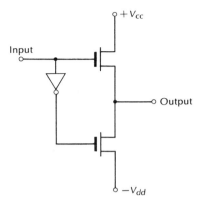

**Figure 10-31**  MOS Push-Pull Output Circuit

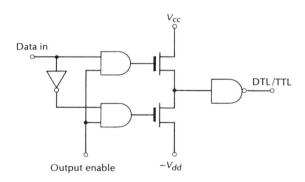

**Figure 10-32**  Tri-State Output Circuit

circuit arrangement for a tri-state MOS output circuit. This is an open circuit when the chip is unselected.

## 10-11  Read-Only Memories (ROM's)

Read-only memories are a permanent data store. In the course of normal operation, they are not volatile and cannot be written into. Permanently held data can be read out during processing. These memories can be used to store lookup tables, microprograms such as algorithms, as a replacement for complex combinatorial logic circuits, for conversion from one code to another, and as CRT character generators.

ROM's are organized for random access but often on an access-to-a-word basis with parallel bit outputs. Word lengths are generally 4, 8, or 16 bits long. Outputs are usually open collector or tri-state to provide for expansion of memory size.

ROM's use much simpler cells than read/write memories. Theoretically, a cell need be no more than a transistor biased to a permanently off state or, in the case of MOS, left off the chip during manufacture. There are three common varieties of ROM's: mask programmed, field programmed, and erasable.

Mask programmed ROM's are programmed to customer order or to certain standard programs during manufacture by controlling transistor base (or gate) potential or by leaving out specific cells. Figure 10-33 illustrates one way this could be accomplished.

In the manufacturing process the resistor of the base of each transistor (cell) is made to be either a low resistance, causing the transistor to conduct heavily thus producing a low (logical 0) output, or it can be made high, causing the transistor to be in the nonconducting state thus producing a high (logical 1) output. The cells are not always quite as simple as that shown in Figure 10-33 because loading factors must be taken into account, cell select provisions must be provided, and very often a chip select input is also provided. However, the basic principle involved is correctly illustrated in Figure 10-33. Once programmed, masked programmed ROM's cannot be altered.

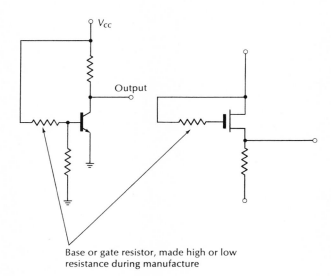

Base or gate resistor, made high or low
resistance during manufacture

**Figure 10-33**   Examples of Masked Programmed ROM Memory Cells

Field programmable units allow us to program our own ROM's for short-run or prototype use. They are available only in bipolar form. Sophisticated programming units are available if much in-house programming is to be done. The principle of operation and the nature of the programming are similar to those of masked programming devices except that the base resistances are provided in the form of fusable nichrome (nickel chromium) links. As delivered to the customer, all links are low resistance. The customer programs the unit by selecting a particular cell in the same way it would normally be selected, and applying an abnormally high voltage (and current) that burns the fusible link open, causing the output of the transistor (cell) to go high. Once the link is opened, that particular cell is forever at a logical 1 and cannot be altered. Each cell is selected in turn, and the link is either fused open or left intact depending upon whether a 0 or a 1 is to be stored in that particular location.

The MOS erasable ROM is similar to the dynamic cell used in RAM's; however, the gate is left open and glass encapsulated. The memory is programmed by applying a relatively high voltage (compared to operating voltages). This produces a trapped charge at the gate-glass interface that is stable unless irradiated by a short wavelength ultraviolet light or some other energetic radiant energy. The memory is erased by removing the protective cover and exposing the chip to ultraviolet light. The chip must then be completely reprogrammed. This program-erase cycle can be repeated several times before the chip must be replaced.

## 10-12    MOS ROM's

MOS ROM's are classified as either dynamic or static even though the actual memory cell is essentially static (although there is no feedback or latching involved). For some larger read-only memories, dynamic decoder circuitry is used. Figure 10-34a shows the basic MOS ROM circuit structure, and part b shows the basic ROM block diagram, which illustrates the clock circuitry that is used only with dynamic memories. No clock system is required for static devices.

## 10-13    The 4096-Bit Dynamic MOS RAM

The 8107, a widely used dynamic 4096-bit MOS RAM, is a low-cost 4096-word-by-1-bit RAM designed specifically for microprocessors. It features tri-state outputs and a 7 $\mu$W/bit power consumption. Like all dynamic devices, it requires refreshing; in this case, one read cycle on each of the 64 rows each millisecond is required. Full on-the-chip decoding is provided, allowing for the use of a 22 pin dual-in-line package.

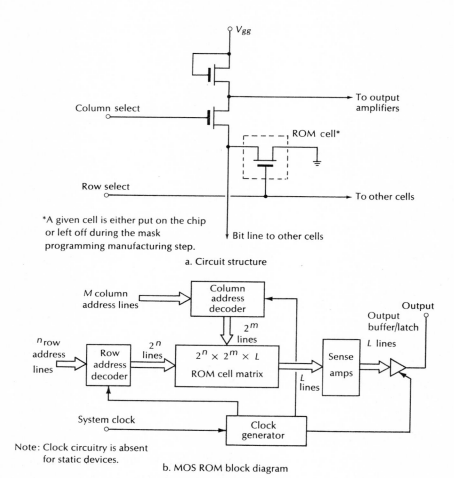

a. Circuit structure

b. MOS ROM block diagram

**Figure 10-34** MOS ROM Memories

Figure 10-35 shows the block diagram of the 8107. Also available are 16K dynamic MOS RAM's, which are becoming increasingly popular.

## 10-14 Static RAM Memory

Static MOS memories use flip-flops as the basic memory element (cell) and are available in both *P*-channel and *N*-channel versions. Static RAM's are slower than dynamic ones but can be operated without complex clock signals or, in most cases, in an asynchronous (no clock) mode. Because flip-flops are used to store data (instead of the charged

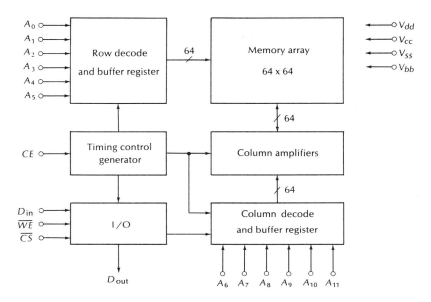

**Figure 10-35**  Functional Block Diagram of the 4096-Bit MOS RAM

capacitor approach used in dynamic MOS), there is no need for refresh circuitry.

The $P$-channel device requires a separate negative supply voltage in addition to the +5V supply. The $N$-channel requires only the single +5V supply and is generally easier to interface with TTL than $P$-channel. Figure 10-36 shows a typical cell structure of both an $N$-channel and a $P$-channel static MOS cell.

In the $N$-channel cell $Q_1$ and $Q_2$ are the active elements of the flip-flop, and $Q_3$ and $Q_4$ function as load resistors for the flip-flop transistors—a common procedure in MOS technology. Transistors used as resistive elements use less chip space and are cheaper to fabricate than conventional resistors. $Q_5$ and $Q_6$ serve to activate the cell as part of the word enable system. $Q_7$ and $Q_8$ function as a pass gate for enabling the particular cell (bit select) for either reading out of or writing into the cell. $A_1$ is a data-in non-inverting amplifier and $A_2$ is an inverting data-in amplifier; $A_3$ is a tri-state sense amplifier. Cell selection for read/write is accomplished by holding the word- and bit-select line high (logic 1); data are written into the cell by selecting the cell and entering a logic 1 or logic 0 via the data-input line.

In the $P$-channel cell in Figure 10-36a $Q_1$ and $Q_2$ are the active transistors in the flip-flop. As in the $N$-channel device, $Q_3$ and $Q_4$ serve

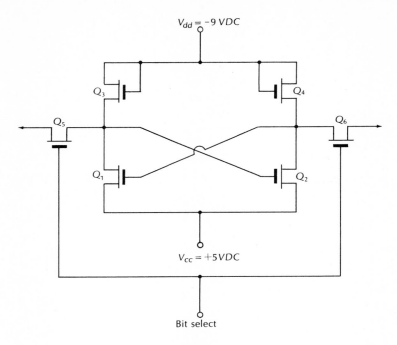

a. P-channel MOS RAM memory cell

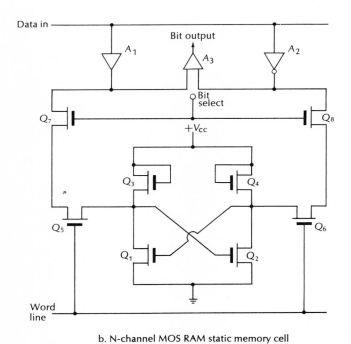

b. N-channel MOS RAM static memory cell

**Figure 10-36**   Typical N-Channel and P-Channel Static MOS RAM Cells

as load resistors for the flip-flops. $Q_5$ and $Q_6$ serve as bit-select pass gates in the same fashion as in the $N$-structure in Figure 10-36b.

Figure 10-37a shows the functional block diagram of a 1024-bit $N$-channel MOS static RAM. A typical $N$-channel device of this type is a 2102 or 2062.

The 2102 is a medium-speed static MOS RAM with an access time of less than 1 $\mu$s. The 2102-1 has an access time of 500 ns, but is otherwise functionally equivalent to the 2102. The 2102 requires no interface circuitry when it is used to drive or is driven by TTL. It requires only a single +5V power supply and features tri-state output and on-the-chip full decoding. It consumes a power of 0.2 mW per bit. Figure 10-37b shows the symbol for a combined inverting and non-inverting data-input amplifier.

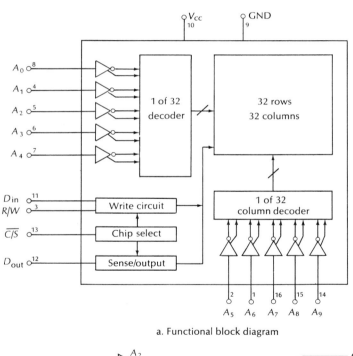

a. Functional block diagram

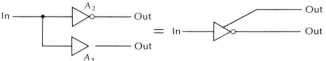

b. Input amplifier symbol

**Figure 10-37** Functional Block Diagram for a 1024-Bit N-Channel MOS Static RAM

## 10-15 Recirculating Shift Registers

Data stored in a shift register can be taken from the output, fed back to the input, and shifted around the loop with the addition of some logic. Recirculating the data can make the readout nondestructive if data is returned to the first stage at the same time it is transferred to the output.

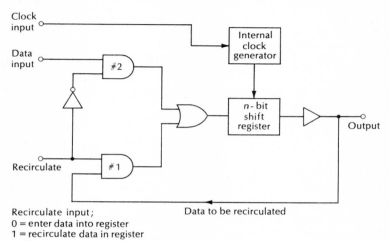

Recirculate input;
0 = enter data into register
1 = recirculate data in register

a. Typical static recirculating register

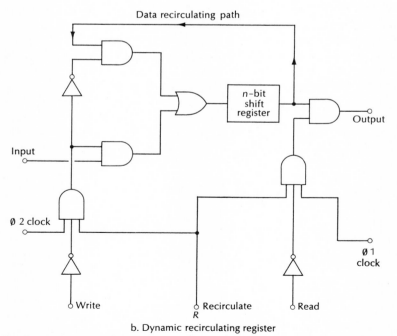

b. Dynamic recirculating register

**Figure 10-38**  Recirculating Registers

Truth table

| Write | Read | Function |
|:---:|:---:|:---|
| 0 | 0 | recirculate, output is 0 |
| 0 | 1 | recirculate, output is data |
| 1 | 0 | write mode, output is 0 |
| 1 | 1 | read/write mode, output is data |

Recirculate input: $R = 0$, data recirculates;
$R = 1$, see truth table

Figure 10-38 continued      c. Dynamic recirculating register truth table

In the case of dynamic registers, recirculating is necessary if data must be held for more than a millisecond because of the dynamic logic's refresh requirement.

The recirculating logic is often included on the chip in MOS devices, but outboard logic can also be used. Figure 10-38a shows a typical MOS static register with recirculating logic. In the circuit in Figure 10-38a output data is always available. A recirculate input at gate 1 determines whether new or recirculated data will enter the $n$-bit shift register. With a 0 on the recirculate input, gate 1 is disabled and recirculated data is locked out. The inverter applies a *high* to the lower input of gate 2, allowing new data to enter the register. With a 1 on the recirculate input, recirculated data is allowed to enter the register and new data is locked out. Most MOS static shift registers have on-chip circuitry to develop the required clock signals from the system clock.

The recirculating gate circuit for dynamic registers in Figure 10-38b is similar to the one used for static registers, except that the output is gated and the two-phase clock is applied to the recirculating control and output gates. The truth table in Figure 10-38c tabulates the gate control functions for the dynamic register circuit.

## 10-16  Dynamic MOS Shift Registers

The following varieties of MOS dynamic shift register memories are commonly available:

1. Quad 256, dual 512, single 1024-bit multiplexed
2. Dual 100-bit
    a. bare drain
    b. with 7.5K pull-down resistor
    c. with 20K pull-down resistor
3. 512 and 1024-bit recirculating

### QUAD 256, DUAL 512, SINGLE 1024-BIT REGISTERS

The quad 256, dual 512, single 1024-bit shift registers are *P*-channel MOS devices capable of a 1 MHz data rate. Because of on-chip multiplexing, the data rate is twice the clock rate. These registers are input compatible with MOS or TTL, and the bare drain output can drive either MOS or one standard TTL load by selecting the appropriate load resistor value. A two-phase clock is required. The clock rate must be greater than 500 Hz and the data rate must be greater than 1 kHz to prevent loss of data due to charge leakage.

### DUAL 100-BIT DYNAMIC SHIFT REGISTER

These devices may be used as two 100-bit registers or a single 200-bit register. Two clock phases are required. The device is available with bare drain or with 7.5K or 20K internal pull-down resistors, making it able to drive most MOS or a single TTL load. Clock and data rates are from 600 Hz to 3 MHz. Figure 10-39 shows the schematic diagram.

### 512- AND 1024-BIT CIRCULATING DYNAMIC REGISTERS

These are single units of 512 or 1024 bits. Internal logic takes care of recirculation and read/write control functions. Both units are bare drain for both MOS and one-unit-load TTL compatibility. A two-phase clock is required with a clock and data rate of from 500 Hz to 3 MHz. Figure 10-40 shows the functional block diagram and function table. A +5V and a −5V supply are required. Other types are available including devices with 2048 or more bits.

## 10-17    Static Shift Registers

The following static shift registers are common off-the-shelf items:

1. Tri-state Output Types
   a. dual 50-bit (for example, Signetics 2509)
   b. dual 100-bit (for example, Signetics 2510)
   c. dual 200-bit (for example, Signetics 2511)
   Output-stage cell structures for static shift registers are very similar to those used in static RAM's. The 2509-10-11 has a DC to 2 MHz clock rate capability and is TTL compatible. These devices require a three-phase clock, but the three-phase signals are generated on the chip and controlled by a 5V logic-level clock.

2. The Hex 32-Bit and 40-Bit Registers
   The hex 32-bit and 40-bit registers (Signetics 2518, for example) use bare drain outputs and clock rates from DC to 3 MHz. They

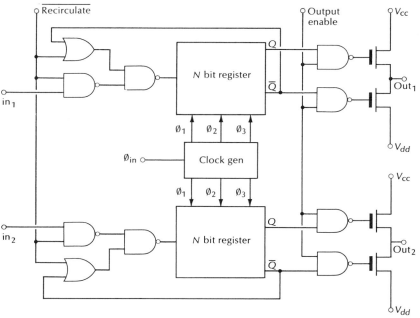

a. functional block diagram

| Recirculate | Input | Function |
|:---:|:---:|:---:|
| 0 | 0 | recirculate |
| 0 | 1 | recirculate |
| 1 | 0 | "0" is written |
| 1 | 1 | "1" is written |

Note: "0" = 0V; "1" = +5V

b. function table

**Figure 10-39**  Dual N-Bit Shift Register and Function Table

are both MOS and TTL compatible. Internal recirculating logic and TTL-compatible clock circuitry are on the chip. A single-phase clock is required.

3. Dual 128-, 132-, 240-, 250-, 256-Bit Static Registers

These devices are one-unit load TTL compatible and use push-pull output stages. The clock-rate range is typically DC to 1.5 MHz. Typically, a three-phase clock is used, but an on-the-chip clock generator is provided and an external single-phase MOS or

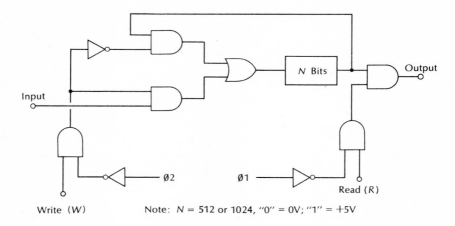

Input

Write (W)     Note: $N$ = 512 or 1024, "0" = 0V; "1" = +5V

a. Functional block diagram

| Write | Read | Function |
|-------|------|----------|
| 0 | 0 | recirculate, output is 0 |
| 0 | 1 | recirculate, output is data |
| 1 | 0 | write mode, output is 0 |
| 1 | 1 | read mode, output is data |

b. Function table

**Figure 10-40**  512 and 1024-Bit Dynamic Shift Registers

TTL clock is all that is required. Two power supply voltages are required.

4. Quad 80-Bit Static Register
   Each of the four registers is provided with independent push-pull outputs and inputs. A single-phase external clock is common to all four registers. An on-the-chip clock generator produces the required three-phase clock signals. On-chip recirculating logic is independent for each of the four registers. Clock rates from DC to 2.5 MHz are typical. Two power supply voltages are required.

5. 1024-Bit Static Shift Register
   This register is similar in most respects to those previously discussed. The three-phase clock generator is on the chip as is most of the required recirculate logic.

The specifications given in the preceding discussion are intended to be typical, if a bit conservative. Improvements occur very frequently and a current data manual should be consulted for more details and exact specifications.

## SUMMARY

### SEMICONDUCTOR MEMORIES

The phenomenal progress made in large capacity semiconductor memory techniques in recent years has begun a revolution in digital technology. Digital systems requiring small memories were not economically feasible because core memories were simply not practical for small systems. Small memories of 64 to 256 bits have been around for some time, but only recently has their cost become attractive. In recent years 1024-bit (or more) memories on a chip have become common and inexpensive items.

### Cost

Cost is a very important factor because of the relatively large number of storage cells required for even a small memory system. The availability of inexpensive memory systems, mostly of the semiconductor variety, is responsible for the current boom in pocket calculators, microprocessors, special remote terminals with auxiliary computing capability (called *intelligent terminals*), digital instrumentation, and industrial process control systems. The availability of inexpensive semiconductor memories has even made it possible for the automotive industry to project the use of a small computer to control fuel mixtures, brakes, transmission, and a variety of other automotive functions—all at a projected cost of less than $50 per car. Memory cost is defined in terms of cents per bit.

### STATIC RAM MEMORY

Static MOS memories use flip-flops as the basic memory element (cell) and are available in both $P$-channel and $N$-channel versions. Static RAM's are slower than dynamic RAM's but can be operated without complex clock signals or, in most cases, in an asynchronous (no clock) mode. Because flip-flops are used to store data instead of the charged capacitor approach used in dynamic MOS, there is no need for refresh circuitry.

The $P$-channel static ROM requires a separate negative supply voltage in addition to the $+5V$ supply. The $N$-channel device requires only the single $+5V$ supply.

MOS RAM's are available with both static and dynamic cells. The static cell is basically a flip-flop latch similar to that used in bipolar memories. The dynamic cell, on the other hand, has no counterpart in bipolar technology. In this type of cell the transistor gate capacitance is charged and the stored charge controls the source-to-drain current. Because of the small capacitance and normal leakage currents, the gate capacitors must be recharged (refreshed) every few milliseconds. The reading out of a memory location automatically refreshes the charge at that location, but this process cannot be relied upon in practice. It is unlikely that each cell will be read frequently enough in the course of normal processing operations. Although the dynamic cell is much faster than the static MOS cell, the time that must be allowed for refresh is a definite drawback. The increased complexity and timing accuracy of the clock also adds to the problem. In addition, some of the potential operating speed is lost as a result of the more complicated gating involved in handling the more complex clock sequence. These peripheral speed losses narrow the speed margin between the P-MOS and the newer N-MOS structures.

### SHIFT REGISTER MEMORIES

There is a variety of both dynamic and static MOS shift register memories that can be used when SISO data storage is available. These memories are relatively inexpensive and easy to implement. All shift register memories can be used as recirculating registers, but not all of them have on-the-chip recirculation logic.

Shift registers can serve as low-cost sequential memories, large bit-number buffer memories, CRT display memories, delay line replacement, and a number of other functions.

Bipolar shift registers are, of course, available but the smaller lengths on each chip make them less suitable for the kinds of applications just mentioned.

### READ-ONLY MEMORIES (ROM'S)

The read-only memory is used for permanent storage such as frequently used control routines, tables of data, and many other computer housekeeping chores. ROM's are available in up to 1K–2K bits in bipolar forms. Bipolar units are faster but more expensive than MOS devices. These devices are available as factory programmed or field (fusible) programmable units (PROM's).

MOS devices are available as factory programmed (mask programmed) and erasable field programmable units. MOS ROM devices are classified as static or dynamic depending upon the kind of logic circuits used in the control and decoder circuitry.

**Problems**

1. Compare the following in terms of access time:
   - a. disc
   - d. core
   - b. drum
   - e. semiconductor main memory
   - c. tape
   - f. semiconductor scratch pad
2. For what purpose is each of the following memories used?
   - a. core
   - b. large-scale integrated circuit memories
   - c. bipolar (LSI) RAM
   - d. cassette
   - e. drum/disc
   - f. computer tape
   - g. punched cards and tape
   - h. ROM
3. What is a cryogenic memory?
4. Describe the advantages or I²L memories over TTL and MOS memories.
5. Is core memory destructive or nondestructive?
6. Describe a stack of core planes. What are the advantages of this configuration?
7. Define DRO in terms of core memory systems.
8. What is a bipolar RAM?
9. Describe the two popular bipolar RAM organizations.
10. What is the basic memory cell in bipolar RAM's?
11. Are bipolar RAM cells classified as static or dynamic? Why?
12. Is the readout of bipolar RAM cells a destructive readout? Why?
13. What is the purpose of memory decoding? (Respond in detail.)
14. A 1024-bit bit organized RAM would require how many inputs when:
    - a. decoded?
    - b. not decoded?
15. What kind of organization is involved in a 16 × 32 memory?
16. A 1K memory probably has an actual bit count of _____ ?
17. Explain the value of tri-state outputs on memory chips.
18. What is another name for a RAM?
19. Why is MOS preferred to TTL type circuitry for larger memories?
20. Compare static and dynamic MOS in terms of complexity, cost, external circuitry, and speed.
21. Draw the schematic diagram of an MOS RAM static cell and briefly describe how it works.
22. Draw and explain the operation of an MOS dynamic memory cell.
23. Explain the term *refresh*. Where is it used and why?
24. Define *precharge*.

25. Why are MOS transistors used as load resistors in MOS memory cells?

26. Draw the schematic diagram of a two-stage MOS dynamic shift register and explain how it works.

27. Why are MOS shift registers preferred over the TTL type for memory applications?

28. If you find a problem with erratic operation in an MOS memory system, what is the first thing you should check?

29. What is a two-phase clock as used in MOS memories? Be specific.

30. List the kinds of output configurations found in MOS memories.

31. What is a read-only memory (ROM)?

32. What are ROM's used for?

33. List the ROM types commonly available.

34. Of what does a bipolar ROM cell consist? An MOS ROM cell?

35. Explain what is meant by *dynamic MOS ROM*.

36. What is a *field programmable ROM?*

37. How is a field programmable ROM programmed?

38. What is an erasable ROM? How is it programmed? How is it erased?

39. What is a recirculating shift register?

40. List 5 types of commercially available MOS shift registers.

41. When MOS memories are classified as TTL compatible, how many standard TTL loads can it drive?

42. Write out the information found on the following punched card.

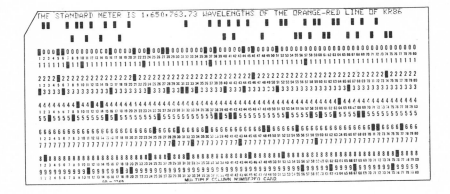

43. (Extra problem) Write out what is encoded on the sample ASCII coded punched paper tape below. Refer to the ASCII code table in Chapter 11 (Table 11-3).

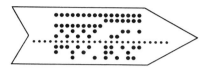

# INTERFACING

*Learning Objectives. Upon completion of this chapter you should:*
1. *Be able to describe the use of bidirectional bus drivers and list the advantages of bus organization.*
2. *Know what kinds of transmission lines are used and be familiar with termination considerations.*
3. *Be able to describe high-level interface devices and know where they are used.*
4. *Be able to define baud rate.*
5. *Be able to describe the most common numerical display devices and the interface devices used with them.*
6. *Know how display multiplexing works.*
7. *Know the principal parameters of MOS-to-LED drivers.*
8. *Be able to draw the block diagram of a phase-locked loop and explain how it operates.*
9. *Be able to explain the phase-locked loop digital frequency multiplier scheme.*
10. *Be able to define FSK (frequency shift keying) and know where it is used.*
11. *Know the purpose of the ASCII and EBCDIC codes.*
12. *Know where the Baudot code is used.*
13. *Be able to draw the block diagram and explain the operation of an alphanumeric video display system.*
14. *Know what code or codes are used as address codes for the video display ROM.*
15. *Be able to describe at least three methods of analog-to-digital conversion.*
16. *Know how digital-to-analog conversion is accomplished.*
17. *Know the meaning of resolution and accuracy in A-D conversion systems.*
18. *Know the principal of operation of the three most common digital voltmeter A-D converters.*
19. *Know what the Gray code is and where it is used.*
20. *Know what bilateral switches are, how they work, and what their important characteristics are.*
21. *Be familiar with the operation and purpose of LSI peripheral interface devices.*
22. *Know the purpose of a UART and how the basic circuit works.*

There are many problems in interfacing digital chips with the outside world. IC chips must ultimately drive relays, solenoids, lamps, digital displays, transmission lines, bus lines, telephone lines, tape recorders, and other peripheral devices.

Because of the diversity in interface problems, data and drive standards have been adopted to make IC interface devices practical. Standard data communications codes (ASCII and EBCDIC) have been adopted, and standards for transmission line levels, bit rates, and so on have been agreed upon.

As a result, manufacturers can produce a line of off-the-shelf interface devices that solve most of the common interface problems. This chapter examines the most common interface problems and the IC devices used to solve them.

## 11-1 Bidirectional Bus Drivers

One of the recent innovations in computer architecture is the bidirectional bus organization system, which has bus organization arithmetic logic units, registers, and so on all connected to a common bus. Data is transferred from any device to any other device on the bus by opening and closing appropriate gates.

The device that interfaces units and the bus is called a *bus interface driver*. Usually bidirectional, it provides directional control *transmit*-to-the-bus or *receive*-from-the-bus and frequently has a high impedance (open-circuit) state. Open collector devices are sometimes used for this purpose, but the tri-state output circuit is more nearly ideal. This output permits 100 or more devices on a single bus, with isolation in the off state that is far superior to that of open collector devices.

Bus (or line) drivers and receivers are available as transmitters only or receivers only, as well as in combination packages.

These interface units are used for a number of machine communication purposes and, consequently, the terminology varies somewhat with different applications. The following are pairs of synonyms that may be interchanged:

  a. Driver—transmitter
  b. Transmitter/receiver—bidirectional bus driver
  c. Receiver—sense amplifier
  d. Bus—line

The input circuit is normally a differential comparator with switching sensitivities of from +5 to 50 mV. Receivers are normally driven in a differential mode when the line length exceeds a very few feet. For longer lines, twisted pairs are preferred. Noise pickup is more nearly the same for each line in a twisted pair, allowing for the cancellation of the common mode noise signal in the differential amplifier. Many of the later IC data bus transmitter/receivers have input impedances high enough to be used with MOS. These devices can be used to interface bus lines where MOS will have to drive TTL inputs. They are commonly used for interfacing MOS memories to TTL.

Figure 11-1 shows how bidirectional driver/receivers are connected on a bus. By varying the control levels at the driver/receivers, any device—*A, B,* or *C*—can have its output connected to the input of any other device on the bus. The output of any device can also drive the inputs to more than one device on the bus. Bus organization provides a simple interconnection system and avoids the limitations of most hard-wired interconnections in which some combinations must be left out because of the impracticality of interconnecting all outputs to all other inputs. The wiring in the bus system can be altered simply by changing the control input levels. What might be very complex wiring can be reduced to a single bus (and few wires) with significant advantages in a high-frequency system.

When longer lines are used, a twisted pair is the most common transmission line, although coaxial lines can also be used. The line is often terminated in the characteristic impedance of the line, typically about 100 ohms for a 100-foot twisted pair.

The terminating resistor may have a capacitor in series with it to avoid loading the system for DC but still maintaining the proper termi-

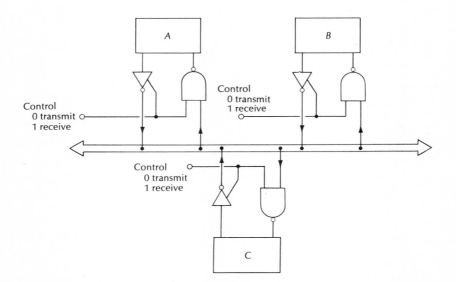

**Figure 11-1**  Bus Interfacing with Bidirectional Bus Driver/Receiver

nation impedance for digital pulses. Terminating the line serves the same purpose as it does in any RF transmission line—to minimize reflections. In digital circuits, reflected pulses could be accepted by some device on the bus as a regular, intended, pulse.

Figure 11-2 shows a *party line* system with terminations. The line drivers must supply the power dissipated by the terminating resistors in addition to the receiver input currents. Most modern drivers can drive as many as twenty receiver inputs and the terminating resistors. Several bus drivers have built-in *D* latches for temporarily holding data on a bus.

## 11-2  Data Communication Line Drivers and Receivers

Line drivers and receivers are required to transmit and receive data on a line between data communication equipment and terminals. The driver converts TTL levels to standard communications levels (usually EIA or MIL-STD). The receiver accepts data at line transmission levels, separates them from line noise, and converts them into standard TTL levels. Hysteresis is normally provided to improve the noise immunity. Because of this feature, receivers are sometimes used in applications that call for a Schmitt trigger.

Table 11-1 compares MIL-STD and EIA communications standards. Mil standards provide for both single-ended and differential lines, but EIA standards apply only to a single-ended line. However, an additional wire that forms half of the twisted pair serves as a noise antenna to provide differential amplifier noise cancellation (see Figure 11-3).

Built-in hysteresis is required for many transmission lines because of inherently high noise levels. Figure 11-4 shows the hysteresis curves for

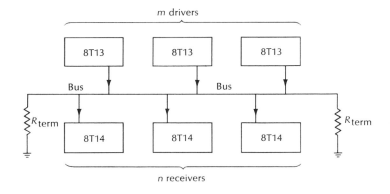

**Figure 11-2**  Drivers and Receivers on a Terminated Bus

**Table 11-1**   Partial Table of Data Transmission Standards

| Specifications | MIL STD 188 B | EIA RS-232 B, C |
|---|---|---|
| Output Voltage: "0" | +6 ±1V | +5 to +15V |
| Output Voltage: "1" | −6 ±1V | −5 to −15V |
| Rise/Fall Time | ±5% of pulse interval | ± 4% of pulse interval |
| Bit Rate | 4 KHz typical | 0 to 20 KHz |

a. One noise cancellation method

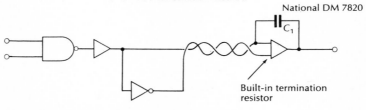

National DM 7820

Built-in termination resistor

Note:  $C_1$ capacitor coupling to terminating resistor

b. Line/driver receiver

**Figure 11-3**   Noise Cancellation Methods

MIL-STD, EIA standard, and EIA fail-safe modes. The EIA fail-safe operation enables the interface on a logical *zero*. In a bus-organized system, if the interface driver disable PC card is removed, it places the interface device at the high impedance state so that it does not affect other devices on the bus.

## 11-3   High-Level Interface Devices

It is sometimes necessary to interface TTL or MOS to devices that require higher voltage current or power levels than standard logic can drive. Typical of such devices are relays, lamps, solenoids, and the like. The Signetics 8T18, 8T80, and 8T90 are intended for this kind of service. These devices typically convert the 5V, 25 mW standard TTL

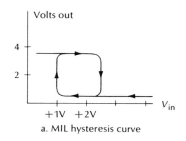

a. MIL hysteresis curve

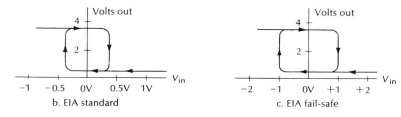

b. EIA standard          c. EIA fail-safe

**Figure 11-4**   Data Communications Hysteresis Curves

level to a 28V, 280 mW level. The 8T80, for example, is a hex device with a two-input NAND gate input with an uncommitted collector. Figure 11-5 shows the schematic and some typical applications for this device.

## 11-4   Baud Rate

The rate at which data is transmitted over a line can be defined in bits per second, but the term *baud rate* is more often used. For a 50 percent duty cycle, the baud rate is twice the bit rate. Figure 11-6 shows a waveform that is not symmetrical (50 percent duty cycle). In Figure 11-6, $T_2$ shows the bit parameters and $T_1$ defines the baud parameters.

$$\text{Bit rate} = \frac{1}{T_2} = \frac{1}{\text{interval per bit}}$$

$$\text{Baud rate} = \frac{1}{T_1} = \frac{1}{\text{minimum unit interval}}$$

## 11-5   Numerical Display Devices

Electronic products continue to demand better display devices for DVM's, frequency meters, calculators, scales, counters, and so on. The

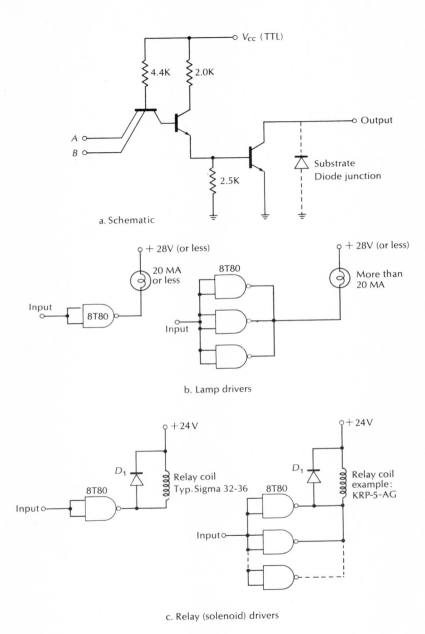

a. Schematic

b. Lamp drivers

c. Relay (solenoid) drivers

**Figure 11-5**  Typical Applications of the 8T80 Interface

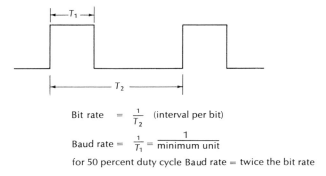

$$\text{Bit rate} \quad = \quad \frac{1}{T_2} \quad \text{(interval per bit)}$$

$$\text{Baud rate} = \quad \frac{1}{T_1} = \frac{1}{\text{minimum unit}}$$

for 50 percent duty cycle Baud rate = twice the bit rate

**Figure 11-6** Baud Rate Defined

result is a wide variety of shapes, sizes, input drive requirements, and principles of operation for display devices. Most electronic display devices use neon, fluorescent, incandescent, electroluminescent, or gallium arsenide (LED) structures to form or illuminate the digital display.

A typical display decoder/driver decodes four-bit (usually BCD) input data into the correct format for the particular display being activated. Outputs must provide sufficient current and voltage and the correct polarity to drive the display. Such decoder/drivers are now available for most display types in a single integrated circuit.

### NIXIE®

One of the oldest numeric displays is the one-of-ten display such as the Nixie tube. An inherent disadvantage is that each number within the tube is not on the same plane. This is very evident when a number of displays are used side by side. Additionally, the red-orange color of the display makes it difficult to change the readout color.

### SEVEN-SEGMENT DISPLAYS

Seven-segment displays have become popular due to their low price and pleasant, modern numeral format. These are available in a wide variety of sizes, colors, and types.

### INCANDESCENT DISPLAYS

Incandescent displays can be made in a wide range of sizes and colors and are among the brightest available. Most newer incandescent dis-

---

® Registered trademark of the Burroughs Corporation.

plays have all seven-segment filaments contained within a single vacuum envelope and are compatible with standard DTL and TTL voltages.

## COLD CATHODE DISPLAYS

Cold cathode displays—also known as neon, gas discharge, or plasma displays—are Nixie-type displays with seven segments instead of ten numeral cathodes. Easily read and red-orange in color, they are available in sizes up to 0.75 inch high.

Fluorescent displays are blue-green and are available to approximately 0.6 inch in height. Their relatively low current and voltage requirements make them easy to multiplex.

## LIGHT-EMITTING DIODE (LED)

The light-emitting diode (LED) is a modern solid-state diode device using either gallium arsenide or gallium arsenide phosphide. These displays are smaller in size, reliable under severe mechanical conditions, and compatible with standard bipolar integrated circuits. LED's are available from 0.1 inch to 0.8 inch heights and are typically red in color; however, yellows and greens are becoming more available. Most of the smaller 0.1 inch LED's are used in small calculators.

## LIQUID CRYSTAL DISPLAYS

Liquid crystal displays are unique because they scatter rather than generate light. There are two basic types: reflective, which requires front illumination, and transmissive, which requires rear illumination. These devices have the lowest power requirements of any display. Liquid crystal displays are becoming increasingly common in consumer items. They are inclined to be slow acting (sometimes an advantage) and the life span is considerably shorter than the other display forms mentioned.

## 11-6   Display Drivers

Each type of display has its own drive requirements, and manufacturers have provided driver packages for each type.

### GAS DISCHARGE DEVICES

The older Nixie device is being replaced largely by seven-segment gas discharge devices such as the Panaplex® and Sperry devices. These require drivers with high voltage breakdown but relatively small cur-

---

® Registered trademark of the Burroughs Corporation.

rent capability (1–5 mA). Some form of current limiting is required to prevent the device from going to a destructive avalanche condition. For seven-segment gas devices some kind of current control is generally required on a segment-by-segment basis. If segments are operated in parallel, using a common current-limiting resistor, a phenomenon known as current hogging occurs which results in some segments being lit dimly, if at all, while one segment hogs most of the available current.

In older systems, individual current-limiting resistors were required for each segment. In modern drivers, individual segment drivers have constant current outputs, eliminating the need for external resistors. In some drivers the output current is programmable by selecting a particular value for a programming resistor. A single current-limiting resistor is all that is required for a Nixie-type device, because only a single element is ever lit at a given time.

All gas devices are common anode configurations; that is, all anodes are connected to a common supply line and individual cathodes are selected for different segments or numerals. In gas devices the visible glow appears around the cathode element but none around the anode. Gas devices are normally operated with all segments or all numerals (in Nixie-type devices) in a common gas-filled envelope.

## LIGHT-EMITTING DIODE

Light-emitting diodes in a seven-segment format are probably the most common of modern display technologies. LED seven-segment devices are available in common cathode (active high) and common anode (active low) versions as well as with multidigits in which the segments are connected in parallel. These devices are intended for operation in a sampling or multiplexed mode. In this mode the segments for forming the digit 3, for example, would be selected for all digits at the same time (they are wired in parallel) but only the desired digit would be enabled. The digits are sequentially enabled at a rate of 250 per second or higher, so that to the human eye they appear constantly lit. Too slow a sampling rate will result in a flickering display. Figure 11-7 shows the common anode and cathode configurations.

## LED DRIVERS

A wide variety of seven-segment LED decoder/driver MSI packages have become available. The most recent type provides internal control of source (or sink) currents to eliminate the need for external current-limiting resistors to insure constant and equal segment brightness. A $16 \times 7$ ROM is included in the package to control the segment patterns, and some of the units include built-in latches for display storage. Inter-

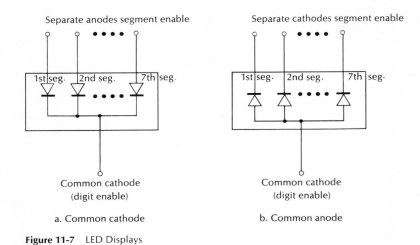

Figure 11-7   LED Displays

nal blanking for leading (or trailing) zeros is also provided. Many units also have provisions for lighting all segments to test the LED display devices.

The constant current sink version is intended for driving common anode LED's, while the constant current source version is a common cathode LED driver. Because of the wide variety of sizes, current demands, and brightness requirements, many of the devices provide programmable output currents. Program resistors are used to set constant output currents to the desired value.

For multiplexed operation the driver must be able to deliver larger than usual currents for short periods. Because of the less than continuous on-time of the display, a larger current is required for the same apparent brightness. Because of a characteristic of the human eye, a multiplexed display has the same apparent brightness as an on-all-the-time display with a significantly lower average power demand.

### INCANDESCENT SEVEN-SEGMENT DISPLAYS

Incandescent seven-segment displays use an incandescent filament for each segment. Segment current and voltage requirements are usually the same as those for LED segments. Because the filaments are non-polarized, either active-high or active-low LED drivers can be used.

### MOS-TO-LED DRIVERS

Display drivers generally fall into two categories: BCD decoded or nondecoded drivers. MOS devices such as calculators normally con-

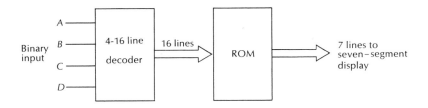

**Figure 11-8**   ROM Decoder

**Table 11-2**   Summary of Decoder and Driver Types
BCD to seven-segment decoder/drivers

| Type | Decoded | MOS/TTL | To _____ |
|------|---------|---------|------------------|
| DM 7856<br><br>DM 8856 | BCD to 7 seg. | TTL (DTL) | direct drive or multiplex LED segment (or electroluminescent) |
| DM 8857 | BCD to 7 seg. | TTL (DTL) | direct drive or multiplex high current LED (many) |
| DM 75491/<br>DM 8861 | No | MOS<br>(Calculators) | LED |
| DM 75492/<br>DM 8863 | No | MOS digit driver high current | LED digit driver drives up to 42-segment (6 digits) at a time |
| DM 8884A | No | MOS | gas discharge 7-segment cathode driver |
| DM 8887 | No | MOS | gas discharge 7-segment anode driver |

tain all decoding and multiplexing circuits on the MOS chip. External driver packages are required because MOS cannot generally provide enough output current to drive the LED's directly. Decoder/drivers are also available to interface MOS-to-LED displays because not all MOS systems have the decoder hardware on the chip.

For those driver circuits that use a ROM for segment pattern control, some manufacturers allow user-specified patterns in addition to (or instead of) numerals 0 through 9. Figure 11-8 shows the functional block diagram of a typical ROM-type decoder/driver. Table 11-2 summarizes a few decoder/driver types that are available from National Semiconductor. Several other manufacturers have a similar line of driver chips available.

## 11-7 Multiplexing Seven-Segment Displays

Multiplexing is a common method used to minimize the number of packages and interconnecting lines in a digital system. In multiplexing operation a single decoder/driver is time shared among the digits in the display. The digits are turned on one at a time in sequence at a 100 Hz or greater rate to insure against flicker.

Because segments are switched on and off rather than operated continuously, brightness will suffer unless the pulse current is increased while a segment is on.

A typical multiplex scheme is illustrated in Figure 11-9a. In the simplified representation (Figure 11-9) the diodes are the LED segments, and mechanical switches are shown in place of electronics. All *a* segments are connected in parallel, all *b* segments are connected in parallel, and so on. The appropriate segment (anode) enable lines to form a given digit are activated. The scanner (counter/decoders 3 and 4) enables the common (cathode) line for the digits in sequence. A coincidence in time between enabled segments and the enabling of the common cathode line selects a particular digit with particular segments activated. The scanner activates the first digit allowing appropriate segments to be activated for a time. It then moves on to the next digit at which time a new combination of segments is selected. Because of the retention of the eye the digits appear to be continuously lit. Placing the current-limiting resistors in the segment enable lines instead of the common lines helps to avoid uneven current distribution among segments with the resulting uneven brightness.

Figure 11-9b shows the functional block diagram (the electronic equivalent of Figure 11-9a) of an LED multiplex system. The following blocks fulfill the function (see Figure 11-9):

1. Decoder/driver decodes BCD input data into the seven-segment display pattern code.
2. Input address selector multiplexer (or shift register) selects the particular BCD group to be displayed at a given time.
3. Scan decoder selects the LED digit to be activated. The input address multiplexer and the scan decoder together see that the proper BCD group is selected and that its corresponding LED digit is activated.
4. Scan counter sequences the input multiplexer and scan decoder through, sampling each BCD group in turn and routing that data to the proper digit in the display.
5. Clock drives the scan counter at the desired rate.

Figure 11-10 shows a typical digital clock circuit using a National 8863 driver and a typical calculator circuit using an 8864 driver.

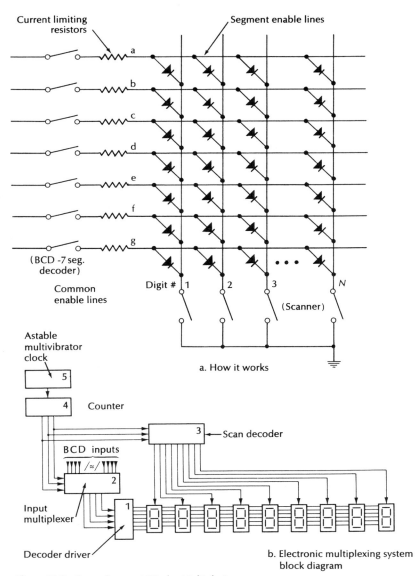

Current limiting resistors

Segment enable lines

(BCD -7 seg. decoder)

Common enable lines

Digit #  1   2   3   N

(Scanner)

Astable multivibrator clock

5

4   Counter

3   Scan decoder

BCD inputs

2

Input multiplexer

1

Decoder driver

a. How it works

b. Electronic multiplexing system block diagram

**Figure 11-9**   Seven-Segment Display Multiplexing

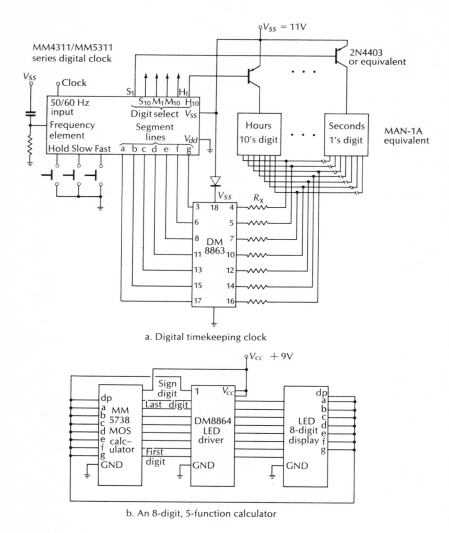

a. Digital timekeeping clock

b. An 8-digit, 5-function calculator

**Figure 11-10** DM 8863 Applications

The multiplex circuitry is on the clock and calculator chips. Figure 11-11 shows a typical counter circuit using the Signetics 8T70 BCD-to-seven-segment decoder/driver latch interface unit.

## 11-8 Phase-Locked Loop

The phase-locked loop (PLL) is a closed-loop feedback, self-regulating system. The basic system has been in use for many years, but until the

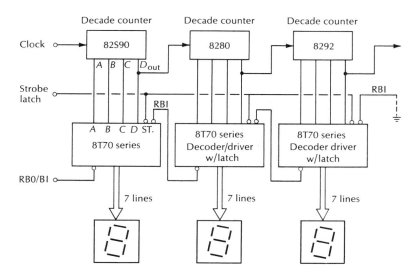

**Figure 11-11** Typical Counter Circuit Using Decoder Driver Latch Interface Unit

implementation of IC technology, its overall complexity and cost prevented its use in many applications.

### THEORY OF OPERATION

The phase-locked loop is a closed-loop electronic servo-mechanism. Figure 11-12 shows the block diagram of a closed-loop servo-mechanism. In the electromechanical servo in Figure 11-12b, $R_1$ and $R_2$ form a bridge. When the reference potentiometer and the error-detector potentiometer are in the same electrical position, the bridge is balanced, the amplifier sees zero voltage, and the gear motor remains off. Suppose that the reference potentiometer is rotated. Because the error-detector potentiometer is connected to the rotary antenna shaft (the load), movement of the reference potentiometer (only) unbalances the bridge. The bridge error signal is amplified to drive the motor. The motor drives the antenna and the error-detector potentiometer in the proper direction to rebalance the bridge. At balance, the error voltage vanishes and the motor stops.

The phase-locked loop consists of the following elements:

1. Load (value to be controlled): frequency
2. Error detector: comparator
3. Error corrector: voltage controlled (voltage variable) oscillator (VCO)
4. Amplifier: electronic amplifier
5. Reference: input frequency

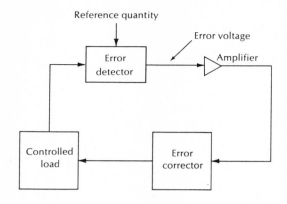

a. Generalized servo-mechanism block diagram

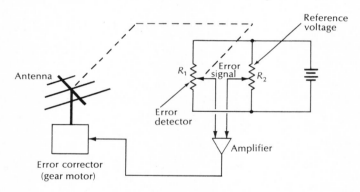

b. Electromechanical servo-mechanism (antenna rotator)

**Figure 11-12** The Servo-Mechanism

Figure 11-13 shows the block diagram of a phase-locked loop. The error detector compares the phase of the input signal with that of the voltage controlled oscillator (VCO). If the two are identical, no error voltage is generated and the VCO runs at its free-running frequency. When there is a difference between the phases of the input signal and the VCO, the two signals are mixed in the phase detector.

Assume that the input frequency is 100 kHz and the VCO is running at 101 kHz. The phase comparator mixes the 100 kHz and 101 kHz to get the sum and different frequencies 201 kHz and 1 kHz. The low pass filter removes the sum frequency. A DC voltage proportional to the frequency difference is fed back to the VCO, changing its frequency to more nearly that of the input signal. The correction continues until the two signals are phase locked. The error-signal output serves as a demodulated FM output. The circuit is designed to make the error

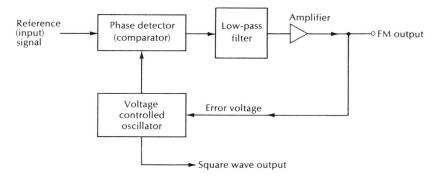

**Figure 11-13**  Phase-Locked Loop Block Diagram

voltage a linear function of the deviation of the input signal. The *capture range* is the range over which the loop can acquire lock. The lock range is generally wider than the capture range.

For use as a frequency multiplier, the VCO can be set to run at a harmonic of the input frequency and it will still lock on the input signal. For larger multiplication factors there is a more satisfactory approach. The VCO output square wave is TTL compatible. Figure 11-14 shows the block diagram of a commercial PLL.

### PLL FREQUENCY MULTIPLICATION

One important application for the PLL is digital frequency multiplication. To accomplish frequency multiplication, the loop is opened and a digital counter (divider) is inserted in the loop as shown in Figure 11-15. The VCO is set to run at the frequency that it is desired to multiply to. For example, to multiply a 10 kHz signal to 100 kHz, a divide-by-10 counter is placed in the loop and the VCO is set (by the external timing $R$ and $C$) to run at 100 kHz. The digital counter divides the 100 kHz VCO frequency down to 10 kHz so that VCO frequency (phase) can be compared with the input signal frequency for each cycle. This results in a precision not obtainable with harmonic-locking techniques; it requires no tuned circuits and can track the input frequency over the range of about an octave.

### SINE-WAVE OUTPUT SYNTHESIS

Some PLL VCO's have two outputs—one a TTL-compatible square wave and the other a triangular waveform. The advantage of the triangular waveform is that it can be easily shaped into a fairly respectable

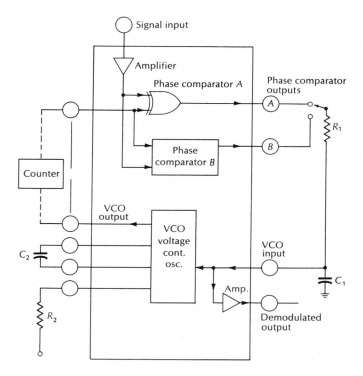

Note: $C_2$ and $R_2$ are VCO frequency determining components;
$R_1$ and $C_1$ form a low-pass filter network.

**Figure 11-14** Typical Commercial Phase-Locked Loop

sine wave with a simple circuit that does not involve frequency-sensitive components. This sine-wave shaping circuit is shown in Figure 11-16.

### FSK (FREQUENCY SHIFT KEYING)

FSK is a form of digital frequency modulation in which a carrier is shifted to one frequency for a logical zero and to another for a logical one. A phase-locked loop can be used as an FSK demodulator. The error voltage output will have distinctly different levels for each of the two frequencies. The output levels can be made directly compatible with TTL.

FSK is frequently used in modems (modulator/demodulators) for interfacing telephone lines with digital equipment. Since phone lines are

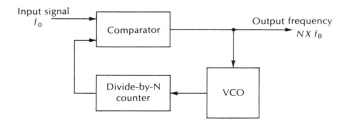

**Figure 11-15**   Frequency Multiplication with Phase-Locked Loop

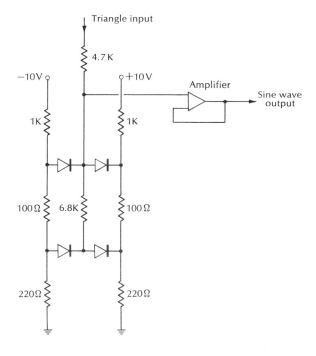

**Figure 11-16**   Triangle to Sine Wave Converter

limited to the range of speech frequencies, the two FSK frequencies in this case would be audio tones.

Another application for FSK is that of interfacing digital equipment to inexpensive audio-type cassette or reel-to-reel tape recorders. These recorders are coming into common use in microprocessor systems as a storage substitute for prohibitively expensive discs, drums, or computer-grade tape machines.

## 11-9 Computer Information Codes

In order to standardize interface hardware between computers and keyboards, printers, video displays, and the like, it is necessary to have a standard interface code. The two most common communications codes are the ASCII (American Standard Code for Information Interchange), and EBCDIC (Extended Binary-Coded-Decimal Interchange Code). These two codes are shown in Tables 11-3 and 11-4.

The ASCII code, the more popular of the two for most applications, is divided into word sets. Sixty-four words are used for the upper case alphabet, numbers, often-used punctuation, and a blank. Thirty-two words are used for machine commands such as carriage return, stop, start, and so on. These "words" do not appear in printouts or displays. Thirty-two additional words are used for the lowercase alphabet and less frequently used punctuation.

In this code, seven bits are required for the 128 ASCII code words. An eighth bit is provided for use as a parity bit, which may be used or left blank. The code may be transmitted one bit at a time, in serial, or all bits simultaneously in parallel. The EBCDIC code is similarly structured but not directly interchangeable with ASCII. The IBM Selectric® input/output typewriter uses a code of its own. Code translating chips are readily available for translating from one code into another.

The Baudot code is a five-bit code used in older model teletype machines. Because so many of these machines are still in operation, code translation chips are available for translating between Baudot and either ASCII or EBCDIC. Table 11-5 shows the Baudot code.

## 11-10 Video Display System

Television screen alphanumeric displays have become increasingly popular for direct human-computer communications. The system often uses a keyboard for human entry and a video display to present rapid reply information from the computer. The video display itself can be an unmodified television receiver, providing the character generator unit includes a low-power transmitter tuned to a TV channel. In most cases, however, the radio-frequency and intermediate-frequency TV receiver circuits are not included.

The heart of the video display system is a character generator, typified by the Signetics 2526. The functional block and timing diagram for the 2526 is shown in Figure 11-17. The characters are presented in dot matrix form on the TV screen (or dot matrix printer). The location of the dots that form each character is determined by memory locations

---

® Registered trademark of International Business Machines Corporation.

**Table 11-3**   American Standard Code for Information Interchange (ASCII)

| Column | 0 | 1 | 2 | 3 | 4 | 5 | 6 | 7 |
|---|---|---|---|---|---|---|---|---|
| Row Bits→ 765 | 000 | 001 | 010 | 011 | 100 | 101 | 110 | 111 |
| 4321 | | | | | | | | |
| 0  0000 | NUL | DLE | SP | 0 | @ | P | \ | p |
| 1  0001 | SOH | DC1 | ! | 1 | A | Q | a | q |
| 2  0010 | STX | DC2 | " | 2 | B | R | b | r |
| 3  0011 | ETX | DC3 | # | 3 | C | S | c | s |
| 4  0100 | EOT | DC4 | $ | 4 | D | T | d | t |
| 5  0101 | ENQ | NAK | % | 5 | E | U | e | u |
| 6  0110 | ACK | SYN | & | 6 | F | V | f | v |
| 7  0111 | BEL | ETB | ' | 7 | G | W | g | w |
| 8  1000 | BS | CAN | ( | 8 | H | X | h | x |
| 9  1001 | HT | EM | ) | 9 | I | Y | i | y |
| 10  1010 | LF | SUB | * | : | J | Z | j | z |
| 11  1011 | VT | ESC | + | ; | K | [ | k | { |
| 12  1100 | FF | FS | , | < | L | \ | l | ¦ |
| 13  1101 | CR | GS | – | = | M | ] | m | } |
| 14  1110 | SO | RS | . | > | N | ⌢ | n | ~ |
| 15  1111 | SI | US | / | ? | O | — | o | DEL |

Example: { bits : 7 6 5 4 3 2 1
Code A = 1 0 0 0 0 0 1

a. Table  of  codes

| | | | |
|---|---|---|---|
| NUL | Null | DLE | Data link escape |
| SOH | Start of heading | DC1 | Device control 1 |
| STX | Start of text | DC2 | Device control 2 |
| ETX | End of text | DC3 | Device control 3 |
| EOT | End of transmission | DC4 | Device control 4 |
| ENQ | Enquiry | NAK | Negative acknowledge |
| ACK | Acknowledge | SYN | Synchronous idle |
| BEL | Bell (audible signal) | ETB | End of transmission |
| BS | Backspace | | block |
| HT | Horizontal tabulation (punched card skip) | CAN | Cancel |
| | | EM | End of medium |
| LF | Line feed | SUB | Substitute |
| VT | Vertical tabulation | ESC | Escape |
| FF | Form feed | FS | File separator |
| CR | Carriage return | GS | Group separator |
| SO | Shift out | RS | Record separator |
| SI | Shift in | US | Unit separator |

b. Legend for control codes in columns 0 and 1

**Table 11-4** Extended Binary-Coded-Decimal Interchange

| | Code (EBCDIC) | | | | | | | | | | *Decimal | | | | | |
|---|---|---|---|---|---|---|---|---|---|---|---|---|---|---|---|---|
| Column (HEX) → | 0 | 1 | 2 | 3 | 4 | 5 | 6 | 7 | 8 | 9 | 10 | 11 | 12 | 13 | 14 | 15 |
| Bits–0 1 2 3 | 0000 | 0001 | 0010 | 0011 | 0100 | 0101 | 0110 | 0111 | 1000 | 1001 | 1010 | 1011 | 1100 | 1101 | 1110 | 1111 |
| Row (HEX) ↓ 4567 | | | | | | | | | | | | | | | | |
| 0 0000 | NUL | DLE | DS | | SP | & | – | | | | | | | | | 0 |
| 1 0001 | SOH | DC1 | SOS | | | | | | a | j | | | A | J | | 1 |
| 2 0010 | STX | DC2 | FS | SYN | | | | | b | k | s | | B | K | S | 2 |
| 3 0011 | ETX | DC3 | | | | | | | c | l | t | | C | L | T | 3 |
| 4 0100 | PF | RES | BYP | PN | | | | | d | m | u | | D | M | U | 4 |
| 5 0101 | HT | NL | LF | RS | | | | | e | n | v | | E | N | V | 5 |
| 6 0110 | LC | BS | EOB ETB | UC | | | | | f | o | w | | F | O | W | 6 |
| 7 0111 | DEL | IL | PRE ESC | EOT | | | | | g | p | x | | G | P | X | 7 |
| 8 1000 | | CAN | | | | | | | h | q | y | | H | Q | Y | 8 |
| 9 1001 | RLF | EM | | | | | | | i | r | z | | I | R | Z | 9 |
| *10 1010 | SMM | CC | SM | | | ! | | : | | | | | | | | |
| 11 1011 | VT | | | | . | $ | % | # | | | | | | | | |
| 12 1100 | FF | IFS | | DC4 | | * | | @ | | | | | | | | |
| 13 1101 | CR | IGS | ENQ | NAK | ( | ) | | ' | | | | | | | | |
| 14 1110 | SO | IRS | ACK | | + | ; | – | = | | | | | | | | |
| 15 1111 | SI | IUS | BEL | SUB | | | ? | " | | | | | | | | |

Example:
```
          ----bits: 0 1 2 3 4 5 6 7
Code for letter D = 1 1 0 0 0 1 0 0
                    column    row
```

a. Table of codes

| | |
|---|---|
| NUL | Null |
| SOH | Start of heading |
| STX | Start of text |
| ETX | End of text |
| PF | Punch off |
| HT | Horizontal tab |
| LC | Lower case |
| DEL | Delete |
| RLF | Reverse line feed |
| SMM | Start of manual message |
| VT | Vertical tabulation |
| FF | Form feed |
| CR | Carriage return |
| SO | Shift out |
| SI | Shift in |
| DLE | Data link escape |
| DC1 | Device control 1 |
| DC2 | Device control 2 |
| DC3 | Device control 3 |
| RES | Restore |
| NL | New line |
| BS | Backspace |
| IL | Idle |
| CAN | Cancel |
| EM | End of medium |

| | |
|---|---|
| CC | Cursor control |
| IFS | Interchange file separator |
| IGS | Interchange group separator |
| IRS | Interchange record separator |
| IUS | Interchange unit separator |
| DS | Digit select |
| SOS | Start of significance |
| FS | Field separator |
| BYP | Bypass |
| LF | Line feed |
| EOB/ETB | End of block/End of transmission block |
| PRE/ESC | Prefix/escape |
| SM | Set mode |
| ENQ | Enquiry |
| ACK | Acknowledge |
| BEL | Bell |
| SYN | Synchronous idle |
| PN | Punch on |
| RS | Reader stop |
| UC | Upper case |
| EOT | End of transmission |
| DC4 | Device control 4 |
| NAK | Negative acknowledge |
| SUB | Substitute |
| SP | Space |

b. Machine control codes for columns 0–4

**Table 11-5** Five-Bit Baudot Teletype Code

| Code | Letters | Figures | Code | Letters | Figures |
|------|---------|---------|------|---------|---------|
| 00000 | blank | blank | 10000 | T | 5 |
| 00001 | E | 3 | 10001 | Z | + |
| 00010 | linefeed | linefeed | 10010 | L | ) |
| 00011 | A | | 10011 | W | 2 |

| Code | Letters | Figures | Code | Letters | Figures |
|------|---------|---------|------|---------|---------|
| 00100 | space | space | 10100 | H | # |
| 00101 | S | ' | 10101 | Y | 6 |
| 00110 | I | 8 | 10110 | P | Ø |
| 00111 | U | 7 | 10111 | Q | 1 |

| Code | Letters | Figures | Code | Letters | Figures |
|------|---------|---------|------|---------|---------|
| 01000 | car ret. | car ret. | 11000 | O | 9 |
| 01001 | D | acknowledge | 11001 | B | ? |
| 01010 | R | 4 | 11010 | G | & |
| 01011 | J | bell | 11011 | Figs. | Figs. |

| Code | Letters | Figures | Code | Letters | Figures |
|------|---------|---------|------|---------|---------|
| 01100 | N | , | 11100 | M | . |
| 01001 | F | ! | 11101 | X | / |
| 01110 | C | : | 11110 | V | = |
| 01111 | K | ( | 11111 | Letters | Letters |

in a 5184-bit ROM, organized in a $64 \times 9 \times 9$ matrix. The 2526 has sixty-four characters and is available with either upper- or lower-case ROM's. Two character generator chips are required for a system with *both* upper- and lowercase characters. The output circuitry is tri-state to allow its use in a bus-organized system. Figure 11-18 shows how both lowercase and uppercase character generators can be put on a bus.

The input to the character generator is standard ASCII code. The actual dot matrix that forms the characters is a $7 \times 9$ array. The column decoder has four inputs for sixteen possible code combinations. However, only nine combinations are used, leaving seven of them unused. The ROM decoder has six inputs for a possible sixty-four combinations. Unused ROM locations are used for EBCDIC and Baudot conversions. The ASCII standard character font is shown in Figure 11-19. The $A_4$ column input is tied to logical zero for character generation. The $A_4$ input is not tied internally to permit the use of extra ROM locations for other purposes. The character generator is also available with the ROM programmed to user specifications.

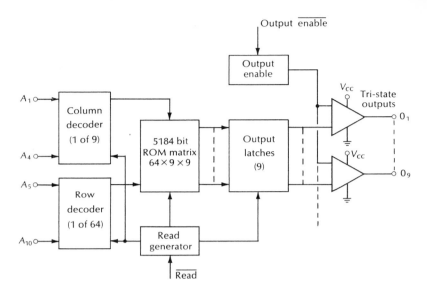

a. Block diagram

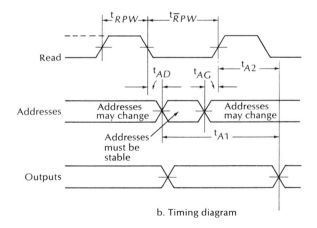

b. Timing diagram

**Figure 11-17**   Block Diagram of the 2526 ROM Character Generator

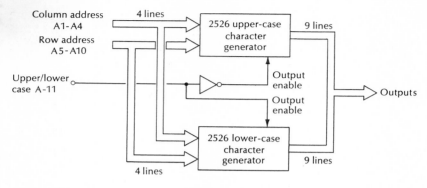

**Figure 11-18** Upper-Lower Case Character Generator

## COMPLETE VIDEO DISPLAY SYSTEM

Figure 11-20 shows the block diagram for a complete video display system. The page memory consists of six shift registers, typically 1024 to 4028 bits in length, and stores enough coded words to fill the entire screen with characters. Additional page memories can be used in a bus organization to store more than one page. The line memory also consists of six shift registers but these must store only the code for the next line to be presented on the screen. The memories store coded address information for the character generator rather than its output information. A six-bit-per-character memory is all that is necessary to store the coded address instead of the sixty-four-bit-per-character memory required to store the character generator output dot pattern.

Six bits of the seven-bit ASCII code are used to define all the characters in either the lowercase or uppercase character group. The seventh bit is used as an enable command to select either the upper or lower character generator, as shown in Figure 11-21.

Code groups are entered into the page memory shift register at whatever rate they come from the keyboard or other device. The display action begins by loading the line memory with the code groups for the first line of characters to be displayed. Nine TV scans are required to complete a row of characters. The row counter addresses the first row of dot locations for all characters in the line, which the character generator then outputs in parallel. They are parallel loaded into the parallel-to-serial converter (PISO) shift register and then fed to the grid on the CRT. As the beam moves across the screen, the 0's and 1's emerging from the PISO register appear as spots of light on the CRT. A 1 turns the beam on and a 0 leaves the screen dark. When the first row of dots for the first character in the line of print has been displayed, the

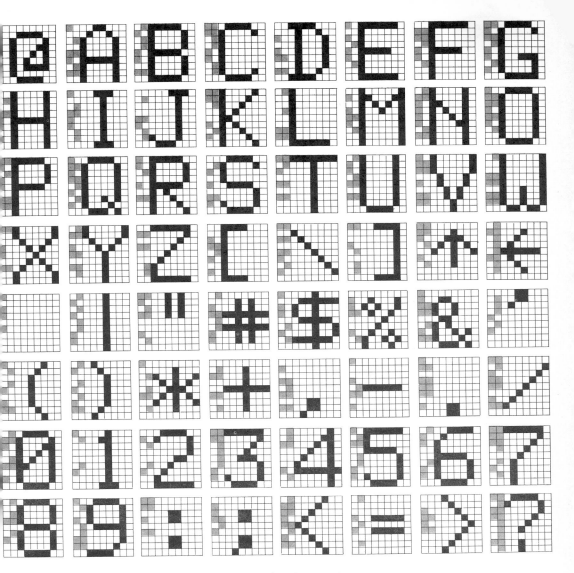

ASCII set, raster scan 7 × 9 with code conversion

Notes:

1. Undefined addresses result in all outputs going low (TTL "0")
2. Black squares in character font are high (TTL "1")
3. See data manual for additional information

© 1974 Signetics Inc. From *Digital Linear and MOS Data Book*, pp. 7 - 94
Used by permission of Signetics Inc., P.O. Box 3004, Menlo Park, Ca. 94025.

**Figure 11-19** Standard Character Font

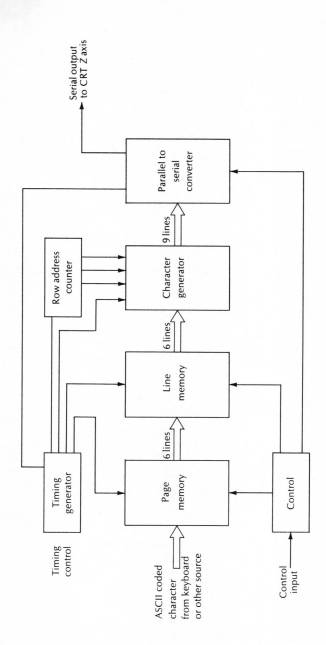

**Figure 11-20**  Video Display System

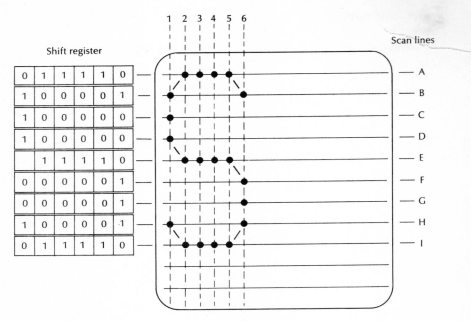

Note: Blanks are not shown on the illustration

**Figure 11-21**    Generating Characters on the CRT

line memory is shifted right for the first row of dots in the second character. The line memory is a recirculating register because these same characters must be presented to the character generator a total of nine times, one for each of the nine CRT traces required to complete the line of displayed characters. When the first CRT row of dots is completed, the row counter advances, causing the character generator to output the dot pattern for the second row of dots in the first line. The line register is now clocked through the characters again for the second CRT trace.

At the end of the first line of characters, the page memory is shifted right to load the line memory for the second line of characters. This process continues until the page memory contents have been used. Figure 11-21 is a simplified illustration showing how the binary combinations out of the PISO shift register form a letter on the screen.

## 11-11    Digital-to-Analog and Analog-to-Digital Conversion

Because digital displays are generally much easier to read than meters, clock hands, or other analog displays, more and more analog quantities

are being displayed in this form. To accomplish this, analog quantities must be converted into equivalent digital quantities. In many process and machine control systems the control functions are handled by digital commands; to control position, motor speed, and other electromechanical functions, digital data must generally be converted into analog form.

Digital-to-analog conversion is more easily accomplished than the reverse. In fact, a digital-to-analog converter is often one important part of an analog-to-digital converter system. Figure 11-22 shows two methods of using resistive networks for D-to-A conversion. In part the outputs of a counter or register are fed to the inputs of level amplifiers, and the outputs of the level amplifiers are fed into an amplifier using weighted input resistance values. The level amplifiers are required because typical TTL (or MOS) output levels are not precise or predictable enough. The approach in Figure 11-22b is essentially the same except that the summing network has been transformed into a ladder form. This resistive arrangement, often called the $R$-$2R$ ladder, has a number of advantages over the summing network shown in part a, particularly when a large number of binary outputs are involved. An examination of the resistance values in part a reveals that each resistor value decreases by a power of 2 as the number of binary outputs increases. The result is a different loading value on each level amplifier, eventually resulting in an unacceptable current in summing resistors for higher order binary outputs.

The kind of ladder network shown in Figure 11-22b has long been popular in constant-input/constant-output audio and RF attenuators. One of its important characteristics is that the equivalent resistance as seen from any node is $2R$ (using $R$-$2R$ ratios) regardless of the state (0 or 5V) of individual inputs to the ladder. The assumption is made that the output resistance of the level amplifiers closely approaches zero ohms at both *high* and *low* levels. This requirement dictates a *low* output impedance for the precision power supply that serves the level amplifiers.

The analog output voltage for each binary input can be determined as follows (assume voltage gain of unity for the amplifier):

$$E_0 =$$

|  |  |
|---|---|
| MSB | $V/2$ |
| 2nd MSB | $V/4$ |
| 3rd MSB | $V/8$ |
| 4th MSB | $V/16$ |
| . | . |
| . | . |
| . | . |
| $n$th MSB | $V/2^n$ |

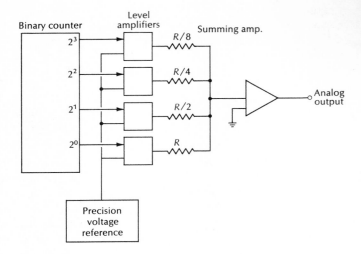

a. Summing amplifier method

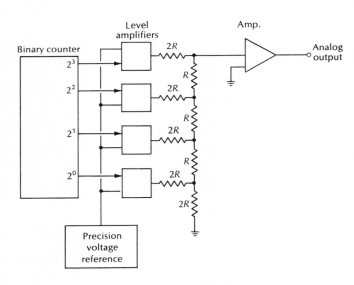

b. Ladder network method

**Figure 11-22**   Digital-to-Analog Conversion Schemes

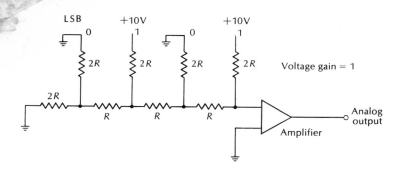

**Figure 11-23**  Ladder Network

where V is the output voltage of all level amplifiers. This can be one of two voltages—either zero volts or V′ which is some arbitrary (specified) value. The total output voltage from the ladder is the sum of the output voltages generated by all individual weighted-bit outputs.

**Example**  Given Figure 11-23, find the analog output voltage. The solution is as follows:

$$\text{MSB} = \frac{10}{2} = 5\text{V}$$

$$\text{2nd MSB} = \frac{0}{4} = 0\text{V}$$

$$\text{3rd MSB} = \frac{10}{8} = 1.25\text{V}$$

$$\text{LSB} = \frac{0}{16} = 0\text{V}$$

$$\text{Sum } 6.25\text{V} = \text{analog output voltage}$$

**Problems**

Given the ladder circuit in Figure 11-23, calculate the analog output voltages for the following binary input values:

1. 1010    3. 1001
2. 1111    4. 0111
5. If a meter is used to read the analog output voltage for Figure 11-23, what would the *full*-scale reading be?

## ACCURACY AND RESOLUTION

Two important parameters of digital-to-analog converters are accuracy and resolution. *Accuracy* is a measure of how close the actual analog output voltage is to the designed (or computed) output voltage. It is dependent largely on the precision of ladder resistors, precision power supply, and other components that have an inherent tolerance. *Resolution* is a measure of the smallest increment that can be resolved and is totally dependent on the number of bits in the input to the converter.

In the four-bit system used in the preceding example, the LSB has a weight of 1/16 ($1/2^4$). The resolution is then 1 in 16 and, if the input voltage levels are 16 volts (full scale), the converter can resolve to the nearest volt. It is always necessary to assume $\pm 1$ count (digitizing error) of the LSB whatever its weight; for example, 14.5 volts could be converted as 14 or 15 volts. The LSB of the digital counter or register must be either *high* or *low,* not halfway between. Resolution and accuracy should generally be within an order of magnitude of the same percentage value. There is little to be gained in constructing a ladder network of $\pm 0.01$ percent for a converter with a resolution of $\pm 1/16$ ($\pm 6.2$ percent).

# ANALOG-TO-DIGITAL CONVERTERS

The heart of nearly all analog-to-digital converters is a comparator with a digitally compatible output. Its operation involves the comparison of a precision reference voltage and the analog input voltage. When the two voltages are equal, the high open-loop gain of the comparator causes it to switch to a logic *high* level.

## 11-12   Simultaneous (Parallel) Conversion A-to-D

Simultaneous conversion, the faster of the two common methods of A-to-D conversion, is by far the more expensive of the two. It involves the use of a number of comparators and a number of weighted reference voltages, a different one for each comparator. Figure 11-24 shows the functional block diagram and truth table for a two-bit A-to-D converter.

An examination of the truth table yields the following equations for the encoding gates:

$$2^0 = C_1\bar{C}_2\bar{C}_3 + C_1C_2C_3$$

$$2^1 = C_1C_2\bar{C}_3 + C_1C_2C_3, \text{ which simplifies to}$$

$$2^1 = C_1C_2$$

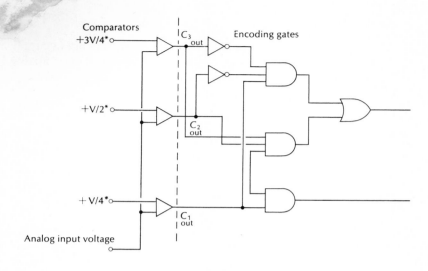

*Reference voltages

| | Comparator output $C_1$ $C_2$ $C_3$ | | | Digital output $2^1$ $1^0$ | |
|---|---|---|---|---|---|
| 0 to +V/4 | 0 | 0 0 | | 0 | 0 |
| +V/4 to +V/2 | 1 | 0 0 | | 0 | 1 |
| +V/2 to +3V/4 | 1 | 1 0 | | 1 | 0 |
| +3V/4 to +V | 1 | 1 1 | | 1 | 1 |

Truth table

**Figure 11-24**   Simultaneous (Parallel) Analog-to-Digital Converter

To convert a voltage into a digital signal of $n$-bits requires $2^n - 1$ comparators and associated encoding gate logic. For any practical number of bits, enough hardware is required to justify the manufacture of MSI analog-to-digital converter chips. A number of IC manufacturers provide these simultaneous analog-to-digital converters in various bit lengths as standard catalog items.

## 11-13   Sequential Approach to A-to-D Conversion

The second common approach to A-to-D conversion uses a single comparator and a varying reference voltage. The method is sequential (se-

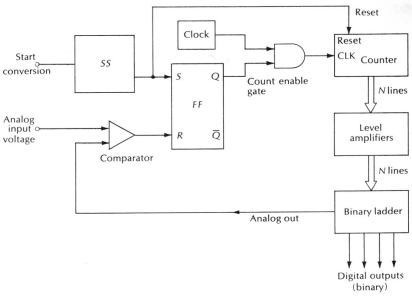

**Figure 11-25**   Counter-Ladder Type of Analog-to-Digital Converter

rial) and considerably slower than simultaneous (parallel) conversion. The sequential method, simpler and less expensive, is the preferred method for digital voltmeters, scales, and similar instruments.

A common form of serial A-to-D converter uses a counter and a digital-to-analog converter based on level amplifiers and a ladder network. Figure 11-25 shows a functional block diagram of this form of converter. The maximum resolving time required is $2^n$ counts at the clock rate. The circuit in Figure 11-25 operates as follows:

1. A pulse is entered to start conversion. That pulse resets the counter to all zeros. The monostable delays the start pulse that sets the ''count/stop-counting'' flip-flop long enough to insure complete reset of the counter. The one-shot then switches the flip-flop long enough to insure complete reset of the counter and then switches it to $Q$ *high,* enabling the clock input to the counter. The counter starts counting at the clock rate.

2. As counting progresses, the level-amplifier binary ladder combination produces a stair-step increasing analog voltage output. This analog staircase is applied to one input of the comparator. This is the varying reference voltage. The analog voltage to be converted is applied to the other input of the comparator.

3. At some point in the counting sequence, the stair-step voltage rises to a point at which it equals the analog input voltage. Then the output of the comparator goes *high*, resetting the flip-flop and stopping the count.

The binary output is the binary digital equivalent of the applied input voltage. Continuous digitizing can be accomplished by constantly resetting and converting at a rate many times greater than the rate at which the analog voltage changes.

## 11-14  Digital Voltmeters

There are three popular methods of converting voltages (analog) to a digital display output: the VCO, the dual slope, and the charge subtracter methods.

### VCO METHOD

The simplest but least accurate method uses a voltage controlled oscillator. The block diagram for a VCO-type digital voltmeter (DVM) is shown in Figure 11-26. The input voltage (DC) determines the frequency at which the VCO runs. The output of the VCO is gated into the counter for a fixed time and then displayed.

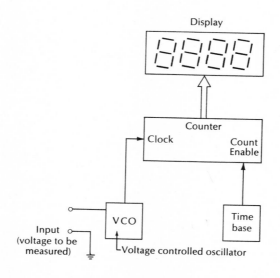

**Figure 11-26**  Voltage Controlled Oscillator (VCO) Digital Coltmeter

Assume that the oscillator runs at 1000 pulses per second at 1 volt. If the VCO output is gated into the counter for a 1 second period and the counting is stopped, the count on the display would be 1000. Proper placement of the decimal yields a count of 1.000 (volts). If the VCO's frequency is a linear function of the input voltage, an input voltage of 2 volts would make it run at 2000 Hz. If allowed to count for a 1-second period, the display will show 2000. Again, placing the decimal behind the 2, we get 2.000 (volts). Recent improvements in IC VCO chips have made this circuit a contender for the position traditionally held by the vacuum tube voltmeter. The Intersil 8038 VCO chip, for example, maintains a 1 percent linearity (voltage-frequency relationship) over a 1000:1 frequency range. One problem that can complicate a basically simple scheme is the fact that VCO's do not produce zero pulses-per-second at zero volts. In general, the voltage-frequency relationship near zero volts tends to be nonlinear. The cure is to let the VCO run at some base frequency and subtract the extra counts from the counter.

## DUAL SLOPE METHOD

For some time, the dual slope method has been the preferred analog-to-digital conversion method for DVM's because it has two primary advantages: a precision time base is not required and errors tend to cancel. The precision reference is a current reference. Figure 11-27 shows the block diagram of a dual slope DVM circuit.

This system involves the measurement of an unknown input current for a fixed time interval. The time base clock need not have long term stability, providing its stability is good during the actual short measurement period, including the time to charge and discharge a capacitor. The integrator charges a capacitor at a linear rate for a specific time period. The capacitor is then discharged for the same period at a constant and precise rate. The counter is clocked until the comparator switches, stopping the count. The measurement is the number of clock pulses that occur during the time the capacitor is being discharged through the precision current reference (back to its initial condition). Because the same circuitry (except for the current reference) is used to ramp the integrator *up* and ramp it *down,* nonlinearities tend to cancel.

Assume a four-digit counter and a 1 kHz clock. The control is a 555 timer in the astable configuration that clears the counter at 1 second intervals. When the counter is cleared, the *overflow* switches the integrator input to take on a charge from the source being measured. The integrator ramps the capacitor *up* until the counter overflows. For a four-decade counter this will occur at a count of 10,000 times the clock frequency. At the instant of overflow the integrator input is switched to

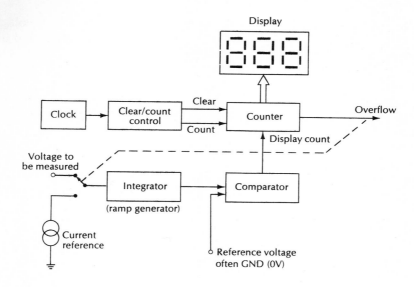

**Figure 11-27** Dual Slope DVM

a ramp-*down* condition, using the precision current reference to control the integrator current. Simultaneously with the beginning of ramp *down,* the counter has gone back to 0000 and has begun to count *up* again. When the integrator has ramped *down* to zero, the comparator stops the count and displays the results.

### LADDER COMPARATOR SYSTEM

A third system uses a counter ladder network, the precision voltage reference, and a comparator. The block diagram is shown in Figure 11-28. The bilateral switch is used as a level amplifier. (Bilateral switches will be discussed later in this chapter.)

The measurement is begun by resetting the counter. The clock then starts feeding pulses to the counter. The ladder network converts the count to its analog voltage equivalent. When the ladder output voltage is equal to the input voltage to be measured, the comparator switches, stopping the count. With proper scaling and decimal placement, the display shows the digital value of the input voltage.

## 11-15 Electromechanical A-to-D Conversion

In machine and process control it is often necessary to translate the angular position of a shaft into digital information. The most common

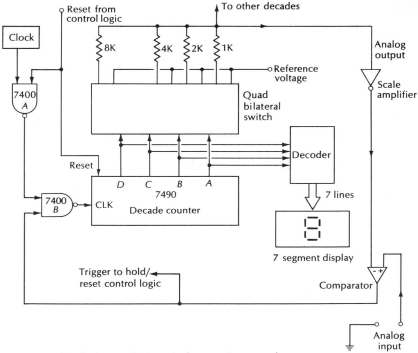

**Figure 11-28**   Digital Voltmeter Circuit

method for accomplishing this task is the use of an optically read binary code disc mounted on the shaft in question. Figure 11-29 shows the arrangement and the code disc layout for Gray code representation.

The Gray code is used because only one bit in the group changes at a time, which improves resolution and minimizes conversion error. The Gray code is not suitable for processing purposes, and data are normally translated into normal binary as an integral part of the conversion process.

## 11-16   Bilateral Switches

The bilateral switch is an MOS or C-MOS device organized as electronically controlled SPSP, SPDT, DPDT, or selector switch. Some are organized as data selectors or multiplexers. Because the channel in an MOS device can carry current in both directions, the switches are called *bilateral devices*. Field-effect devices have no offset voltage as all

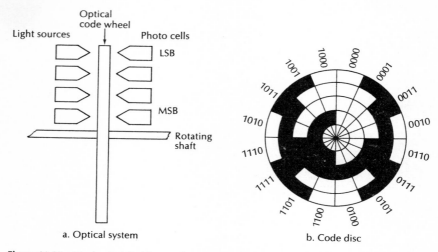

**Figure 11-29** Mechanical Position Analog-to-Digital Conversion Using a Coded Optical Disc

bipolar junction devices have. The result is a switch element that is very similar to its mechanical equivalent. Another important consideration is the transient-free switching that cannot be obtained with bipolar devices because of junction potentials. Control inputs are also better isolated from the switching elements than in bipolar switches.

Bipolar devices provide lower *on* resistances than MOS devices. The bipolar devices often have field-effect control inputs to improve isolation between control and switching elements and to minimize the control current.

Figure 11-30 shows a simple quad bilateral switch. The circuit is typical of the National Semiconductor AH0014 (c), AH0015 (c) and AH0019 (c) devices, all of which feature a switching speed of 500 ns, an *on* resistance of 200 Ω and an *off* resistance of 10 MΩ. They are fully compatible with TTL and DTL and can be used for TTL/MOS level shifting, in A/D and D/A converters, data acquisition switching commutation, and multiplexing. Control signals are TTL standard. The switch element can control voltages (digital or analog) up to ±10 volts. The switches are available in DPDT, Quad SPST, and dual DPST configurations.

These devices can switch voltages up to ±20V at a frequency or bit rate of 1 MHz. Typical switching time is from 400 to 1000 ns. All three are available with either logic gate or internal comparator control circuits. Their applications are similar to those of the bipolar-MOS device previously discussed.

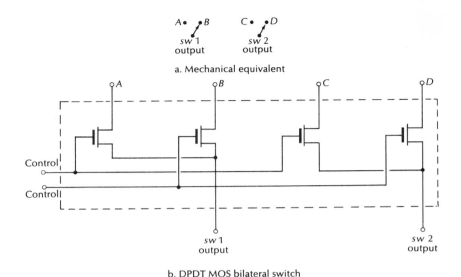

a. Mechanical equivalent

b. DPDT MOS bilateral switch

**Figure 11-30**   DPDT MOS Switch

The *on* resistance is approximately 10 to 100 Ω. As is the case with all reverse-biased junction devices, the leakage current in the *off* condition is independent of the applied voltage and varies only with temperature. The typical leakage current (off) for this kind of device is 10 PA at 25°C.

## MOS AND C-MOS SWITCHES

An increasingly popular form of bilateral switch uses only MOS structures, either MOS or complementary MOS. Such switches are particularly well suited for large or complex switching arrays such as commutators and multiplexers. Figure 11-31 shows a six-channel P-MOS multiplexer. The following are typical switching characteristics for this device:

1. *On* resistance: 150–200
2. *Off* leakage current: 100 PA
3. Switching range: 10V
4. 1 MHz switching rate
5. Zero volts offset
6. Switch normally off with zero gate voltage

The zener diodes are gate protection diodes. Control inputs are generally TTL compatible. These devices are available in a wide variety of switching configurations.

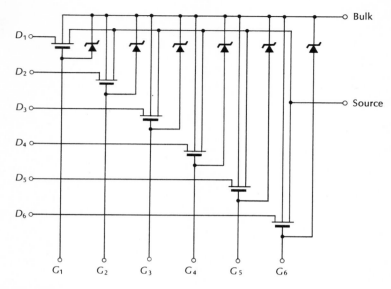

**Figure 11-31** MOS Six-Channel Multiplexer

C-MOS devices such as the CD 4066 quad bilateral switch also have many applications in the interface between the digital and analog worlds. Figure 11-32 shows the schematic of one switch and the block diagram of the quad switch. Single or dual power supplies can be used. The following are typical switching parameters of this device:

1. *On* resistance: $80\Omega$
2. *Off* leakage current: 10 PA @ 25°C
3. Control input impedance: $10^{12}$ $\Omega$
4. Frequency response of on channel: 40 MHz
5. Switching rate 100 to 400 ns depending upon system capacitances

A variety of MOS and TTL control logic is available as well as analog control capability.

## 11-17 Optical Isolators

An increasingly important interface device consists of an LED and a phototransistor optically connected in a light-tight package. This device eliminates reflected loading because the only coupling is by way of a light beam. Variations in the load are not reflected back to the source as happens in nearly all other coupling devices. Optical isolators are particularly useful for coupling devices with incompatible voltage re-

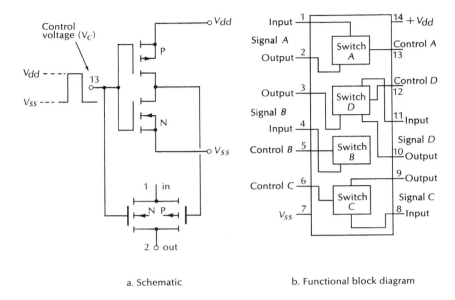

a. Schematic

b. Functional block diagram

**Figure 11-32**  C-MOS Bilateral Switch

quirements. Figure 11-33 shows a typical optical isolator application. Optical isolators provide isolation between LED and phototransistor up to several kilovolts.

## LARGE-SCALE INTERFACE DEVICES

### 11-18  Programmable Peripheral Interfaces

These devices are designed to interface microcomputers to peripheral devices such as teletype terminals, CRT terminals, printers, keyboards, punched card and tape readers and punches, and magnetic memories (floppy-disc and so on). The peripheral interface device generally has two or more bidirectional output ports of eight bits each and an eight-bit bidirectional data input port that is compatible with the computer's internal bus system. It also has inputs for various controls that select individual output ports and control the direction of the data on the input and output lines. The peripheral interface operation is controlled by the computer. Figure 11-34 shows the functional block diagram of a typical peripheral interface unit. The outputs are normally

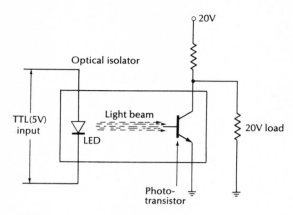

**Figure 11-33**   Optical Isolator

tri-state and inputs are buffered to a high input impedance. Several interface devices can be tied to the computer to provide for the connection of a variety of peripheral devices.

## 11-19   Universal Synchronous/Asynchronous Receiver/Transmitter (USART)*

A common problem in microcomputer systems is that of interfacing to communications channels that operate in an asynchronous serial mode, such as telephone lines and cassette recorders. The most common solution to the problem is an LSI chip that can take the parallel synchronous data from the computer and convert it into serial data at some specific bit rate other than the computer clock rate. This universal SART can also receive data in asynchronous, serial form from the communications channel, convert it into parallel form, and synchronize it with the computer's clock.

The USART is controlled by the computer and can communicate its status to the computer. It can be a complex device with up to six internal registers and considerable control logic. Separate registers are used for outgoing and incoming data. Figure 11-35 shows a simplified block diagram of a USART. Figure 11-36 shows one of the most complex of available USART's, the Motorola MC6850.

In Figure 11-35 when the transmit/receive control line is in the transmit condition, the transmit shift register is loaded with eight bits in parallel. The transmit shift register produces a train of serial output

---

* An asynchronous only device is a UART.

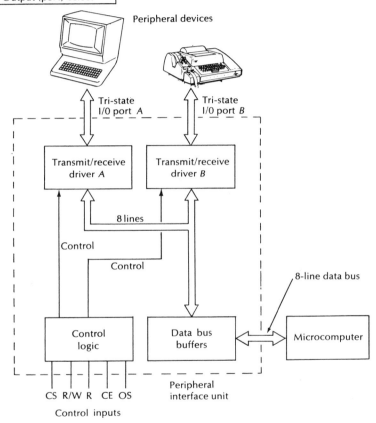

Control functions

| R | Reset |
|----|---------------------|
| CS | Chip select |
| CE | Chip enable |
| R/W | Read/write control |
| OS | Output (port) select |

**Figure 11-34** Peripheral Interface Unit

pulses at the transmit clock rate. The transmitter interfaces the data stream to the communications channel. In the receive mode, data is loaded into the receive shift register serially. When the register is full, the next receive-clock pulse unloads the register in parallel onto the computer data bus through the data buffer amplifiers. The data buffers generally have a high impedance input to allow several USART's to be connected to the same data bus.

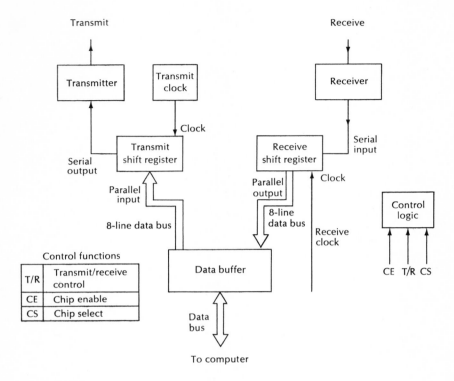

**Figure 11-35** Simplified Block Diagram of a USART

## SUMMARY

The most common interface problems involve interfacing IC chips to the following:

1. Relays, lamps, solenoids (for printers, etc.)
2. Digital display devices
3. Data buses
4. Transmission lines
5. Telephone lines
6. Alphanumeric display systems

IC devices in data communication systems have been greatly simplified through the adoption of standard data communications codes (ASCII and EBCDIC).

Interfacing can involve changes in power level, translation from serial to parallel data transmission, translation of data between synchro-

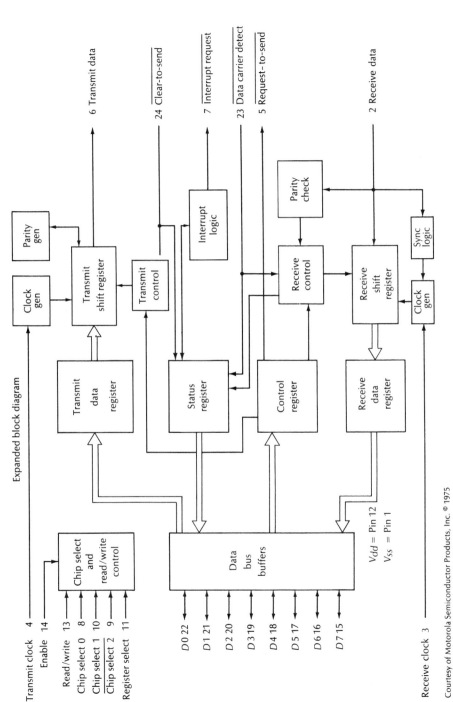

Expanded block diagram

Transmit clock 4
Enable 14

Read/write 13
Chip select 0 8
Chip select 1 10
Chip select 2 9
Register select 11

Chip select and read/write control

Parity gen

Clock gen

Transmit shift register

Transmit data register

Transmit control

6 Transmit data

24 Clear-to-send

Interrupt logic

7 Interrupt request

Status register

Control register

23 Data carrier detect

5 Request-to-send

Receive control

Parity check

Receive shift register

Receive data register

2 Receive data

Sync logic

Clock gen

Data bus buffers

$V_{dd}$ = Pin 12
$V_{ss}$ = Pin 1

D0 22
D1 21
D2 20
D3 19
D4 18
D5 17
D6 16
D7 15

Receive clock 3

Courtesy of Motorola Semiconductor Products, Inc. © 1975

**Figure 11-36** Motorola 6850 UART

nous and asynchronous devices, and any other problem involving the connection of a chip to some outside world device.

**Problems**

1. Describe the advantages of bidirectional driver/receivers in a bus-organized system.
2. What is the reason for terminating resistors in a data transmission line system?
3. What kind of line is most commonly used for distances of 100 feet or so?
4. What are high-level interface devices used for?
5. Define *baud rate*.
6. List the four most common numerical display types.
7. Explain the theory of operation of numerical display multiplexing.
8. Explain the reasons for constant current output stages in LED drivers.
9. Explain why leading and trailing zero blanking is often desirable.
10. List the two kinds of LED displays available.
11. Draw a block diagram of a phase-locked loop.
12. Explain how a phase-locked loop works. Use a block diagram.
13. Draw the block diagram of a phase-locked loop digital frequency multiplier.
14. Define *frequency shift keying* and describe one or more applications for it.
15. What is the Baudot code used for?
16. Draw the block diagram of an alphanumeric video display system. Explain how it operates.
17. What kind of ROM is used in video display systems?
18. Draw the block diagram of and explain the principle of operation for three analog-to-digital conversion methods.
19. Explain the digital-to-analog conversion method using a ladder network.
20. What is the difference between resolution and accuracy in A-D converters?
21. What is the Gray code and where is it used?
22. List the most common forms of bilateral switch. What do they do?
23. Why are MOS switches (particularly C-MOS) electrically quiet? What makes the bipolar devices electrically noisy?
24. What is a UART (USART) and what is it used for?
25. What is the purpose of an LSI peripheral interface device?

# CHAPTER 12

# AN INTRODUCTION TO MICROPROCESSORS AND MINICOMPUTERS

*Learning Objectives.    Upon completion of this chapter you should:*
1. *Know how microprocessors differ from random logic in dedicated systems.*
2. *Be able to define programming.*
3. *Be able to list the hierarchies of programming languages.*
4. *Be able to describe the principal characteristics of:*
    *a. machine language*
    *b. assembler language*
    *c. procedure-oriented language*
5. *Be able to define the following:*
    *a. hardware*
    *b. firmware*
    *c. software*
6. *Be able to list and describe the function of each of the 6800 microprocessor registers.*
7. *Be able to describe one-byte, two-byte, and three-byte microprocessor instructions.*
8. *Know how various kinds of programs are stored in a computer.*
9. *Be able to define mnemonics.*
10. *Be able to describe one-, two-, and three-byte instruction codes.*
11. *Be able to describe the operation of pushdown stack and explain how zero-address instructions can be used.*
12. *Be able to explain the bus concept.*
13. *Be able to define RALU and ALU.*
14. *Be able to define the term branch.*
15. *Be able to define and explain link-bit (or carry bit).*
16. *Be able to explain how the ALU output is tested and the reason for such testing.*
17. *Be able to explain indexed branching.*
18. *Be able to describe the operation of the RALU control memory system.*
19. *Be able to define microinstruction and microprogram.*

*20. Be able to define system-level operation.*
*21. Be able to write a simple program for the 6800 microprocessor.*

The microprocessor is probably the most exciting digital development since the introduction of integrated circuits. The basic idea behind large-scale, fully programmable computers was to have a single basic machine that could be made to handle nearly any computing or data processing task simply by giving it an appropriate set of instructions. Implementing these instructions—called a *program*—required only that the program and data be loaded into a memory, and the machine could take it from there. Obviously such a powerful, truly general-purpose machine could also be used for such things as traffic signal control, electronic instrumentation, electronic scales, automobile systems control, and the like. Just as obviously, it could do the chores of inventory control, tax computation, payroll, and so on for a small company having perhaps 20 employees. All of these tasks have become too complex to do well manually, but the cost of a general purpose digital computer is enormously prohibitive.

Now the microprocessor is available and its cost is dropping just as the price of pocket calculators fell shortly after their introduction. The microprocessor is roughly a less powerful equivalent of the CPU (central processing unit) of a full-scale digital computer.

The microprocessor is the heart of a system called a *microcomputer*. There is no hard and fast rule as to how much of the microcomputer is put on a single chip. An entire microcomputer can be put on a single chip, although this practice, until recently, has been limited mostly to military applications. A large part of the computer is commonly put on a single chip and called a *microprocessor*. The percentage of the computer system put on the microprocessor chip varies among manufacturers. The microprocessor unit (MPU) nearly always contains the ALU (arithmetic logic unit), minimum necessary working and control registers, and perhaps some specifically committed ROM cells, along with counters and delay circuits.

The exact capabilities and limitations of a given system are determined by three things: hardware, software, and firmware. Limitations imposed by hardware are relatively inflexible. They are designed in according to design philosophies, cost considerations, technological limitations, and so on. As much as is possible, the MPU is designed so that it has very little internal direction—it is virtually uncommitted to anything but the simplest operations common to any computer operation. Although the MPU is the central part and coordinator of the system, it is virtually a slave to external control. Nearly every action is dictated by external programming in the form of firmware or software. The firmware is a programmed ROM that determines what kind of machine the processor will become. The ROM is external to the MPU chip and can be programmed for the functions required of a general purpose machine or of a dedicated (special purpose) machine.

The following are some examples of dedicated machines:

| | |
|---|---|
| Automotive ignition control | Automated gas pumps |
| Automotive brakes | Fast-food cash registers |
| Home appliances | Cash registers |
| Vending machines | Communication line controllers |
| Electronic scales | Printer controllers |
| Specialty calculators | Traffic light controllers |
| Adaptive control systems | Copiers |
| Film processing | Point-of-sales inventory control |
| Automotive analyzers | Electronic typesetting |
| Medical instruments | Character generation |
| Machine tool control | Automatic drafting systems |
| Electronic games | |

Once programmed, the firmware becomes permanent software that directs the activities of the processor and facilitates communication with keyboards and other peripheral devices. The firmware contains a number of short programs called *subroutines*. In dedicated systems firmware may constitute the entire program (stored in the ROM).

In this chapter we will examine processor structure and support systems and introduce microprocessor programming.

## 12-1   The Bus

The bus is one of the fundamentally important interconnecting ideas in current microprocessor architecture. A basic problem with any large-scale integrated circuit is getting the signals into and out of the chip. An excessive number of leads can cause a drastic increase in circuit board cost and a serious decrease in overall reliability. The multiplexing arrangement used in calculators serves that purpose, but it is too restrictive and much too slow.

The bidirectional bus reduces the required pin count to an acceptable number without being too slow. Even more important, the bus concept permits almost unlimited expansion of the machine by simply adding chips and tying them into the bus.

Figure 12-1 is a simplified illustration of how a bidirectional bus might operate. In Figure 12-1a the phase 2 clock level is *high* and the MPU is in the *input* condition. The ROM and RAM are both connected to the

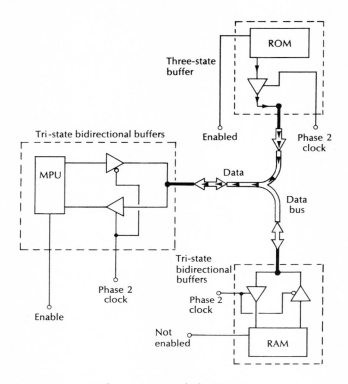

a. The processor reads the ROM

**Figure 12-1**   The Bus

data bus. The bidirectional buffer *amplifiers* $A_1$ and $A_2$ are enabled to flow data out of the memories (they are in the read mode). However, only the ROM chip is enabled and passes its data down the bus. The RAM is in the high-impedance or open-circuit state and is effectively off the bus.

In Figure 12-1b the phase 2 clock is *low* and the data flow is directed out of the MPU and into the memories (write). Again, both memories are in the write condition as controlled by the phase 2 clock. In this case, only the RAM chip is enabled, and the ROM is in the high-impedance state and off the bus.

## 12-2   An Introduction to Programming

Programming is a broad term covering all methods of providing instructions for a computer or processor to follow. Some programs are hard-

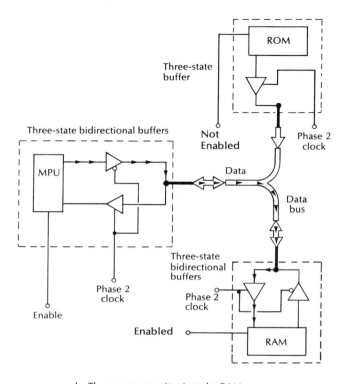

b. The processor writes into the RAM

Figure 12-1 continued

wired and permanent, some are in the form of read-only memories (called firmware), and others are in the form of software, requiring no physical changes to change the program. A logic system designed for a specific job is hardware programmed and cannot be adapted for other tasks without physical modification and possibly a complete redesign. A logic system using only ROM devices is firmware programmed and can be transformed into a completely different system for an entirely different task by changing or reprogramming the ROM's. The most flexible of programs is software. The program is created on paper and transferred to the logic system by means of a keyboard, punched or magnetic tape, or punched cards. The machine stores the instructions in some kind of random-access memory and is dedicated to the performance of the special task directed by the instructions in the RAM. While a particular program is in the RAM, the machine is just as dedicated to a special task as a hard-wired logic system. However, all that is necessary to rededicate it to an entirely new task is to erase the RAM and load in a new program. Once a library of programs has been built up, it takes but minutes to convert the machine from the performance of one task to another.

Many microprocessors are used in so-called dedicated systems rather than for general-purpose computing. For example, assume that a city is in the process of installing traffic signal controls. This process could involve activities such as sampling current traffic patterns and adjusting to them, varying signal behavior according to the season or time of day, and so on. The basic function of the controller for each signal is essentially the same, but each has its own unique problems. If the microprocessor controllers are used throughout the city, the controller at each signal can be adapted to its unique set of conditions by simply programming a ROM or a RAM for each signal. If a street is widened or other conditions changed, the controller for that signal does not have to be redesigned or modified. All that is required is inserting a ROM programmed for the new situation or loading a new software program into a RAM.

### MACHINE-LANGUAGE PROGRAMMING

Machine language consists of groups of binary digits that direct the actions of the logic circuits controlling the transfer and handling of logic-level data within the machine. Machine-language instructions consist of two basic parts: the operation to be performed and the address or addresses of the data (operands) to be operated upon. Because machine language consists entirely of many zeros and ones, it is not very suitable for direct human use. A hierarchy of languages has therefore been developed to interface human language and machine language. Each successively higher level of language more closely approaches standard American English.

### CHARACTERISTICS OF MACHINE LANGUAGE

In machine language all instructions must be expressed in binary code, generally octal or hexadecimal. An instruction set consisting of nothing but ones and zeros is nearly impossible to remember, tedious to look up, and impossible to use without frequent errors.

The single advantage of machine language is its direct access to even the simplest of operations. The directness of machine language permits direct, efficient programming.

In addition, actual numerical addresses must be spelled out for every instruction and piece of data.

Editing or error correction in machine language is difficult because a single change usually requires that the entire program be rewritten.

## ASSEMBLY LANGUAGE LEVEL

One step up in the language hierarchy is assembly language. In this language a single instruction is machine translated from a mnemonic (memory aid) code* such as ADD MOV CLA (clear and add) into the appropriate binary code groups. The human programmer can make statements in easily remembered mnemonic terms. A specially programmed ROM is often used to convert mnemonic codes into appropriate machine-language groups of ones and zeros.

Assembly language is closely related to the machine language of a specific machine except that mnemonic symbols are used instead of zeros and ones to specify operations and memory addresses. Both machine and assembly languages are machine dependent; that is, their construction is dependent upon the organization of the hardware of a particular machine.

## PROCEDURE- (OR PROBLEM-) ORIENTED LANGUAGES

Higher-level languages—such as FORTRAN (FORmula TRANslation), a mathematically oriented language, COBOL (COmmon Business/ Oriented Language), and BASIC—are not machine dependent. A translator interfaces these standard languages to any given machine. With an appropriate translator these high-level languages can be used without regard to the kind of machine involved. They are called procedure-oriented languages because they are concerned strictly with the problem, not with internal machine operation.

A characteristic of these procedure-oriented languages is that a single statement results in a number of machine-language instructions and the housekeeping functions of loading data into memory, keeping track of data locations, and retrieving the data when required are handled automatically.

A sample BASIC statement might be similar to the following:

## IF THEN/GO TO

This statement would finally be translated into control signals that cause addition and other operations to take place within the machine.

Many high-level languages contain a vocabulary of key or reserved words that cause the system to act, along with a set of optional words that can be used to make written statements more easily understood by humans. These optional words are ignored by the machine and are for human use only.

---

* Example: STB might mean *store* in register *B*. STA would then mean *store* in register *A*.

Programming languages are carefully constructed artificial languages. While we might debate about the use of commas in a term paper, there is no room for debate in programming languages. The syntax and punctuation must be correct or the computer will refuse to act on a statement and will call the programmer's attention to an error. At the machine-language level, an incorrect 1 or 0 entry would be executed by the machine and the final results would be in error. Because programming errors are inevitable, many mistakes are avoided by using high-level languages.

## 12-3    Machine-Language Instructions

Instructions for machine language consist of binary numbers, $n$-bits in length. The binary numbers are divided into sections called *fields*. One field is usually devoted to defining the operation to be performed and one or more fields give the memory location of the operands to be operated on. Instructions may contain from one to four addresses depending upon the type of machine involved. Some machines use two or more address formats.

**FOUR-ADDRESS INSTRUCTIONS**

| Operation code | Source of operand #1 | Source of operand #2 | Destination | Location of next Instruction |
|---|---|---|---|---|

The four-address instruction contains a field that specifies the address in memory of each of the two operands (sources), the address where the result of the operation is to be stored, and the address where the next instruction will be found.

**THREE-ADDRESS INSTRUCTIONS**

| Operation code | Source of operand #1 | Source of operand #2 | Destination |
|---|---|---|---|

When three-address instructions are used, a special register called a *program counter* keeps track of the address of the next instruction. In this case, it is not necessary to specify the next instruction as part of the initial instruction. The instructions are stored in sequence and branch locations are ordered. The program counter simply advances one location at a time or branches to another location.

## TWO-ADDRESS INSTRUCTIONS

| Operation code | Source of operand #1 | Destination |
|---|---|---|

If one of the operands is always in a known location in an accumulator register and the system includes a program counter to keep track of the location of the next instruction, a two-address instruction will be sufficient.

The two-address instruction makes it difficult to perform subtraction and division if the subtrahend or divisor happens to be stored in the accumulator. This difficulty can be overcome, however, by adding MOVE or LOAD and STORE instructions to the instruction set. The MOVE instruction transfers the memory contents from one location to another. Symbolically this MOVE can be indicated by the following form:

$$Y \leftarrow X$$

This is interpreted as: MOVE the contents of location $X$ into location $Y$. The problem in division and subtraction occurs because neither is commutative, that is:

$$A - B \neq B - A \text{ and } A/B \neq B/A$$

Many computers have LOAD and STORE instructions instead of MOVE instructions. These are usually more convenient in one-address machines.

a. The LOAD instruction moves data to the accumulator.
b. The STORE instruction moves data out of the accumulator to some other memory location.

## ONE-ADDRESS INSTRUCTIONS

| Operation code | Address |
|---|---|

In the one-address instruction, the counter is used, and one operand is always in the accumulator. The address of one operand is specified. The destination of the result is always the accumulator, so it does not have to be specified. Again, MOVE or LOAD and STORE instructions are often necessary for subtraction or division.

## PUSHDOWN STACK INSTRUCTIONS

The pushdown stack memory permits zero-address instructions. The instruction contains only an operation code. A binary group is loaded on the top layer of the stack. It is then *pushed down* to the next lower level to make room for an additional group. The last information to be loaded is the first out. Loading a number into the stack is called *pushing* and extracting the data is called *popping*.

The principal disadvantage of the stack is that only the data resting on the top of the stack is accessible. Normally, the two operands destined for the next operation are resting in the top two positions in the stack.

## MICROPROCESSOR INSTRUCTIONS

Microprocessor instructions consist of one, two, or three bytes. Data must follow instruction commands in successive memory locations.

### One-Byte Instructions

| $b_7$ | $b_6$ | $b_5$ | $b_4$ | $b_3$ | $b_2$ | $b_1$ | $b_0$ | $\leftarrow$ Op-code |
|---|---|---|---|---|---|---|---|---|

One-byte instructions, often called inherent instructions, are used primarily for manipulating accumulator registers. No address code for the operand needs to be specified because it is inherent in the instruction. For example, CLRA (clear accumulator register $A$) requires no definition of the data to the operated on, nor is it necessary to specify an address for the data to be operated on (operand). Clearing the register clears whatever data is stored in it.

### Two-Byte Instructions

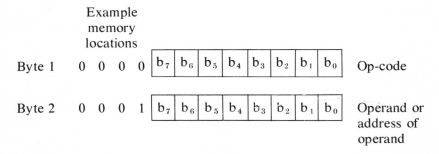

Example
memory
locations

Byte 1    0  0  0  0  | $b_7$ | $b_6$ | $b_5$ | $b_4$ | $b_3$ | $b_2$ | $b_1$ | $b_0$ |    Op-code

Byte 2    0  0  0  1  | $b_7$ | $b_6$ | $b_5$ | $b_4$ | $b_3$ | $b_2$ | $b_1$ | $b_0$ |    Operand or address of operand

In two-byte instructions the operand must be in the memory location immediately following the op-code location.

**Three-Byte Instructions**

Memory
address

0003 | $b_7$ | $b_6$ | $b_5$ | $b_4$ | $b_3$ | $b_2$ | $b_1$ | $b_0$ |    Op-code

0004 | $b_7$ | $b_6$ | $b_5$ | $b_4$ | $b_3$ | $b_2$ | $b_1$ | $b_0$ |    Higher 8 bits of the address of the operand

0005 | $b_7$ | $b_6$ | $b_5$ | $b_4$ | $b_3$ | $b_2$ | $b_1$ | $b_0$ |    Lower 8 bits of the address of the operand

Three-byte instructions are used in the *extended* address mode. The three bytes are located sequentially in memory as shown above.

## 12-4 A Sample Processor

In this section we will examine a TTL processor system. This discussion is intended only to bridge the gap between familiar hardware concepts and microprocessor software. The sample used is not actually representative of most microprocessors. We will examine a typical microprocessor in subsequent sections.

The diagram in Figure 12-2 is that of a TTL processor unit. The register/arithmetic/logic unit (RALU) performs the necessary arithmetic and logic operations and contains enough memory (registers) to provide temporary storage for its internal operation.

The control memory provides commands to tell the RALU unit what specific arithmetic or logic operation to perform and how and when to move data in the RALU registers. The control memory also gets signals back from the RALU that permit the alteration of the control memory's instruction sequence. This allows a sequence to be altered if the result of an ALU operation is zero, for example. Conditional control permits a jump to an alternate sequence, multiple repetitions of short sequences, and other capabilities essential to fully programmed operation.

The interface logic generally takes the form of bidirectional bus drivers to allow for a variety of input/output and memory devices with a minimum of interface hardware.

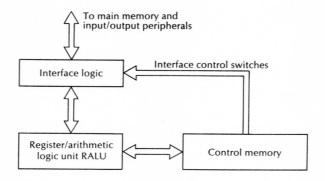

**Figure 12-2**    Sample Processor Block Diagram

## 12-5    The RALU (Register/Arithmetic/Logic Unit)

Figure 12-3 is the block diagram of a TTL RALU. The operands are stored in the four-bit latch and four-bit shift register until the ALU is commanded to use them. The $S_0$, $S_1$, $S_2$, and $S_3$ inputs to the ALU are the control inputs that tell it what operation to perform on the operands.

An ALU of the 74181 TTL type (discussed in Chapter 9) can be combined with a small $16 \times 4$ bit RAM, a 7495 shift register, a 7475 quad latch, and a quad bus driver to form a simple but workable processor. Most processors currently available contain all of these basic elements and often some others on a single MOS or I²L chip. The TTL version would be faster than MOS but a good deal more costly and power hungry and would require more space than its equivalent LSI package.

The circuit in Figure 12-3 is extremely versatile in spite of its obvious simplicity. Any of the $16 \times 4$ bit RAM memory locations can be treated as a four-bit bidirectional counter. Incrementing—advancing the counter one step (or decrementing back one step)—can be accomplished by passing the data in a given memory location through the ALU and back to the memory. In addition, moving a four-bit word through the shift register allows for the right or left shift required for multiplication, division, and other processing operations.

By loading one word into the latch and another into the shift register, the ALU can perform sixteen (or more) arithmetic and sixteen (typical) logical operations by combining the data in the two registers. The system can handle most common arithmetic and processing operations by simply instructing the RALU to perform specific operations in a specific sequence (with conditional or unconditional branches).

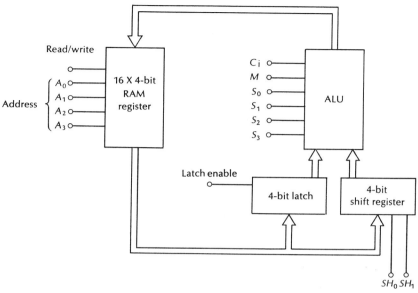

**Figure 12-3**   Block Diagram of the RALU

This system does, however, have limitations, probably the most serious of which is the four-bit word length limitation. The solution is simply to expand the existing hardware in one of two directions, either by simply adding more (parallel) ALU shift registers or providing some overflow storage and recirculating additional words through the same basic system. Both methods are commonly used, with a trade-off between the speed and the amount of hardware required. The addition of more ALU's is sometimes referred to as lateral expansion. This parallel mode of operation is faster, but the extra hardware requires considerable chip space and is usually used with larger, faster machines rather than with single-chip microprocessor units.

In most microprocessors, the word length ranges from four bits to sixteen bits. Many situations require two (or more) words. In order to handle multiple word lengths in the basic RALU system shown in Figure 12-3, it is necessary to add two one-bit memories, known as carry or link-bit memories, to accommodate a carry-out of the ALU and any bit that is shifted "off the end" of the shift register. The overflow bit in this application is generally known as a carry/link bit because it provides the link between parts of the composite word.

In Figure 12-4 the insertion of the carry/link bit or a constant 1 or 0 is controlled by a multiplexer. The shift register operation is controlled by

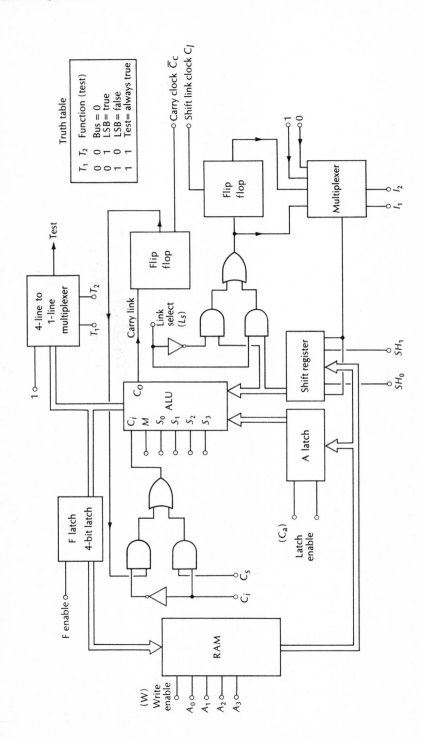

**Figure 12-4** Complete RALU System

**Table 12-1**  Multiplexer and Shift Register Truth Tables

| $I_1$ | $I_2$ | Function |
|---|---|---|
| 0 | 0 | Rotate |
| 0 | 1 | Insert link |
| 1 | 0 | Insert zero |
| 1 | 1 | Insert 1 |

a. Multiplexer truth table

| $SH_0$ | $SH_1$ | Function |
|---|---|---|
| 0 | 0 | Load |
| 0 | 1 | Shift right |
| 1 | 0 | Shift left |
| 1 | 1 | Hold |

b. Shift register truth table

the control inputs $SH_0$, $SH_1$. Table 12-1a is the truth table for the multiplexer and part b is the shift register truth table.

One of the most important capabilities in a microprocessor is that of being able to branch to another part of the control sequence. Branching instructions can be either conditional or unconditional. For conditional branches, a test for conditions at the output of the ALU is made. In the sample machine we are discussing the following conditions can be tested for:

1. Are all outputs 0?
2. Is the LSB 1?
3. Is the LSB 0?
4. Are all outputs 1?

Assume that a program requires a branch when the LSB = 1. The program would progress in the normal sequence until the test indicated the LSB = 1 condition. At that time the instructions would come from a different part of the program memory as directed by the memory address part of the instruction. Some machines also offer *indexed branches* in which the memory location for the branch is found by adding to it or subtracting from it the contents of a RALU register. In the example shown in Figure 12-4 an ALU latch and link control gates are also provided. The carry/link gate structure allows for selection of the source for the carry's input to the ALU. Carry input data can be taken from the link-bit flip-flop or from the program control circuit (to be discussed shortly). The shift register logic permits selection of either the first or the last bit in the register.

## 12-6  The RALU Control Memory System

The control memory system is centered in a ROM array. Two four-bit counters select the various memory locations. Each word in the ROM is called a *microinstruction;* it produces all the control signals required by the RALU for a given operation. A sequence of RALU specific

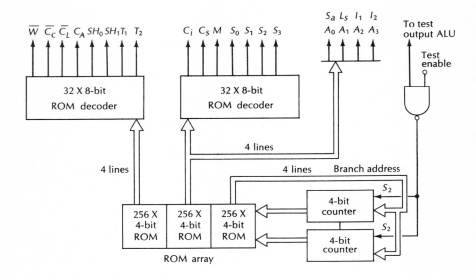

**Figure 12-5**    Control Memory System

microinstructions generates a systems-level operation such as multiplication. Such a sequence of microinstructions is called a *microprogram*. The block diagram of the control memory system is shown in Figure 12-5.

The two 32 × 8 bit ROM decoders provide RALU control signals that are a function of the ROM programming. Because of the decoder, there need be no relationship between memory locations in the 256 × 4 bit control ROM memory and specific RALU control inputs. This allows for an arbitrary but convenient program set.

Table 12-2 is a sample list of microinstructions for the control memory system in Figure 12-5. These instructions are based on the RALU shown in Figure 12-4.

A sequence of the available microinstructions constitutes a microprogram, the lowest machine-language programming level.

### MICROPROGRAMMING

Microprogramming is a technique that may pave the way for better communications with the microprocessor and perhaps make new processor-oriented languages a reality. Traditional internal computer control systems are composed of random logic, counters, flip-flops, and so on. Machines using microprogramming have a computer within a computer. The internal control computer has a processor and a memory (ROM); it is a complete computer on a small scale. The user is not

**Table 12-2** Microinstruction Set

| | 4 BITS | | | | 4 BITS | | | | 4 BITS | | | |
|---|---|---|---|---|---|---|---|---|---|---|---|---|
| RAM to $A$ LATCH | 0 | 0 | 0 | 1 | RAM ADDRESS | | | | | | | |
| RAM to SHIFT REGISTER | 0 | 0 | 1 | 0 | RAM ADDRESS | | | | | | | |
| F LATCH to RAM | 0 | 0 | 1 | 1 | RAM ADDRESS | | | | | | | |
| ALU operation ($A$, $B$ to $F$) | 0 | 1 | 0 | 0 | $C_1$ | $C_s$ | $M$ | $S_0$ | $S_1$ | $S_2$ | $S_3$ | |
| SHIFT RIGHT | 0 | 1 | 0 | 1 | $I_1$ | $I_2$ | $L_s$ | | | | | |
| SHIFT LEFT | 0 | 1 | 1 | 0 | $I_1$ | $I_2$ | $L_s$ | | | | | |
| SPARE | 0 | 1 | 1 | 1 | BRANCH ——— ADDRESS | | | | | | | |
| UNCONDITIONAL BRANCH | 1 | 0 | 0 | 0 | BRANCH ——— ADDRESS | | | | | | | |
| BRANCH IF BUS = 0 | 1 | 0 | 0 | 1 | BRANCH ——— ADDRESS | | | | | | | |
| BRANCH IF LSB = 1 | 1 | 0 | 1 | 0 | BRANCH ——— ADDRESS | | | | | | | |
| BRANCH IF LSB = 0 | 1 | 0 | 1 | 1 | BRANCH ——— ADDRESS | | | | | | | |

aware of the internal computer and has no access to it. The control computer executes the user's programmed instructions by executing a sequence of its own pre-programmed microinstructions. By simply altering a ROM program, the machine becomes a completely different computer, emulating some specific machine or having a highly specialized instruction set. Microprogramming ROM's may also be available as an off-the-chip device allowing the microprocessor architecture to be altered from the outside.

## 12-7  A Typical Microprocessor System, the Motorola 6800

The Motorola 6800 system consists of a family of the eight-bit 6800 microprocessor itself and basic support chips. The support chips consist of the following:

1. An eight-bit, 1000-byte (8K) ROM, the 6830. Traditionally, a byte has been defined as half a word. In most current microprocessors it is considered to be eight bits, even though a functional word typically may be one, two, or three bytes, depending on the nature of the operation involved.

2. An eight-bit by 128-byte (1024 or 1K) RAM, the 6810.
3. A two-port, bidirectional universal peripheral interface adapter, PIA.
4. An asynchronous communications interface adapter (ACIA), the 6850.

The memory capacity can be expanded by adding more memory chips, a basic principle in modern microprocessor philosophy. All of the chips in the family are N-MOS LSI and can be operated from a single +5 volt power supply. All outputs are TTL compatible and can drive one TTL load or ten (or more) MOS loads.

A two-phase clock is used. All computers operate on a regular *fetch-execute* cycle. Data are *fetched* from memory in one clock phase and operated upon during the other. More than one fetch-execute cycle may be required depending on the addressing mode. For example, a fetch-fetch-execute or some other combination may be required to gather up and operate on all necessary data.

### THE 6800 PROCESSOR CHIP

Figure 12-6 is a photomicrograph of the 6800 chip showing the function of the various areas on the chip. Figure 12-7 shows the functional block diagram of the microprocessor. The data bus in the 6800 is eight bits wide and capable of carrying data in both directions (bidirectional).

The sixteen-bit-wide address bus specifies memory locations. The 6800 does not use special instructions or special input/output ports for addressing input/output (I/O) devices. Communications of the MPU with the outside world are treated simply as communications with memory locations. Peripheral devices are selected by using appropriate memory location.

### MEMORY

The two memory packages in the 6800 family are the $128 \times 8$ (6810) RAM and the $1024 \times 8$ ROM (6830). Both devices are static and require no clock or refresh cycle. Both operate on a single +5 volt power supply and are TTL compatible. Figure 12-8 shows the functional block diagram for the two memories and Figure 12-9 shows how the memories are connected to the MPU.

### INPUT/OUTPUT AND PERIPHERAL INTERFACE ADAPTER

There are two peripheral interface devices: one (PIA) to interface data in parallel form and a second (ACIA) for interfacing data in serial form. Both are bidirectional and programmable. Between the two, nearly any

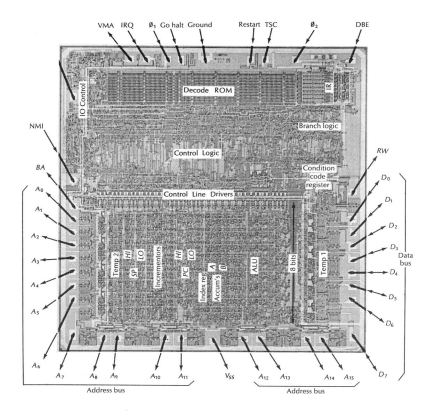

Courtesy of Motorola Semiconductor Products, Inc. ® 1975

**Figure 12-6** Photomicrograph of the Motorola 6800 Microprocessor Unit (MPU)

common input/output devices can be interfaced to the MPU. The flexibility designed into these two units is intended to make them almost universal. Between the two devices, they can interface teletype, keyboards, various printers, CRT displays, cassette and floppy-disc memories, and a variety of other input/output machines. This considerable built-in capability makes each of these devices nearly 20 percent as complex as the MPU itself. Figure 12-10 shows the 6800 system.

## 12-8    Programming the 6800 Microprocessor

The 6800 has two accumulators (registers), designated as ACCA and ACCB, which are eight-bit, one-byte registers. In most modes of operation, data enter and leave the processor via the accumulators. Data directed to memory is entered into the accumulator and then transferred into memory.

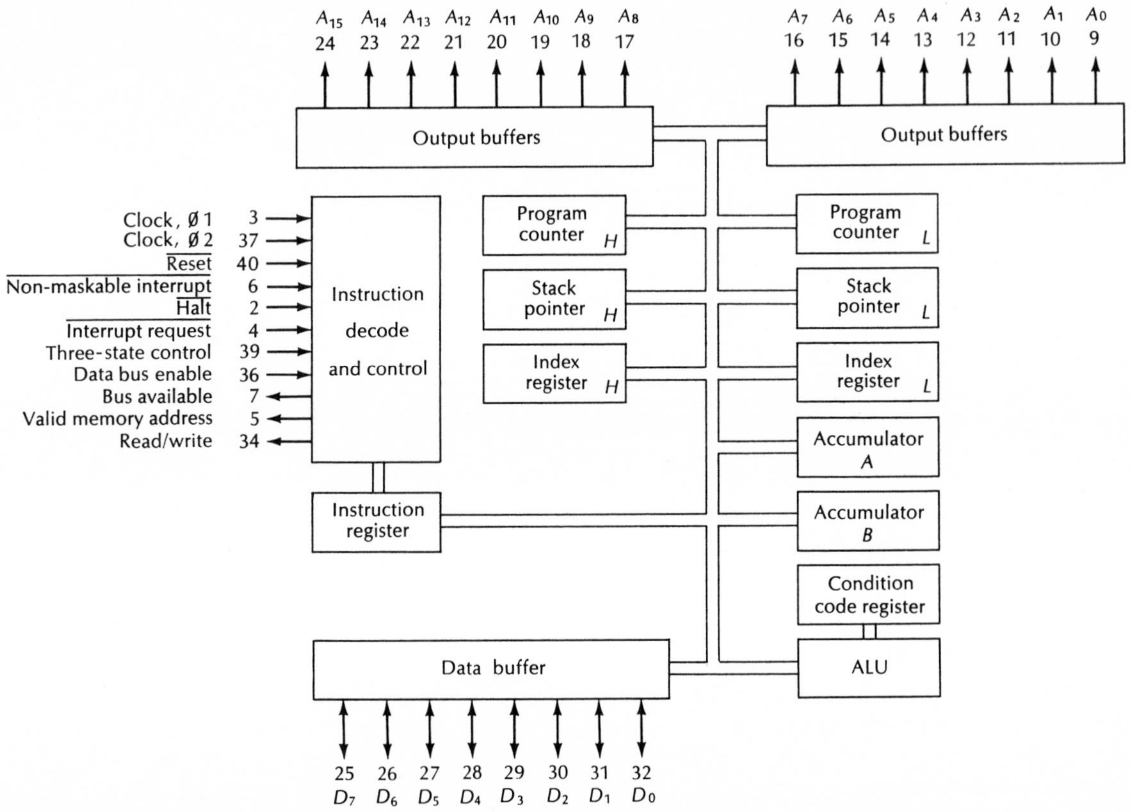

**Figure 12-7** Functional Block Diagram of the 6800 MPU

Courtesy of Motorola Semiconductor Products, Inc. © 1975

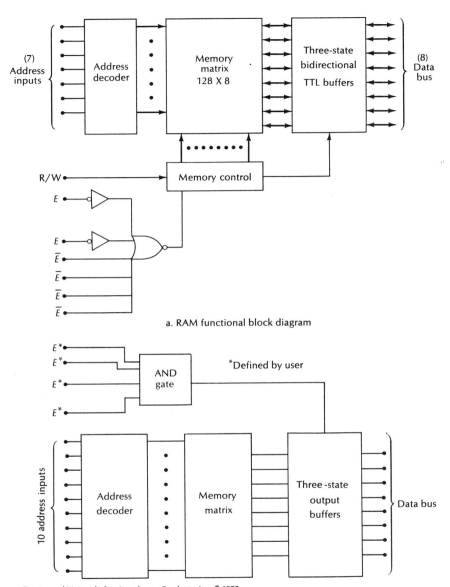

a. RAM functional block diagram

**Figure 12-8**   Functional Block Diagram of the RAM and ROM Memories

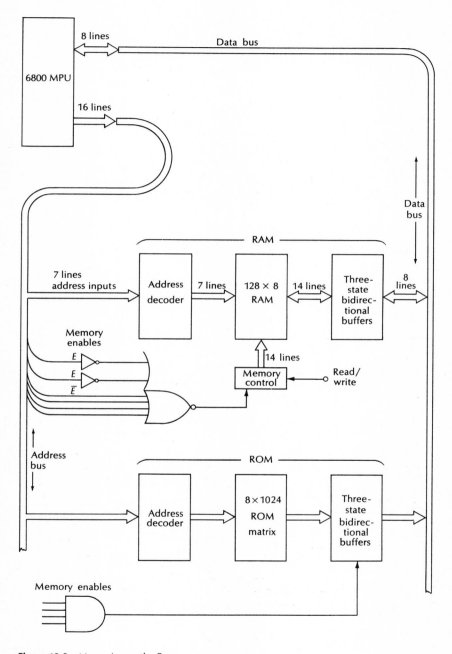

**Figure 12-9**    Memories on the Bus

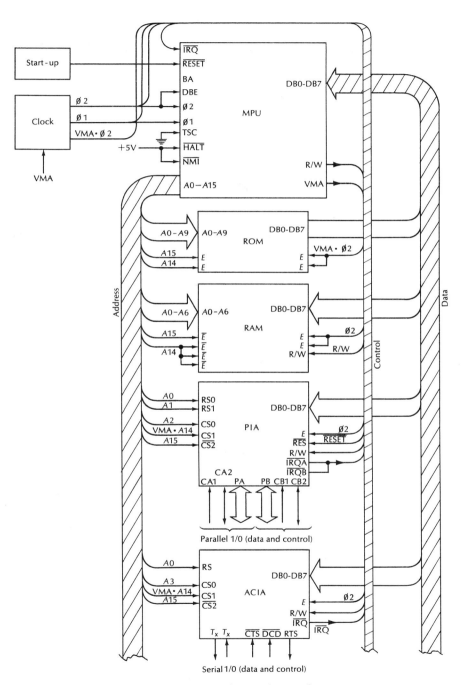

Courtesy of Motorola Semiconductor Products, Inc. © 1975

**Figure 12-10**   The 6800 System

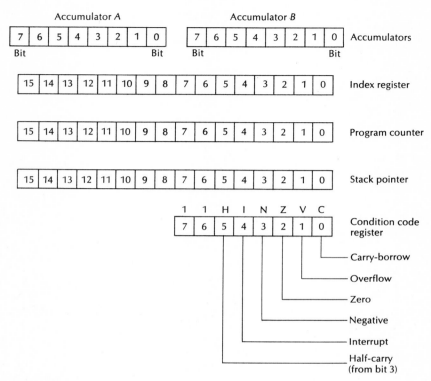

**Figure 12-11**   The 6800 Registers

Figure 12-11 shows the 6800 MPU register group. The accumulators are eight-bit registers, but they can be split in half for some operations. The *index* register is a sixteen-bit register for handling three-byte instructions in the indexed addressing mode. The program counter keeps track of program locations in memory. The stack pointer is a register that keeps track of data locations in the stack. The stack is a dedicated part of the memory used to store the contents of all registers in the MPU when processing is interrupted. The *condition* register is an eight-bit register that uses only five of the available bits. (The two unused bits are held at a logical 1.) This register provides the necessary test bits for jumps and other conditional operations. The 6800 has seven addressing modes and can execute 72 instructions. A summary of the instruction set is shown in Table 12-3.

### ADDRESSING MODES

Each instruction defines one of the seven addressing modes, which are as follows:

Inherent addressing (or implied addressing)
Immediate addressing
Accumulator addressing
Direct addressing
Relative addressing
Extended addressing
Indexed addressing

### Inherent Mode (Implied)

There are 25 inherent mode instructions in which the instruction contains only an op-code. No operand or memory location for an operand is required. For example, the instruction ABA (add the contents of accumulators A and B) is an inherent mode instruction. The operands need not be specified because they are already stored in the two accumulators.

### Immediate Addressing

Immediate addressing, involving only the lower 256 memory locations, is one of the fastest modes. Immediate instructions are two-byte instructions in which the operand itself, or a symbolic representation of it, is contained in the second byte of the instruction.

### Relative Addressing

Relative mode addressing uses a two-byte instruction, with the relative address specified by the second byte. The relative address is stored as an eight-bit number in two's complement (binary) form to allow for a range of relative addresses from $-128$ (dec.) to $+127$ (dec.). The relationship between the relative address and the absolute address of data is given by the following:

$$D = (PC + 2) + R$$

where $PC$ = the first byte of a branch instruction
$D$ = the address of the destination of the branch instruction
$R$ = the eight-bit, two's complement binary number stored in the second byte of the branch instruction

### Indexed Mode Addressing

In this mode the numerical address is variable and depends on the contents of the index register. The current address is obtained during program execution rather than being held at a predetermined fixed location as with other addressing modes. The operand field contains a numerical value which, when added to the contents of the index register, yields the current address of the operand.

# Table 12-3  6800 Instruction Set

Courtesy of Motorola Semiconductor Products, Inc. © 1975

## ACCUMULATOR AND MEMORY INSTRUCTIONS

| OPERATIONS | MNEMONIC | IMMED OP | ~ | = | DIRECT OP | ~ | = | INDEX OP | ~ | = | EXTND OP | ~ | = | IMPLIED OP | ~ | = | BOOLEAN/ARITHMETIC OPERATION (All register labels refer to contents) | H (5) | I (4) | N (3) | Z (2) | V (1) | C (0) |
|---|---|---|---|---|---|---|---|---|---|---|---|---|---|---|---|---|---|---|---|---|---|---|---|
| Add | ADDA | 8B | 2 | 2 | 9B | 3 | 2 | AB | 5 | 2 | BB | 4 | 3 | | | | $A + M \rightarrow A$ | ↕ | • | ↕ | ↕ | ↕ | ↕ |
| | ADDB | CB | 2 | 2 | DB | 3 | 2 | EB | 5 | 2 | FB | 4 | 3 | | | | $B + M \rightarrow B$ | ↕ | • | ↕ | ↕ | ↕ | ↕ |
| Add Acmltrs | ABA | | | | | | | | | | | | | 1B | 2 | 1 | $A + B \rightarrow A$ | ↕ | • | ↕ | ↕ | ↕ | ↕ |
| Add with Carry | ADCA | 89 | 2 | 2 | 99 | 3 | 2 | A9 | 5 | 2 | B9 | 4 | 3 | | | | $A + M + C \rightarrow A$ | ↕ | • | ↕ | ↕ | ↕ | ↕ |
| | ADCB | C9 | 2 | 2 | D9 | 3 | 2 | E9 | 5 | 2 | F9 | 4 | 3 | | | | $B + M + C \rightarrow B$ | ↕ | • | ↕ | ↕ | ↕ | ↕ |
| And | ANDA | 84 | 2 | 2 | 94 | 3 | 2 | A4 | 5 | 2 | B4 | 4 | 3 | | | | $A \cdot M \rightarrow A$ | • | • | ↕ | ↕ | R | • |
| | ANDB | C4 | 2 | 2 | D4 | 3 | 2 | E4 | 5 | 2 | F4 | 4 | 3 | | | | $B \cdot M \rightarrow B$ | • | • | ↕ | ↕ | R | • |
| Bit Test | BITA | 85 | 2 | 2 | 95 | 3 | 2 | A5 | 5 | 2 | B5 | 4 | 3 | | | | $A \cdot M$ | • | • | ↕ | ↕ | R | • |
| | BITB | C5 | 2 | 2 | D5 | 3 | 2 | E5 | 5 | 2 | F5 | 4 | 3 | | | | $B \cdot M$ | • | • | ↕ | ↕ | R | • |
| Clear | CLR | | | | | | | 6F | 7 | 2 | 7F | 6 | 3 | | | | $00 \rightarrow M$ | • | • | R | S | R | R |
| | CLRA | | | | | | | | | | | | | 4F | 2 | 1 | $00 \rightarrow A$ | • | • | R | S | R | R |
| | CLRB | | | | | | | | | | | | | 5F | 2 | 1 | $00 \rightarrow B$ | • | • | R | S | R | R |
| Compare | CMPA | 81 | 2 | 2 | 91 | 3 | 2 | A1 | 5 | 2 | B1 | 4 | 3 | | | | $A - M$ | • | • | ↕ | ↕ | ↕ | ↕ |
| | CMPB | C1 | 2 | 2 | D1 | 3 | 2 | E1 | 5 | 2 | F1 | 4 | 3 | | | | $B - M$ | • | • | ↕ | ↕ | ↕ | ↕ |
| Compare Acmltrs | CBA | | | | | | | | | | | | | 11 | 2 | 1 | $A - B$ | • | • | ↕ | ↕ | ↕ | ↕ |
| Complement, 1's | COM | | | | | | | 63 | 7 | 2 | 73 | 6 | 3 | | | | $\overline{M} \rightarrow M$ | • | • | ↕ | ↕ | R | S |
| | COMA | | | | | | | | | | | | | 43 | 2 | 1 | $\overline{A} \rightarrow A$ | • | • | ↕ | ↕ | R | S |
| | COMB | | | | | | | | | | | | | 53 | 2 | 1 | $\overline{B} \rightarrow B$ | • | • | ↕ | ↕ | R | S |
| Complement, 2's (Negate) | NEG | | | | | | | 60 | 7 | 2 | 70 | 6 | 3 | | | | $00 - M \rightarrow M$ | • | • | ↕ | ↕ | ① | ② |
| | NEGA | | | | | | | | | | | | | 40 | 2 | 1 | $00 - A \rightarrow A$ | • | • | ↕ | ↕ | ① | ② |
| | NEGB | | | | | | | | | | | | | 50 | 2 | 1 | $00 - B \rightarrow B$ | • | • | ↕ | ↕ | ① | ② |
| Decimal Adjust, A | DAA | | | | | | | | | | | | | 19 | 2 | 1 | Converts Binary Add. of BCD Characters into BCD Format | • | • | ↕ | ↕ | • | ③ |
| Decrement | DEC | | | | | | | 6A | 7 | 2 | 7A | 6 | 3 | | | | $M - 1 \rightarrow M$ | • | • | ↕ | ↕ | ④ | • |
| | DECA | | | | | | | | | | | | | 4A | 2 | 1 | $A - 1 \rightarrow A$ | • | • | ↕ | ↕ | ④ | • |
| | DECB | | | | | | | | | | | | | 5A | 2 | 1 | $B - 1 \rightarrow B$ | • | • | ↕ | ↕ | ④ | • |
| Exclusive OR | EORA | 88 | 2 | 2 | 98 | 3 | 2 | A8 | 5 | 2 | B8 | 4 | 3 | | | | $A \oplus M \rightarrow A$ | • | • | ↕ | ↕ | R | • |
| | EORB | C8 | 2 | 2 | D8 | 3 | 2 | E8 | 5 | 2 | F8 | 4 | 3 | | | | $B \oplus M \rightarrow B$ | • | • | ↕ | ↕ | R | • |
| Increment | INC | | | | | | | 6C | 7 | 2 | 7C | 6 | 3 | | | | $M + 1 \rightarrow M$ | • | • | ↕ | ↕ | ⑤ | • |
| | INCA | | | | | | | | | | | | | 4C | 2 | 1 | $A + 1 \rightarrow A$ | • | • | ↕ | ↕ | ⑤ | • |
| | INCB | | | | | | | | | | | | | 5C | 2 | 1 | $B + 1 \rightarrow B$ | • | • | ↕ | ↕ | ⑤ | • |
| Load Acmltr | LDAA | 86 | 2 | 2 | 96 | 3 | 2 | A6 | 5 | 2 | B6 | 4 | 3 | | | | $M \rightarrow A$ | • | • | ↕ | ↕ | R | • |
| | LDAB | C6 | 2 | 2 | D6 | 3 | 2 | E6 | 5 | 2 | F6 | 4 | 3 | | | | $M \rightarrow B$ | • | • | ↕ | ↕ | R | • |
| Or, Inclusive | ORAA | 8A | 2 | 2 | 9A | 3 | 2 | AA | 5 | 2 | BA | 4 | 3 | | | | $A + M \rightarrow A$ | • | • | ↕ | ↕ | R | • |
| | ORAB | CA | 2 | 2 | DA | 3 | 2 | EA | 5 | 2 | FA | 4 | 3 | | | | $B + M \rightarrow B$ | • | • | ↕ | ↕ | R | • |
| Push Data | PSHA | | | | | | | | | | | | | 36 | 4 | 1 | $A \rightarrow M_{SP},\ SP - 1 \rightarrow SP$ | • | • | • | • | • | • |
| | PSHB | | | | | | | | | | | | | 37 | 4 | 1 | $B \rightarrow M_{SP},\ SP - 1 \rightarrow SP$ | • | • | • | • | • | • |

| Operation | Mnemonic | IMMED OP | ~ | # | DIRECT OP | ~ | # | INDEX OP | ~ | # | EXTND OP | ~ | # | IMPLIED OP | ~ | # | Boolean/Arithmetic Operation | H | I | N | Z | V | C |
|---|---|---|---|---|---|---|---|---|---|---|---|---|---|---|---|---|---|---|---|---|---|---|---|
| Pull Data | PULA | | | | | | | | | | | | | 32 | 4 | 1 | SP + 1 → SP, MSP → A | ● | ● | ● | ● | ● | ● |
| | PULB | | | | | | | | | | | | | 33 | 4 | 1 | SP + 1 → SP, MSP → B | ● | ● | ● | ● | ● | ● |
| Rotate Left | ROL | | | | | | | 69 | 7 | 2 | 79 | 6 | 3 | | | | M | ● | ● | ↕ | ↕ | ↕(6) | ↕ |
| | ROLA | | | | | | | | | | | | | 49 | 2 | 1 | A | ● | ● | ↕ | ↕ | ↕(6) | ↕ |
| | ROLB | | | | | | | | | | | | | 59 | 2 | 1 | B | ● | ● | ↕ | ↕ | ↕(6) | ↕ |
| Rotate Right | ROR | | | | | | | 66 | 7 | 2 | 76 | 6 | 3 | | | | M | ● | ● | ↕ | ↕ | ↕(6) | ↕ |
| | RORA | | | | | | | | | | | | | 46 | 2 | 1 | A | ● | ● | ↕ | ↕ | ↕(6) | ↕ |
| | RORB | | | | | | | | | | | | | 56 | 2 | 1 | B | ● | ● | ↕ | ↕ | ↕(6) | ↕ |
| Shift Left, Arithmetic | ASL | | | | | | | 68 | 7 | 2 | 78 | 6 | 3 | | | | M | ● | ● | ↕ | ↕ | ↕(6) | ↕ |
| | ASLA | | | | | | | | | | | | | 48 | 2 | 1 | A | ● | ● | ↕ | ↕ | ↕(6) | ↕ |
| | ASLB | | | | | | | | | | | | | 58 | 2 | 1 | B | ● | ● | ↕ | ↕ | ↕(6) | ↕ |
| Shift Right, Arithmetic | ASR | | | | | | | 67 | 7 | 2 | 77 | 6 | 3 | | | | M | ● | ● | ↕ | ↕ | ↕(6) | ↕ |
| | ASRA | | | | | | | | | | | | | 47 | 2 | 1 | A | ● | ● | ↕ | ↕ | ↕(6) | ↕ |
| | ASRB | | | | | | | | | | | | | 57 | 2 | 1 | B | ● | ● | ↕ | ↕ | ↕(6) | ↕ |
| Shift Right, Logic | LSR | | | | | | | 64 | 7 | 2 | 74 | 6 | 3 | | | | M | ● | ● | R | ↕ | ↕(6) | ↕ |
| | LSRA | | | | | | | | | | | | | 44 | 2 | 1 | A | ● | ● | R | ↕ | ↕(6) | ↕ |
| | LSRB | | | | | | | | | | | | | 54 | 2 | 1 | B | ● | ● | R | ↕ | ↕(6) | ↕ |
| Store Acmltr. | STAA | | | | 97 | 4 | 2 | A7 | 6 | 2 | B7 | 5 | 3 | | | | A → M | ● | ● | ↕ | ↕ | R | ● |
| | STAB | | | | D7 | 4 | 2 | E7 | 6 | 2 | F7 | 5 | 3 | | | | B → M | ● | ● | ↕ | ↕ | R | ● |
| Subtract | SUBA | 80 | 2 | 2 | 90 | 3 | 2 | A0 | 5 | 2 | B0 | 4 | 3 | | | | A − M → A | ● | ● | ↕ | ↕ | ↕ | ↕ |
| | SUBB | C0 | 2 | 2 | D0 | 3 | 2 | E0 | 5 | 2 | F0 | 4 | 3 | | | | B − M → B | ● | ● | ↕ | ↕ | ↕ | ↕ |
| Subtract Acmltrs. | SBA | | | | | | | | | | | | | 10 | 2 | 1 | A − B → A | ● | ● | ↕ | ↕ | ↕ | ↕ |
| Subtr. with Carry | SBCA | 82 | 2 | 2 | 92 | 3 | 2 | A2 | 5 | 2 | B2 | 4 | 3 | | | | A − M − C → A | ● | ● | ↕ | ↕ | ↕ | ↕ |
| | SBCB | C2 | 2 | 2 | D2 | 3 | 2 | E2 | 5 | 2 | F2 | 4 | 3 | | | | B − M − C → B | ● | ● | ↕ | ↕ | ↕ | ↕ |
| Transfer Acmltrs | TAB | | | | | | | | | | | | | 16 | 2 | 1 | A → B | ● | ● | ↕ | ↕ | R | ● |
| | TBA | | | | | | | | | | | | | 17 | 2 | 1 | B → A | ● | ● | ↕ | ↕ | R | ● |
| Test, Zero or Minus | TST | | | | | | | 6D | 7 | 2 | 7D | 6 | 3 | | | | M − 00 | ● | ● | ↕ | ↕ | R | R |
| | TSTA | | | | | | | | | | | | | 4D | 2 | 1 | A − 00 | ● | ● | ↕ | ↕ | R | R |
| | TSTB | | | | | | | | | | | | | 5D | 2 | 1 | B − 00 | ● | ● | ↕ | ↕ | R | R |

**LEGEND:**

OP    Operation Code (Hexadecimal);
~     Number of MPU Cycles;
=     Number of Program Bytes;
+     Arithmetic Plus;
−     Arithmetic Minus;
•     Boolean AND;
MSP   Contents of memory location pointed to be Stack Pointer;

+     Boolean Inclusive OR;
⊕     Boolean Exclusive OR;
M̄     Complement of M;
→     Transfer Into;
0     Bit = Zero;
00    Byte = Zero;

Note — Accumulator addressing mode instructions are included in the column for IMPLIED addressing

**CONDITION CODE SYMBOLS:**

H    Half-carry from bit 3;
I    Interrupt mask
N    Negative (sign bit)
Z    Zero (byte)
V    Overflow, 2's complement
C    Carry from bit 7
R    Reset Always
S    Set Always
↕    Test and set if true, cleared otherwise
●    Not Affected

a.

# INDEX REGISTER AND STACK MANIPULATION INSTRUCTIONS

| POINTER OPERATIONS | MNEMONIC | IMMED OP | ~ | # | DIRECT OP | ~ | # | INDEX OP | ~ | # | EXTND OP | ~ | # | IMPLIED OP | ~ | # | BOOLEAN/ARITHMETIC OPERATION | H | I | N | Z | V | C |
|---|---|---|---|---|---|---|---|---|---|---|---|---|---|---|---|---|---|---|---|---|---|---|---|
| Compare Index Reg | CPX | 8C | 3 | 3 | 9C | 4 | 2 | AC | 6 | 2 | BC | 5 | 3 | | | | $X_H - M, X_L - (M+1)$ | • | • | ⑦ | ↕ | ⑦ | • |
| Decrement Index Reg | DEX | | | | | | | | | | | | | 09 | 4 | 1 | $X - 1 \rightarrow X$ | • | • | • | ↕ | • | • |
| Decrement Stack Pntr | DES | | | | | | | | | | | | | 34 | 4 | 1 | $SP - 1 \rightarrow SP$ | • | • | • | • | • | • |
| Increment Index Reg | INX | | | | | | | | | | | | | 08 | 4 | 1 | $X + 1 \rightarrow X$ | • | • | • | ↕ | • | • |
| Increment Stack Pntr | INS | | | | | | | | | | | | | 31 | 4 | 1 | $SP + 1 \rightarrow SP$ | • | • | • | • | • | • |
| Load Index Reg | LDX | CE | 3 | 3 | DE | 4 | 2 | EE | 6 | 2 | FE | 5 | 3 | | | | $M \rightarrow X_H, (M+1) \rightarrow X_L$ | • | • | ⑨ | ↕ | R | • |
| Load Stack Pntr | LDS | 8E | 3 | 3 | 9E | 4 | 2 | AE | 6 | 2 | BE | 5 | 3 | | | | $M \rightarrow SP_H, (M+1) \rightarrow SP_L$ | • | • | ⑨ | ↕ | R | • |
| Store Index Reg | STX | | | | DF | 5 | 2 | EF | 7 | 2 | FF | 6 | 3 | | | | $X_H \rightarrow M, X_L \rightarrow (M+1)$ | • | • | ⑨ | ↕ | R | • |
| Store Stack Pntr | STS | | | | 9F | 5 | 2 | AF | 7 | 2 | BF | 6 | 3 | | | | $SP_H \rightarrow M, SP_L \rightarrow (M+1)$ | • | • | ⑨ | ↕ | R | • |
| Indx Reg → Stack Pntr | TXS | | | | | | | | | | | | | 35 | 4 | 1 | $X - 1 \rightarrow SP$ | • | • | • | • | • | • |
| Stack Pntr → Indx Reg | TSX | | | | | | | | | | | | | 30 | 4 | 1 | $SP + 1 \rightarrow X$ | • | • | • | • | • | • |

b.

# JUMP AND BRANCH INSTRUCTIONS

| OPERATIONS | MNEMONIC | RELATIVE OP | ~ | # | INDEX OP | ~ | # | EXTND OP | ~ | # | IMPLIED OP | ~ | # | BRANCH TEST | H | I | N | Z | V | C |
|---|---|---|---|---|---|---|---|---|---|---|---|---|---|---|---|---|---|---|---|---|
| Branch Always | BRA | 20 | 4 | 2 | | | | | | | | | | None | • | • | • | • | • | • |
| Branch If Carry Clear | BCC | 24 | 4 | 2 | | | | | | | | | | $C = 0$ | • | • | • | • | • | • |
| Branch If Carry Set | BCS | 25 | 4 | 2 | | | | | | | | | | $C = 1$ | • | • | • | • | • | • |
| Branch If = Zero | BEQ | 27 | 4 | 2 | | | | | | | | | | $Z = 1$ | • | • | • | • | • | • |
| Branch If ≥ Zero | BGE | 2C | 4 | 2 | | | | | | | | | | $N \oplus V = 0$ | • | • | • | • | • | • |
| Branch If > Zero | BGT | 2E | 4 | 2 | | | | | | | | | | $Z + (N \oplus V) = 0$ | • | • | • | • | • | • |
| Branch If Higher | BHI | 22 | 4 | 2 | | | | | | | | | | $C + Z = 0$ | • | • | • | • | • | • |
| Branch If ≤ Zero | BLE | 2F | 4 | 2 | | | | | | | | | | $Z + (N \oplus V) = 1$ | • | • | • | • | • | • |
| Branch If Lower Or Same | BLS | 23 | 4 | 2 | | | | | | | | | | $C + Z = 1$ | • | • | • | • | • | • |
| Branch If < Zero | BLT | 2D | 4 | 2 | | | | | | | | | | $N \oplus V = 1$ | • | • | • | • | • | • |
| Branch If Minus | BMI | 2B | 4 | 2 | | | | | | | | | | $N = 1$ | • | • | • | • | • | • |
| Branch If Not Equal Zero | BNE | 26 | 4 | 2 | | | | | | | | | | $Z = 0$ | • | • | • | • | • | • |
| Branch If Overflow Clear | BVC | 28 | 4 | 2 | | | | | | | | | | $V = 0$ | • | • | • | • | • | • |
| Branch If Overflow Set | BVS | 29 | 4 | 2 | | | | | | | | | | $V = 1$ | • | • | • | • | • | • |
| Branch If Plus | BPL | 2A | 4 | 2 | | | | | | | | | | $N = 0$ | • | • | • | • | • | • |
| Branch To Subroutine | BSR | 8D | 8 | 2 | | | | | | | | | | | • | • | • | • | • | • |
| Jump | JMP | | | | 6E | 4 | 2 | 7E | 3 | 3 | | | | See Special Operations | • | • | • | • | • | • |
| Jump To Subroutine | JSR | | | | AD | 8 | 2 | BD | 9 | 3 | | | | | • | • | • | • | • | • |
| No Operation | NOP | | | | | | | | | | 02 | 2 | 1 | Advances Prog. Cntr. Only | • | • | • | • | • | • |
| Return From Interrupt | RTI | | | | | | | | | | 3B | 10 | 1 | | ⑩ | | | | | |
| Return From Subroutine | RTS | | | | | | | | | | 39 | 5 | 1 | | • | • | • | • | • | • |
| Software Interrupt | SWI | | | | | | | | | | 3F | 12 | 1 | See Special Operations | • | • | • | • | • | • |
| Wait for Interrupt | WAI | | | | | | | | | | 3E | 9 | 1 | | • | ⑪ | • | • | • | • |

c.

**CONDITION CODE REGISTER MANIPULATION INSTRUCTIONS**

| OPERATIONS | MNEMONIC | IMPLIED OP | ~ | # | BOOLEAN OPERATION | COND. CODE REG. 5 H | 4 I | 3 N | 2 Z | 1 V | 0 C |
|---|---|---|---|---|---|---|---|---|---|---|---|
| Clear Carry | CLC | 0C | 2 | 1 | 0 → C | • | • | • | • | • | R |
| Clear Interrupt Mask | CLI | 0E | 2 | 1 | 0 → I | • | R | • | • | • | • |
| Clear Overflow | CLV | 0A | 2 | 1 | 0 → V | • | • | • | • | R | • |
| Set Carry | SEC | 0D | 2 | 1 | 1 → C | • | • | • | • | • | S |
| Set Interrupt Mask | SEI | 0F | 2 | 1 | 1 → I | • | S | • | • | • | • |
| Set Overflow | SEV | 0B | 2 | 1 | 1 → V | • | • | • | • | S | • |
| Acmltr A → CCR | TAP | 06 | 2 | 1 | A → CCR | ⑫ | | | | | |
| CCR → Acmltr A | TPA | 07 | 2 | 1 | CCR → A | • | • | • | • | • | • |

**CONDITION CODE REGISTER NOTES:** (Bit set if test is true and cleared otherwise)

1 (Bit V) Test: Result = 10000000?
2 (Bit C) Test: Result = 00000000?
3 (Bit C) Test: Decimal value of most significant BCD Character greater than nine? (Not cleared if previously set.)
4 (Bit V) Test: Operand = 10000000 prior to execution?
5 (Bit V) Test: Operand = 01111111 prior to execution?
6 (Bit V) Test: Set equal to result of N⊕C after shift has occurred.
7 (Bit N) Test: Sign bit of most significant (MS) byte = 1?
8 (Bit V) Test: 2's complement overflow from subtraction of MS bytes?
9 (Bit N) Test: Result less than zero? (Bit 15 = 1)
10 (All) Load Condition Code Register from Stack. (See Special Operations)
11 (Bit I) Set when interrupt occurs. If previously set, a Non-Maskable Interrupt is required to exit the wait state.
12 (All) Set according to the contents of Accumulator A.

d.

Table 12–3 continued

The formula for the current indexed address is:

$$D = \text{numerical value} + X$$

where $X$ = contents of the index register
$D$ = the address of the operand
The numerical value is often referred to as offset or bias.

### Direct and Extended Addressing

In direct addressing, the second byte (eight bits) contains the absolute memory address. In extended addressing, three bytes are used. The first byte contains the op-code, the second contains the highest eight address bits, and the third contains the lowest eight bits of the address. The address in this case is also absolute.

### INSTRUCTIONS EXPLAINED

The following are instructions for performing operations on data in the accumulator. These are one-byte (inherent) instructions.

| Mnemonic | Op-code* | Meaning |
|----------|----------|---------|
| ABA | 1B | Add the contents of accumulators $A$ and $B$. The result is stored in accumulator $A$. The contents of $B$ are not altered. |
| CLA | 4F | Clear accumulator $A$ to all zeros. |
| CLB | 5F | Clear accumulator $B$. |
| CBA | 11 | Compare accumulators: Subtract the contents of ACCB from ACCA. The ALU is involved but the contents of the accumulators are not altered. The comparison is reflected in the condition register. |
| COMA | 43 | Find the one's complement of the data in accumulator $A$, and replace its contents with its one's complement. (The one's complement is simple inversion of all bits.) |
| COMB | 53 | Replace the contents of ACCB with its one's complement. |
| NEGA | 40 | Replace the contents of ACCA with its two's complement. This operation generates a negative number. |
| NEGB | 50 | Replace the contents of ACCB with its two's complement. This operation generates a negative number. |

---

* Op codes are given in hexadecimal.

| Mnemonic | Op-code | Meaning |
|----------|---------|---------|
| DAA | 19 | Adjust the two hexadecimal digits in accumulator $A$ to valid BCD digits. Set the carry bit in the condition register when appropriate. The correction is accomplished by adding 06,60 or 66 to the contents of ACCA. |
| DECA | 4A | Decrement accumulator $A$. Subtract 1 from the contents of accumulator $A$. Store result in ACCA. |
| DECB | 5A | Decrement accumulator $B$. Store result in accumulator $B$. |
| INCA | 4C | Increment accumulator $A$. Add 1 to the contents of ACCA and store in ACCA. |
| INCB | 5C | Increment accumulator $B$. Store results in AACB. |
| ROLA | 49 | Rotate left, accumulator $A$ or $B$. |
| ROLB | 59 | |

Carry/borrow in condition register.

| RORA | 46 | Rotate right, accumulator $A$ or $B$ |
| RORB | 56 | |

| ASLA | 48 | Shift left, accumulator $A$ or $B$ (arithmetic). |
| ASLB | 58 | |

In condition code register     Always enters zeros

| ASRA | 47 | Shift right, accumulator $A$ or $B$ (arithmetic). |
| ASRB | 57 | |

Retains sign bit

| Mnemonic | Op-code | Meaning |
|----------|---------|---------|
| LSRA | 44 | Logic shift right, accumulator $A$ or $B$. |
| LSRB | 54 | |

$$0 \rightarrow \boxed{b_7 \mid b_6 \mid b_5 \mid b_4 \mid b_3 \mid b_2 \mid b_1 \mid b_0} \rightarrow \boxed{C}$$

| Mnemonic | Op-code | Meaning |
|----------|---------|---------|
| SBA | 10 | Subtract the contents of accumulator $B$ from the contents of accumulator $A$. Store results in accumulator $A$. |
| TAB | 16 | Transfer the contents of ACCA to accumulator $B$. The contents of register $A$ are unchanged. |
| TBA | 17 | Transfer the contents of ACCB to accumulator $A$. The contents of ACCA are unchanged. |

## 12-9  A Programming Example

The first step in writing a program is to make a flowchart showing what is to be accomplished and in what order. In this example we will set up a program for the following:

> Find $N$ (in decimal)
> Equation: $X \times Y = N$
> Where: $X = 09$
> $Y = 08$

Figure 12-12 shows the flowchart for this example. Block #0 in the flow chart indicates the start of the program. The notation "Find $N$" is a code word description of the purpose of the program. The second and third (#1 & #2) blocks get the two operands into the accumulator registers where they are added in block #3. In block #4, the hexadecimal result in the accumulator is corrected (adjusted) to a BCD result that can be conveniently printed out as an ordinary decimal number.

Table 12-4 is the programming sheet for the example, and Figure 12-13 shows the conditions in the two accumulator registers for each step in the program. It is common practice to reserve memory locations 0000 through 0100 for branch instructions. We will arbitrarily begin at location 0106.

The student should compare the flowchart, program sheet, and register contents (Figure 12-13) for each program step.

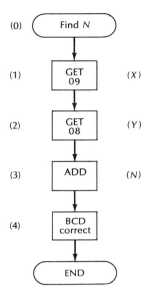

Equation:  $X + Y = N$   find  $N$

**Figure 12-12**   Flowchart for Programming
Example

**Table 12-4**   Programming Sheet for Programming Example

PROGRAM SHEET
TITLE:                         $X + Y = N$      Find $N$

| Memory address | Instruction byte 1 | byte 2 | byte 3 | Label | Op-code | Mode | Op-erand | Comment | Step |
|---|---|---|---|---|---|---|---|---|---|
| 0106 | 86 | X | X | | LDAA | IMM. | | load accumulator A | 1 |
| 0107 | X | 09 | X | | | | :09 | with  :09 | |
| 0108 | C6 | X | X | | LDAB | IMM. | | load accumulator B | 2 |
| 0109 | X | 08 | X | | | | :08 | with  :08 | |
| 010A | 1B | X | X | | ABA | INH. | | add the contents of accumulators | 3 |
| 010B | 19 | X | X | | DAA | INH. | | make BCD correction   (A register) | 4 |
| | | | | | | | | | |
| | | | | | | | | | |
| | | | | | | | | | |

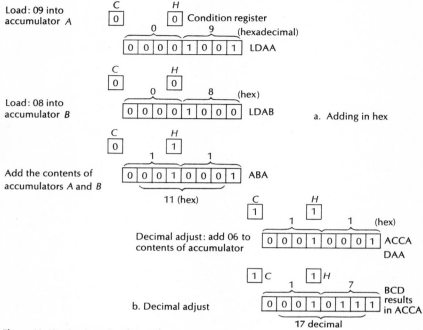

Load: 09 into accumulator *A*

Load: 08 into accumulator *B*

a. Adding in hex

Add the contents of accumulators *A* and *B*

Decimal adjust: add 06 to contents of accumulator

b. Decimal adjust

**Figure 12-13** Register Conditions for Programming Example

## Analysis

1. In step 1, accumulator *A* is loaded with 09. This is stored in the register in hexadecimal form. At this point there is no difference between the BCD and hex representations.
2. In step 2, accumulator *B* is loaded with 08.
3. In step 3, the contents of the two accumulators are added to yield the hex result (11). The sum is stored in accumulator *A*.
4. In step 4, 06 is added to the *A* accumulator contents to convert the hex result into BCD.

## 12-10   A Cooperative Programming Example

In this example it will be necessary for you to follow the changing status of the carry and half-carry bits (H & C) in the condition code register. The program for this example is like the previous example until the completion of the decimal adjust operation for the sum $X + Y$.

The 6800 programming manual makes the following statement about the condition code register carry and half-carry bits for the instruction ABA:

Equation: $X + Y + Z = N$
$X = 65, Y = 58, Z = 9$
Find $N$

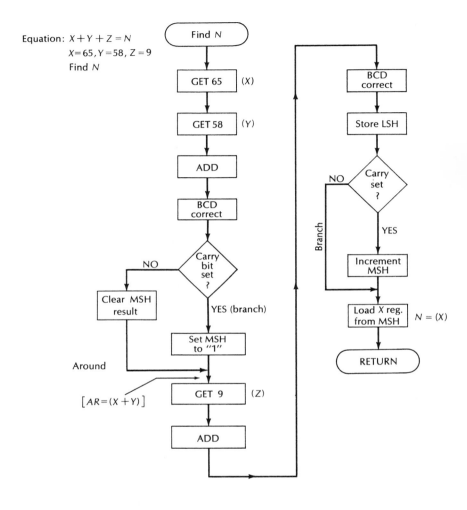

**Figure 12-14** Flowchart for Programming Example

H: Set if there is a carry from bit 3; cleared otherwise.
C: Set if there was a carry from the most significant bit of the result; cleared otherwise.

The condition code register is not an appropriate place to keep the carry. The carry must eventually end up as part of the final result. The branches shown in the flowchart represent one way of accomplishing carry manipulation. Figure 12-14 is the flowchart, Table 12-5 is the program sheet, and Figure 12-15 shows the register status.

**Table 12-5**   Programming Sheet for Programming Example

PROGRAM SHEET

TITLE: _____ $X + Y + Z = N$     $X = 65, Y = 59, Z = 9$     Find $N$ _____

| Memory address | Instruction byte 1 | byte 2 | byte 3 | Label | Op-code | Mode | Op-erand | Comment | Step |
|---|---|---|---|---|---|---|---|---|---|
| 0106 | 86 | X | X | | LDAA | IMM. | | load ACCA | |
| 0107 | X | 65 | X | | | | 65 | with 65 | |
| 0108 | C6 | X | X | | LDAB | IMM. | | load ACCB | |
| 0109 | X | 58 | X | | | | 58 | 58 | |
| 010A | 1B | X | X | | ABA | INH. | | ADD accumulators | |
| 010B | 19 | X | X | | DAA | INH. | | Decimal (BCD) adjust | |
| 010C | 25 | X | X | | BCS | REL. | | branch if carry set | |
| 010D | X | 05 | X | | | | 0005 | branch to 0005 | |
| 010E | 7F | X | X | Clear | CLRM | EXT. | | Clear memory at | |
| 010F | X | 00 | X | | | | 0000 | 0000 | |
| 0110 | X | X | 00 | | | | 0000 | 0000 | |
| 0111 | 20 | X | X | | BRA | REL. | | branch always (unconditional) | |
| 0112 | X | 04 | X | | | | Around | around (skip SET instructions) | |
| 0113 | C6 | X | X | SET 1 | LDAB | IMM. | | SET memory | |
| 0114 | X | 01 | X | | | | 01 | to 01 | |
| 0115 | D7 | X | X | | STAB | DIR. | | store accumulator B..... | |
| 0116 | X | 00 | X | | | | 00 | at 0000 | |
| 0117 | C6 | X | X | Around | LDAB | IMM. | | load accumulator B with ..... | |
| 0118 | X | 09 | X | | | | 09 | the next addend, 09 (Get 09) | |
| 0119 | 1B | X | X | | ABA | INH. | | ADD contents of accumulators | |
| 011A | 19 | X | X | | DAA | INH. | | correct to BCD (decimal adjust) | |
| 011B | 97 | X | X | | STAA | DIR. | | store ACCA (save LSH, BCD | |
| 011C | X | 01 | X | | | | 01 | corrected result) | |
| 011D | 24 | X | X | | BCC | REL. | | branch if carry <u>clear</u> | |
| 011E | X | 03 | X | | | | "SAME" | | |
| 011F | 7C | X | X | SET 2 | INCM | EXT. | | Increment memory at | |
| 0120 | X | 00 | X | | | | 00 | | |
| 0121 | X | X | 00 | | | | 00 | | |
| 0122 | DE | X | X | Same | LDX | DIR. | | load index register | |
| 0123 | X | 00 | X | | | | 00 | | |
| 0124 | 3F | X | X | | SWI | INH | | software interrupt | |

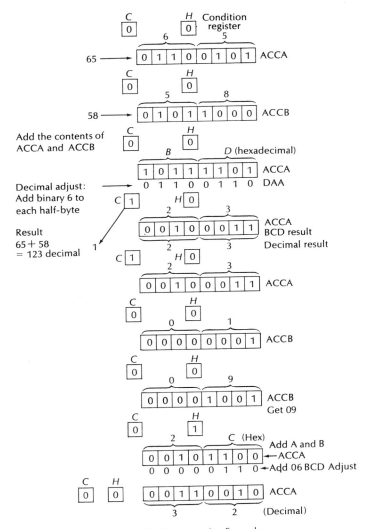

**Figure 12-15** Register Conditions for Programming Example

## SUMMARY

In addition to the tasks normally associated with computers, the microprocessor can perform many systems tasks that were once the exclusive territory of extremely complex, hard-wired, random logic systems. Hard-wired logic systems are totally committed. If the nature of the job they were designed for changes, they must be redesigned and rebuilt. If a microprocessor is being used to perform the same task, a change in the nature of the task does not make the logic system obsolete. The microprocessor needs only to be reprogrammed, a process that may involve removing and replacing one or more read-only-memory IC's or simply typing new instructions on a keyboard.

The use of microprocessors allows large-scale (cheap) mass-produced devices to replace a myriad of expensive, highly specialized logic systems. As a result, many control activities in which digital control was desirable but prohibitively expensive are becoming economical candidates for digital control.

There are four important programming levels for microprocessors. The highest levels include the various problem-oriented mnemonic program languages that have become popular with larger computing systems. Below the problem-oriented languages are mnemonic assembler languages that vary for different machines. The lowest level is machine language, which is the binary control language of logic systems. Microprogramming, which involves firmware at the machine level, is growing in importance in many microprocessor areas of application.

**Problems**

1. Define *dedicated* (committed) *system.*
2. In a dedicated system, how do microprocessors differ from hard-wired logic?
3. Define *programming.*
4. List the hierarchies of programming languages.
5. Contrast the following:
    a. Machine language
    b. Assembler language
    c. Procedure-oriented language
6. Match the following with (1), (2), and (3) below.
    a. The least flexible program form
    b. The most flexible program form
    c. Requires *no* physical modification to change the machine's task
    d. Requires replacement or programming of a ROM
        (1) Hardware    (2) Firmware    (3) Software
7. List the seven address modes for the 6800.
8. Contrast one-, two-, and three-byte instructions.
9. How is a software program used by the computer? Explain in detail.
10. Define the term *mnemonics* and explain how it applies to programming.
11. What are the advantages of assembler language over machine language?
12. What are the advantages of high-level procedure-oriented languages over assembler and machine languages?

13. How is assembler language converted into machine language?
14. Does it make any difference to the programmer what kind of machine COBOL, BASIC, FORTRAN is used with?
15. Make a sketch of the fields for:
    a. Four-address instruction
    b. Three-address instruction
    c. Two-address instruction
    d. One-address instruction
16. In a three-address instruction, how is the location of the next instruction defined?
17. In a two-address instruction, the source of one operand is given; how is the location of the second operand specified?
18. In a one-address instruction, how is the destination specified?
19. What advantages does the bus arrangement have over multiplexing?
20. What is the purpose of the ALU? What additional hardware is required to make up an RALU?
21. Define the term *branch*.
22. Define *link bit*. Of what does the link-bit (or carry) memory consist?
23. What is the purpose of the *test* output in the RALU system? How does it relate to branching?
24. Define *indexed branches*.
25. What is the reason for counting the operations in the multiplication process?
26. What is the function of the RALU control memory system? How does it relate to microprogramming?
27. Define *microinstruction*.
28. What is a microprogram?
29. What is a systems-level operation?
30. Write a program for the 6800 to perform the following: $X - Y = N$ (in decimal), where $X = 12$, $Y = 9$.
31. Write a program for the 6800 to perform the following logical operation: $f = (A \cdot B) + (\bar{A} \cdot C)$.

# INDEX